THE Classroom Instruction Book

Creating lessons for maximum student achievement

Harry K. Wong and Rosemary T. Wong

with

Sarah Powley

"To make an Impact on your students and yourself, improve your instructional capacity."

Harry and Rosemary Wong

HARRY K. WONG PUBLICATIONS, INC.
www.EffectiveTeaching.com

This book is printed on environmentally friendly paper. Join us in making a choice to save the planet.

ISBN: 978-0-9963350-9-6

Library of Congress Control Number: 2021946524

15 14 13 12 11 10 9 8 7 6 5 4 3 2 1

Printed in Singapore by Pristone Pte. Ltd.

Executive Producer: Rosemary T. Wong
Graphic Design: Mark Van Slyke
Editor: Katharine Sturak
Indexer: Kelly Burch
Administrative Assistant: Lacey Imes

HARRY K. WONG PUBLICATIONS, INC.
943 North Shoreline Boulevard
Mountain View, CA 94043-1932
T: 650-965-7896 F: 650-965-7890
www.HarryWong.com

Front Cover QR Code: Harry and Rosemary have a special message for you.

Dedicated to John Hattie

Your tireless commitment to culling the research provides a clear and "visible" direction for what impactful instruction looks like and how to deliver it.

Introduction

> You Can Be a Super Successful, Extremely Effective, and Very Happy Teacher.

This book doesn't promote a program, fad, or philosophy. **THE Classroom Instruction Book** contains sensible, evidence-based instructional practices that have been thoroughly researched and proven to be highly effective. Its purpose is to show you how to create and organize lessons on your students' behalf so that their success is assured no matter what their demographics or circumstances.

These practices can be adopted and implemented in your classroom at no cost without any changes to schedules or class size. They can help you become the teacher you have always hoped to be, a teacher who is capable of making an enduring impact on the lives and futures of your students.

Amazon and Customer Obsession

Successful global businesses and organizations practice "customer obsession." They collect feedback regularly and prioritize the needs and wants of their customers. Their goal is to cultivate trust through consistency. **Jeff Bezos**, Amazon's founder, says, "Customers are always dissatisfied. They always want a better way, yet they don't know what that will be. Therefore, we are always inventing on their behalf." What they now want and expect is convenience and speed.

Teaching and Student Obsession

To be an effective teacher, you must practice "student obsession." The effective teacher's goal is to create lessons so clear and comprehensive that students know exactly what to expect and what is expected of them. Such students take tests without anxiety because they know how their tests have been constructed and, if they make the appropriate effort, passing is assured. Students in the classroom of a teacher who practices student obsession are eager to come to school because they trust that their teacher is focused on their success.

John Hattie, the educational researcher and analyst, says, "There is no deep secret to teaching and learning. In the classrooms of successful teachers and students, teaching and learning are evident. The teacher knows when learning is occurring—or not—because the teaching is clearly visible to the student and learning is visible to the teacher."

Practicing student obsession grows success for teachers and students.

In classrooms where learning is clearly happening, every student is engaged and in the moment.

Focus on Teachers and School Leaders

THE Classroom Instruction Book **is focused on teachers and school leaders.** Studies have conclusively determined that teachers who are knowledgeable and experienced in research-based instructional practices are effective.

In countries that consistently excel in standards of student achievement, there is always a concentrated process to develop the instructional capacity of teachers and school leaders. They then **empower** teachers and school leaders to exercise their knowledge and skills so that they are able to deliver the best possible instruction for every student. *THE Classroom Instruction Book* shows what effective teachers and administrators know and do to create a consistent school environment where students thrive and succeed.

It is the administrator that creates an effective school.

It is the teacher that creates an effective classroom.

Your Success. Our Passion.

These are the words that greet you on our home page at www.HarryWong.com. To write this book, we have combed the research to find what works in the classroom and then provided you with the means to put these ideas, concepts, and skills into your toolbox of techniques and practices—all for one reason only—student achievement.

THE Classroom Instruction Book was written for teachers by three master classroom teachers with input and examples from more than fifty educators. It will inspire you to empower yourself through proven and effective instructional practices. It will change the way you approach lesson construction and implementation by focusing on your students' needs and actively involving them in the learning process.

When you are empowered through effective practices, you will empower your students. Your teaching will have a profound effect on them that will impact their lives and futures. Together you will be capable of achieving astounding results.

Empowerment leads to growth and change for the future. Your students will forever thank you.

Contents

The Impact of Teacher Effectiveness on Student Achievement

The work of **William Sanders** emphasizes the importance of the individual teacher on student learning. Sanders collected data on what happened to students whose teachers produced high achievement versus those whose teachers produced low achievement results. He discovered that when students, beginning in third grade, were placed with three high-performing teachers in a row, they scored on average at the 96th percentile on Tennessee's statewide mathematics assessment at the end of the fifth grade.

When students with comparable achievement histories starting in third grade were placed with three low-performing teachers in a row, their average score on the same mathematics assessment was at the 44th percentile, an enormous difference of 52 percentile points for students who had comparable abilities and skills.

His research found that the difference was attributable to the difference in the wide variation in effectiveness among teachers. He also found that effective teachers appear to be effective with students of all achievement levels, regardless of the demographic diversity of the students.[1]

In a comparable study by researchers in Dallas, Texas, similar results were found in both math and reading during the early grades. When first-grade students were fortunate enough to be placed with three high-performing teachers in a row, their average performance on the Iowa Tests of Basic Skills increased from the 63rd percentile to the 87th percentile. In contrast, a student with similar scores placed in classrooms with low-performing teachers showed their performance decreased from the 58th percentile to the 40th, a percentile difference of 42 points.[2]

In clear terms, it is obvious that not only does teacher *quality* matter when it comes to how much students learn, but also that, for better or worse, a teacher's *effectiveness* stays with students for years to come.

The conclusion is emphatic.

- *A teacher who uses effective instructional practices is the single biggest school-based influence on student achievement.*

- *Teachers, more than most other aspects of a student's classroom experience, are the key to determining a student's educational outcomes.*

---

[1] William L. Sanders and June C. Rivers, *Cumulative and Residual Effects of Teachers on Future Student Academic Achievement* (Knoxville, TN: University of Tennessee Value-Added Research and Assessment Center, 1996).

[2] Robert L. Mendro, Heather R. Jordan, Elvia Gomez, Mark C. Anderson, and Karen L. Bembry, "An Application of Multiple Linear Regression Determining Longitudinal Teacher Effectiveness" (paper presented at the Annual Meeting of AERA, San Diego, California, April 1998).

UNIT A Learning and Achievement

Chapter

How to Ensure Effective Instruction

Effective instruction is essential for student learning and achievement.

Learning Is the Core of Education

Every sport, every company, every organization has a purpose or core—a central and foundational reason for existing. What is the core business of an airline? A restaurant? A bank? A dental office? You can answer those questions quite easily—flying safely, serving food, handling money, and healthy teeth.

What is the core business of a school?

This is what Stonefields School in Auckland, New Zealand, states as its core business.

Learning is our Core Business.

They are committed to delivering learning. They are committed to imparting the necessary knowledge and competencies for students to thrive and succeed at school and in life.

Be an Instructional Leader

"We've got to teach for mastery."

Elaine Farris
Chairwoman of the Board
Kentucky State University

Kentucky's first black superintendent reflects on her journey and 'mastery for every child' education philosophy. Elaine Farris went from P.E. teacher to the highest office in the district.

We've got to teach for mastery. We have the curriculum, the content and we have the standards that the kids have to master. *If you want to be an administrator, you've got to understand instruction.* You've got to be an instructional leader first; you've got to understand teaching and learning. That's where you have to hang your hat. That's where you get your credibility with teachers.[1]

The core business of every school is learning, to build the learning capacity of all students.

If you are in education, you have a set of knowledge and skills to impart. This is called the curriculum. Instruction begins with the curriculum, the course of study that determines what knowledge and skills students are to learn.

---

[1] Autumn A. Arnett, "Kentucky's First Black Superintendent Reflects on Her Journey and 'Mastery for Every Child' Education Philosophy," *Education Dive* (February 26, 2018).

What is the core knowledge of a school? That would be the curriculum.

The most basic task in a school is teaching and learning. Teaching is what teachers do and learning is what students do. And what they each respectively teach and learn is the curriculum. This is why school districts should have a curriculum and instruction department.

What to Teach

Beth was so excited. Her family had moved into a new community. Her husband had a new job, the children were enrolled in their respective schools, and Beth got a job at the district's middle school.

She showed up at the school's office and was greeted by the school secretary who gave her the schedule and keys to her classroom. Beth asked, "Can I have a copy of the school's curriculum?"

The secretary replied, "Humma, humma . . . Oh, you'll figure it out."

If you are a new player on a team, you will ask for the playbook. If you are hired as a financial consultant for an investment company, you will be told what financial plans are available for sale. If you are working in a supermarket and are asked, "Where are the organic heirloom tomatoes?" you know the answer because you have received training in products and display.

It's obvious that a teacher wants to know what is to be taught and what students are to learn.

There is a curriculum for every grade level and subject:

- Head Start curriculum
- Early Childhood curriculum
- Liberal Arts curriculum
- Third-grade curriculum
- Science curriculum and other content areas

But what do you do if your school or school district does not have a curriculum guide for the grade level or subject you need to teach? Chapter 21 will give you some ideas on how to work collaboratively with colleagues and school leaders to create your own.

Curriculum ⟶ Instruction

Curriculum
The content that is to be taught and learned in a class or subject

Instruction
Instruction is the act or practice of instructing or teaching the content.

It Takes Knowledge

Far too often, the rhetoric that emanates from schools is made up of platitudes that say students must be problem solvers, discoverers of their own learning, and purposeful citizens. Google 21st century skills and you will see columns of idealistic and overwhelming skills. These are admirable traits, but they cannot be done in a vacuum that lacks knowledge and competencies.

Knowledge aids the acquisition of more knowledge.[2]

Daniel Willingham

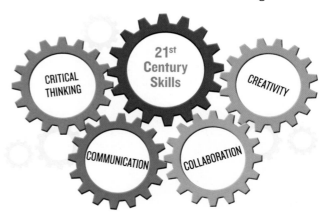

As a Harvard physicist said, "You can't think like a physicist unless you know a whole lot about physics." You cannot play symphonies until you have first mastered the notes. You can't be a pharmacist until you are trained in medicines and its side effects. You cannot discover something until you first know what you are trying to discover.

---

[2] Daniel T. Willingham, "It Speeds and Strengthens Reading Comprehension, Learning—and Thinking," *American Educator* (Spring 2006).

The "Crayola Curriculum"

by Mike Schmoker

A couple of years ago, I found myself touring a school that had received an international award for excellence in staff development. Roaming from class to class—on what was clearly a "showcase day"—I went from being puzzled to astonished by what I saw.

Two things were terribly wrong. One, a majority of students were sitting in small, unsupervised groups, barely, if at all, engaged in what were supposedly learning activities. Many of the children were chatting. Second, but more important, was that the activities themselves seemed to bear no relation whatsoever to *reading*, the presumed subject being taught at the time. After seeing this pattern in several classes, I finally asked my host what kinds of gains had been made in this award-winning but high-poverty school. I was regretfully informed that there had been no gains, what with the hardships these children faced at home and in their neighborhoods.

I began to tour early-grade classrooms *during the reading period*. I purposely took several people along with me each time—building and district administrators, teachers, even an occasional superintendent. I briefed them on what to look for: (1) reasonably good reading activities, the kind almost anyone would agree on, and (2) the majority of students at least nominally attending to them. Along the way, I asked the group how the lessons stood up to our scrutiny.

From the start, the virtually unanimous impression was that (1) most of the activities had very little relation to reading—to acquiring the ability to read, and (2) students were barely, if at all, engaged in their work. We weren't looking for perfection; we were looking for a reasonable amount of student engagement in garden-variety literacy activities.

Students were not reading, they weren't writing about what they had read, they weren't learning the alphabet or its corresponding sounds; they weren't learning words or sentences or how to read short texts.

They were coloring. Coloring on a scale unimaginable to us before these classroom tours. The crayons were ever-present. Sometimes, students were cutting or building things out of paper (which they had colored) or just talking quietly while sitting at "activity centers" that were presumably for the purpose of promoting reading and writing skills. These centers, too, were ubiquitous, and a great source of pride to many teachers and administrators, but tragically counterproductive.

The question in my mind, never uttered, was, "Why wouldn't they be learning the alphabet? Why are they coloring instead of being taught to read?"

None of these tours was conducted in a spirit of accusation. On the contrary, we were looking for patterns. It was those patterns, not individual teachers, that were discussed. Rather than condemn teachers, it is time for us to condemn the traditions, the institutional inertia, that account for these practices. They represent nothing less than a crisis in teaching, in teacher training, in supervision and supervisory training, and in reading research itself, which is still far too esoteric and remote from the trenches where teachers teach and students learn.

It is worth emphasizing that the most important single activity to promote reading is reading.

The logic is pretty plain. Kids, especially those in disadvantaged settings, don't have a chance unless we teach them to read, early and well. This can happen the moment we charge teachers and administrators in every school and district to give reading and language arts instruction the thorough, common-sense review it so desperately needs.[3]

---

[3] Abridged from Mike Schmoker, "The Crayola Curriculum," *Education Week* 21, no. 8 (October 24, 2001).

**You cannot have a school unless
you have a curriculum.**

Students must learn before they can achieve anything. This is why good instruction is so valuable to a student's future.

- **Learning:** Learning is the process of acquiring basic knowledge and skills about a subject. For example, how to use correct grammar and punctuation, how to apply PEMDAS when solving math problems.

- **Achievement:** Achievement is when a student is able to take what has been learned and demonstrate an act of accomplishment or attainment. For example, producing a report, writing a poem, performing a weld, singing a song, or solving a problem. Achievement is not about test scores; it is about producing results.

What Is Instruction?

**Instruction is the act or practice
of instructing or teaching.**

An Internet search for the definition of "teacher" will bring tears to your eyes:

n. 1) One who provides knowledge and insight. 2) One who inspires, motivates, and opens up minds to the endless possibilities of which one can achieve. 3) One who makes a positive difference in the lives of many. 4) One who is admired, appreciated, and held in the highest esteem.

Those definitions are all true. But the basic responsibility of a teacher is to instruct. **As a teacher, you are hired to manage an instructional program and teach the grade level or subject you are assigned to teach.** When you come to teach each day, your every wish is to see each student learn and achieve, and this can happen. You can indeed do wonders.

If schools want to improve student learning, every student needs to receive excellent instruction every day in every classroom.

Why is there a need for a book on instruction? We know that the single most decisive factor in student achievement is effective teaching or instruction. **It is astounding what teachers who practice effective instruction can do for their students.**

> *The only way to improve student learning is to improve teacher instructional practice. Good instruction is fifteen to twenty times more powerful than family background, income, race, gender, and other explanatory variables.*[4]

Theodore Hershberg

The purpose of instruction is to help people learn. The goal of a teacher is to expedite instruction to make learning easier, quicker, and more enjoyable. A teacher's job is to help everyone learn and be successful. Education should always be about student learning. And students learn from instruction that is effectively provided.

All students, all ages need a teacher skilled in effective practices.

[4] Theodore Hershberg, "Value-Added Assessment and Systemic Reform: A Response to the Challenge of Human Capital Development," *Phi Delta Kappan* 87, no. 4 (December 1, 2005): 276–283.

The Three Characteristics

The three characteristics of effective teacher practices have been known for well over fifty years. It is these characteristics that effective districts, schools, administrators, and coaches use to teach teachers and principals how to be effective. They have been researched, defined, and validated by research conducted by Thomas Good, Jere Brophy, Robert Pianta, and Charlotte Danielson, among many others.

The Three Characteristics of Effective Teaching

1. **Classroom Management:** The practices and procedures that a teacher uses to organize an environment in which instruction and learning can occur.

2. **Lesson Mastery:** The instruction provided so students will comprehend and master a concept or skill as determined by the lesson objective and assessment.

3. **Positive Expectations:** What the teacher believes will or will not happen that greatly influences the achievement and success of students.

The subject of *THE Classroom Instruction Book* is characteristic 2: Lesson Mastery. **A significant body of research and knowledge about effective instruction is in this book.** Every teacher has the potential to translate the body of knowledge to reach great heights. Every moment of each day is an opportunity for teachers to grow and learn and reach the top of their profession.

Madeline Cheek Hunter, considered one of the ten most influential people in education, emphasized this.

- There is an extensive body of research and knowledge about teaching that must be known by the teacher.

- The teacher must be a decision-maker who is able to translate the body of research and knowledge about teaching into increased student learning. (Several of those teachers are described in this book.)

The research about teachers and instructional practices is abundant.

Robert Pianta, Dean of the University of Virginia's Curry School of Education and Human Development, developed an observation instrument in 2008 to assess classroom quality and help teachers become more effective. He called it a "Classroom Assessment Scoring System" (CLASS). The CLASS examined effective teacher and student interactions. He concluded that effective teachers excel in three domains:

- Organizational support
- Instructional support
- Emotional support

The National Center for Mental Health at UCLA studied classroom success among students with social-emotional issues. The report published in 2008 found that there are three major barriers to learning and school improvement:

- Management component
- Instructional component
- Enabling component

Bruce Torff, Hofstra University, surveyed principals in high-achieving and under-performing schools. Torff found these deficiencies as the most common causes of teacher ineffectiveness:

- Lack of classroom management skills
- Lack of lesson implementation skills
- Inability to establish rapport with students

In summary, these are the three characteristics of effective teachers.

1. They are **organized**.
2. They are **knowledgeable**.
3. They are **kind**.

The Research in Support of Effective Teachers

Hundreds, if not thousands, of research studies, journal articles, and educational commentaries support the thesis that effective teaching produces the greatest effect on student achievement—without contradictions. This is a small sampling of the findings.

The Power of Teachers

◆ The single greatest effect on student achievement is the teacher to whom a student gets assigned. *Rivkin, Hanushek, and Kain (2005)*[5]

◆ Teacher expertise accounts for more difference in student performance—40 percent—than any other factor. *Ferguson (1991)*[6]

◆ More can be done to improve education by improving the effectiveness of teachers than by any other single factor. *Wright, Horn, and Sanders (1997)*[7]

◆ To improve student learning, do not change the school structure. Change the instructional practice to focus on learning. *Elmore (2002)*[8]

◆ Good teachers, effective teachers, matter much more than content materials, pedagogical approaches, or programs. *Sanders and Rivers (1996); Duffy (1997); Darling-Hammond (1999); Taylor, et al. (2000); Allington and Johnston (2001); Pressley (2001); Allington (2002)*[9]

◆ The classroom teacher is widely regarded as the most influential school-related factor that affects student achievement. *Mendro, Jordan, Gomez, Anderson, and Bembry (1997); Muijs and Reynolds (2003); Stronge, Ward, and Grant (2011)*[10]

◆ The effect of increases in teacher quality swamps the impact of any other educational investment, such as reductions in class size. *Goldhaber (2010)*[11]

◆ Teacher quality is one of the few school characteristics that significantly affects student performance. *Goldhaber (2016)*[12]

Teachers who use effective instruction techniques tend to stay effective even when they change schools. Research evidence suggests that a teacher's impact on student achievement remains reasonably consistent regardless of whether the new school is more or less advantaged than the old one.

Teachers who use effective instructional techniques matter more to student achievement than any other aspect of schooling.

Research on Effective Teaching

Scan the QR code for the complete citations for these studies.

Additionally, access this information and all QR code files at www.EffectiveTeaching.com on the QR code tab for **THE Classroom Instruction Book**.

[5] Steven G. Rivkin, Eric A. Hanushek, and John F. Kain, "Teachers, Schools, and Academic Achievement," *Econometrica* 73, no. 2 (March 2005): 417–458.

[6] Ronald F. Ferguson, "Paying for Public Education: New Evidence on How and Why Money Matters," *Harvard Journal of Legislation* 28 (Summer 1991): 465–498.

[7] S. Paul Wright, Sandra P. Horn, and William L. Sanders, "Teacher and Classroom Context Effects on Student Achievement: Implications for Teacher Evaluation," *Journal of Personnel Evaluation in Education* 11, no. 1 (1997): 57–67.

[8] Richard Elmore, "The Limits of 'Change,'" *Harvard Education Newsletter* 18, no. 1 (January/February 2002).

[9] Richard L. Allington, "What I've Learned from Effective Reading Instruction" *Phi Delta Kappan* 83, no. 10 (June 1, 2002): 740–747.

[10] James H. Stronge, Thomas J. Ward, and Leslie W. Grant, "What Makes Good Teachers Good? A Cross-Case Analysis of the Connection Between Teacher Effectiveness and Student Achievement," *Journal of Teacher Education* 62, no. 4 (September 1, 2011): 339–355.

[11] Dan Goldhaber, "Teacher Pay Reforms: The Political Implications of Recent Research," *CEDR Working Paper*, no. 2010-4.0 (2010).

[12] Dan Goldhaber, "In Schools, Teacher Quality Matters Most," *Education Next* 16, no. 2 (Spring 2016).

The Four Stages of Teaching

In Chapter 2 of **THE First Days of School**, the four possible stages in a teacher's professional life are described. Here is how they pertain to instruction:

- **Stage 1—Fantasy.** Many neophyte teachers in the initial Fantasy stage only have the most basic instructional skills. They rarely talk about standards, assessment, or student achievement. They want to be liked, and they search for fun activities to keep students occupied.

- **Stage 2—Survival.** Teachers in the Survival stage are still struggling with organizational and instructional skills. Conflicts in the classroom arise, and they ask for more counselors and smaller class sizes.

- **Stage 3—Mastery.** Teachers who have reached Mastery employ effective instructional practices. They use objectives, scaffolding, formative assessment, guided practice, gradual release of responsibility toward independent practice, and evaluation. They have a classroom management plan and an instructional plan.

- **Stage 4—Impact.** Teachers who have Impact have mastered effective instructional strategies. They are dedicated teacher-leaders who contribute to their profession and fulfill their fantasy of making a difference in the lives of their students.[13]

If you are currently in Survival mode, **THE Classroom Instruction Book** can take you to Mastery, and if you are in Mastery, it can take you to Impact.

The Power of Principals

Next to an effective teacher, extensive research and observation have shown that principal leadership is second only to classroom instruction among all school-related factors that contribute to student learning. Highly effective principals had more of an impact on students than a reduction in class size, and they added two to seven months of growth for every student on their campuses. Ineffective principals lower achievement by the same amount.[14]

Elaine Farris worked her way from an elementary school P.E. teacher to being Kentucky's first black superintendent and now serves as chairwoman of the board of Kentucky State University. And the great distance of her career trajectory says as much about her tenacity and determination as it does her commitment to standing with those she loves and standing up for the things she believes in.

We've got to teach for mastery. We have the curriculum, the content and we have the standards that the kids have to master. If you want to be an administrator, you've got to understand instruction. You've got to be an instructional leader first; you've got to understand teaching and learning. That's where you have to hang your hat. That's where you get your credibility with teachers.

What I say to principals is this—You have to know who are the students who are not getting there [in terms of progress]. Once you identify who those students are, then you have to look at the data on a daily basis. You're teaching this particular curriculum every day, so what are the deficits that they're not mastering? You surround those students with the support systems that they need. It's really not rocket science. It's really about teaching and learning—I taught it, did they learn it?

We've got to teach for mastery. We can't teach and say, "Well, they didn't get it," and move on. That doesn't mean re-teaching and just saying it louder. We've got to understand what skill deficits there are, and we've got to teach to those skill deficits.[15]

[13]Kevin Ryan, *The Induction of New Teachers* (Bloomington, IN: Phi Delta Kappa Educational Foundation, 1986).

[14]Gregory F. Branch, Eric A. Hanushek, and Steven G. Rivkin, "School Leaders Matter," *Education Next* 13, no. 1 (Winter 2013).

[15]Arnett, "Kentucky's First Black Superintendent Reflects on Her Journey and 'Mastery for Every Child' Education Philosophy."

**A classroom is only as good as its teacher.
A school is only as good as its principal.**

Researchers from the universities of Minnesota and Toronto conducted a large-scale study of school leadership in 2004 and discovered that there are virtually no documented instances of troubled schools being turned around without leadership by an effective principal.[16]

Principal leadership is second only to teacher effectiveness among school influences on student success.

"

I once had the smartest principal I have ever been around. He knew how to teach.

When you have leadership like this, you have to raise your own game.

A teacher

Robert Marzano reported on a national meta-analysis of sixty-nine studies involving two thousand eight hundred schools that found that 25 percent of the variation in student achievement could be explained by principal leadership skills.[17]

These are the major differences between successful and unsuccessful schools.

◆ **Unsuccessful schools** stress programs. They spend millions of dollars adopting programs and bandwagon fads searching for the quick fix.

◆ **Successful schools** stress effective practices. They wisely invest in their teachers and the effective practices of their teachers. They don't adopt programs; they teach basic, curriculum-based academic content, prioritizing the instructional practices of their teachers because that is the major factor for improving student achievement.

Effective principals teach effective instructional practices because it is these practices that make teachers effective.

We know the following about administrators—superintendents and principals:

◆ **Superintendents.** There is a direct link between superintendent leadership and student achievement. A Mid-continent Research for Education and Learning (McREL) report found that superintendents positively influenced student achievement, especially when they kept their districts focused on teaching and learning.[18]

◆ **Principals.** In a study of thirty years of research, McREL also found that principals who concentrate on the right practices (they list twenty-one leadership characteristics) can elevate a school scoring in the 50th percentile up another ten to nineteen percentile points.[19]

A recently retired superintendent shared the following wise advice. He said, "The best thing you can do for a superintendent is not to give him or her more money, more buildings, or another program to adopt. Instead, give him a tool to make his average teachers just a little bit better, and you'll see a vastly greater impact across the district than any model school or program will ever bring."

The effective principal recruits and trains new talent and ensures that all teachers receive the professional development and support they need. Teachers come to a school certified and eager to teach. The challenge is to put them in the classroom as trained teachers who have effective instructional skills.

---

[16] Karen Seashore Louis, Kenneth Leithwood, Kyla Walhstrom, Stephen Anderson et al., *Learning from Leadership Project: Investigating the Links to Improved Student Learning* (University of Minnesota, University of Toronto, Wallace Foundation, 2010): 9.

[17] Robert J. Marzano, Timothy Waters, and Brian McNulty, *School Leadership that Works: From Research to Results* (Alexandria, VA: ASCD, 2005).

[18] Timothy Waters and Robert J. Marzano, *School District Leadership that Works: The Effect of Superintendent Leadership on Student Achievement* (Denver, CO: Mid-continent Research for Education and Learning, 2006).

[19] Timothy Waters, Robert J. Marzano, and Brian McNulty, *Balanced Leadership: What 30 Years of Research Tells Us About the Effect of Leadership on Student Achievement. A Working Paper* (Denver, CO: Mid-continent Research for Education and Learning, 2003).

Investing in Teachers

**Effective principals invest
in the instructional skills of teachers.**

Successful schools have principals who know that it's much better to spend time and resources developing teachers' skills and abilities to steer students to achievement rather than buying packages of hyped and untested quick fixes for academic woes.

They regard teachers as their greatest asset.

Richard Elmore of Harvard University observed that to improve student learning, you do not change the structure (that is, block scheduling, smaller class size, small school size, and so on); you change the instructional practices of the teachers.

The schools that do best are those that have a clear idea of what curriculum is to be taught, what kind of **instructional practices** they want to implement, and then design a structure to support the curriculum and instructional practices.[20]

An effective teacher knows and accepts that it is their instructional practices—how they teach— that improve student learning. It's not the demographics of the student population, or class size, or technology, or how the school is structured.

**The more knowledgeable and skillful the teacher,
the greater the asset the teacher is to the students,
the school, and the community.**

At a school in Montreal, where crime—including murder, violence, and theft—was epidemic, 92 percent of the students dropped out. In a statistical study of the students examining birth dates, socio-economic factors, and racial and national backgrounds, one first grade teacher's name reappeared frequently because 40 percent of her students completed school with a diploma.

**One teacher
can make an impact on a student's life.**

The achievement gap facing poor and minority students is not due to poverty or family conditions, but to systematic differences in teacher effectiveness. A student who is taught by a teacher using ineffective techniques for two years in a row can almost never recover the learning lost during those years. As a teacher's effectiveness increases, the first students to benefit from this improvement are those from lower-achieving groups.

*The ineffective teacher produces inadequate,
if any, growth in students.*

*The effective teacher, even in an ineffective
school, produces improved student learning
and increased student achievement.*[21]

Robert Marzano

**If schools want to improve student learning,
the only route is to have teachers who are trained in
effective instructional practices.**

Training is essential to create skillful and informed teachers.

---

[20] Elmore, "The Limits of 'Change.'"

[21] Robert J. Marzano, Jana S. Marzano, and Debra J. Pickering, *Classroom Management That Works: Research-based Strategies for Every Teacher* (Alexandria, VA: ASCD, 2003).

A Framework for Producing Effective Teachers

A district can use the three characteristics of effective teacher practices to form the framework of an effective professional development program to train teachers to be effective:

- **Classroom Management**
- **Lesson Mastery**
- **Positive Expectations**

2 Binder Covers

Download covers for your Classroom Instruction Plan binder.

THE Classroom Instruction Book will teach you how to create your own classroom instruction plan so that you can teach effectively. If you have not done so, start a binder like **Kara Howard** did, with everything you collect on how to have an effective instructional program.

Mastering Instruction

 For students to learn, there must be a curriculum and there must be a teacher who instructs effectively.

 A teacher who uses effective instructional practices is the single biggest school-based influence on student achievement.

 Principal leadership is second only to teacher effectiveness among school influences on student success.

 The characteristics of effective teacher practices must be the central focus of an administrator's vision for a school.

 A district can use the three characteristics of effective teacher practices to form the framework of an effective professional development program to train teachers to be effective.

...Produces Achievement!

2

How to Teach for Student Achievement

Effective teachers use well-researched, evidence-based methods that have a profound influence on learning and achievement.

Visible Learning

Chapter 1 established these beliefs.

- The single greatest effect on student achievement is the effectiveness of the teacher.

- Students learn from how well teachers use effective instructional practices.

There is extensive research on how to instruct and improve student achievement. The research is visible; it is in plain daylight and in language that is easily understood. It can be found in *Visible Learning: A Synthesis of Over 800 Meta-Analyses Relating to Achievement.*

VISIBLE LEARNING: A SYNTHESIS OF OVER 800 META-ANALYSES IN EDUCATION

JOHN HATTIE

Visible Learning is the work of **John Hattie**, formerly of New Zealand, now at the University of Melbourne in Australia. The key word in the title of the book is "achievement," which is what every student, teacher, administrator, parent, and stakeholder wants. His research focuses on answering a basic and essential question—**What effect does a teaching practice have on student achievement?**

Teaching and Learning

" **The more the student becomes the teacher and the more the teacher becomes the learner, then the more successful are the outcomes.** "

John Hattie
Visible Learning

Visible learning is used by teachers to become evaluators of their own teaching. Visible teaching and learning occur when teachers see learning through the eyes of students and help them become their own teachers.

It is critical that the teaching and the learning are visible. There is no deep secret called "teaching and learning." What is most important is that teaching is visible to the student, and that the learning is visible to the teacher. The more the student becomes the teacher and the more the teacher becomes the learner, then the more successful are the outcomes.[1]

There is overwhelming research on the instructional methods that influence and enhance student learning. This research has been done by thousands of educational researchers worldwide. What Hattie has done is the

[1] Hattie, *Visible Learning.*

monumental task of compiling and correlating all this research—which is why it's called a meta-analysis—to present the most comprehensive review of educational literature on student achievement ever conducted—and it is still ongoing.

Hattie's work, first published in 2009, included
- 800 meta-analyses encompassing over
- 50,000 individual studies of more than
- 250 million students worldwide.

In 2018, the database increased to
- 1,200 meta-analyses encompassing over
- 70,000 individual studies of more than
- 300 million students worldwide.

A meta-analysis is a statistical tool for combining findings from different studies. In Hattie's work, the goal is identifying teaching methods that have an effect on student achievement. Because of the preponderance of similar research, meta-analyses have statistical power in measuring what works best in effecting improved student achievement.

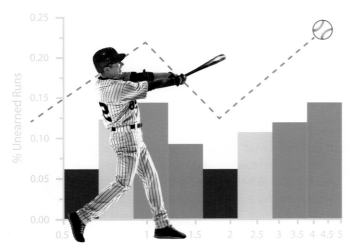

Analytics, as used in baseball, can be used to improve team dynamics, and can be used in other fields as well.

When conducting a meta-analysis, a researcher translates the results of a given study into a unit of measurement referred to as an *effect size*. In this instance, effect size is a way of showing how well a teaching strategy or technique works in advancing student achievement.

Meta-analyses are commonly used in sports, business, and medicine to measure performance. Perhaps you have seen the word "analytics" used in sports or seen the movie *Moneyball,* which illustrated that analytics can be used to identify what works best for a baseball team. The same concept is used in medicine. For instance, if a doctor is recommending a medicine or treatment, you should ask, "How well will it work?" "Will it perform to make me well?" Doctors don't prescribe "nostrums," dubious potions that have been mixed up in some back room by some unknown semi-professional. They prescribe medicines based on extensive meta-analyses of what works.

Nor does the medical profession operate from information or strategies used by one doctor, nurse, or organization with its own agenda. The Cochrane Collaboration, now called Cochrane, is an international organization that summarizes, similar to what John Hattie has done, the results of medical research to help people in the health profession make evidence-based decisions.

Likewise in education, you should only instruct your students using evidence-based instructional strategies. **Hattie's research provides evidence of which education practices work better than others to improve teaching and learning.**

Evidence-Based Instruction

One should be careful when reading articles about innovative educational practices, because all educational innovations work—in the eyes of the innovator. Something could work—for a moment in time and in someone's classroom—but is there corroborating research or evidence to support its continuing efficacy?

Hattie acknowledges that many new ideas and methods in education have the potential to work. But, there is no evidence that student achievement will be advanced across-the-board and in all circumstances when individual teachers say, "Well, it worked for me." Principals like to brag about what program they have just used, but they never tell you what previous programs they tried to implement or the amount of money spent on past, failed programs.

Educators are to be commended for their eagerness to try new and different approaches, but often their comments and articles do not provide a compelling, refereed research basis that can be shared to improve student achievement. In contrast, Hattie's research is truly monumental in size and statistical accuracy.

Evidence-based instruction, instruction based on accurate, thorough research, shows you how to approach your work in ways that will help students achieve the best results they possibly can. This does not mean you have to work harder—most teachers work hard enough already! It means you use the research evidence to structure your work.

The question an effective teacher asks is, "To what degree does a teaching strategy work?"

Evidence-based medicine is used to treat illnesses. Evidence-based instruction is used to increase achievement.

John Hattie's Effect Size

Effect size is a statistical number that tells the influence of a strategy used in the classroom. What Hattie has done is organize teaching strategies and practices and place them in numerical order. The larger the number, the greater its influence on supporting student achievement. There is no need to ponder the statistical definition of effect size. All a teacher should be asking is, "What has a better influence on learning?" Or, perhaps, "What will help my students to perform their best?"

An effect size is the size of statistical significance that a teaching technique has in influencing student achievement.

When *Visible Learning* was first published in 2009, Hattie found 130 teaching techniques, or zones of influences, that have an effect size in the classroom. He arranged those influences in numerical order from those that work best to those that work least.

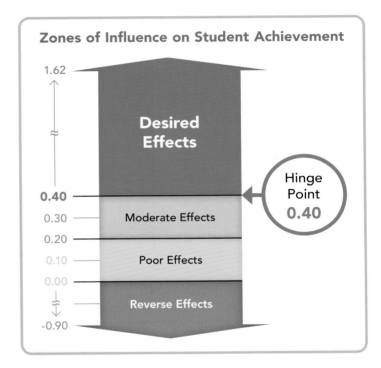

Hattie calls 0.40 the "hinge point," or balance point. This is the tipping point where the higher the effect size is above 0.40, the better the influence will have on improving student achievement. **Conversely, it is also extremely important to know that influences under 0.40 can cause regression in student learning.**

Three of the Most Effective Influences on Student Achievement

1. Teacher estimation (Chapter 12)
2. Collaborative impact (Chapter 21)
3. Self-reported grades (Chapter 13)

**Just think how much progress could be made
on student achievement
if priority time was spent daily
on the most effective classroom influences.**

Influences with Positive Effects on Student Achievement[2]		
Influence	Effect Size	Page
Teacher estimation	1.62	18
Collaborative impact	1.57	250
Self-reported grades	1.33	143
Teacher clarity	0.75	239
Reciprocal teaching	0.74	201
Feedback	0.70	89
Direct instruction	0.60	28
Spaced vs. mass practice	0.60	192
Mastery learning	0.57	235

Influences with Poor Effects on Student Achievement[3]	
Influence	Effect Size
Class size	0.21
Single gender	0.08
Student control over learning	0.02
Retention	-0.32

3

Ranking of Effect Sizes

See **John Hattie's** complete list of influences on student achievement.

2,3"Hattie Ranking: 256 Influences and Effect Sizes Related to Student Achievement," *Visible Learning*, accessed November 1, 2021, https://visible-learning.org/backup-hattie-ranking-256-effects-2017/.

Many of the positive influences that impact student achievement are explained and demonstrated in this book—feedback, teacher clarity, reciprocal teaching, direct instruction, and mastery learning.

It is significant, and some teachers may be surprised to learn, that class size has a low effect size. But the most startling finding is that retention has a minus effect size of -0.32. Yes. That is below zero, yet we waste an inordinate amount of time and money focusing on retention, class size, single gender schools, and various other negligible factors when student achievement, or lack of it, is discussed.

Another teaching technique that has a very low effect size is student control over learning, that is, when students are allowed to pick their own books and projects and even tell the teacher what they want to learn. **The effect size indicates that very little learning is accomplished when students design their own curriculum.**

4

Effect Size

Read more information on effect size and the statistical implications for learning.

How Is Effect Size Derived?

The effect size of an earthquake is called the Richter scale, which assigns a number to quantify the size of an earthquake. Most people do not ask how the Richter scale number is derived. We accept it just as we do many other statistics we see daily. We don't question them. So, it would be best to accept the statistical fact that teaching practices have an effect size indicating which ones have more effect or influence on student achievement than others.

The use of a classroom influence above 0.40 will significantly enhance learning and achievement.

Statistics We Accept in Life

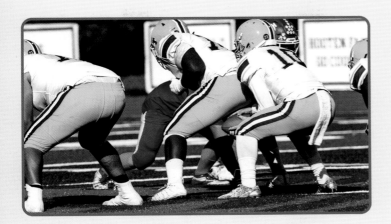

Passer Rating or Quarterback Rating

The passer rating, also called the quarterback rating, is the number given to indicate how well a quarterback did during a game. A perfect passer rating is 158.3 (yes, 158.3 is perfect—just go with it), yet very few can tell you how a passer rating is calculated. Nonetheless, the average sports fan doesn't care, and only wants to know how well a quarterback can pass; that is, the higher the passer rating, supposedly, the better the quarterback.

Dow Jones Industrial Average

The Dow Jones Industrial Average is a stock market index that shows how thirty large, publicly-owned companies in the United States have traded during a session or day on the stock market. A similar bellwether for the U.S. economy is the S&P (Standard & Poor's) Index. The average person hears these numbers daily along with the weather report yet has no concept of how both indexes are calculated. They only care that the higher the index, the better a person's stock is performing, which is all most people want to know.

Television Ratings

No one has ever knocked on your door to ask you what you are watching on TV, yet the public seems to know what the country is watching. The rating is based on a random sampling of thousands of people compiled by Nielsen Media Research to produce a statistical sampling. The average person does not care how this is done, other than to smile if others are enjoying the same programs. Accept it—you like it when people share your likes and dislikes. (In this instance, of course, it's the advertisers who really want to know what people are watching.)

From the Middle to the Top

An effect size gain of 0.70 in international comparative studies in mathematics would have raised the score of a nation that falls in the middle of the list of forty-one countries (the U.S., for example) to one of the top five.

5

Rising to the Top

See the list of countries and how to move to the top of the list.

The Highest Effect Sizes

The immediate question every teacher wants to know is this—**What is the classroom strategy or practice with the highest effect size?** In the most recent update to Hattie's influences, this is the top influence on student achievement:

◆ Teacher estimation of student achievement with an effect size of 1.62

These are the next two highest effect sizes that influence student achievement:

◆ Collaborative impact (collective teacher efficacy) with an effect size of 1.57

◆ Self-reported grades (students predicting their own grades) with an effect size of 1.33

Research shows that when teachers work together in teams to design lessons, they make a significant collaborative impact on student achievement. This concept will be discussed in Chapter 21.

Teacher estimation and self-reported grades are directly related to each other. When teachers know how to design a lesson, they can predict what students will learn and that they will succeed. And when students know how the lesson is designed, they have the knowledge to complete the assignment successfully and learn.

Students who succeed are in a classroom run by a teacher who structures well-organized lessons. They know what they are expected to learn.

How this is done is explained in Units B, C, and D—the core of **THE Classroom Instruction Book**.

◆ Each lesson, if not each day, begins with objectives so students know where they are going and what they are to accomplish. (Unit B)

◆ As students work on the activities, the teacher is monitoring them and supplying feedback to help them make progress—this is called assessment. (Unit C)

◆ The teacher uses guided practice activities that are all correlated to, and reinforce, the learning of the objectives. (Unit D)

◆ At the end of the lesson, each question on the test is correlated to the lesson objectives. (Unit D)

Everyone wants good grades. Teachers want their students to achieve and succeed. What students hate the most is uncertainty. They want to be assured that their work and the efforts they are making are taking them in the right direction. Students who know how a lesson is organized can predict their probability of success.

When there is consistent instructional design in the classroom, students are given the possibility of having an impact on their own lives.

The Effect of Visible Learning

As **John Hattie** says, there is no deep secret to teaching and learning. In the classrooms of successful teachers and students, teaching and learning are visible. The teacher knows when learning is occurring—or not—because lesson objectives are visible at all times and the teacher is constantly assessing the learning. Teaching is visible to the student, and learning is visible to the teacher.

It is imperative to have lessons that are transparent. Many students have never been provided with lessons that are transparent. So, the confused students passively trudge along, day in and day out, apathetic and uninspired, hoping for the best but unsure what is required of them to progress.

Teacher Clarity

> Teachers who practice "student obsession," that is, teachers who are firmly focused on each student's potential to succeed, create and invent lessons that ensure their students will succeed no matter what their circumstances are.

Students are often dissatisfied even if they don't know what it is they need or want. They may want a better way of learning and working, but they usually have no idea what that way would be like. Many have been discouraged and failed in school for so long that they do not even know what it is like to learn and succeed. Achievement is beyond their experience or comprehension. *THE Classroom Instruction Book* will show you how to provide lessons that are clear and understandable.

We know how to improve student achievement because there are teaching methods that positively influence student achievement.

Teacher clarity has an effect size of 0.75. Students achieve when there is teacher clarity. Examples of what has been described as an organized lesson will be shown in Unit D. Simply, students learn more when the teacher clearly outlines and communicates the learning they are expected to master. With teacher clarity, learning is not a mystery.

Carpenters, doctors, farmers, and mechanics all know what tools to use—the tools of the trade. They know what they need to accomplish and can explain what they are doing to their clients or patients. Likewise, effective teachers have the tools of their trade, and they know which are the better tools to use. **Students learn from teachers who know which instructional practices are more effective than others.**

Mastery, Not Mystery

I feel like I specialize in "visible learning" when I teach because I liked teachers who did that for me—clearly stating what we needed to learn, how we were going to learn it, and how we would show that we learned it. I call it being a "mastery teacher" not a "mystery teacher."

Karen Rogers
Kansas

Principals need to know even more. They need to know how to lead the school so that teaching effectiveness occurs. When this is done, results have shown that student achievement rises dramatically.

Baseball coaches know baseball; orchestra leaders know music; bank managers know money matters. **Principals are expected to be knowledgeable in instruction.** They must know pedagogy—basically, how to manage the classroom and how to manage instruction. (Refer back to page 9 and what Elaine Farris says about mastery and instruction.)

If a principal is not knowledgeable in pedagogy or instruction, then the principal has no right to evaluate the teachers.

A child only has one chance at being eight years old. A student only has one chance at third grade. That student's teacher is the most important person that school year. Don't ask, "What program can I use," "What game can we play," or "What project can we do?" Ask, **"What instructional method or influence can I use that will exceed effect size 0.40?"** That can happen in your classroom.

Setting the base point at 0.00 and assuming every student will learn no matter what method is used is

Clear, Not Confused

"She explained everything. I can't get confused in her class. She was very clear."

student of Juanita Radden
Washington, DC

a dangerous and false assumption. If every teaching fad or program or method works equally well, then the result would be that we do not need to make any changes in our school systems. But it is obvious that many students are floundering and not realizing their potential. So we keep asking for more money, more resources, more programs, and smaller class sizes even though research has shown that these are not the issues that need addressing. Setting the bar at an effect size of 0.00 is simply a disaster. It leads to stagnation and inefficiency.

THE Classroom Instruction Book shows you the efficacy of methods used by effective teachers that are ranked above the 0.40 level.

Mastering Instruction

 There is extensive research on how to instruct and improve student achievement.

 The effective teacher uses evidence-based research methods that have a profound influence on learning and achievement.

 An effect size is the size of a teaching technique that has a statistical significance in influencing student achievement.

 By implementing the influences with effect sizes above 0.40, the potential for a student to experience academic growth increases.

 Effective teachers use visible learning techniques to help students become their own teachers.

...Produces Achievement!

The Learning Triangle is the basis for organizing a lesson for effective instruction.

The Learning Triangle

The idea of The Learning Triangle is used to create a strong and stable lesson, a lesson that has integrity. Start with a clear idea of what it is students should learn—the lesson objectives; then determine the instructional methods that will best lead them to grasp those objectives; then assess their learning.

The process is best explained by the shape of a triangle, in which the three sides fit together and support each other. Please note that there is no strict linear order to the three sides of the triangle—

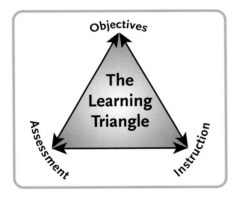

The
Learning
Triangle

Objectives

Assessment

Instruction

that is, Objectives, Instruction, and Assessment don't necessarily have to be addressed in that order when designing a lesson. The three components just have to work as a meaningful, coherent whole.

What the effective teaching process does is put learners first—and effective teachers meticulously design instruction with clarity and integrity so that students master what they are to learn. Students deserve to be given every opportunity to achieve and succeed in life using what they have learned in school.

Strength of the Triangle

> **The triangle is a foundation to an offense.**
>
> Bill Cartwright
> Retired NBA player and coach

The triangle offense combines perfect spacing with the actions of players with a high basketball IQ and great fundamentals to produce optimal spacing of players on the court.

You have probably sat at a table that rocked annoyingly, most probably a four-legged one. A table with three legs will not rock because the three points form a plane. In the "old days," milking stools were three-legged so that the stool would not wobble under the weight of the dairy farmer. The tripod that a photographer uses prevents the camera mounted on it from moving even slightly. The triangle is the most stable geometrical shape.

It is the responsibility of teachers to organize an instructional process that ensures their students learn to the best of their ability.

What Every Student Deserves

Every student deserves an effective teacher, not by chance, but by design. You would want to be assured of the professional expertise and effectiveness of a dentist, pilot, accountant, or hairdresser—and it is the same in education. The person a student gets for a teacher should not be left to the luck of the draw, where "good enough" is acceptable. Every student's future depends on having dedicated teachers who are trained professionals.

There is a belief by some teachers that students should do what they like, whereas effective teachers create classrooms where students like what they do.

Education should not be a haphazard process where students design their own curriculum, determine what they want to learn, choose their own books, and do their own work at their own pace—where it is left up to them to figure out what content is to be discovered and what skills they are to learn. That is not the approach taken here.

Learning takes place when effective teachers create and manage classrooms that are learning-centered— where they organize and structure Objectives, Instruction, and Assessment.

The Essence of Teaching

The essence of teaching and the magic of learning truly happen when

- the teacher says, "I am the one that makes learning possible in the classroom and I am committed to making it happen," and

- the student says, "I trust that my teacher will make it possible for me to learn and I will do everything that I can to learn."

There is no one definitive way to teach or learn. Students, teachers, schools, classes, and communities are all different. You don't teach band the same way you teach third grade spelling, middle school history, or high school AP English. You don't teach immigrant students with limited English the same way you teach a class of young nerds in Silicon Valley. You don't teach students in math class the same way you teach a class in Career Technical Education.

There are myriads of approaches a teacher can use, as described by John Hattie's list of effect size influences.

Basically, effective teaching boils down to

- **I do**—The teacher clearly explains what students are to learn and how they will learn.

- **We do**—The teacher checks for understanding while students are practicing and working on lesson objectives.

- **You do**—Students are asked to produce work that shows they have learned the objectives.

Take an example, such as when you taught someone how to ride a bicycle. You taught (I do); you held on with the rider (We do); you let go (You do). Teaching a lesson is the same. The academic term for this process of "letting go" is Gradual Release of Responsibility (page 210).

Teaching to ride a bike: One of life's great learning achievements.

A Culture of Consistency

The most effective teachers create a culture of consistency. In a classroom that is consistent, predictable, reliable, dependable, and stable, students know, from day to day, how lessons are structured and organized. This gives students a sense of security. They know they are in capable, trustworthy hands. They know exactly what to do to learn and succeed.

> **CONSISTENCY is the hallmark of an effective classroom.**

Educational literature is filled every day with stories of students who come from dysfunctional homes coping with poverty and many other problems. What these students deserve more than anything else is a teacher who teaches content using the best possible effect size techniques so that they are given every opportunity to succeed despite the challenges they face. Their life, their livelihood, and their dreams depend on being in a classroom that is organized so that learning is assured.

Students have only one chance in your classroom.

Students at all levels of the academic spectrum need teachers who use well-organized, research-based instructional practices.

Targeted Lessons

The real challenge in teaching is to apply focused, targeted instruction to address particular skill areas. Doctors target treatment; they do not adopt a program. **Effective teachers always teach lessons with targeted objectives so both teacher and students know what they will accomplish and how.**

To create targeted instruction plans, ask these questions.

- What are students to learn? (Chapter 4)

- How does the teacher show and model what learning is to take place? (Chapter 17)

- How does the teacher assess learning to help students make progress? (Chapter 8)

- How do students practice what is to be learned in a group? (Chapter 11)

- How do students independently practice and demonstrate what is being learned? (Chapter 18)

- How does the teacher finally evaluate what students have learned? (Chapter 19)

Good Teaching Is Content-Driven

The effective teacher recognizes solid academic instruction as essential to teaching. The greater a teacher's knowledge of the subject they teach, the more learning will be enhanced. The more you know, the better you will be able to teach what you want students to learn.

All students learn more when content drives the purpose of instruction.[1]

Daniel T. Willingham

When students (and parents) clearly see an emphasis on high-quality, meaningful instruction, they are confident that learning will result. Effective teachers orchestrate consistency and organization in their classrooms to allow the central focus of classroom time to be on teaching and learning.

**The key word is organization.
A comprehensive curriculum that is organized around meaningful and engaging instruction will produce student learning.**

Organized Instruction

In an effective classroom, the instruction is organized. This removes uncertainty for both the teacher and students. Students are given every opportunity to succeed because there is teacher clarity in an organized instructional plan for all to see.

Effective teachers establish an organized pattern so that students can be active participants the minute they enter the classroom without being bullied, teased, or bored while waiting for the teacher to announce that class has started.

Effective teachers have an agenda and an opening, bellwork assignment posted before students arrive to maximize instructional time. Students know before class begins what they will learn and how they will learn. This knowledge and certainty enable them to predict how well they will do on a lesson.

---

[1] Willingham, "Ask the Cognitive Scientist."

The Well-Organized Lesson

A well-organized lesson has the following visible parts.

◆ Students know what they are learning. (Lesson objectives, Chapter 4)

◆ Students know if they are learning. (Assessment, Chapter 8)

◆ Students know what it means to be good at this learning. (Self-assessment, Chapter 13)

◆ Students know what it means to have learned it. (Evaluation, Chapter 19)

When instruction is well organized, there is visible learning.

When there is visible learning, the more students will learn.

The Three Components of Effective Instruction

The three core components of good instruction and effective lesson design have been known for decades and are supported by cumulative research. Objectives, assessment, and instruction are found in units B, C, and D:

1. **Objectives—Unit B**
   What students are to learn and what the teacher is to teach

2. **Assessment—Unit C**
   What progress the learner is making

3. **Instruction—Unit D**
   What the best influences are, by effect size, for the teacher to use to teach

These components form The Learning Triangle, the organizing structure of *THE Classroom Instruction Book*.

However, as was said before—the three core components are not a sequential list. There is no beginning or end to The Learning Triangle. The components are related to each other and have coherence, that is, they fit together, work together, and form an instructional design model that works.

The Most Stable Shape

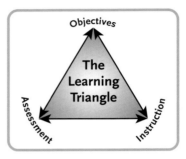
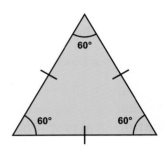

An equilateral triangle has three equal sides of equal length connected by three identical 60-degree angles, giving the triangle a consistent shape.

The Learning Triangle can be found as a lesson design model at Carnegie Mellon University.[2]

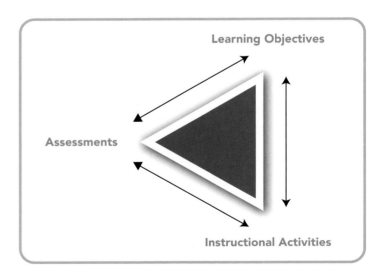

---

[2] "Teaching Principles," Teaching Excellence & Educational Innovation, Eberly Center, Carnegie Mellon University, last accessed October 1, 2021, https://www.cmu.edu/teaching/principles/teaching.html.

It is also part of the national curriculum in Singapore.[3]

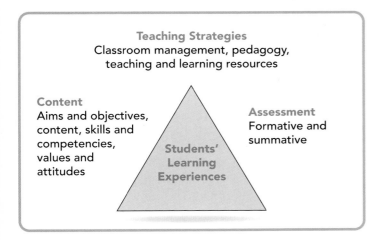

Teaching Strategies
Classroom management, pedagogy, teaching and learning resources

Content
Aims and objectives, content, skills and competencies, values and attitudes

Students' Learning Experiences

Assessment
Formative and summative

The equilateral triangle is the strongest geometric shape. If you press down on an equilateral triangle, its angles cannot change because the force is distributed along all three sides, keeping the triangle in place. Each side supports the other two. If you put weight on a square, on the other hand, the square will lean to the side and become a rhombus. A triangle will not change shape and it will not collapse under a weight. That is the reason bridges, roof lines, trusses, and many objects in our daily lives are in the shape of triangles. That is why the equilateral triangle is being used as a teaching and learning model.

We use triangles to develop strong and stable items for use in our lives.

We use a triangle to model a strong and stable lesson, a lesson where all components fit together, work together, and learning results.

The Objectives, the Instruction you choose to teach the objectives, and the Assessment of student learning are the three sides of the triangle. Introduce a fourth leg—for instance, content that is irrelevant or a test question about something that wasn't taught—and you destroy the integrity of the lesson. The integrity of The Learning Triangle is a simple concept, and it applies to the development of a lesson, a unit, a semester plan, or even a whole course.

[3] Winston Hodge, "Singapore Basic Education Curriculum Revisited: A Look at the Current Content and Reform," *Multilingual Philippines*, June 28, 2012.

You Start with a Triangle

" Crafting the perfect triangle has been the work of a lifetime. "

Sarah Powley
Coauthor
High school English teacher and instructional coach
Tippecanoe School Corporation, Lafayette, Indiana

Love Happens

I am an English teacher, but I spend my days drawing triangles and circles: sometimes imperfect ones, but identifiably these basic geometric shapes.

Once, during college, I created a unit on utopian literature for a hypothetical twelfth grade class. I assembled a glorious reading list that chronicled the history of the topic, covered all the major writers, and led my fantasy students to explore related issues in depth. The list was long and comprehensive. But that's all it was.

My professor wrote a single sentence at the bottom: What will the students learn?

I hadn't a clue. I think they were supposed to learn through osmosis. I wanted them to fall in love, as I had, with the texts and the ideas, but I had no sense of how I would orchestrate that love affair. I just supposed that they would open their books and read—and tumble head over heels into an embrace of what I thought was quite wonderful.

It was another teacher who taught me about the triangle. You start with a clear idea of what it is the students should learn, determine the instructional methods that will best lead them to grasp those objectives, and then assess their learning. Objective, Instruction, Assessment.

You don't test what you didn't teach, and you don't teach what you won't test. A triangle is stable just because there are three points. It's a simple concept, and though

it is second nature to me now, I still keep that triangle foremost in my mind every single day—whether it's a lesson, a unit, a semester plan, or even a whole course that I'm putting together.

In the beginning, my objectives were limited, even superficial—or they were too grand. It takes time to analyze content and pick out the important concepts. Over time, I learned to identify the gaps in some students' learning and figured out how to remediate those students while I was accelerating others. I learned to anticipate what every student would need to understand big ideas, and then to sequence my instruction accordingly.

I learned strategies that reach students by accommodating exceptionalities, that differentiate for ability, that touch every level of learning—or at least I try to do all this. A smorgasbord of instructional strategies exists, and I still try new ones and invent others as much and as often as my ingenuity, stamina, and the available resources allow.

Finally, I learned to write assessments that match the objectives precisely, and to select appropriate methods for assessment. The standardized format—multiple choice—usually isn't the best way to test depth of knowledge or critical thinking. Essays work often, but not always. Some situations call for the right rubric. Choosing the right assessment tool is a learned skill, too.

Crafting the perfect triangle has been the work of a lifetime (student obsession).

And that's only the half of it. A student can learn from a teacher who is technically skilled, but a student loves learning when the teacher loves the student, too. The geometry of a successful classroom includes a circle that, like the arms of parents around their children, makes the students feel important and secure, a circle that opens them up to learning.

*Some people think teaching is easy. You just stand in front of the class, tell them to open the book, and boom: love happens. No. You start with a triangle, the structure of **THE Classroom Instruction Book**. "*

1. Objectives

Effective instruction begins with clearly-defined objectives so that students can see where they are going and what they are to learn. Objectives produce student achievement results because there is no confusion as to what the teacher will teach or what the students will produce to show learning. **An important principle in successful teaching and learning is to be very specific in what is expected from students.** Post the objectives so students can constantly see what they are aiming for and how well they are progressing, like road signs are posted to guide us when driving.

Although it is usually recommended that the objectives be written before instruction and assessment, there will be times when you will find, even stumble over, an activity that is so good and workable that after trying it out you will want to write an objective and assessment afterwards. Regardless, there must be an objective for everything students do in the classroom.

If there are no objectives, it is just busywork.

Objectives may even be more important for the teacher than the students. This is because the teacher uses the objectives to craft the lesson. They serve as the foundation when designing the information and activities necessary for students to successfully complete the lesson. Without objectives, the teacher will resort to teaching in a panic mode. (More on objectives is found in Unit B.)

2. Assessment

Assessment is the process of helping students make progress. Every teacher knows the common term for assessment—it is "check for understanding." As the lesson is being taught, the teacher stops frequently to see how well students are learning the objectives. **The effective teacher does not separate the objectives from the assessment.**

Assessment is not evaluation;
it is not testing;
it is not grading.
It is checking for understanding.

Assessment is planned at the same time objectives are written and while the instructional activities are chosen. Assessment is how you will know your students have learned. Because you want your students to be successful at the end, you help them plan their progress for their success. To do this, effective teachers use assessment tools. (More on assessment is found in Unit C.)

Some teachers, like music, art, or physical education teachers, know precisely what they are looking for and how they will assess students. Thus, they can write the objectives after knowing what they are looking for in the assessment.

Truthfully, what effective teachers do is write and tweak the objectives and assessment simultaneously, going back and forth.

> *It is teachers seeing learning through the eyes of students, and students seeing teaching as the key to their ongoing learning.*[4]
>
> John Hattie

Since objectives, and possibly even the assessment, drive the instruction, the instructional activities can be incorporated at any time.

3. Instruction

The instruction part of the triangle is made up of the activities you use to teach the lesson objectives. This is where you can be inspired and use your imagination. This is where the effective teacher turns teaching into a creative art form. Be very creative. Go online. Ask your colleagues. Read the literature and find different ways to teach the objectives. (More on effective instruction is found in Unit D.)

All three parts of a lesson are directly related. They cannot be separated from each other. The objectives drive the instruction and are the basis for the assessment. Some teachers write the objectives first and then write the assessment, as the assessment will tell the teacher if the student is learning the objectives.

---

[4] Hattie, *Visible Learning.*

However, teachers are constantly looking for new and better activities that teach objectives, so an objective for an activity may be written after an activity is chosen.

As you select activities, always ask yourself this one essential question: What do I want students to learn?

6

Don't Teach in Panic Mode
See if you're teaching in panic mode and how to get out of it!

Direct Instruction

One of the most significant influences on student achievement is direct instruction—an effect size of 0.60. Direct instruction is not lecturing. It is based on the research finding that when teachers explicitly explain what students are expected to learn, and demonstrate and assess the steps needed to accomplish a particular academic task, students learn more. It is an instructional approach that is structured, sequenced, and led by the teacher.[5] In other words, teachers are "directing" the instructional process and showing students how to learn what is to be learned. There is no panic when instruction is planned, organized, and direct.

Direct instruction is teaching students how to learn.

Direct instruction does not mean repetition, drill and kill, or spoon-feeding students. Instead, most importantly, direct instruction is based on the assumption that knowing how to learn may not come naturally to all students, especially beginning and low-performing learners. Just as piano teachers teach students how to play the piano in a direct manner, effective teachers teach students how to learn in a direct and explicit manner. They can do this by showing students how a lesson is organized and structured, and then giving them the means, resources, and responsibility to learn.

Direct instruction is used to establish learning objectives for lessons, activities, and projects, and then making sure that students have understood how they are to proceed. Direct instruction takes students through learning steps systematically, helping them see both the purpose and the result of each step. Direct instruction is for leading students through a process and teaching them to use that process as a skill to master other academic tasks. In this way, students learn not only a lesson's content, but also methods and techniques for learning all subsequent content.

Direct instruction has been particularly effective in teaching basic skills to young and at-risk students, as well as in helping older and higher-ability students to master more complex materials and develop independent study skills. When someone teaches you how to use a food processor or how to write an essay, what you are getting is structured, direct instruction.

When teachers explain exactly what students are expected to learn, and demonstrate the steps needed to accomplish a particular academic task, students are given the ways and means to learn more.

When students see the path to success, the greater is the opportunity to learn.

---

[5] U.S. Department of Education, *What Works: Research About Teaching and Learning* (Washington, DC: U.S. Department of Education, Office of Educational Research and Improvement, 1986): 35.

With the use of direct instruction, effective teachers know

- the content to be taught,
- how to assess the success of the lesson being taught,
- how to motivate students to delve and explore, and
- how to expand student learning and creative skills that lead to the gradual release of responsibility.

Everything you need to succeed as a teacher is right in front of you. There are no secret menus. There are no magic formulas. There are no passwords to enter. Nothing is hidden.

THE Classroom Instruction Book will direct you by providing a clear, transparent roadmap based on The Learning Triangle for you and your students to achieve outstanding results.

Mastering Instruction

 Students need structure and consistency to learn and achieve.

 Effective teaching occurs when teachers create an effective instructional program.

 Instruction that is organized using the three components of The Learning Triangle—Objectives, Assessment, and Instruction—gives students the best opportunity to learn.

 Well-organized instruction results in visible learning.

 One of the most significant influences on student achievement is direct instruction with an effect size of 0.60.

...Produces Achievement!

UNIT B Objectives

Chapter

How to Use Objectives

Simply, tell students what they will be learning (objectives) and student achievement can be raised by as much as 27 percent.

Objectives Blaze the Trail

The Appalachian Trail is roughly 2,170 miles long. All along the way, you will see white blazes, not fires, but white marks like those on a horse's face. These 2-inch by 6-inch vertical rectangles are painted on trees, rocks, and signposts, showing hikers the trail. You can't get lost while hiking as these signs "blaze the trail" for you. A blaze tells you you're on the right track.

A blaze guides you on a trail.

Unit B is about how objectives effectively and efficiently blaze a trail for students.

Unit B focuses on three types of objectives:

- **Objectives that begin with a verb (Chapter 4)**
- Learning targets (Chapter 5)
- Essential questions (Chapter 6)

Learning Is Not Left to Chance

My students are able to focus on what they are expected to learn or be able to accomplish. Objectives provide direction to their learning; it is not left "to chance."

Jeff Gulle, NBCT
Middle School Teacher
Danville, Kentucky

"Hey, Mr. Gulle. What do we have to do today?" Before he could answer, another student responded. "You should know what we're doing. He puts it on the screen every day. If you don't know then it's your own fault!"

The teacher, **Jeff Gulle**, smiled because he has found that posting objectives sets the tone for the day's lesson and gives his students something to focus on throughout the class period. As instruction progresses, he regularly refers back to the objectives. This, in turn, provides his students with opportunities to construct their own knowledge by explaining to him (rather than vice versa) how the objectives are progressively being met—that is, how and what they are learning.

The Most Effective Learning Is Intentional

Teaching should be intentional. Effective teachers write objectives for a purpose. They want students to understand what they are supposed to learn. They refer to the objectives during the lesson and review them at the end for the same reason. **Teaching with objectives is intentional teaching.**

Students learn best when they understand what they are to learn and what is expected of them.

Objectives tell students **what they should know, do, and understand in a lesson**. Without objectives learning will be a mysterious, muddled process that does not lead to mastery. As explained in Chapter 2, students can predict their own success if they know what they are to do and learn in class.

Objectives
- help students understand the goal of a lesson.
- enable students to plan accordingly.
- help students manage their learning.

Many Names, One Aim

Learning objectives go by many names:

- Learning targets
- Learning goals
- Performance goals
- Mastery goals
- Goals
- Purpose statements
- Learning intentions
- Instructional objectives

What they are called is not important. What they tell students they are going to learn *is*.

Know Where You Are Going

To begin with the end in mind means to start with a clear understanding of your destination. It means to know where you're going so that you better understand where you are now so that the steps you take are always in the right direction.[1]

Stephen Covey
The 7 Habits of Highly Effective People

How often have you heard students ask, "What are we supposed to be doing?" Or, embarrassingly, have you overheard students say, "I'm lost. I don't know where the teacher is going." Worst yet, when you teach a lesson, are there times when you don't know where you are going yourself? If that is the case there will be no trail for students to follow.

The following conversations may sound familiar. You are relaxing in the faculty lounge during a break when a colleague asks you the kinds of questions you've heard a hundred times before, "Where are you in class," "What are you up to," or "What are you on now?"

The all too usual replies are, "I'm up to Chapter 22," "I'm on Chapter 17," "I'm covering the Civil War," or "I'm doing astronomy now." In the classroom, in the upper left corner of the board, something like this is probably written: Assignment—Read Chapter 22 and answer questions 1 to 7.

Honestly, objectively, and specifically, what does "I'm up to Chapter 22" or even "Read Chapter 22" really mean? If questions 1 to 7 are answered, what's the purpose? If there are no specific intentions or clear objectives, there is no purpose. **The textbook is not the curriculum.** The curriculum is a course of study that determines what students are to learn. Textbooks can be useful supplements to support the curriculum.

When students work without a purpose, they become lost in class with no clear idea of what to do in an assignment. That's what may cause them to fail.

---

[1] Steven Covey, *The 7 Habits of Highly Effective People* (New York: Free Press, 1989, 2004).

Lack of direction leads to lack of engagement in learning.

> *Without goals and plans to reach them, you are like a ship that has set sail with no destination.*
>
> Fitzhugh Dodson

The Importance of Objectives

No matter what instructional strategy you are using, start by posting the objectives.

Objectives produce superior student achievement results because the teacher knows exactly what is being taught and the students know exactly what they are learning. In precise, simple, and clear language, they state the aim of the lesson. There is no confusion or ambiguity about what the teacher will teach or what students will produce to show learning. With an objective, the teacher is able to craft the information or skills necessary for students to successfully complete the lesson.

Vague classroom assignments are similar to someone inviting you for a ride and saying, "Come with me and we'll cruise around Michigan." You would soon feel uneasy, bored, and lost with the lack of direction or purpose. Yet this is what *often* happens in classrooms. We don't give students any choice. They get in the car and are taken for a cruise around Chapter 1. And then they cruise around Chapter 2, and on and on it goes.

Soon we're like Alice in *Alice's Adventures in Wonderland* as she talks to the Cheshire Cat.

> *"Would you tell me, please, which way I ought to walk from here?"*
> *"That depends a good deal on where you want to get to,"* said the Cat.
> *"I don't much care where—"* said Alice.
> *"Then it doesn't matter which way you walk,"* said the Cat. *"—so long as I get somewhere,"* Alice added as an explanation.[2]

Setting achievable, measurable objectives for your students is a hallmark of effective teaching. Depending upon the format you select, the age of the students, and the complexity of the instructional goals, objectives can last for one day, several days, or for the length of a unit. Whatever their timespan or complexity, the benefits of establishing objectives are unquestionable.

- **John Hattie**, education researcher in New Zealand and Australia, studied over 800 possible influences on achievement. **He says that telling students the objectives before the lesson can raise student achievement by as much as 27 percent.**[3]

If you and your students do not know what is expected from a lesson, you're not likely to stumble across it. **Unless you know where you are going, how do you know you've arrived when you get there?**

---

[2] Lewis Carroll, *Alice's Adventures in Wonderland* (London: Macmillan & Co., 1865).

[3] Hattie, *Visible Learning.*

◆ **Robert Marzano**, education researcher in the United States, identified nine instructional strategies that have the greatest impact on learning. **Setting objectives and providing feedback** for students is one of those nine.[4]

◆ **Connie Moss** and **Susan Brookhart**, education researchers in the United States, write that **achievement is directly correlated with goal-setting**.[5]

◆ **Grant Wiggins** and **Jay McTighe**, education researchers in the United States, explain how **"Backward Design," or beginning with the end in mind**, significantly increases students' understanding.[6]

Very simply, you start where you want to end up. Knowing your destination sets the course for instructional success.

Objectives Are Based on Academic Standards

Lay out a sound set of standards and then actually teach these standards and there will be an immense increase in levels of achievement.[7]

Mike Schmoker

Objectives are derived from standards. You do not choose an objective out of thin air or because there is a particular topic, book, or idea that you want to teach. Objectives must be aligned with an official set of standards or your district's curriculum for your grade, subject, or class.

Standards are commonplace in life. Tradespeople must comply with standards called codes. You want buildings to meet code. Hairdressers, school bus drivers, and dry cleaners all must meet standards. The Food and Drug Administration (FDA) has standards. The Federal Aviation Agency (FAA) has standards.

Industries that serve the public have standards that must be met.

[4] Robert J. Marzano, Debra J. Pickering, and Jane Pollock, *Classroom Instruction That Works* (Alexandria, VA: ASCD, 2001, 2012).

[5] Connie M. Moss and Susan M. Brookhart, *Learning Targets: Helping Students Aim for Understanding in Today's Lesson* (Alexandria, VA: ASCD, 2012).

[6] Grant Wiggins and Jay McTighe, *Understanding by Design* (Alexandria, VA: ASCD, 2005).

[7] Mike Schmoker, *Results: The Key to Continuous School Improvement* (Alexandria, VA: ASCD, 1996, 2007).

There are standards in education also. **Content standards** are usually stated by grade level. They are broad statements that outline the scope of a particular course or grade and show how knowledge and skills accumulate, broadening and deepening, as students advance from grade to grade. They outline the ultimate aims of instruction in each realm of knowledge.

Standards are not the curriculum; they are not curriculum guides; they do not give examples of classroom activities; nor do they suggest books or topics that a teacher might use for instruction. Standards are not designed to be used as daily objectives.

Standards are written in general terms. It is up to the teacher to write objectives derived from those standards in user-friendly language that students can understand and accomplish.

An objective describes what you will teach your students to do. It describes what students will be able to do successfully and independently because of a classroom lesson. Students will find it much easier to succeed if they know what the objectives are.

Standards need to be "unpacked" to make them manageable for daily lessons. Here are three examples of a standard and the "unpacked" objectives.

◆ **Texas Essential Knowledge and Skills (TEKS)**
7.4A: Analyze the importance of graphical elements (e.g., capital letters, line length, word position) on the meaning of a poem.

Objectives
- Identify the poem's various graphical elements.
- Explain the significance of the poem's graphical elements such as word position.
- Determine the meaning of the poem.

◆ **Indiana Academic Standards (IAS), high school (Historical Thinking)**
9.2: Locate and analyze primary sources and secondary sources related to an event or issue of the past; discover possible limitations in various kinds of historical evidence and differing secondary opinions.

Objectives
- Using Internet and library resources, locate primary source documents or materials related to a controversial topic or event in US history.
- Using Internet and library resources, locate secondary source documents or materials that address the same topic or event.
- Complete a chart identifying the author, date, occasion, intended audience, and purpose for each document.
- Using evidence from your search, write an essay discussing the role variations in the author's profile; the date and occasion of the event; the intended audience for the document or material; and how the author's purpose can limit a reader's perspective on the event in question; and, more generally, on one's perception of any event.

◆ **Next Generation Science Standards, MS-ESS1-1 (The Universe and Its Stars)**
Patterns of the apparent motion of the sun, the moon, and stars in the sky can be observed, described, predicted, and explained with models.

Objectives
- Use a model to describe the motion of the sun, moon, Earth, and stars.
- Describe the life cycle of a star.
- Explain why the sun is an important star.
- Predict the amount of sunlight at the poles and equator on any given date.

My Thirty-Fourth Year Has Been the Most Rewarding

I plan my lessons with a structured, consistent daily routine in mind. From the moment my students enter the classroom, they know what we will be doing on that particular day, and how we will be doing it. Content standard, bellwork, and the day's objective are posted every day in the front of the room. They know what I expect of them before I begin teaching the lesson.

My instructional strategies, guided and independent practice, and daily assessment are all executed in the same way every day. My daily lessons and assessments come from an assessment system aligned to the South Dakota content standards. In both my teaching and assessing of the lesson, I use the same terminology that the state assessment uses so as to keep those skills "fresh" in their minds.

At Sisseton Middle School we have a culture of consistency! Our teachers and paraprofessionals follow the same procedures throughout the day, from greeting our students at the door as they enter the classroom, to being at the door again as they leave the classroom with a friendly, "Have a nice day," "Good work," etc. All teachers have the same expectations of students. Along with the implementation of procedures, all teachers use the same lesson plan format.

This is my thirty-fourth year of teaching, and I can honestly say last school year and this school year have been the most rewarding. *I am so grateful that our principal,* **Mrs. Karen Whitney,** *believed in our staff and trusted that we could come together as a team for our students.*

Deb Thompson
Sisseton Middle School, South Dakota

Curriculum Guides

Expect the Best. Expect Success.

In addition to standards, school districts typically have a curriculum guide. It may also be called the course guide, the curriculum map, or the scope and sequence. Curriculum guides are usually written by a committee or small group of teachers, administrators, and curriculum experts in the district—your peers. A curriculum guide provides a roadmap for all of the teachers of a particular subject or grade to use. **The curriculum guide is the trailblazer to use when creating the objectives and teaching to them.**

School districts develop curriculum documents to help their teachers as they design daily lessons and units of study that will ultimately convey the content of the standards. Curriculum guides begin the process of breaking the standards down into manageable chunks.

A set of curriculum documents builds and outlines, one grade at a time, one course upon another, from kindergarten to twelfth grade, the whole body of learning required by the district. Curriculum guides also outline the sequence of instruction if a particular sequence is critical.

If a teacher does not adhere to and teach the curriculum, gaps and redundancies in learning occur. The result is impaired achievement for students.

Curriculum guides tell teachers which texts or sources they must use or can choose from. Curriculum guides present required units of study, usually breaking those down into specific concepts and skills that are to be learned. Curriculum guides often provide sample activities to give teachers an even more concrete idea of what kind of instruction and what level of learning is expected.

Curriculum guides differ in its design from district to district, but every district in a state must align its curriculum with the state standards. At each grade level and in each subject area, the curriculum must match the state standards in scope and in depth because the state's standardized assessments are based on those standards.

Teachers must adhere to the local curriculum because it is aligned with the state's standards and assessments. Teachers are not free to teach whatever they want whenever they want to. However, they are encouraged to be innovative and creative in conveying the information, skills, and values required by the standards.

Curriculum guides provide the scope and sequence that teachers must follow. But teachers are usually free to decide how they implement the teaching in their own classrooms.

Writing Objectives

The effective teacher does not cover. The effective teacher uncovers—uncovers what students are to learn.

Objectives can be stated many ways. Districts may require written objectives, but not dictate the style.

Objectives all begin with a verb, an action word that requires a student to do something.

- ◆ **Explain** the difference between a conductive hearing loss and a sensory-neural hearing loss.

- ◆ **Debate** an issue from both the affirmative and the negative position.

- ◆ **Prove** that two triangles are congruent.

Make It Clear, Keep It Simple

During the first week of school, a new English teacher optimistically began the year by assigning an independent project to his eleventh-grade students. His intent was for his students to review, in groups, the content and concepts he thought they should have mastered in their previous English classes. Each group would take an aspect of the English curriculum—for example, the comma rules—and create a PowerPoint presentation on the topic to present to the rest of the class. In this way, the class would cover the basics, and the students would be ready to move on to new material.

As it turned out, the concepts were so complicated, and the project so complex, that most students gave up. They used their time together to socialize or play on their computers. They did not even ask questions because they did not know what to ask. **There was a complete lack of clarity.**

The teacher's expectations were high, but these students needed smaller, more manageable topics, and much more guidance from him. He had assumed they understood all the concepts and were capable of working productively in groups. However, they did not all know one another and had not worked together

before. The teacher did not provide step-by-step directions, a rubric (Chapter 12), or an example to guide the presentation each group would make. His assignment was just too big. By the end of the week, he had scaled back his expectations, and the next week, he started over. Fortunately, this teacher learned what to do about objectives during that week of struggle.

A single explanation or example, broken into manageable steps, would have provided the direction needed to blaze a trail.

- State an objective in terms of what students should be able to do or know by the end of the lesson. (Unit B)

- Plan the assessment instrument that will be used to measure students' achievement of the objective. (Unit C)

- Select the best learning activity or instructional strategy to guide students to mastery of the objective and successful performance on the assessment. (Unit D)

Some objectives are written in an "I can" form (Chapter 5) and are called learning targets.

- I can create a pie chart to show the results of the survey.
- I can distinguish between rational and irrational numbers.
- I can relate the gas laws to a real-world example.

Then there are objectives written as an essential question (Chapter 6).

- What makes a "classic" in literature?
- Nature or Nurture: Which is more powerful in child development?
- How can we prevent genocide?

No matter what style you use, providing your students with objectives will have a significant impact on their achievement and on your effectiveness as a teacher.

Objectives Using Bloom's Taxonomy

Benjamin Bloom created a Taxonomy of Educational Objectives in 1956. His taxonomy is a guide to understanding the hierarchical nature of our thinking processes. The taxonomy has recently been revised, but it is still one of the most widely-used tools for educators who want to move their students from simply parroting information to independent, analytical thinking and original, creative thought.[8]

Writing an objective using Bloom's Taxonomy is a straightforward process.

1. **Choose a verb from Bloom's Taxonomy.**
2. **Complete the sentence.**

- **Describe** endotosis and exotosis.
- **Explain** the difference between a primary and secondary source.
- **Convert** fractions to decimals.
- **Use** the imperfect tense of regular verbs in French.
- **Write** a well-structured argumentative essay about global warming.

The verb should match the level of thinking you expect from your students. The level depends upon whether the knowledge and skills to be learned are these:

- Remembering
- Understanding
- Applying
- Analyzing
- Evaluating
- Creating

Objectives Are Precise

Objectives begin with a precise, measurable verb.

You will be writing, posting, and referring to the objectives throughout your teaching, and they must be visible and comprehensible to all students. It is imperative that objectives are well-written in "student-friendly" language. That does not mean talking down to students and over-simplifying. **It means writing clearly, directly, and precisely.**

Some universities prepare students to enter the teaching profession by modeling good classroom practice. Students describe **Stacey Allred's** class this way:

She puts the objectives up on the board every day and meets those objectives. The objectives are explained not only for the course, but for the entire lesson every single day.

Preservice teachers in **Stacey Allred's** class at Ball State University produce their own classroom organization plan.

[8] Benjamin S. Bloom and David R. Krathwohl, eds., *Taxonomy of Educational Objectives Handbook 1: Cognitive Domain* (London: Longmans, Green, and Co. Ltd., 1956).

She targets our learning, reminds us of due dates, and is so forward in her teaching.

She explains everything clearly and adds humor from her own teaching career as well as others.

We never fall behind in her class.

Because she is a role model for her students, students like **Kasey Oetting** were able to go forth in the profession and write clear and direct objectives.

Kasey Oetting's classroom in Muncie, Indiana, has clearly posted objectives to guide students each and every day.

Bloom's Taxonomy

Recently, revisions have been made to Bloom's Taxonomy. Levels 5 and 6 have been reversed. The point for the teacher is not which level is the highest. For the teacher, the point is to structure learning so that objectives reach all six levels at appropriate stages in the learning process.

Pages 231 and 232 in **THE First Days of School** show lists of verbs that describe the thinking processes at Bloom's six levels of thought with descriptions for each of the six levels.

Access the code to see Bloom's Taxonomy.

Over time, you will write objectives at many different levels, taking care to sequence the objectives so that you do not ask students to perform a higher-level thinking process before they know the fundamentals.

Conversely, you do not want to spend so much instructional time on recall and comprehension tasks that you never get to the more challenging levels of analysis, evaluation, and synthesis.

Another important aspect of using objectives is that the tasks you ask your students to perform should be age- and stage-appropriate. The tasks must be doable.

Novice teachers may discover that students are not able to complete a task if it requires more independence than they are prepared to demonstrate. In some cases, especially for young students, for students with accommodations, and for any student when being introduced to a concept for the first time, the teacher needs to begin where students can all succeed and then scaffold (Chapter 16) and sequence to a higher order of learning.

Producing worksheet after worksheet (also called "drill and kill") are signs of lower-level expectations. However, asking students to analyze a complex topic for which they have no prior knowledge, no context, and no vocabulary is an exercise in frustration for everyone. Ask yourself what your students need to know before they will be able to accomplish any large task.

As students develop experience and skill, they will be able to work more independently. Finding the right balance between guided learning and independent learning will become easier as you gain experience and develop skill.

To support student success, objectives must be achievable and based on realistic expectations.

Imprecise Words

There are verbs that are not precise and are therefore not in Bloom's taxonomy. Avoid using vague verbs such as "know," "understand," or "appreciate." These soft verbs are not measurable and make it hard to determine whether the student has successfully completed the objective.

"Understand" is not a Bloom verb because it is difficult to pin down exactly what we mean when we say a student "understands" something. For example, how will you know when a student understands the distinction between an autobiography and a memoir? What will the student do or say to show you? How will you know that a student understands the causes of the Civil War? How will you know that a student understands the implications of the ice melt in the Arctic? Understand is not a precise verb. Choose a verb that tells the student exactly what you expect.

♦ If you want students to explain the difference between an autobiography and memoir, then "explain" is the right verb to use. You know that it is because you have thought about how you will assess knowledge of the difference between the two. You already know you will have a short answer question on your test that will require students to define the terms.

♦ If you want students to "contrast" the attitudes of the North and the South toward slavery, it is because you will post an essay question asking students, on the test at the end of the unit, to contrast the two stances.

♦ If you want students to "predict" what the rising sea level will mean for various parts of the world, it is because you will ask them to apply what they know about the impact of global warming on ice melt and the resulting ecological impact on areas of the world they are familiar with or can research.

The beginning and the end of instruction are directly linked. Knowing what you want each student to be able to do at the end of the lesson will help you choose the right verb for the objective at the beginning of the lesson. **To be effective, lesson objectives, instruction, and assessment must be aligned.**

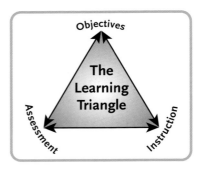

The Learning Triangle is an instructional model that works. You start with a clear idea of what it is students should learn, determine the instructional methods that will best lead them to grasp those objectives, and then assess their learning.

Posting the Objectives

In **Jeff Gulle's** classroom, he posts objectives with his daily agenda. When objectives are made clear to students, they are more readily able to self-assess and determine for themselves what they have learned and what they have not.

Begin class by pointing to the objectives and stating them aloud. Remind students periodically throughout the lesson that the activities they are doing will help them master the objectives. You cannot assume that students will read the objectives themselves and make the connection between them and what you are doing that day in class. If you do not draw attention to the objectives, students will not pay attention to them. They will become decorative wallpaper.

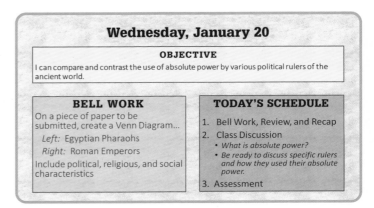

Wednesday, January 20

OBJECTIVE
I can compare and contrast the use of absolute power by various political rulers of the ancient world.

BELL WORK	**TODAY'S SCHEDULE**
On a piece of paper to be submitted, create a Venn Diagram... *Left:* Egyptian Pharaohs *Right:* Roman Emperors Include political, religious, and social characteristics	1. Bell Work, Review, and Recap 2. Class Discussion • *What is absolute power?* • *Be ready to discuss specific rulers and how they used their absolute power.* 3. Assessment

Because objectives provide direction to their learning, students in **Jeff Gulle's** classroom are able to focus on what they are expected to learn and accomplish.

Creating Objectives as Learning Goals

- Align with the state standards for your grade
- Follow your district's curriculum
- Sequence logically
- Write with students' prior knowledge and experience in mind

Post objectives every day in a place where students can easily see them. Write them in large letters so they can be read from the back of the classroom. If you write the objectives on the whiteboard, use black or blue markers so they can be seen. **The more visible learning is, the more capable and motivated students will be.**

> *Do not begin to think about technology until you have identified a clear objective for the lesson. Begin by asking, "How clear is the learning objective? What is the target?"*
>
> *Then, the objective should be in writing or posted for the students to see.*
>
> Howard Pitler
> McREL, Chief Program Officer

Timeframe for Objectives

The amount of time it takes to accomplish objectives will vary. Some can be accomplished in a day, and some need several days. For example, suppose you want students to be able to explain the distinctions among the various points of view in third-person narratives: objective, limited, and omniscient. Depending upon how much prior experience your students have had with this sort of task, teaching them the mechanics of identifying the point of view might only take one day.

You would state the objective this way.

- Identify the point of view in the short story.

On the other hand, suppose you wanted students to consider why an author chose a particular point of view. To do that, you might ask them to revise the story under discussion—or any story—by changing the point of view. If they did not already know the mechanics of identifying point of view, you would need time to teach that. Then, you would model changing the point of view and students would try doing the same thing.

Finally, the class would discuss the impact of the changes they made. You would guide them to make the connection with the author's purpose. Doing all that might take longer than one day because the objective is larger than simple identification. This larger objective would involve discussion of what effects changing the point of view has on the story and lead to a discussion of the choices authors make and why they make those choices. The objective calls for analytical thinking.

Blazing Ahead

An important principle in successful teaching and learning is to be very specific in what is expected from students. Put everything up front.

- What to read
- What to do
- The objectives
- What they must know
- When the deadlines are
- How they will be tested

What we need is a system that is so sure and so sound, so clear and so consistent, that there is no way a student can cop out or take a wrong turn. What we need is a system that gives the teacher and the student constant directions, continuous blazes, so progress is assured.

When you teach, you have expectations of what students will learn and achieve. This means you need to tell students exactly what is expected of them.

In this case, the objective could be stated like this.

◆ Infer the author's purpose for writing the story from the third-person limited point of view.

When both students and teacher are moving towards the same objectives, that's when you get learning.

The use of objectives ranks 0.42 on Hattie's influences of student achievement. Anything above 0.40 will significantly impact learning and achievement.

Tip for ELL Students

Begin class by pointing to the objectives and saying, "Here are our goals for the day." Refer to them during the lesson. Come back to them at the end. Following this procedure will help ELL students in the early stages of language acquisition understand that the instruction and activities during class are connected to the objectives. It will help them understand and process academic language.

All students in the class will benefit from knowing where you are headed and why they are doing the activities you have designed for that day.

Mastering Instruction

 Students learn best when they understand what they are to learn and what is expected of them.

 Objectives are based on academic standards.

 No matter what instruction strategy you are using, post the objectives first.

 Objectives begin with a precise and measurable verb.

 Learning happens when both students and teacher are moving towards the same objectives.

...Produces Achievement!

How to Use Learning Targets

Learning targets are manageable daily goals that students can feel personally responsible for achieving.

The "I Can" Objectives

In Chapter 4, you learned how to write objectives that begin with a verb. You were also made aware of the levels of thinking as categorized by Bloom's Taxonomy— from Remembering to Creating—which should be taken into consideration when scaffolding learning. Objectives written in that format are appropriate for older students who have longer assignments, and those who have prior background in a subject.

Learning targets are another form of objective. They are written in a distinctive way, readily identifiable because they begin with the two words:

"I can," followed by an action verb

Learning targets are useful for all students when a concept is introduced for the first time. They are particularly appropriate for younger, challenged, and ELL students because a learning target is designed to capture a daily goal—a bite-sized piece of learning.

Unit B focuses on three types of objectives:

- Objectives that begin with a verb (Chapter 4)
- **Learning targets (Chapter 5)**
- Essential questions (Chapter 6)

What Is Expected

❝ I teach with learning targets because my students know exactly what is expected of them and how they will be able to show that they have learned. ❞

Aundrea Beck
Holland, Indiana

"I can" statements are also beneficial for special education students. Objectives written in this way are specific, time-limited, and clear. Whether they are placed in a regular classroom or learn in a self-contained environment, special education students

"I can" statements guide students to aim clearly and hit the bullseye of the learning expected of them.

benefit when learning targets are written the same way each day and posted in the same place each day.

Learning targets are objectives that begin with "I can." They are specific, time-limited, and clear.

Learning Targets Instill Confidence

The "I" in "I can" is critical. When a student reads a statement that begins with "I can," the learning target becomes personal. Learning targets speak to the student because they are written from the student's point of view. They allow students to take ownership of their learning.

Students also understand the term "I can" immediately because it states precisely what they are aiming for. They know what they are responsible for learning and what exactly they will be able to do.

When students know what they are aiming for, they become responsible for learning.

When you write an "I can" statement, you must know what you want students to be able to do at the end of instruction. Learning targets tell students exactly what will be taught and what they are going to learn. "I" speaks directly to the student and encourages the student to respond with "I can" or "I cannot."

The response "I cannot" is just as important as "I can." **It is absolutely essential that students are not hesitant or afraid to say "I cannot." When they say "I cannot," it indicates that they know that you are there to guide and help them make progress.** Developing students'

confidence and understanding is your goal as a teacher. They have to be assured that they are allowed to be confused and unclear and that you are there to clarify, support, and assist.

Learning targets instill confidence and promote self-reliance. They ensure students take responsibility for learning. They permit them to say "I cannot" when they need assistance and to announce "I can" when they accomplish a task successfully.

Learning Targets Are Paced

Learning targets are not just a series of stand-alone lessons. They are lessons that build from the previous day's lesson toward the next day's lesson. They are paced appropriately. When you plan lessons in terms of learning targets, you move from day to day asking yourself, "What is the next step?" A lesson starts when you ask yourself, "What will I do tomorrow?" Then you create an "I can" statement that describes the teaching and learning that you will tackle that day.

You
- write the learning target,
- shape the lesson around the target, and
- ask students to demonstrate understanding of the target by completing a specific task that you have prepared them for during the lesson.

The learning target must be referred to repeatedly as the lesson progresses, not only mentioned at the beginning of class. Post it where it can be seen at all times. With a learning target visible, students are continuously aware of what they are aiming for. At the same time, the teacher explicitly focuses on the target and steers instruction toward the task each student will be asked to complete. This combination of aim and direction assures students that they **are** competent, that they **can** complete the task, and that you, the teacher, are there to ensure that they do it successfully.

Achieving proficiency in one day's learning target leads to proficiency in the next day's target. Students become ever more confident and competent when learning targets are paced appropriately.

> ### The learning target . . .
>
> - must provide a clear focus,
> - is something specific students will **do**,
> - is a concrete task that students will be expected to complete, and
> - should be at a level that students will be able to perform.

Learning Targets Are Quick and Easy

All teachers want to begin where students can succeed. When learning targets are simply and clearly written, students are capable of achieving the lesson goal so that they can experience the pride of accomplishment. Then they will be ready and eager to progress even further.

Learning targets are a joy to use. They are easy to write and easy for students to understand. It is also simple to adjust learning targets. You can quickly tweak or change a learning target when the need arises and the time has come to move forward (without having to stay up late at night devising new objectives for every subject every day). The consistent phrase at the beginning helps students stay focused even though the remainder of the sentence changes.

For example, in teaching what plants need for growth, the learning target could be "I can name one component that a plant needs for growth." Based on the lesson reading, discussion, and questions, the class might agree on "sunlight."

The next day, the learning target might be, "I can name one component, other than sunlight, that a plant needs for growth." All the teacher has to do is modify the part after the initial phrase to advance learning. This "student-friendly" design creates consistency that students can easily follow as the lessons build to reveal the four components that plants need: sunlight, water, minerals, and carbon dioxide.

By stating the learning target at the beginning of the lesson, students know what the focus should be, and as they progress through a lesson, they can refer back to the learning target to see if they are on track. And when students refer to the learning target at the end of a lesson, they can see if they actually met the goal they started out with.

It's much like having a shopping list that you have in hand to refer to before, during, and after shopping. Not having a shopping list is like not having a learning target. A learning target helps both you and your students to concentrate and work with a specific purpose in mind instead of wandering around aimlessly in the dark without a flashlight.

A shopping or "to do" list provides focus for getting tasks done.

Remember TSWBAT?

The beauty of learning targets is their simplicity. Not only are they personal, they are doable. This is in contrast to the antiquated five-step format many were told to adhere to that had to include the phrase "The student will be able to." Teachers fretted over and hated to write objectives because of the unwieldy format, not to mention that students often had no idea what the teacher was talking about as they tried to decipher the educational jargon. "The student will be able to" was such a redundant and obvious phrase that teachers started to abbreviate it to TSWBAT, which only served to confuse students further when they read the objective:

You may remember when you had to write an objective with the following five parts:

1. **The condition**—What will be provided as the basis of the lesson.
2. **TSWBAT**—"The student will be able to . . ." (It goes without saying that the objective is for the student!)
3. **The verb**—An action word from Bloom's taxonomy
4. **The content**—The parameters or condition of what is to be done.
5. **The evaluation criteria**—The test or proficiency used to indicate a score or grade.

Following that model, this is what a teacher may have provided to the class:

> Given three examples of a Shakespearean sonnet (numbers 3, 6, and 10) and four classifications (iambic pentameter, octave, closing couplet, and ABABCDCDEFEFGG rhyme scheme), the student will be able to bracket and label the four classifications correctly.

Now that you have recovered from your exasperation, know that it's possible to give students a learning target that states the objective quite simply, clearly, and succinctly.

◆ I can label an iambic pentameter, octave, closing couplet, and ABABCDCDEFEFGG rhyme scheme in a Shakespearean sonnet.

For the Love of a Closing Couplet

If you are curious, scan the code to see a correct response for the Shakespearean sonnet objective.

Objectives, learning targets, and essential questions (Chapter 6) function as tools of formative assessment. They help the teacher determine what the student has learned and what instruction is needed to master the content. They are visual roadmaps for effective instruction that eventually lead to testing and a formal, summative evaluation that shows student proficiency of the information.

Writing a Learning Target

Writing clearly defined lesson targets is the first step to guide you and your students in reaching their final destination—mastery of the content.

A learning target is a statement of an instructional goal.

◆ It is the basis for the assessment of the lesson. (Unit C)
◆ It is connected to the activities that the teacher selects. (Unit D)
◆ It is sequenced. It builds on instruction from the day before and leads to the next day's instruction.
◆ It is written in language that the student can easily understand.
◆ It is shared with the student at the beginning of instruction, during the instruction, and at the end of the instruction.

A learning target is easy to write. There are two steps.

1. Start with the stem "I can . . . ."
2. Add what the students will be able to *do*, prefaced with a verb at the beginning of the instruction.

Here are some examples.

◆ I can find the volume of a cylinder.
◆ I can convert a passive voice sentence into an active voice sentence.
◆ I can use indirect and direct Spanish object pronouns correctly in an affirmative command.
◆ I can use a Punnett square to predict the probability of a particular trait in an offspring.
◆ I can summarize the main idea of the article.
◆ I can solve a two-digit division problem.
◆ I can label the New England states on a blank map of the United States.
◆ I can explain the water cycle by drawing a picture and labeling the stages.
◆ I can create a still-life drawing of a three-dimensional object.
◆ I can predict the amount of sunlight based on the phases of the moon.
◆ I can write sentences with correct ending punctuation marks.

With older students, some teachers use "The student will . . ." or "I will . . ." to make the learning target sound more age-appropriate. And with students who are working in groups or projects, use "We can . . ." or "We will . . . ."

A learning target begins with "I can," "I will," or "We can," "We will," followed by a verb that states what students will do.

Create a display board of objectives for each subject with the headings of "I can," "I will," "We can," "We will," or "We are learning to . . . ." Such reinforcement and clear statements of purpose and direction will make students feel like active participants in the teaching and learning process.

Sarah Jondahl posts her learning targets so that students are continuously reminded of what they are expected to accomplish as they work throughout the day.

Converting Standards into Learning Targets

Objectives and learning targets are achievable daily goals based on standards and district curriculums.

Objectives and learning targets are determined by a set of academic standards, or a district's curriculum for particular grades, subjects, or classes. They are written in general terms and need "unpacking" to make them accessible and manageable for daily lessons.

Some teachers post the state standard alongside the accompanying lesson targets.

- ◆ **State Standard**
  - Interpret and compute quotients of fractions, and solve word problems by fractions, e.g., by using visual fractions models and equations to represent the problem.

- ◆ **Student-Friendly Lesson Target from the State Standard**
  - I will use models to multiply fractions.
  - I will multiply fractions by fractions.

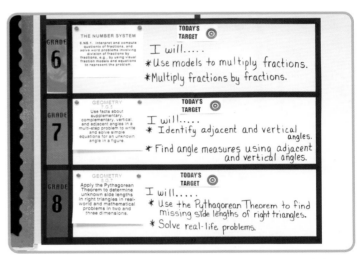

Some teachers post the state standards alongside their daily lesson targets in order to make the connection clear and explicit.

Maria Sanchez, a high school teacher, is often saddled with implementing new programs with new standards. Sometimes these standards are overly complex, as they are put together by groups of academics, curriculum people, and philanthropists who have no concept of what it is like to teach in an urban setting with many students bordering on being at-risk. Maria teaches in such a setting. Here is an example of a standard she had to grapple with.

- ◆ The student will explain that paleoclimatological evidence is analyzed to reveal historical patterns of warming and cooling on Earth.

Paleoclimatology is the study of changes in climate taken on the scale of the entire history of Earth.

The historical scale is so vast that it may even go back further than the big bang theory, yet many of Maria's students have difficulty remembering or caring about what happened yesterday. So she devised some student-friendly learning targets that her students would be able to accomplish successfully.

- ◆ I can read rings on a tree trunk and tell what the Earth was like at that time.
- ◆ I can read charts on the melting of ice in the Arctic and tell what the Earth is like at this time.

Tree rings tell the story of what the tree has experienced each year of its existence. Learning targets tell students what they will experience and accomplish during the lesson.

Long-Term Projects

"I can" statements work with complex and long-term projects or performances as well as daily assignments. Most teachers require students to complete projects that take time, and learning targets can be used effectively by dismantling the final performance or project into smaller steps.

When working on long-term projects with several stages, present learning targets one at a time in their logical sequence. It may take several days of instruction to accomplish the final task, but you will have broken the task down so that students will have been progressing toward the end from the beginning.

For example, writing an essay is a daunting task for some students no matter how old they are. Breaking

the task down into sequential steps that can be accomplished one at a time makes the task easier.

In this case, the progression of "I can" statements might look like this:

Day 1: I can write a proposal for a persuasive essay.
Day 2: I can write the introduction to my essay.
Day 3: I can write the first paragraph of support.
Day 4: I can write the second paragraph of support.
Day 5: I can write the third paragraph of support.
Day 6: I can write the conclusion of my essay.
Day 7: I can correct grammar, punctuation, and spelling errors in my whole essay.

Long-term and complex projects can be broken down into achievable tasks using daily learning targets.

9

From Paragraphs to Essay

See an example of how a student can convert paragraphs into an essay, bit-by-bit and step-by-step.

The Criteria for Success

The criteria for success is a map to the learning destination. It provides direction for teacher instruction and serves as continual motivation for students.

A learning target calls for students to complete a specific task and demonstrate that they can do what was asked for in the "I can" statement.

For example, the performance task is clear in the statement, "I can find the volume of a cylinder." At the conclusion of the lesson, the student should be able to use the formula for finding the volume of a cylinder to solve just such a problem.

Or success may mean accomplishing something that is spelled out in the "I can" statement. For example, "I can run one mile."

Students Know What Is Expected of Them

"For my high school special education class, I created a PowerPoint that was projected at the beginning of the period. As students entered our classroom they saw on the board the Question of the Day (QOD). The QOD would be a question that reframed yesterday's learning expectation (learning target). If students answered the QOD correctly I went to the next slide on my presentation that listed that day's "I can" statement and an "I know that I am successful when I can . . ." that would help students identify when they have met the learning expectation.

I would explain to my class what I expected them to learn for that day, how they would know that they were successful at meeting that expectation, and why it is important for us to learn the following skill or content area. I think it is vital for students to know the What, Why, and How of learning.

At the end of the class, the slide would be projected again, and students would attempt to answer the "I can" question as an Exit Ticket* in order to determine if they met that day's learning expectation. I would use those Exit Tickets to determine what adjustments I would need to make in the next day's lesson.

If students did not answer the QOD correctly at the start of class, then I would flip back to the previous day's learning expectation and have a class discussion on the previous day's materials and "I can . . ." criteria question. Sometimes I would reteach the lesson to try to discover why students struggled to carry over the previous day's learning expectation. The learning expectations were informal assessments that I used to gauge student understanding. The Exit Ticket also allowed me at the end of class to see who did not reach the learning expectation and I would use the start of class the next day to reteach to those few who did not meet the learning expectation instead of them working on the QOD.

I teach with learning targets because my students know exactly what is expected of them and how they will be able to show that they have learned. Learning expectations allow my students to be involved in the education process and be stakeholders in their own education because it sets clear criteria of success for them. It allows them to leave my room feeling successful and positive that they have learned something new and met their expectations. My students are excited when they are able to meet the learning expectation."

*(See Chapter 10 for more on Exit Tickets.)

Aundrea Beck
Holland, Indiana

The criteria for success of the learning task should be absolutely clear. Learning targets are designed to capture daily progress. When you teach using "I can" statements, it is imperative that you share with students not only what the task at the end of the day will be, but the criteria you will use to assess their performance. That is how they will know what to do and how they will know ahead of time if they are close to, or far from, meeting your expectations.

**What you teach should align with
your expectations
of student performance and achievement.**

In some cases, getting the right answer will let you and your students know that they have reached the goal of the learning target.

- I can label the parts of speech in a sentence.
- I can measure distance in kilometers.

In some cases, the success criteria are embedded in the wording of the target.

- I can perform ten push-ups.
- I can write a sentence that is fifteen to eighteen words long.

WALT and WILF
We Are Learning To and What I'm Looking For

The WALT and WILF acronyms will help students understand your learning intentions as well as the criteria for success.

Begin with a learning target that states what "**W**e **a**re **l**earning **t**o . . . (WALT)."

Then follow by telling students "**W**hat **I**'m **l**ooking **f**or . . . (WILF)" as they do the work. These statements form the basis of your assessment as to whether or not the students accomplished the WALT statement.

Post both the WALT and WILF so students can see what they are to produce to achieve success.

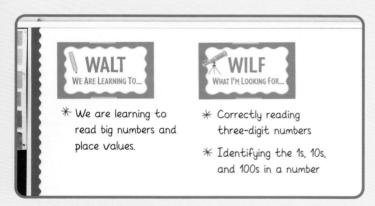

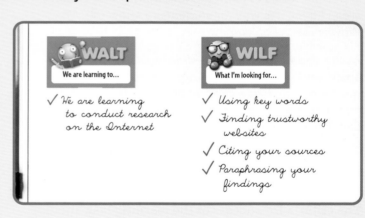

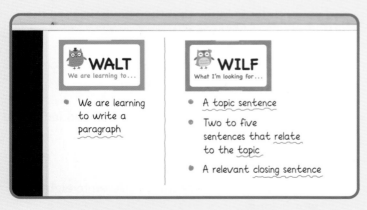

WALT and WILF

Use these and other ready-made WALT and WILF graphics to bring clarity to your instruction.

The Importance of Examples

In some cases, students will need concrete examples of what a successful task looks like. It is one thing to post the objective or learning target, but to help students reach proficiency, they need to be shown an example of a successfully completed task. Coaches do this all the time—they demonstrate and show examples of what a successful end result looks like. Students should have plenty of examples to understand what they are to do. Provide examples of diagrams, charts, models, and demonstrations.

Diagrams and Charts. Perhaps the task requires that the student will label a diagram or fill in a chart:

- A diagram of a cell with blanks to name the cell parts
- A Frayer model for learning vocabulary words
- A grid with fourteen rows and ten columns for writing a sonnet

The diagram or chart should be shared with the student from the beginning. Help and guide students so that what they are to do is clear. As stated before, what you teach should reflect what you expect.

Examples, Models, and Demonstrations. Examples help students understand what they are expected to learn and do. Textbooks, depending upon the subject, often provide the examples students need. Sometimes, a model of what is expected is helpful for students. Models clarify expectations, especially when the quality of the student's work will be evaluated.

You can share past examples of student work so that your current students know what you expect. If there are no past examples, you can demonstrate or create a model yourself.

Students should be supported with plenty of examples and models so they understand exactly what they are to do, what your expectations are, and how they will be assessed.

Using a past example as a model, **Kara Howard** of Coal Grove, Ohio, asks her students to explain Newton's law of conservation of energy by building a model of Newton's cradle.

Display numerous examples so students can see what you expect them to produce and achieve at the completion of a lesson or project.

Cell Anatomy Worksheet

Frayer Model Example

Definition:	Characteristics:
A living creature with feathers, wings, and a beak	Ability to fly

Bird

Examples:	Non-Examples:
Dove Eagle Penguin	Bee Bat Flying fish

Example Sentences

- **Incorrect:** *Their* being very rude
- **Correct:** *They're* being very rude

- **Incorrect:** Who would *where* that silly hat?
- **Correct:** Who would *wear* that silly hat?

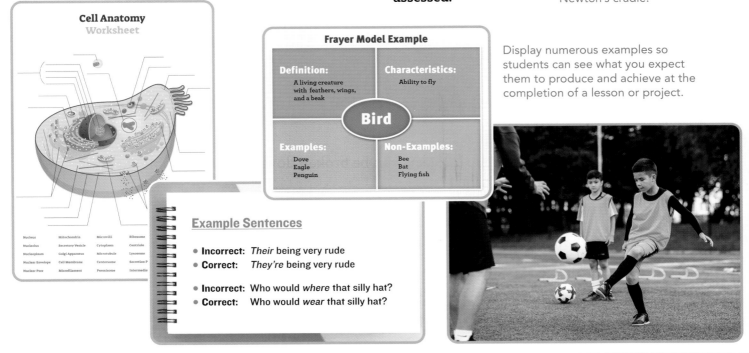

- In math, the teacher can select problems from the textbook to use as supplementary examples.

- Photographs in textbooks are intentional. In Earth Science, for example, a student who does not understand what a moraine is can see a captioned picture in the textbook.

- In language arts texts, sentence after sentence is provided to show students how to correctly form the specific sentence construction under study.

If the textbook does not have examples—or if you aren't using a textbook—the Internet is only a few keystrokes away. Students often need many examples to guide them as they attempt to complete a task.

Sentence Patterns	Examples
Subject + Verb	The bell rang. He danced.
Subject + Verb + Object	She likes eggs. I met my brother.
Subject + Verb + Adjective	Martin is busy. She was sick.
Subject + Verb + Adverb	The truck came here. He ran fast.
Subject + Verb + Noun	They are teachers. Marilyn was the class president.

Mastering Instruction

 Learning targets are objectives that begin with "I can." They are specific, time-limited, and clear.

 Learning targets instill confidence. They ensure students say, "I can" and take responsibility for learning.

 Objectives and learning targets are based on standards and district curriculums.

 Long-term and complex projects can be broken down into achievable tasks using daily learning targets.

 Align what you teach with your expectations of student performance.

...Produces Achievement!

How to Use Essential Questions

Essential questions engage students in issues that will recur throughout life.

Essential Questions Are Also Objectives

What is an essential question? Well, it's a question that is essential—to life, or the subject being learned. Essential questions are relevant and help students link what is being studied to personal experience. They are questions that address core issues and help learners make sense of important, complicated ideas.

Essential questions are often designed for larger units of learning. They cannot be answered in one short day or even in a few days. Essential questions are designed to drive a unit of study. They can drive a semester of study or even a year-long investigation.

For instance, an essential question in a Spanish class might ask how a meal is prepared—in Spanish, of course. When students enter the Spanish 3 class taught by **Noah Roseman** at Brockton High School in Massachusetts, they first see their placemats with goals, essential questions, and objectives. They also see four boards around the room spelling out the different aspects of the lesson for the day. Noah never has to say a word as students settle into their seats and

Unit B focuses on three types of objectives:

- Objectives that begin with a verb (Chapter 4)
- Learning targets (Chapter 5)
- **Essential questions (Chapter 6)**

Essential Questions on a Placemat

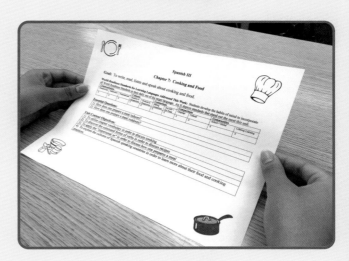

"They can't help but know exactly what they are doing in class at all times."

Noah Roseman
Brockton High School
Brockton, MA

There are restaurants where the menu is written on a placemat. **Noah Roseman**, a Spanish teacher, has incorporated such an idea in his classrooms as a prelude to his daily lessons.

A new placemat is generated for every unit of study. It lists the goals, essential questions, and content objectives. Students adopt the routine of examining their placemat immediately upon sitting down. They can't help but know exactly what they will be learning at all times and what they are aiming to achieve. They are told up front before instruction begins.

prepare themselves. The class is organized so that the learning is visible, and students know exactly what is expected of them.

To their left, students see the driving or essential question written on the board. This sets the tone or purpose of the lesson.

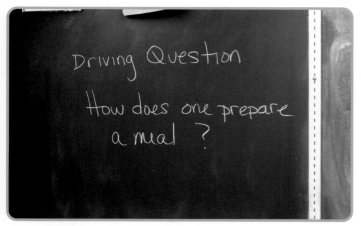

The driving, essential question challenges students to start thinking when they enter the classroom and prepare for the lesson ahead.

Next, they see *El horario* or the schedule for the class period.

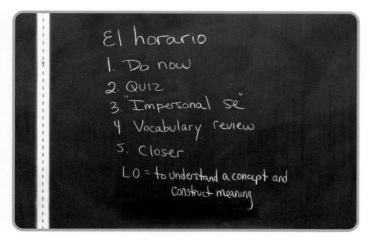

The schedule provides the flow of instruction and tells students what to expect as the lesson progresses.

The first task, the Do Now, is presented on another board.

The Do Now engages students in a purposeful activity the moment they enter the classroom.

And finally, they read the lesson or content objectives.

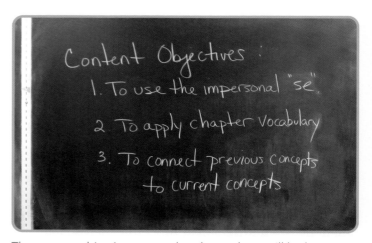

The content objectives state what the students will be learning during the course of instruction and what the teacher expects them to achieve.

Students can't get lost in this class. They know what's happening because all the components that make up a lesson are explicitly displayed, and each day is consistent. The class is organized, the students are engaged, and learning starts right away. Students look at the four boards and see a span of what is needed to successfully execute the lesson.

It all starts with an essential question.

Essential Questions Are Part of the Agenda

The four boards in **Noah Roseman's** classroom create the learning agenda for students to follow. In addition to the information on the placemat listing the essential question, goals, and content objectives, students are able to see in detail how the day's instruction works coherently to enable the learning necessary for accomplishing the goals and objectives as they address the essential question guiding the lesson.

Board 1: Essential or Driving Question

The driving question is the essential question and provides the big picture for students. Its purpose is to help them realize that the most important thing is not memorization of individual facts or concepts as it relates to the lesson. Rather, the most important thing is that they will be able to apply the new information as they go through life in school and in the real world.

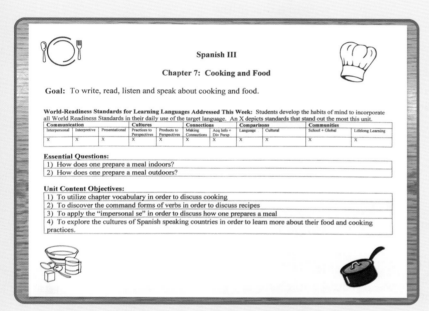

Spanish III

Chapter 7: Cooking and Food

Goal: To write, read, listen and speak about cooking and food.

World-Readiness Standards for Learning Languages Addressed This Week: Students develop the habits of mind to incorporate all World Readiness Standards in their daily use of the target language. An X depicts standards that stand out the most this unit.

Communication			Cultures		Connections		Comparisons		Communities	
Interpersonal	Interpretive	Presentational	Practices to Perspectives	Products to Perspectives	Making Connections	Acq Info + Div Persp	Language	Cultural	School + Global	Lifelong Learning
X	X	X	X	X	X	X	X	X	X	X

Essential Questions:
1) How does one prepare a meal indoors?
2) How does one prepare a meal outdoors?

Unit Content Objectives:
1) To utilize chapter vocabulary in order to discuss cooking
2) To discover the command forms of verbs in order to discuss recipes
3) To apply the "impersonal se" in order to discuss how one prepares a meal
4) To explore the cultures of Spanish speaking countries in order to learn more about their food and cooking practices.

Cooking Up Success

To demonstrate that students have executed the lesson successfully, they produce a recipe booklet as a culminating independent practice activity. The concept of independent practice is explained in Chapter 18.

Noah Roseman generates a new placemat with an essential question, a list of goals, and content objectives for every unit of study.

Board 2: Schedule

The schedule provides an outline of what students will do that day. They are trained to immediately connect the schedule to the content objectives on the placemat. This organizing technique helps students understand how the current lesson connects to previous lessons.

The last item on the schedule is the closer. **The closer is a prompt that students answer during the last few minutes of class. It is a type of formative assessment to see if students understood the lesson.** Often, they are asked to write in response to the closer. The papers are then collected and placed in three piles. The first pile is for students who understood the lesson; the second is for those who more or less understood the lesson; the third is for those who did not understand the lesson. This important information is used by the teacher to create instruction for the next day. The next day's opener will target any evident weaknesses.

Board 3: Opener or Do Now

The opener is a prompt designed to get students on task immediately in order to ensure instruction from bell to bell. The opener is always relevant to the work on that day. Ideally, the opener targets a weakness noticed from the previous lesson through formative assessment.

Board 4: Content Objectives

The content objectives tell students exactly what they are expected to learn that day. Perhaps they have already worked with an objective but are strengthening their skills during that class period. The content objectives provide a clear focus for what students will be able to do by the end of the class period.

Origin of Essential Questions

Ted Sizer, chair of the Department of Education at Brown University, coined the term "essential questions" in his book, *Horace's Compromise*.[1] Sizer stressed that teachers need to make decisions about what students need to know and be able to do, and that they should use essential questions to engage students and structure their lessons.

Grant Wiggins and **Jay McTighe** further developed the related idea of backwards design, that is, beginning with the end in sight when designing lessons, in their book, *Understanding by Design*.[2] Wiggins and McTighe suggest that there are four types of essential questions:

1. Questions that recur throughout our lives
2. Questions that get at core ideas and inquiries within a discipline
3. Questions that are essential to help learners make sense of important, complicated ideas
4. Questions that most engage a specific and diverse group of learners

Some essential questions blend lifelong questions on relevant topics with historical examples. For example, the essential question, "The Code of Hammurabi: Were the laws just?" encourages students to decide what is just and what is not, and to evaluate the code in those terms. It challenges them to ask questions about issues of justice and social contracts that will recur throughout their own lives. A good question to ask to further the inquiry and provoke deeper thinking is "If you could, what in Hammurabi's code would you change?"

The Code of Hammurabi, an ancient Babylonian code of law from about 1754 BC, was the first to create penalties for crimes and to establish the presumption of innocence.

[1] Theodore R. Sizer, *Horace's Compromise: The Dilemma of the American High School* (New York: Houghton Mifflin, 2004).

[2] Wiggins and McTighe, *Understanding by Design*.

Essential Questions Are Important

An essential question can be used to focus or drive the lesson, but essential questions are not the commonly asked factual questions. They are not the usual, run-of-the-mill lesson objectives that are familiar to students.

Essential **questions require intensive investigation, where students are asked to think about something rather than do something.** There is no definitive answer as there would be for a lesson target. **Essential questions are often challenging and involve ongoing inquiry.** They are discussion points rather than an assignment, which is a clever way to get students engaged.

Essential questions engage students in issues that are challenging, complex, and intriguing. They address issues that will recur throughout their lives.

Essential Questions Are Excellent Group Questions

Lessons driven by essential questions allow students to explore compelling ideas and learn important skills at the same time. **With an essential question, a teacher can plan a framework for instruction for an entire unit that spans a much longer length of time than a learning target, which is typically for a day.**

Essential questions are the most intriguing kinds of questions to ask in class. For one, they rarely provoke often-asked, apathetic questions from students like "Why are we studying this?" or "How does this apply to my life?"

This is because essential questions speak directly to students and ask them to give serious thought to

Essential Questions in a Yearlong Course

Janet Stearns, a middle school music educator in Indiana, suggests a sample list of essential questions for the classroom.

- What inspires a composer to write music?
- When can you call yourself a music reader?
- When is it music? When is it noise?
- How does music affect culture? How does culture affect music?
- When is it music? When it is written down or when it is heard?
- What does it mean to be really good at something?
- What is the difference between singing along and performing?

These questions are then turned into targeted questions.

- How did Duke Ellington's music affect culture? How did culture affect Duke Ellington's music?
- Did the evolution of the keyboard create music? Or did the evolution of the keyboard create noise?
- Is Karaoke really singing? Or is Karaoke a performance art?

Janet has also designed three courses in General Music around year-long essential questions.

- Sixth grade: What inspires a composer?
- Seventh grade: When is it music and when is it noise?
- Eighth grade: How does society influence music and how does music influence society?

Even if you are not a music educator, these examples are useful guides. Learn how to adapt what others are doing to what you are teaching.

11

Note This Essential Question

See an example of how a single essential question can be utilized in a year-long general music class.

things that do apply to their lives, like "What will be the greatest invention of the 21st century?" or "If a tech-filled city were built, would you move there?"

Students will blink and think when asked such questions. These are some of the characteristics of essential questions.

- Essential questions are questions that recur throughout life.
- They spark discussion, incite engagement, and provoke inquiry.
- They allow students to transfer their learning outside the school—into their lives.
- They are important, timeless, and foundational to learning.
- They can potentially open a whole new world to students.
- They allow students to express and communicate what they have learned.
- They are non-judgmental, open-ended, meaningful, and purposeful.
- They structure a unit of study as a problem to be investigated and explored.

Essential questions spark discussion, curiosity, and introduce new ideas.

Take the question, "How does one prepare a meal?" This is more than a question with a simple, correct answer asked in class on a particular day. This question

Essential questions create opportunities to communicate with classmates.

will provide the trigger for lively discussions, as everyone has opinions, health considerations, cultural influences, and social circumstances, not to mention their own favorite kinds of food. In the process of considering all these various factors, students learn to read and write, speak and listen, debate and defend.

Everyone can be involved in discussing how to prepare a meal, even those students who do not cook, because meals are essential. The discussion can be extended by having students bring in dishes to share from the meals they talk about. Students will expand their knowledge and taste buds, and in **Noah Roseman's** class the conversation is all in Spanish. **That's learning, and it's exciting, and will cause students to blink, think, and drink in new thoughts and experiences.**

Essential Questions Reflect Big Ideas

Essential questions spring from "big ideas." They are open-ended inquiries that can never be completely and definitively answered. They stimulate thought-provoking debate. Essential questions are never finally answered, so teachers and students can return to them over and over again in an ever-widening, ever-deepening spiral.

Essential questions may be ones that people have been pondering for centuries. They may elicit the underlying concepts of a discipline. They cross disciplines and boundaries of time and place. They may provide guidance for navigating one's life. **And last, but not least, they are just fun and interesting because they engage everyone in serious, profound, and complex thinking!**

Here are more examples of essential questions.

- Why do we study the past?
- What is a hero?
- What is true friendship?
- How does the language we use shape our thoughts?
- How do our beliefs shape our responses to advancements in bioengineering?
- What constitutes proof in geometry?
- How can a story be interpreted?
- What are the potential pitfalls of applying modern standards to historical events?

These are essential, "big idea" questions that pertain to specific subjects.

Science
- Are genetically modified foods safe to eat?
- How can studying evidence from the past help us prevent future problems?

Math
- Should the metric system be universal in use?
- How is geometry used in the world?

Social Studies
- What are the effects on the world economy as it moves to Asia?
- How does the economy of a society depend on the geography of the region?

Language Arts
- Do stories need a beginning, middle, and end? Why?
- Should one take notes with pen and paper or a laptop?

Physical Education
- How can classrooms be designed more ergonomically?
- Should the probability of concussions deter someone from playing a sport?

Art
- Does everyone have artistic talent inside of them?
- How does history affect art?

Foreign Language
- What is your opinion that in Singapore and Poland, a student is required to learn two languages and encouraged to learn a third?
- In what ways would learning a foreign language be beneficial?

Essential Questions Are Derived from Standards

Although essential questions are stimulating and exciting, they are not to be used arbitrarily in isolation. They must enhance and be part of the curriculum and lesson. Like an objective or learning target, they are

Posing an essential question can lead to new thoughts and ideas about what is to be learned.

derived from academic standards. In fact, on the last board to the right in **Noah Roseman's** class, there is a set of lesson objectives that add coherence (scope and sequence) to what is being taught.

An essential question must be derived from academic standards and aligned to the content and skills of the district's curriculum.

For instance, here is a life science standard.

- Standard: LS2.A: Interdependent Relationships in Ecosystems

  - Ecosystems have carrying capacities, which are limits to the numbers of organisms and populations they can support. These limits result from such factors as the availability of living and nonliving resources and from such challenges as predation, competition, and disease. Organisms would have the capacity to produce populations of great size were it not for the fact that environments and resources are finite. This fundamental tension affects the abundance (number of individuals) of species in any given ecosystem.

That seventy-eight-word standard can be made not only student-friendly, but student-inquisitive in an essential question of five words.

◆ Should human population be limited?

Units that are written using essential questions are related to content and skills derived from the state standards and the district curriculum.

◆ **Social Studies** A question suggested by the content (perhaps the French Revolution and the American Revolution):
  ● What conditions must be present to precipitate a revolution?

◆ **English** A question suggested by a particular text (possibly *Great Expectations* or *Hamlet*):
  ● How are people's lives affected when their aspirations conflict with their limitations?

◆ **Music** A question suggested by styles and periods (maybe baroque, jazz, or hip-hop):
  ● How does music reflect and shape a society?

◆ **Math** A question suggested by mathematical concepts (such as mean, median, and mode):
  ● What do we mean by average and when should each type of average be used?

As shown, an essential question relates to prescribed content, but it provides a line of inquiry for considering the ideas and information inherent in the content. Essential questions provide a basis for considering the important ideas in a subject area and across the curriculum. Essential questions—and the key ideas that they encompass—must be written in language that students can easily understand. Fundamental to the learning process, essential questions should be shared with students at the beginning of instruction, during instruction, and at the end of instruction.

12

Sources for Essential Questions

See this listing of websites for additional essential questions.

Designing a Unit with Essential Questions

Developing a unit of instruction around an essential question is like the creative process of producing a blueprint for a home. The essential question in that context is, "What is my ideal house?"

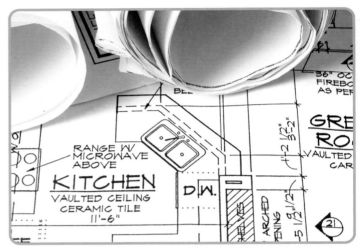

Designing a unit, a blueprint for learning, involves the same kind of thought, preparation, and creativity required for any significant enterprise, like designing an ideal home.

You would, in the beginning, consider the styles of architecture you could choose from and the local building codes that your house would have to comply with. You might hire an architect, and together you would discuss the essential questions involved in designing your house.

◆ How will the architecture of the house reflect the customs and practicalities of the geographic region?
◆ How will the environment impact the design of the house and how will building the house impact the environment?
◆ What financial costs will be incurred by the design of the house?
◆ How will the design be impacted by the availability of materials?
◆ How will the house reflect your physical needs and personal lifestyle?
◆ How will the house reflect your personal aesthetic?

The architect creates a blueprint incorporating all of your ideas and calling out the technical skills needed to satisfactorily complete the project such as laying the foundation, framing the structure, wiring and plumbing, laying the floors, tiling, painting, and landscaping. The construction is then ready to begin, and your ideal home will be the final product.

Just as in planning and constructing a house, the preparation and instruction that takes place in the classroom leads to the final product—a culminating project, product, or performance. To drive instruction, the unit design (the blueprint) uses both the ideas that are relevant to the essential question and the technical skills that are necessary for accomplishing the desired outcome.

**The teacher is the architect
and builder of a unit
based on an essential question.**

Key thoughts will arise when an essential question is discussed. These ideas or key concepts might become conclusions students will reach following an activity or in the course of their reading and studies. They are the ideas that will stay with a student when the unit of instruction is finished.

For instance, imagine this as the essential question.

◆ What relevance do ideas in books from or about another time period have today?

Suppose the novel is *To Kill a Mockingbird*. As the teacher, you would structure lessons so that students would uncover the major themes in this novel.

◆ Prejudice is a disease.
◆ The justice system is imperfect.
◆ All human beings should be treated with dignity and compassion.

These themes are the key thoughts and ideas that you, the teacher, would guide the students to discern. These key ideas are timeless. They are open-ended and thought-provoking. They will stick with students long after they have forgotten the plot details of *To Kill a Mockingbird*.

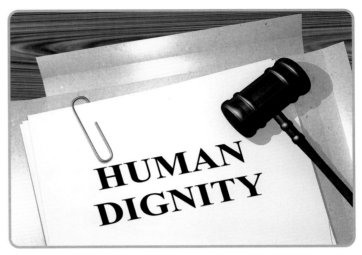

Essential questions open the door to timeless discussion. They tackle complexities, intricacies, and different points of view. They stimulate curiosity; they encourage investigation and further questioning. They challenge platitudes and set opinions by exercising and expanding the mind.

Once students understand these key ideas, they will be able to relate the text to modern times. They will be able to discuss the essential question broadly and in depth. They will be able to create a final product that relates the ideas in the novel to the world today in a meaningful way.

How to Create a Unit Using an Essential Question

Essential Question Unit Steps in Planning Order

1. Devise the question.
2. Select the main text or body of knowledge and make a list of its key ideas.
   (Steps 1 and 2 can be reversed; that is, you can start with the question or the text.)
3. Select the supplementary texts.
4. Determine the final project.
5. Determine the content knowledge and skills that students must learn.
6. Plan the instructional activities.

The essential question is an all-encompassing idea.

Step 1: Devise the question.

The question could arise naturally from the critical content of your curriculum or from an idea or issue in your content area.

- Should the United States adopt a national service program? (Social Studies)
- How can an emergency room be designed for maximum efficiency? (Biomedical Innovations)
- Are income equality and capitalism mutually exclusive concepts? (Economics)
- How does diet relate to health? (Family and Consumer Sciences)

The question could arise from the theme of a particular book or text.

- *The Iliad:* What defines a hero?
- *The Great Gatsby:* What is the American Dream?
- *The Declaration of Independence:* When is war justified?
- *The Bridge to Terabithia:* How can we cope with profound loss?

The essential question could arise from considering an abstract noun:

- Courage
- Responsibility
- Mercy
- Loyalty
- Wisdom
- Justice

Step 2: Select the main text and make a list of its key ideas.

The main text may actually come first. It may be the source of the essential question. You may base your essential question on the themes of a required novel or on the critical content of your curriculum.

If you begin your planning with the essential question, you then assemble texts for students to read to consider the question. The first book or reading to select will be the main text that will provoke the essential question. Many districts require students to read particular texts; for example, *The Odyssey* is often taught in the ninth grade. Essential questions for this classic might look like these.

- What is universal about the hero's quest?
- Is the epic hero alive today?
- What does it mean to be "civilized"?
- Are we subjects to fate, or do we have free will?

The main text could be chapters in a textbook. Any content-specific book, important document, or critical reading can become the central text for a unit driven by an essential question. For example, in Earth Science, in a study of the water cycle, one might ask, "How is our ecosystem—especially the quality of our water—affected by pollution?" In this case, the focus is on the interaction between the air we breathe, the earth we walk upon, the water we drink, and the various forms of pollution in our environment. The focus of instruction goes beyond the simple facts of the water cycle.

Your decision about the principal text may be a practical one.

- Are there chapters in the textbook that deliver the content necessary to understanding the essential question?
- What paperback books do you have access to?
- Are classroom sets of books available to you?
- Can you order books?
- What is your budget?
- What texts can you access via the Internet?

Consult your district curriculum so that you do not choose a text that students have already read or that is mandated for a grade beyond the one you are teaching.

Make a list of the key thoughts in that main text. Any supplemental readings you select will revolve around the key ideas in your principal text.

Step 3: Select the supplementary texts.
When you teach using essential questions, you can expose students not only to the main text and the core content of your curriculum, but to other readings that extend or challenge students' understanding of the principal text's key ideas. You can ask students to consider multiple points of view and alternate ways of looking at a question. A collection of readings that bring ideas and information to bear on an essential question is called a *text set*.

Many textbook companies have organized their literature into text sets. Especially in English Language Arts textbooks, you will find the principal text and accompanying stories, nonfiction articles, essays, and poems.

Online companies and non-profit organizations have assembled and provide text sets for teachers in all disciplines. The Digital Public Library of America is one of many companies that provides primary source text sets. Search "free text sets" to find companies that can help you with this task.

Going beyond the textbook exposes students to multiple ways to interact with an idea.

You can also assemble your own text sets.

♦ You may find old textbooks still in your building that contain reading selections you can use. If you are selecting nonfiction, check that the information is not out-of-date.

♦ The Internet is a great source for essays and articles. Select pieces that are up-to-date, credible, and well written. If you are planning a debate, choose pieces from opposing points of view.

♦ If you want to include poems, the Library of Congress and the Poetry Foundation provide search engines to help you find poems by author, title, and subject.

♦ Films, videos, artistic representations, and guest speakers can provide supplementary information.

♦ Your media specialist can help you find books in your school library and locate online resources for various instructional purposes.

♦ Depending upon their age, the course you are teaching, and the task, the students themselves may have ideas for supplementary texts.

Your aim is to find texts that deepen thought about the essential question by extending a definition, providing another point of view, comparing two ideas, contrasting concepts, or challenging a key idea. With supplementary texts, you can consider a question from different perspectives or through the eyes of someone from another country.

Step 4: Determine the final project.
The essential question is connected to the performance task—the culminating project—at the end of the unit. The final project is a demonstration of what students have learned. It is the way that you will assess the impact of your instruction on student learning. Therefore, as you shape the essential question and select your texts, you should be thinking at the same time about what you want your students to do at the end of the unit.

Your goal in a unit designed with an essential question is for your students to internalize the ideas they have considered during instruction and apply their knowledge to a culminating project, a new problem to solve, or an investigation suggested by the content of the unit. They will use the skills you have taught them to demonstrate their understanding of the essential question and its key ideas. They will go beyond recitation of the specific content they have learned to show you they have a deep understanding of the essential question.

Although you will naturally begin thinking about instructional activities early in the planning process, put off making final decisions about those activities until you have settled on the demonstration of understanding at the end; that is, the final project. That way, you will plan instruction intentionally.

You will plan your activities to prepare your students to show you that they have learned.

By the end, they will have the technical skills and the content knowledge they need. They will be able to put everything together and complete a final project, presentation, or performance that will demonstrate what they have learned.

Examples of Culminating Activities

A class book	Model
Architectural plan	Musical Composition
Art object	Portfolio
Community service project	Photo book
Documentary	Poster presentation
Essay	Research project
Film or play	Simulation
Game	TED Talk
Instruction manual	Web or radio program

Students should know the criteria for success on their projects. As you teach various skills, you should make clear to students that the degree of mastery of these skills will affect the quality of their final projects. Rubrics and checklists are critical for students to understand your expectations. (Chapter 12)

Step 5: Determine the content knowledge and skills that students must learn.

List the content you will need to teach that addresses the essential question and the technical skills your students will need to learn to complete the project. Use your state standards and local curriculum to help you identify any specific content and the technical skills that are required learning.

◆ If the final project calls upon students to write a comparison/contrast paper, you will need to teach them the structure of such an essay.

◆ If the final project asks students to make a poster presentation of information gathered from primary and secondary sources about a historical topic, make sure they know the difference between primary and secondary sources. You also will need to teach them—or review with them— a format for documenting their sources.

◆ If the final project calls for students to present a TED Talk about a topic in modern medicine, you will have to teach them the structure of a TED Talk and rehearse specific oral and visual presentation skills.

Clearly then, within the larger unit that is powered by the essential question, you will have daily learning targets or two to three single-day objectives. These short-term learning targets or learning objectives will be based upon the content knowledge and specific technical skills your students need to be successful at the end of the unit. These short-term objectives will always be connected to the essential question and to the final project.

Step 6: Plan the instructional activities.

Plan the instructional activities last. You have decided what you want your students to do to show that they have learned. You know what content knowledge and technical skills they will need to do that. You are now ready to begin planning the day-to-day activities. You are ready to think about how you will lead your students to the key ideas of the unit, and how you will teach the content knowledge and skills they will need to be successful at the end. You are ready to plan the instructional activities that will take the student from the beginning to the end of the unit.

You can use whatever teaching methods that are best suited to conveying the content you know is crucial for success. You may teach using a combination of direct instruction for the whole class, facilitating small group inquiry, or directing individual investigation and practice.

Strategies such as Socratic seminars, Fishbowl discussions (page 206), debates and other formal class discussions are effective in helping students understand the key ideas. Simulations, inquiry-based activities, experiments, and countless other instructional activities can also help your students learn key concepts.

No matter what instructional methods you use, your instruction over the course of the unit must tie to the objectives students need to know to carry out the performance task at the end.

Essential Questions Conform to the Learning Triangle

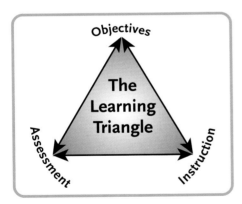

Objectives

The design of a unit begins with an essential question. The teacher identifies key ideas or concepts that contribute to understanding the question and responding to it. The teacher plans instruction so that students can explore these key ideas and learn relevant content knowledge and the specific technical skills that they will use in a final project. The key ideas,

content knowledge, and specific technical skills are the learning objectives.

Assessment

The final project (or culminating activity) and how it will be assessed is planned in advance of instruction. The students' final projects will demonstrate understanding of the essential question and ideas related to it. Students will need relevant content knowledge and specific technical skills to present their projects confidently. The final project provides evidence of student learning.

Instruction

The teacher plans instruction so that students can explore the key ideas and concepts and learn relevant content knowledge and the specific technical skills that they will use in a final project. Instruction is sequenced. It builds from day to day, intentionally, so that students are prepared to demonstrate, in the end, understanding of the essential question.

You Are the Architect of Learning

When you teach with essential questions, you plan instruction from start to finish before you begin teaching a unit.

Planning takes time up front, but as instruction and learning progress, you feel confident because you know where you and your students are headed. You know what you will do. You have thought everything through.

Units planned using essential questions are engaging because students are given the opportunity to grapple with ideas. They know their responses are valued. They know they are learning and expanding their outlook and they like working on projects that demonstrate their understanding.

For you, the teacher, teaching with essential questions is satisfying, too. You are not frantically thinking and planning every day about what you will do the next day. While the unit progresses, you are able to guide your students to understanding the ideas generated by the essential questions.

You can concentrate during class on helping your students master the objectives that they need to learn. You can really listen as your students discuss an issue.

As you monitor their discussions and ask questions along the way, you will guide them as they work together or independently.

You are the architect of their learning.

> *I like planning ahead and then building towards the end. It's productive. The students are learning more, and I'm prepared.*
>
> Terah Slawnikowski
> First-year teacher
> Lafayette, Indiana

Mastering Instruction

✓ Essential questions engage students in thought-provoking life issues.

✓ Essential questions engage students in complex thinking.

✓ An essential question reflects a big idea.

✓ An essential question must be derived from academic standards and the district's curriculum.

✓ Units constructed using essential questions allow for teacher creativity.

...Produces Achievement!

How to Drive Instruction Using Objectives

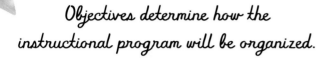

Objectives determine how the instructional program will be organized.

Why Students Are Bored

You may remember this happening. You were reading a classic novel in English class. Your teacher had prepared study guide questions for each chapter. The questions were largely recall. In class, the teacher asked questions and students volunteered answers, but it seemed like all that mattered was whether you gave the teacher the right answer. There was never an essential question asked, such as, "What's the major theme? What do you think of the author's plot?" Your teacher spent only a little time at the end of the book on the theme of the book. You did not discuss the author's intent in writing the story. You did not understand why the book had become a classic. It ended up on your "most disliked" list and the word "classics" left a bad taste in your mouth.

Or this. You were studying world history. Your teacher plodded through the timeline of history chronologically, highlighting everything, and testing for details. The rise and fall of each empire was a roller coaster ride. The wars ran together. You wished you could talk about a unifying idea, for example, "What makes a civilization great? Why do great civilizations die out? Is war inevitable?" History seemed to be about facts and memorizing dates.

Or this. You were learning about genetics in biology class. Your teacher taught you about phenotypes, genotypes, and alleles. You learned about cloning and genetic mutation. You learned about DNA and the Genome Project. But you did not discuss the

Students Value Objectives

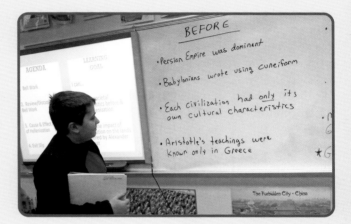

> ## The students value the objectives.

Jeff Gulle, NBCT
Danville, Kentucky

A few years ago, one student delighted in arriving before I was able to put the agenda/objective slide on the screen for the next class. He was a "history buff" and liked to see what material was left on the board from the previous class. From that he would try to guess what the day's objective would turn out to be. He was usually pretty close!

advancements in medical science and forensics that genetic research has facilitated. You did not discuss or debate the social, legal, and ethical issues that arise from research in genetics. There was no debate about genetic engineering.

You were bored.

You, the Teacher

When a coach, or an executive, or an artistic director is being interviewed for a job, they outline and explain how they personally will implement an effective program. They show their projected organization, their plans, and the results they intend to achieve.

If members of a school board or superintendent are interviewing a prospective teacher, they don't want to hire someone who says, "I am going to introduce this commercially prepared current fad or outside program." The essential thing they want to know is, "How are you, the teacher, going to organize this district or this school and, in particular, your classroom for student learning?"

A classroom management plan
is how the teacher will organize
the class and classroom for student learning.

An instructional plan
is how the teacher will organize
instruction for student learning.

Jeff Gulle has classroom management and instruction plans. This kind of organization and clarity ensures his success and his students' success.

**Effective teachers know how to organize
an instruction program, just as they know how
to organize a classroom.**

The Architect of Learning

In all of these cases, the class was rudderless. Teaching does not mean standing in front of the room and transferring information mindlessly and endlessly to the class. **Teaching is the skill of organizing the instructional program to stimulate and expand students' outlooks while they learn what the curriculum expects them to learn.**

The key word is "skill." As a teacher, you are a master of your profession, the architect of learning. You have the skill set to organize a meaningful instructional program that begins with a set of objectives, learning targets, or essential questions. They ensure students and teacher are united on a mission to explore, investigate, and achieve together. Objectives, targets, and essential questions create a learning environment that is personal and focused.

The relationship between teacher and student is based on learning expectations and predicated on trust. **The effective teacher begins a lesson by telling students the lesson objectives so that everyone— students, administrators, parents, and the teacher— know what students are expected to learn and accomplish.** Effective teachers garner respect by using their skills to give everyone goals, purpose, and equal opportunity to learn.

What Kind of Objectives Should Be Used?

You have learned that there are three basic kinds of lesson objectives:

1. Objectives that begin with a verb (Chapter 4)
2. Learning targets (Chapter 5)
3. Essential questions (Chapter 6)

The question is what kind of objective should a teacher use in the classroom? The answer is all kinds. Just like a tradesperson with a box full of different tools for various jobs, there is no such thing as teaching in only one way, as in using projects or inquiry only. You use the tool or objective appropriate at a given moment depending on students' needs and the subject matter to teach effectively and ensure learning.

The effective teacher knows how to use different kinds of objectives for different purposes and may well use more than one kind in a given lesson.

Research on learning supports the conclusion that novice to intermediate learners may find direct, strong "I can" instructional guidance most beneficial, while advanced learners may benefit from more autonomy and opportunities for exploration with essential questions.

It's often most effective to "scaffold" (page 190) a lesson, beginning with an objective or learning target and building towards an essential question that can be presented and explored during guided or independent practice when the basics have been mastered.

It makes no difference what kind of objective you use, how many you use, and in what sequence. **The most important concept is that all lessons need to be crafted around an objective.**

Three Methods, One Triangle

As has been discussed repeatedly, Objectives are one of the three components of The Learning Triangle. Objectives are inextricably connected to the other two sides of the triangle—Instruction and Assessment. All three components are essential and interrelated.

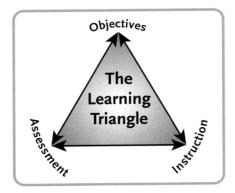

The three components of The Learning Triangle are not only connected but depend upon that connection for their integrity.

Objectives drive the instruction and are the basis for assessment. The activities you choose must lead students to achieving the objectives.

Objectives drive instruction. They give direction, focus, and purpose. They ensure lessons are meaningful.

Objectives are the reason students come to class. If there are no objectives, students have every right and reason to ask, "Why are we doing this?" Without objectives, it's as though they are on a mystery ride when they enter the classroom. They ask, "Where are we going?" or "When will we get there?" or "What will we do there?"

Students want to know what your intentions are, what they will achieve, and how they will learn.

There are differences among the three ways of writing objectives, but they are alike in their adherence to the three points on The Learning Triangle. The table on page 70 summarizes the similarities and differences among the three methods.

Choosing a Style for Writing Objectives

Some teachers prefer one type of learning objective over another. Elementary teachers are more likely to choose "I can" statements because lessons in the early grades often focus on one skill at a time. Secondary teachers often need several days to accomplish one objective, so for them using the verbs and thought processes of Bloom's Taxonomy might be more practical and appropriate. However, "I can" statements can work at the secondary level, even with extended projects, and many elementary teachers write objectives using Bloom's Taxonomy.

Teachers at all grade levels may prefer constructing units framed by an essential question. Teachers in any subject area who conceive of their lessons as integrated pieces of a larger and deeper unit of instruction find that using essential questions for their objectives is a sure way to spark curiosity, discussion, and debate.

There are school districts that require teachers to use a particular format for writing objectives. Other

Comparison Among Three Types of Objectives

	Verbs and Bloom's Taxonomy	"I can" Learning Targets	Essential Questions
Planning begins with the assessment in mind	✓	✓	✓
Objectives are explicitly stated	✓	✓	✓
Objectives are shared with students	✓	✓	✓
Instruction is sequenced	✓	✓	✓
Assessment informs teacher and student that objective goals have been reached	✓	✓	✓
Criteria for success are shared with students	✓	✓	✓
Time span of the objectives	Flexible—one to three lessons, possibly more	One lesson	A unit or longer—possibly a semester or even a year of units could all be focused on one essential question.
Number of objectives in a lesson	One lesson could include several objectives	Each lesson has one objective	The unit includes multiple objectives—key ideas, content knowledge, and specific skills
How understanding is shown	Demonstration of the thinking skill	Performance of a specific task	Application of knowledge and skills to a new performance task
Nature of the assessment	Formative and summative	Emphasis on formative assessment	Formative assessment throughout the unit; emphasis on summative assessment via a culminating performance task
Criteria for success	Clarified for students through alignment with the objective; use of rubrics, checklists, etc., which are shared with students beforehand	Emphasis placed on transparent communication to students of the criteria for success; use of rubrics, checklists, etc.	Rubrics, checklists, etc., shared with students and, in some cases, generated by students

I Want Teachers in the Classroom

Many states have education service centers, such as the Cooperative Educational Service Agencies in Wisconsin; Educational Cooperatives in Kentucky; Regional Education Associations in North Dakota; and others. The director of one of these centers shared that sixteen superintendents gathered for their monthly meeting, and they started to talk. "Have you tried this program? Have you tried this approach? Have you tried . . . ?"

Then one of the superintendents, with infinite wisdom, said, "No. I want teachers in the classroom—teaching." The discussion ended.

Yet, that discussion is indicative of how many schools and districts haphazardly construct their instruction, trying this new program and that method or system, not succeeding, trying something else that comes along, and failing and floundering again. Schools throughout the country have been doing this for seventy-five years and the results are abysmal.

The focus needs to be on teachers so that they are supported and trained to be experts of organization and instruction. There is one well-researched, tried and true formula for student success, and it is led by effective teachers.

Programs do not teach. They don't reach hearts and minds. Effective teachers teach because they plan, they organize, and they know how to design instruction based on objectives that are aligned to standards and the district's curriculum. Effective teachers care and want to ensure that all their students learn and achieve.

Objective = Instruction + Assessment = Instruction + Assessment (X ∞) = Evaluation

districts leave the style up to the teacher. Unless a particular format is required by your district, choose the style that makes sense to you. **Choose the style that serves your purpose, makes the target clear to your students, and paves the way to visible learning in your classroom.**

What matters is that you are ready, willing, and able to teach with objectives.

- What matters is that you communicate the objective to your students—at the beginning, throughout, and at the end of your instruction.
- What matters is that the instructional strategies you use and the activities with which you engage your students are tied to the objective.
- What matters is that the objective and instructional strategies are planned with the assessment in mind.

By using objectives to plan a lesson, and clearly communicating those objectives to your students, you plan for success.

The more visible the teacher makes the learning goals, the more likely the student is to engage in the work needed to meet the goal.[1]

John Hattie

Other Strategies for Writing Objectives

The three kinds of objectives that have been presented are not the only ways to write objectives. There are other methods that can be used to communicate objectives to students.

---

[1] Hattie, *Visible Learning.*

Daily Questions. You can pose a daily question at the beginning of class. These kinds of questions are not unit-sized essential questions. They are designed for one objective only, usually lasting for one class period only, to focus students on the main idea of a lesson.

- What is a primary resource?
- What is a pronoun antecedent?
- What is a tessellation?
- How did Elizabethans view the universe?
- What does the term "manifest destiny" mean?

Both non-essential and essential questions can be used advantageously in class. Non-essential questions are asked often as they are necessary for the teacher to determine current learning.

- What do you know about the events that sparked WWI?
- What steps did you take to get your answer?

These are comparable essential questions.

- Is war necessary?
- What do good problem solvers do when they are stuck?

Essential questions do not seek correct answers because they have no definitive answers. Non-essential questions, however, have an answer.

A Variety of Stems. Not all objectives need to begin with "I can" or a verb from Bloom's taxonomy. You can write objectives beginning with a variety of stems.

- Today I will have learned . . .
- The purpose of today's lesson is to . . .
- By the end of class today, you will know . . .
- By the end of class today, you will be able to . . .

"We" Objectives. It's also important to include "We" objectives in your instructional program. Our world is interconnected. We no longer live in isolated communities in distant countries. More than ever, we are part of a global community. Social media is making connectivity easier and faster each day. Connectivity offers an infinite number of opportunities to enhance learning and cooperation.

Educators like to say that we are preparing our students for their future careers in the work world. In the work world, almost no one works alone. Companies and businesses have teams, and employees and managers plan and work together. There are project teams, customer service teams, sales teams, and production teams, and each team is charged with producing results.

Although "I can" is a perfectly suitable stem for an objective in many instances, it's also beneficial to incorporate "We can" objectives to encourage an awareness of the kind of collaboration and cooperation that reflects the realities of the work world. More often than not, essential questions are "We can" questions.

As you determine what form of objective to use, include "We can" or "We will" objectives and organize your students so that they collaborate, cooperate, and achieve together in teams.

General Objectives. You may also want to have these aspirational types of general objectives on display in the classroom.

- We can ace this class.
- We can solve problems.
- We can work together in groups.
- We can support each other.
- We can help each other improve.

The Objective of Class Activities

There are many things a teacher can creatively use to teach objectives, ranging from hands-on activities, discussions, lectures, field trips, computer work, and projects. Whatever activity you use, it must provide an answer to the question, "What have students learned?" or "What have students mastered?"

**Every activity used in the classroom must be correlated to lesson objectives.
The purpose of every activity is to ensure those objectives are taught.**

It's nice to find a fun, new activity in a book, magazine, or on the Internet and use it in class. Students laugh, enjoy themselves, and are engaged, but have they

Examples of Team or "We" Objectives

Language Arts

- We can create a chapter in a book. (Or an essay. Or a poem.)
- We can work together to find examples of figurative language in a text.
- We can diagram compound-complex sentences.
- We will practice vocabulary words by playing word games.
- We will meet with our literature circle groups each week to continue our novel study, working on reading fluently and discussing the story by using different comprehension skills and strategies.

Science

- We will work in groups to discover and explain karyotypes.
- We can list properties of water.
- We can explain why water is important in biology.
- We can draw a food chain and show how energy flows through it.
- We can observe how yeast uses sugar for energy.

Music

- We can clap a steady beat to music.
- We can perform music with uniform articulation/bow strokes.
- We will accurately tune our instruments in under five seconds by matching the pitch of the strings to the tuner.
- We can identify, define, and perform syncopation.
- We can classify instruments into the four families of the orchestra.

Mathematics

- We can solve a quadratic equation by working together in groups.
- We will work with our math partners throughout the week to complete math activity games in order to practice our multiplication and division facts.
- We can find and count the three types of beans that our teacher threw in the courtyard.

History

- We can uncover and explain the barriers to housing for African-Americans in Chicago during the 1950s.
- We can recreate the events leading up to WWII by working in groups to represent key countries.
- We will work together in small groups to research an American landmark and then organize a presentation board to share with the class.

Career and Technical Education

- We can design, plan, and operate a restaurant in our school.
- We will create business cards, advertisements, and brochures using computer technology.

13

How to Design an Efficient and Effective Emergency Room

This blog essay is a great example of Career and Technical Education where high school students work in teams.

---

learned anything? The word "engagement" is bantered around so much in education that one would think it is the magic potion to learning—that if students are "engaged" they are automatically absorbing the knowledge and skills they need for their futures. The reality is that, more often than not, engagement is merely busywork that involves little or no actual learning. In fact, many students themselves will wonder, "Why are we doing this?"

For students to be engaged in real learning, there must be a purpose to what they are doing—that is, there must be an objective. Just as a builder needs a blueprint, a pilot a flight plan, and a chef a recipe, both teacher and students need to engage in the visible learning provided by objectives. That is why it is important to continuously analyze how best to teach (the instruction) so students will learn, and how best to check to see (the assessment) if students have learned what has been taught.

The integration of objectives into the instructional plan assists students in understanding how the work they do will be assessed, giving the student and the teacher an indicator of success.

> *The objective itself can be used as part of the daily bellwork or Do Now assignment. In some years, I have had the students keep a journal and on each day's page they were required to start class by writing the objective.*
>
> *Then, at the end of each period my students wrote down how that objective was met.*
>
> Jeff Gulle, NBCT
> Danville, Kentucky

Same Objectives for All

The objective should be the same for all students in the classroom. The last thing you want to do is communicate that some students do not need to participate on a project or in learning that day because they are advanced or, conversely, that you think others are incapable of learning certain skills or content knowledge at that point because they are behind. Conveying messages of unequal expectations is detrimental to everyone and will seriously undermine your efforts to create a consistent, caring learning environment where every student is given every opportunity to succeed. You must convey that you, their teacher, have every expectation that all of the students in your classroom will succeed to the best of their ability.

It is essential to provide equal opportunity for all students to learn with the expectation that every student is capable of succeeding.

14

Study Guidelines Define Lesson Objectives

See an example of a study guide or find it in **THE First Days of School** on page 240.

Your state's standards are written for all students and standardized tests are administered to almost all students. Even students who take alternate assessments or receive accommodations in standardized testing situations are tested on the standards. You show that you have positive expectations for all of your students when you write objectives that apply to everyone in the class.

Objectives, however you write them, should be the same for all students in the class. They unite students around a common purpose to explore, investigate, and achieve together.

It is the instructional strategies you choose to use, the activities you design, and the texts you use that will vary depending upon your students' prior knowledge, academic readiness, and whatever learning challenges they may have.

Your assessments may be modified for students' readiness whether they have an IEP (Individualized Education Program), ILP (International Language Program), Section 504 accommodations (rights of students with disabilities), or no accommodations.

If necessary, instructional strategies may vary to accommodate individual leaning abilities.

But all students must be taught the standards called for in their grade level each year. Students should receive the same rigorous education whether they are enrolled in your class, the class across the hall, or a class across the state. This is how schools and teachers operationalize "equal opportunity to learn" and "high expectations." You can't provide equal opportunity unless you have positive expectations for all students and provide equal access to grade-level content.

Thorough and effective grade-level instruction is crucial. Teachers throughout the school must work collaboratively to ensure that students are prepared with the knowledge and skills they need to move seamlessly from grade to grade.

Students taught below grade level will obviously and inevitably perform below grade level. In fact, when students are taught below grade level, they are, in reality, precluded from doing well on grade-level state tests. Be very aware that your students need every opportunity to prepare for these tests. The results will affect their confidence and influence their future possibilities. Don't minimize their significance; these tests exist for the very good reason that they try to ensure and enforce equal opportunity for all students.

Assessment Tools

Always keep The Learning Triangle in the forefront of your mind. Along with organizing instruction and designing activities to teach objectives, you prepare formative assessment tools to determine whether the objectives have been taught.

**Assessment is not an afterthought.
It is a critical component of The Learning Triangle
and an integral part of your lesson design.**

Formative assessment is how you will know if your students are learning, what they have learned, and how instruction needs to be modified or improved to help them progress and ensure that they succeed when the time comes for summative assessment or evaluation.

Unit C is on assessment.

Mastering Instruction

 Teaching is the skill of organizing an instructional program.

 Each component of The Learning Triangle is a critical component for success.

 Different kinds of objectives can be used for different learning purposes.

 Objectives determine what activities will be used in the instructional program.

 Although instructional strategies may vary, all students should have the same objectives and the equal opportunity to learn.

...Produces Achievement!

UNIT ◆ C ◆ Assessment

Chapter

How to
Use Assessment

The number one factor for improving student achievement is frequent formative assessment.

Student Improvement at No Extra Cost

What if you were told that your students could advance one and possibly two grade levels in a year? What if you were told that this could be done

- without extra cost,
- without adopting another program,
- without extending the school year,
- without reducing the class size, and
- without changing any teacher's schedule or assignment?

How can it be done? The answer is in one word—assessment. You may know assessment as "check for understanding." As the lesson progresses, the teacher monitors and checks to see if the students have learned what is being taught or that they have "caught what is being taught." The teacher then provides whatever help is needed.

Assessment defines what students are to learn.

Unit C is the most important unit in this book. It is based on extensive research that validates the significance of assessment. It explains what assessment is and how to use it effectively. Effective assessment will also significantly enhance your professional life and your students' success.

- Research has confirmed that students who are given clear objectives and frequent assessment

Assess the Learning

" Bad dog! "

Every frustrated pet owner

Pointing a finger and harshly belittling a dog does nothing to help it learn. This teaching technique just forces the animal to try to figure out what they should or should not be doing through trial and error. Dogs are eager to please, but without guidance and constructive feedback they don't know what to do in order to become a "good dog."

Assessment is at the heart of effective teaching. It is one of the most powerful influences on student achievement. When both the student and the teacher are moving towards the same objective, that's when you get learning.

aligned to those objectives can learn in six or seven months what would take other students an entire year to learn.[1]

- Research has determined that one of the most powerful influences on student achievement is assessment, producing an overall effect size of 0.75. This is equivalent to more than two years

---

[1] Paul Black and Dylan Wiliam, "Assessment and Classroom Learning," *Assessment in Education: Principles, Policy, & Practice* 5, no. 1 (1998): 7–74.

of student progress within a single academic school year.[2]

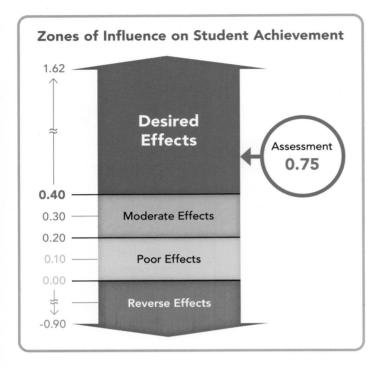

Zones of Influence on Student Achievement

- Assessment 0.75
- 1.62
- Desired Effects
- 0.40
- 0.30 — Moderate Effects
- 0.20
- 0.10 — Poor Effects
- 0.00
- Reverse Effects
- -0.90

Two Kinds of Assessment

Assessment gives students information about their progress and gives teachers information about their instruction. There are two kinds of assessment and they are often confused: formative and summative.

> The role of a teacher is to assess that the students have mastered the material, identify which students have not, and make sure that those students get additional time, instruction, and practice to master what the curriculum specifies.

Formative Assessment

- ◆ Used to FORM students' knowledge and skills as they learn lesson objectives
- ◆ Used by the teacher to determine what modifications need to be made to instruction
- ◆ Used along with continual feedback during the course of a unit of study.

Summative Assessment

- ◆ Occurs at the conclusion of a unit of study to SUM up how well the student has achieved the lesson objectives
- ◆ Used as a culminating test with a grade, rating, or ranking given to the student

Another term for summative assessment is evaluation.

Formative assessment is used to further learning. Summative assessment is used to test and grade.

Assessment = Formative Assessment

This book, the terms assessment and formative assessment will be used synonymously. Summative Assessment = Evaluation and it is the subject of Chapter 19.

> **When the cook tastes the soup, that's assessment. When the guests taste the soup, that's evaluation.[3]**
>
> Michael Scriven

Assessment is for growth in learning. Assessment is not testing. Testing is for scoring, marking, or grading. After classroom management, which is all too often confused with discipline, **the second most misused word in education is assessment, which is all too often confused with testing.** Formative assessment is NOT about testing. Summative assessment is about testing.

---

[2] Hattie, *Visible Learning*.

[3] Michael Scriven, "Beyond Formative and Summative Evaluation," in *Evaluation and Education: At Quarter Century*, eds. M.W. McLaughlin and D.C. Phillips (Chicago: University of Chicago Press, 1991).

There Is No Way to Fail

Assessment strategies are essential for ensuring progress in teaching and learning. Many teachers use the technique of sharing two pieces of paper at the start of every lesson. One piece of paper lists the objectives, goals, targets, or outcomes for the lesson. Their students always know, upfront, what they will be learning by participating in the instruction. The teacher is assuring students that they need not be anxious or worried—teaching is visible and every moment is focused on helping them learn and succeed.

The second piece of paper is the assessment tool that will be used to keep students on track toward achieving the lesson objectives. In this example it is a rubric. The type of assessment used will not always be the same for every lesson. (See chapters 10, 11, and 12 for multiple methods to assess students.)

Providing students with an assessment tool is the same as a score card in a game. When you play a game, you keep score. Why? Because you want to track your progress towards winning or achieving a goal. Assessment gives students the tool they need so that they know where they are in the flow of the lesson and if they are making steady progress towards the objective—or not. Assessment tells the teacher what additional instruction is needed so that all students are given every opportunity to succeed.

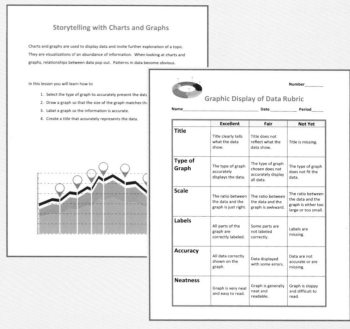

Students become active participants in their learning when the objectives of the lesson are stated and the rubric for assessment is provided—before the lesson begins.

Sharing objectives and an assessment tool takes the mystery out of the age-old question, "What are we going to learn today?" There is no way students will fail when this becomes your consistent instructional practice.

You may take a test home to score, but you cannot take an assessment home to score. Assessments are used for immediate feedback to help students. Assessment is done in the classroom in real time.

Evaluations end learning.
Assessments continue learning.

Differences Between Assessment and Evaluation

Assessment is based on where teachers and students are going (the learning objectives and performance targets for a particular class and task). It determines where they are in relation to those objectives and targets and informs them what they need to do to close any gaps between the objectives and their current performance.

- ◆ **Assessment** focuses on learning and teaching and provides direction for student progress and instructional improvements. It is centered on the learner, based on objectives, and not graded.

- ◆ **Evaluation** focuses on grades and results, and it may reflect issues in the classroom other than course content and mastery level. These could include participation in discussion, cooperation, attendance, and, incorrectly, even behavior.

This Is <u>NOT</u> Teaching

Cover, test, grade. Cover, test, grade.

- **Cover:** The teacher covers the material, mostly by lecture, but videos, computer work, worksheets, and an activity may also be used. And the teacher says, "Everything covered will be in the test."

- **Test:** The test is a mystery and students try to guess what will be on it. If students ask, "What will be in the test?" The answer could be, again, "Everything we've covered this week." Or, they are offered the more cryptic, "You'll see." The test is written the night before and the teacher looks for any source to find questions.

- **Grade:** The test is corrected and a grade is given. Some teachers grade on a curve, and then students are pitted one against another and left feeling superior, inferior, or just mediocre.

Note that these kinds of teachers do little or no assessment for learning. They never stop to check for understanding during a lesson, nor do they give feedback for assistance when needed. They moan, "Oh, I have so much to cover and so little time to do it." They just cover and test, cover and test. That's not teaching. That's mindless covering.

Furthermore, teachers shouldn't be **giving** grades. Rather, students should be **earning** grades based on their mastery of the lesson objectives as explained in Chapter 19.

Assessment is used to guide students in learning the lesson objectives. Evaluation is used for grading to see if students have learned the objectives.

The problem with focusing more on evaluation than assessment is that it is just a rating or ranking system. Grades can pit students against other students. They can make some feel inadequate, and some feel smug and complacent. They can leave at-risk students behind in learning because their grades seem to indicate that they can't be helped. **In too many classrooms, giving marks and grading are overemphasized, while giving useful assessment advice or feedback is underemphasized.**

Why the Term Assessment Is Misused

During the last few decades, various government and philanthropic programs have decided to improve

Assessment vs. Evaluation		
Area of Difference	**Assessment**	**Evaluation**
Time	Continuous and ongoing to improve learning	Final, to measure quality
Observation	How learning is progressing	What has been learned
Results	Assistance in areas needing improvement	Only interested in end results
Content	Constant diagnosis and adjusting instruction	Rating or ranking to arrive at a grade or score

education outcomes by testing teachers and students. This has resulted in school districts spending hundreds of millions of dollars buying test programs made by test-making companies under the guise of assessment. As already stated, the second most misused word in education is assessment, which is all too often confused with testing.

For instance, a governor says, "We need to assess (meaning test) students at least three times a year." A company that produces tests advertises, "We produce assessment tests. Our tests are customized to increase the accuracy in scoring your tests." A government program announces, "We enforce rigorous and challenging standards and assessments."

Companies have made millions producing these tests. Regretfully, none of them have improved how teachers teach or how students learn. Standardized tests do nothing to encourage and enhance learning. Why? Tests don't teach. **There must be teaching—effective teaching—before testing.**

Educational testing companies are constantly promoting the sales of formative tests. **There is no such thing as a formative test.** There are only summative tests. Formative assessment is used to help students make progress in their learning and, ultimately, to prepare for a summative test.

Never give a summative test until prior instruction and formative feedback support has been provided.

The Tragedy of Testing

The tragedy is that governing bodies, districts, and schools have permitted and passively accepted the evaluation (not assessment) of students based on commercially available computer-generated tests. These standardized tests are then used to judge and categorize students—and their teachers—by the number of correct responses.

People who buy formative assessment tests don't understand their error in not realizing that assessment is not a testing process. Tests discourage so many students. **It is important for students to understand**

Assess the Learning

"Good dog!"

A satisfied pet owner

Pointing a finger and harshly belittling a dog does nothing to help it learn. This teaching technique is void of guidance and constructive feedback. It just forces the animal to figure out, through trial and error, what it must do in order to please you. Ensuring pets experience and register moments of accomplishment leads to greater success with training and a happier life with your furry friend.

Instead of pointing a finger at students and chastising them because they failed to learn, give them opportunities to access and refine their own understanding as they work towards the lesson objectives. **Assessment is the tool to use to measure progress towards a goal.** Students are rewarded when they can visibly see how much they have accomplished. There is no trial and error or guessing with assessment. The path to learning is clearly defined by signposts the entire way so that students are confident they are on the road to success and a feeling of accomplishment.

that the assessment process is designed to HELP them learn. **The immediate perfection or getting the right answer is not the goal.** When students are in the process of improving their performance as they strive to achieve a goal, it is important for them to know that making mistakes is perfectly alright. The mistakes we all make help us figure out how to get better.

Judging or grading with no indication of how to improve will not produce student achievement. It will erode confidence and motivation to learn.

Computers—machines—can't assess students accurately, whereas teachers—human beings—can. There must be lesson objectives, there must be observation and assessment feedback during the lesson, and only teachers who know and care about their students can provide these services. Once the purchased test is given, the invaluable interaction between teacher and student is lost and learning stops. But when a

teacher uses formative assessment, the learning process expands and continues. And guess what? That process does not cost the district a single penny as compared to the cost of a company's test.

Why Do Districts Test?

In the United States, there is no federal curriculum and no federal mandate that districts must follow. So, how does the government get districts to test their students? The only course of action the federal government can use to motivate districts to test is to dangle money in front of them knowing that there are people who believe that money can be spent to improve test scores. So, grant writers are hired to chase after government money to install another test-preparation program when, at a fraction of the cost, if money were spent on improving teacher effectiveness, the result would be improved student achievement.

Of course, there are superintendents who, in their infinite wisdom, have refused to chase after such government grants. But there are also many superintendents who do spend time chasing after them, receive them, and then stand tall on a soapbox and brag as if they had just won the lottery. A few years later, ask them what resulted from "winning" the grant. Most probably nothing much, and yet they usually think they must continue doing what they are doing, hoping that something will work—eventually.

> **Just think how much a district could improve its educational system if it used a fraction of the money spent on testing or other program fads to improve the effectiveness of its teachers.**

Student achievement has little to do with money, class sizes, latest programs, or technology. To produce success

- ◆ assess and re-assess how students are learning, and
- ◆ use the assessment results to teach and reteach.

[4] Howard Nelson, "Testing More, Teaching Less: What America's Obsession with Student Testing Costs in Money and Lost Instructional Time," *American Federation of Teachers* (2013): https://www.aft.org/pdfs/teachers/testingmore2013.pdf.

Testing and More Testing

When researchers looked at the assessment and testing calendars of two midsize school districts, they found that their testing schedule had spiraled out of control. Here are some of their findings.[4]

- Students in heavily tested grades spent between twenty and fifty hours annually taking tests.

- Students in high-stakes testing grades spent between sixty and one hundred ten hours annually in test preparation—that is, taking practice tests and learning test-taking strategies. One hundred ten hours equals one full month of school.

- Including the cost of lost instructional time, the estimated annual testing cost per pupil in grades that had the most testing ranged from $700 (approximately 7 percent of per-pupil expenditures in the typical state) to more than $1,000 (approximately 11 percent of per-pupil expenditures in the typical state).

- If testing were abandoned altogether, one school district in this study could have added twenty to forty minutes of instructional time to each day, whereas the other could add almost an entire class period to each day for grades 6–11.

Research has clearly shown that test scores do not provide the information or motivation students need to help them make progress. Tests do not tell teachers how to improve instruction. They are just tests with no follow-up assessment for learning or feedback assistance.

> Testing does not produce progress;
> assessment produces progress.
> Testing does not improve student test scores;
> effective teachers improve test scores.

There Should Be Testing

This does not mean that students and teachers should not be tested. There should be tests, but not until there has been adequate instruction and assessment, and the assessment has been used to improve instruction and learning. Can you imagine the Department of Motor Vehicles giving you a driver's test before giving you the information and help you need to pass the test?

The purpose of assessment is to inform, not to punish with a test. If you find yourself wanting to spring a "gotcha" quiz on your students, don't do it. Formative assessments are not about surprising students, but about guiding where instruction needs to go next.

Assessment in Daily Life

The simplest example of assessment is when you look in a mirror and adjust your hair or clothes. Assessment is what you do when you check how the cooking is coming along and you adjust the seasoning or temperature.

When you are in pain you go to a dentist. The dentist asks questions about your problem and does an examination. When the results are assessed, the doctor does not say, "I give you a D-." The doctor prescribes a treatment or medication to improve your health. You may even need a recommendation for a specialist because of your particular need. Assessment in the classroom is the educational equivalent of a medical checkup.

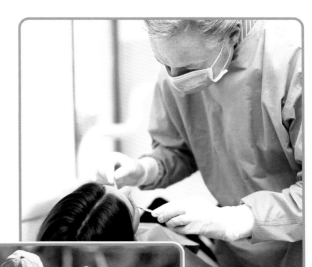

The manager of a baseball team is always hanging over the dugout railing assessing the progress of a game— in real time. Adjustments are made, often almost immediately. Coaches watch, assess, and develop a plan to assist athletes to improve their performance. Hairdressers continuously assess their work and adjust their technique to achieve results wanted. When you drive a car or write a paper, you are constantly assessing and making adjustments.

That's the process teachers use to become more and more effective.

Assessment in the Classroom

Assessment is one of the most powerful influences on student achievement. Research has shown that regular assessment produces significant and substantial learning gains and student success over time.[5]

The primary function of assessment is to inform students of progress in reaching desired performance levels and to help teachers identify strengths and weaknesses—what students know and what they still need to learn. If assessment finds that the student does not understand what is to be learned, the teacher provides additional instruction and directions, called feedback, to guide the student to mastering the objective of the lesson.

Assessment is for learning.
Feedback is for assistance.

Assessment measures understanding and performance. The teacher uses it to analyze each student's needs; provide constructive, personalized feedback; and make decisions on how to improve instruction. It is the most important tool a teacher has to create a classroom environment where learning and achieving are paramount and students' efforts are recognized and respected.

The two most important aspects of teaching are assessment and feedback. Over the past twenty years, educational research has confirmed the value of

- ◆ linking instruction to assessment,
- ◆ assessing student work to inform instruction, and
- ◆ using assessment practices to drive learning.

Effective teachers use assessment and feedback as THE major strategy in their teaching.

The research is clear. What teachers do in their classrooms matters. When **John Hattie** conducted an extensive meta-analysis that focused on student achievement, formative assessment topped his list as one of the most influential practices that improve student outcomes.[6]

15

Outperform 98 Percent of Regular Students

Read and learn from studies that show that assessment for learning is comparable to individual tutoring in its effectiveness.

Assess and Assist

Assessment in the classroom is like the GPS voice that is hidden in your vehicle's dashboard. It gets you from where you are to where you want to go no matter how many wrong turns you may make. Effective teachers use assessment techniques to get students from where they are to where they should be no matter how many mistakes they make.

The purpose of assessment is to assess and assist.
Effective teachers assess and assist.

Reviews of more than 4,000 research investigations show clearly that when formative assessment is well-implemented and effectively used during instruction, it can essentially double the speed of student learning. The process is so robust that different teachers can use it in diverse ways, yet still get significant results with their students to produce substantial increases in students' achievement.[7]

---

[5] Siobhan Leahy, Christine Lyon, Marnie Thompson, and Dylan Wiliam, "Classroom Assessment: Minute by Minute, Day by Day," *Educational Leadership* 63, no. 3 (November 2005): 19–24.

[6] Hattie, *Visible Learning*.

[7] W. James Popham, "Formative Assessment—A Process, Not a Test," *Education Week* 30, no. 21 (February 22, 2011): 35.

Assessment is the interaction between teaching and learning, between what teachers do and what students accomplish. Many students are academically lost in schools. The purpose of assessment is not to rate, rank, and sort students, or to pit them against each other. It is to provide the kind of meaningful feedback to each student that leads to higher performance for all students. Assessment is the minute-to-minute and day-to-day interaction that teachers use to gather the information they need to make productive adjustments to instruction and teaching.

Assessment is not something we do TO our students. The purpose of assessment is to provide feedback FOR our students, to guide and enhance their learning.

To guide students, keep four factors in mind for sound formative-assessment practice.

1. Clearly lay out what you want students to learn.
2. Monitor evidence of that learning.
3. Provide helpful feedback to individual students.
4. Adjust teaching and reteaching the lesson.

Practice this by asking three questions.

1. What will students learn?
2. Did they learn it?
3. How will I reteach to mastery?

Assessment is to be used in real time by both students and teacher. It helps students make progress while on task and is used by the teacher to modify lesson plans and instruction to further student learning. This must be done in real time, also.

Ineffective Teaching
Cover and test. Cover and test. Cover and test.

Effective Teaching
Assess and assist. Assess and assist. Assess and assist.

Once again, when people outside of education talk about testing, many incorrectly use the word assessment. Keep the distinction between the two very clear in your mind. Are you assessing for student learning or are you testing?

Assessment Is for Teachers Also

Assess the Teaching

Assessment is used to improve teaching practices.

- Diagnose and discuss student work based on learning objectives.
- Identify challenges, observe strengths and weaknesses, and devise strategies for improvement.
- Adjust instruction to keep students on track.

It is the practices of teachers that have an impact on student learning.[8]

James Stronge

James Stronge, who has researched and written on the qualities of effective teaching, states it is not about what program or approach is used, what technology has been purchased, the number of students in the classroom, the neighborhood the school is located in, or any other external factor. It is what teachers DO to design and adjust lessons in the classroom.

So, assessment is not just for students. It is for teachers, too. In addition to using assessment to monitor and promote student learning, classroom assessment should also be used to examine and improve teaching practices. Assessment helps teachers determine where students are so they can adjust lessons to support student learning.

---

[8] James Stronge, *Qualities of Effective Teachers* (Alexandria, VA: ASCD, 2018).

Immediately, Continually

- Assessment is conducted as immediately as possible and continually throughout the lesson.
- Teachers must adjust their instruction to keep students on track.
- No grades or scores are given and record keeping is primarily anecdotal and descriptive.

Assessments are correlated to lesson objectives so students can always see the expectations you have for learning. Assessments are not conducted in isolation. They build upon each other toward an overarching purpose. They create a classroom where teaching and learning are coherent, consistent, and continuous.

Praise and Rewards Are Not Assessment

The highest effect sizes were reported when students receive feedback about a task and how to do it more effectively. Lower effect sizes were related to praise, rewards, or punishment.[9]

John Hattie and Helen Timperley

General praise and rewards do not motivate students to do better. Assessment feedback is not about giving rewards—it is providing concrete, authentic information about the task and specific praise about accomplishments related to the task. Teachers often use rewards such as candy and stickers in an attempt

[9] John Hattie and Helen Timperley, "The Power of Feedback," *Review of Educational Research* 77, no. 1 (March 2007): 81–112.

How Do I Motivate Students?

Here's a common classroom scenario. The teacher talks endlessly. Students are given a hodgepodge of videos, worksheets, reading tasks, programs on the computer, and coloring activities. These are assigned without rhyme or reason, scope or sequence, coherence or consistency, objectives or targets—and then the students are blamed for being bored, distracted, and unmotivated.

Believe it or not, students come to school wanting to learn. In a class with no objectives or assessment, students are understandably apathetic. They do not know what they are to achieve or what they have accomplished. Students are motivated when they see a purpose and direction to what they are learning.

Focus more on progress and less on grades. Students need different opportunities to showcase their learning. Create lessons and assessments that focus more on mastery and progress rather than percentages and grades. Give students small tasks to accomplish successfully. Students need to take risks, ask questions, and know that mistakes are acceptable.

The research is emphatic. Achievement is increased with objectives and targets, assessment, and feedback assistance. Learning should not be a mystery and mastery

should be made an achievable goal. It is imperative that what is being taught is clearly stated and students receive a clear message that feedback help is being given. This hinges on an essential teaching technique—**Clarity** (Chapter 20).

When there is teacher clarity, students will listen, make an effort, and do what needs to be done. Achievement gives confidence. When students are confident, they motivate themselves to be productive learners. They become **intrinsically** motivated. Even a small success will spark enough confidence to achieve another success. As teachers, our goal is to perpetuate this cycle of intrinsic motivation. Extrinsic motivation—the desire to please a teacher, parents, or other authority figures—does not have a lasting effect.

The only way to motivate students is to awaken and foster intrinsic motivation so that they motivate themselves to become productive learners.

For their sake, at school and in life, students must come to the realization that their capacity to achieve and succeed comes from the tenacity and grit they themselves can muster intrinsically. **Feedback will be the motivating procedure.**

to encourage students to complete tasks. When the classroom culture focuses on rewards, "gold stars," grades, or class ranking, then students look for ways to outdo each other and obtain the best grades rather than focusing on improving their learning.

Indeed, it is doubtful whether rewards should be thought of as feedback at all. There is no research to support that students learn more when they receive rewards, or that students need praise to establish and maintain feelings of self-worth. True, praise may make students happy, but only momentarily, and it may inspire them to keep trying, momentarily, but it does not assist them to learn or help them develop the internal drive they need for challenges they will encounter throughout life.

We know of no research finding suggesting that receiving praise itself can assist a person to learn or to increase their knowledge and understanding.[10]

John Hattie

The effects of praise are particularly negative not when students succeed, but with students who are not really succeeding. Artificial or undeserved praise should be avoided at all costs. When praise is not based on real evidence of progress, the false praise can undermine trust and embarrass a student. Students know when praise is deserved.

Praise can discourage effort. Perhaps the most harmful effect of praise is that it creates students who come to depend on praise to be involved in their schoolwork. Praise can have little or no effect when students are successful. But is likely to be a negative effect when students are not successful, because this leads to learned helplessness.[11]

Often students come to school to be with their friends. Just tell your students how happy you are to see them.

Make them feel worthwhile as learners and welcomed to your class. There is no need to praise students for coming to class or school.

If you wish to make a major difference to learning, leave shallow praise out of feedback. Feedback is about learning, not rewards.

I Believe in You

A teacher returned an essay to the students, but the students who tended to be low-achievers received an extra sentence at the end of the feedback. Remarkably, those very students achieved at significantly higher levels in school a year later, with higher grade point averages. What was the sentence that those students read at the end of the feedback that caused such a dramatic result?

It simply said, "I'm giving you these comments because I have very high expectations and I know you can reach them."

Assessment Gives Hope for All Students

Teachers must be aware of students' progress minute by minute, so that they can provide feedback to help close gaps in understanding. There is no time to score papers traditionally and return them days later. To help underachievers meet learning goals, both the teacher and students must know immediately where they stand on the content being taught.

Assessment is to be used in real time so that students make progress while on task and the teacher can modify instruction then and there to further student learning.

Achievement is directly linked to frequent assessment and timely feedback. One of the best ways to help students who are not achieving is to use frequent

---

[10] John Hattie and Gregory C. R. Yates, *Visible Learning and the Science of How We Learn* (New York: Routledge, 2014).

[11] C.I. Diener and Carol Dweck, "An Analysis of Learned Helplessness: II" *Journal of Personality and Social Psychology* 39, no. 5 (December 1980): 940–952.

assessments to pinpoint where they need specific help. Examples of these can be seen in the assessment tools in chapters 10 and 11 and the rubrics in Chapter 12.

Using graded tests to evaluate what students have learned can too often just remind them again of what they have NOT learned. They then avoid investing effort in learning because they get another unsatisfactory message about their ability and believe that they lack the ability to overcome their poor performance.

With assessment for learning, students get a clear picture of the final learning targets. When feedback for assistance is timely, practical, and understandable, low-performing students begin to realize small successes. With each subsequent success, they become more likely to persevere and become more confident learners—**transforming them into successful students.**

Effective teachers use immediate and continual assessment to prevent learners from losing hope. They use it to rebuild hope that has been eroded or destroyed. They use it to convince students that they are there to help, not judge, test, and evaluate. They use it to create classrooms in which there are no surprises and no excuses. They use assessment to build trust and confidence.

There are three major ways to do assessment:

- Provide feedback (Chapter 9)
- Use an assessment tool (Chapters 10, 11)
- Use a rubric (Chapter 12)

Mastering Instruction

 Assessment is what a teacher does to monitor student work to see if the student is learning what has been taught.

 The effective teacher uses assessment and feedback as THE major strategy in their teaching.

 Assessment and feedback continue learning; testing and evaluation end learning.

 Assessment is not used just to determine student progress, but also to determine teacher effectiveness.

 Just as assessment of students must be done in real time, modifying instruction must be done in real time, also.

...Produces Achievement!

How to
Use Feedback

> *Feedback, along with effective instruction, is a powerful strategy to enhance and promote learning.*

What Is Feedback?

After a teacher assesses for understanding, the information given to students about their work is known as feedback.

Feedback is the bridge between teaching and learning.

Feedback is an integral part of the assessment process. It helps students understand where they are in their learning. It highlights what has been accomplished and what still needs to be achieved. It tells them what adjustments they need to make to do better and informs them what to do next. It helps them improve and make progress. Once they feel they know what to do and why, most students feel that they have control over their own learning, which is a big motivational factor to continue learning.

For feedback to work, there must be a clearly defined set of objectives to determine if a gap in performance exists. Feedback gives specific guidance for corrective action and engages students in review, analysis, reflection, and planning to attain the aim of the lesson.

◆ **Assessment** is what the teacher does to check if students have learned what has been taught.

◆ **Feedback** is the method the teacher uses to help students make progress in attaining the learning objective.

He Guarantees
That No One Will Fail

> **It's great to see the light bulb go on for my students and even greater when they see the light bulb go on for me as I see how I can improve my teaching. Once I understood where they were coming from, I was better able to teach them.**
>
> Brad Volkman
> Alberta, Canada

Brad **Volkman** teaches high school and does something unusual—almost unheard of—in his class. He GUARANTEES his students that if they work with him and follow his system, they WILL NOT FAIL his course, no matter how bad they think they are at math.

Feedback helps students stay on track. It helps them make progress towards a goal. It gives students control over their own learning.

In Chapter 8, you learned that studies have shown that formative assessment or "check for understanding" produces significant and often substantial learning gains. This can be done in three ways:

- **Using feedback** (Chapter 9)
- Using an assessment tool (Chapter 10 and Chapter 11)
- Using a rubric (Chapter 12)

Research Basis for Feedback

When I completed the first synthesis of one hundred and thirty-four meta-analyses of all possible influences on achievement, it soon became clear that feedback was among the most powerful influences on achievement.[1]

John Hattie

The effectiveness of feedback to improve learner performances has been recognized from the beginnings of behavioral science, some 150 years ago. **Feedback is incredibly empowering as it enables students themselves to plot, plan, and understand how to move forward successfully.**

The work of the Education Trust has shown that one key to promoting very high levels of achievement in low-performing schools is the effective use of day-to-day classroom assessment and feedback.[2]

Research has shown that assessment with feedback has produced significant and substantial learning gains.[3]

Paul Black and Dylan William

The average effect size of feedback is twice the average effect of all other teaching effects. **Feedback has an average effect size of 0.70, which translates into substantial student growth.** Feedback is indisputably one of the top influences on student achievement.

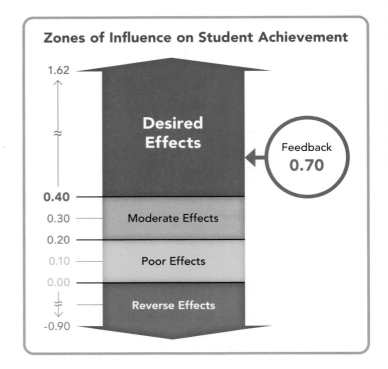

More than four thousand research investigations over forty years clearly show that when feedback, coupled with teacher clarity, is well used with students, it can essentially double the speed of student learning.[4,5]

Clarity and Intention

Feedback must always be aligned to explicit objectives.

To expedite student achievement, there must be a clear vision of what it means to succeed. Students need to know where they are headed to participate actively in their own learning. Teachers must be clear themselves about the intended learning, teach intentionally to it,

---

[1] John Hattie, *Visible Learning.*

[2] Dylan Wiliam, "Content Then Process: Teacher Learning Communities in the Service of Formative Assessment," in *Ahead of the Curve: The Power of Assessment to Transform Teaching and Learning*, ed. Douglas Reeves (Bloomington, IN: Solution Tree Press, 2007), 182–204.

[3] Paul Black and Dylan Wiliam, "Inside the Black Box: Raising Standards Through Classroom Assessment," *Phi Delta Kappan* 92, no.1 (September 2010): 81–90.

[4] Frank Fendick, "The Correlation Between Teacher Clarity of Communication and Student Achievement Gain: A Meta-Analysis" (PhD diss., University of Florida, 1990).

[5] Shaun Killian, "Teacher Clarity: A Potent Yet Misunderstood and Often Abused Teaching Strategy" (Australian Society for Evidence Based Teaching, June 16, 2017) https://www.evidencebasedteaching.org.au/teacher-clarity/.

and let students in on the purpose from the outset.

◆ Be clear about what you want your students to know and be able to do.

◆ Clearly explain new content to students.

◆ Post examples and check that students have a clear understanding of the new material.

◆ Clearly demonstrate relevant skills and processes that you expect students to do.

◆ Give students practice tasks visibly focused on what you want them to know and be able to do.

First, the objectives. You have the lesson objectives posted. They are visible—just as you have a shopping list in hand or a GPS that you refer to when you drive. You know what to buy or where to go. With the objectives posted, both you and your students know what is to be taught and what is to be learned. Students can even monitor their own learning.

Second, the assessment. Next, you assess for student learning constantly, just as you check your shopping list and GPS constantly—in real time. You don't check for understanding after the work has been turned in. Assessment is the process of checking to see if the student is making progress towards the objectives.

Third, the feedback. Feedback is the process of delivering information to the student to help the learning progress towards the objectives. Thus, feedback is the bridge to effective teaching. It fills the gaps between teaching and learning. It's the structure that keeps teaching and learning focused and on the same path.

For feedback to be effective, students need to know **where** they are going, **why** they are going there, and **what** is required for them to get there. To help them, provide the following:

◆ An **understanding** of the desired goal

◆ **Evidence** about their present position in relation to that goal

◆ **Guidance** on the way to close the gap between the two

The Power of Feedback

The impact of feedback translates into student achievement.

■ It positively increases learning capacity by twenty to thirty times.

■ It adds six to nine months of additional learning growth per year.

■ It enables students to learn four times as quickly with consistent use.[6]

When you begin teaching the lesson, before students start the learning process, you should be able to convey the final outcome to students and what they are expected to achieve.

Closing the Gaps

Feedback is not ranked, graded, or even recorded. It provides understanding, evidence, and guidance.

Students are motivated by knowledge gaps they can see and close. They perform best when they understand the target they are working towards. Unless students understand the lesson objectives, feedback is of no value. When students are told to "Read Chapter 3; Complete this worksheet; Play this computer game; Find an essay topic to write about;" there is no learning destination.

[6]Craig D. Jerald, *Dispelling the Myth Revisited: Preliminary Findings from a Nationwide Analysis of "High Flying" Schools* (Washington, DC: Education Trust, 2001).

The activity is not the objective. Too often, students— even teachers—believe that the activity they are doing is the learning objective. If there are no precise, clearly articulated objectives, students will believe that *finishing an activity* rather than *learning* is the purpose of the lesson.

The key to effective assessment is a teacher who has strong subject knowledge, knows the curriculum and what students should be learning, and then combines it with effective feedback practice. This is critical in "closing the gap" for students. Students who receive clear feedback have the information they need to take responsibility and monitor progress themselves to improve their learning.

When students are given the kind of feedback they can use constructively, they will experience a feeling of control over their learning. This empowerment is the foundation for motivation and self-sufficiency.

The ultimate purpose of feedback is to get students to learn the skills of teaching themselves—to self-assess their learning.

Positive Feedback

Feedback is used to let students know what they have done right, not just to correct and improve what they have done wrong. Learning is enhanced when people see what they have done correctly and what they need to do to improve.

It is common for students to make an inadvertent mistake. Just help them correct the mistake by pointing out the errors in the process that they used. This can be as simple as listening to them think out loud and describe the steps they used. Much can be learned when students are made aware of how a mistake was made.

The Right Kind of Questions

Asking a question, the right kind of question, is the quickest way to check understanding and provide the precise feedback students need to achieve lesson objectives.

To provide constructive feedback, evidence of learning, or lack of it, must be gathered. One way to do this is to ask questions. Asking questions is the most common way for teachers to determine what feedback is needed for students to progress and succeed.

These are the three questions that you, the teacher, need to ask.

1. What is the learning objective for this lesson?
2. Where are my students now in relation to the learning objective?
3. What do I need to do now to adjust my instruction to close any gaps between achieving the objective and my students' current performance?

Students should also feel free to ask you, the teacher, questions during the course of a lesson. Guide and help students to focus on these three basic questions.

1. What knowledge or skills do I aim to develop?
2. How close am I to achieving the learning objectives?
3. What do I need to do next?

The power of feedback is greatest in influencing student achievement when the answers tell them how to perform a task more effectively. For this to happen, learning objectives must be clearly expressed and feedback information must clearly define what to do in order to achieve the objectives.

The most important question to ask a student at the conclusion of feedback is, "Given the information I have just given you, do you have some idea of how to improve what you have just done?"

Feedback should provide a clear picture of how to progress.

The Wrong Kind of Questions

Knowing how to ask the right questions is an essential skill when determining how to provide constructive feedback. It's important to realize that not all questions are effective at gathering useful evidence of learning.

These questions are pointless.

- "Do you all understand?" (as all students will nod "Yes" even if most do not really understand)
- "Can we move on?" (as all students will nod "Yes" because they want to get out of class)

Refrain also from asking questions that elicit one-word responses or that have a single right answer.

- "What is photosynthesis?" (as you will get a terse definition; someone may even just say "green.")
- "How many sides to a trapezoid?"

Instead, probe to get student responses that cause thinking. For example, consider this classroom scenario, beginning with a direction.

- "Saul, Justin, and Grant, please go to the board and each of you draw a trapezoid without looking at each other's drawing."

While the students are at the board, engage the rest of the class in a discussion of the trapezoid.

- Describe and define a trapezoid.
- What do you notice about the three trapezoids drawn on the board?
- What do you notice about the lines on a trapezoid? And the angles?

Make the Teacher Happy

This, unfortunately, is a familiar classroom routine. The teacher stands in front of the classroom and asks a question, supposedly to gather information for feedback. Five or six hands go up, and they are usually the same five or six hands. Because the rest of the class knows that the teacher will call on one of these students, they sit out the ritual and feel no incentive to even try to participate. The teacher selects a student and receives a correct response. The teacher assesses the response and says to self, "I just heard the correct answer, so I must be doing well." The teacher then moves on and the cycle begins again.

This model is played out it in the vast majority of classrooms in every country of the world. Teachers believe they are assessing their students. In reality, they are judging how well the lesson is proceeding based on isolated answers from a confident few. The major problem with asking the entire class a question is that the only person who actually receives feedback is the teacher. Teachers pick students to hear what they want to hear—the right answer—assumes every student understands, and plows right on.

When teachers ask general recall questions and then accept the "correct" answer from a select few, those students learn to take the path of least resistance and give the answers the teacher expects to see or hear. They play the game called, "Make the teacher happy." Other students are not given the opportunity to say, "I don't really understand. I am here to learn, achieve, and succeed and I want to know what I have to do to improve."

- Each of you draw your own trapezoid.
- How would you calculate the area and perimeter of the trapezoid you just drew?
- In England, the trapezoid is called a trapezium. Please report tomorrow if it is just a difference in name or if they are two different shapes.

When to Provide Feedback

The most effective use of feedback occurs on a daily basis and determines the teacher's minute-by-minute decision making.

**Feedback is used
to modify instruction in real time.**

After providing clear, specific learning objectives at the beginning of the lesson, deliver feedback as immediately and frequently as possible. **Feedback should permeate a class period.** Feedback is most effective while students are still engaged in the lesson. That's when there is time to act on it. Structure your lessons and student assignments so that all or most of your feedback is given on student work in progress, not when it is too late to help students improve and instruction has moved on to the next unit or learning objective.

**For an effective teacher,
feedback is not secondary to what they do—
it is the core of their professional work.**

Assessment is a process for uncovering misunderstandings and encouraging deeper understanding. **Assessment takes time, patience, and dedication. It is personal and focused.**

In sports, coaches and players are constantly assessing a game's progress and making immediate adjustments. They do not wait until the game is over to make corrections. They do not wait until the team meets the next day in the clubhouse. **In the classroom, there should be a continual flow of feedback assistance based on careful observation of student progress. Assess promptly, patiently, and persistently.**

Frequent feedback produces strong gains because it gives students timely information about their work. It enables teachers to make immediate adjustments to instruction. Students are assured that the teacher cares and truly wants to help. **A climate of trust, risk-taking, collaborative support, transparency, and continuous improvement results when there is frequent feedback.** The trust that develops between students and teacher results in openness, honesty, and genuine dialogue.

In contrast, when feedback is scarce or inconsistent, students are surprised by the "help" when it suddenly appears. They may be puzzled or even suspicious of it; they wonder, "What's wrong?" When there is ongoing feedback, students learn to appreciate that it is used to continuously improve their performance.

Effective feedback is frequent, timely, and consistent.

Ongoing assessment and continuous feedback have been consistently shown to have a powerful effect on student learning. Feedback provides moment-to-moment results in classrooms in which there are no surprises and no excuses.

A Student of Students

**An effective teacher is a habitual student
of his or her students.**

An effective teacher is constantly assessing—walking, watching, and listening for clues about students' understanding, asking questions that probe their thinking, and taking notes.

During this process, it becomes evident that the most powerful aspect of assessment is the feedback students give to the teacher. This information allows teachers to see learning through the eyes of their students. When teachers can see what students know, what they understand, and where they make errors, then teaching and learning can work together to help students make progress. Feedback to teachers makes learning, or lack of it, visible. It facilitates the planning of next steps.

> **Assessment is not just used to determine student progress; it is also used to determine teaching progress.**
>
> **Although the emphasis may seem to be from the *teacher to the student*, the most powerful benefit of feedback is when it is from the *student to the teacher*.**

Feedback guides instruction. It tells the teacher whether to move on and continue or modify instruction to help students reach mastery. This is the same when cooking—you check to see how the chicken is roasting or how the cake is baking. When teaching, you monitor how well students are doing so that you ensure they do indeed learn.

It is teachers seeing learning through the eyes of students, and students seeing teaching as the key to their ongoing learning.[7]

John Hattie

The Power of Examples

Students understand best what a goal or objective really means when they can see examples of good work.

The teacher's role in helping students understand the final outcome is to
- diagnose student work based on learning objectives.
- provide verbal or written feedback, describing strengths and making suggestions for improvement.
- show examples and provide the necessary guidance so students can make progress and achieve learning targets.
- adjust instruction to keep students on track.

Just as learning objectives must be posted so students can continually see where they are going, post examples of good work. Give them an idea of what they are striving to accomplish. When students have an idea of what the desired outcomes are, the mystery is taken out of learning. They are given the opportunity to rise to the occasion and meet the challenges presented. Examples are particularly effective if a student is struggling with a new concept or if a student is unfamiliar with English.

To ensure students are doing a task correctly, the teacher should monitor student work and not assume that one correction is sufficient. Draw their attention to the examples and be ready to intervene and correct over and over again until "practice makes perfect."

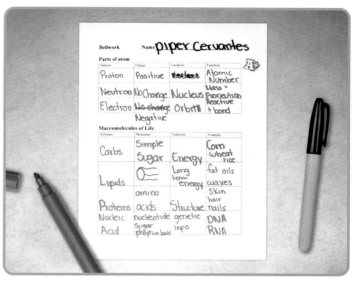

Save examples of acceptable work to share with future students so they have a visual reference of what it takes to succeed.

Then, praise their accomplishment specifically so that they are made aware of what exactly they have achieved.

Feedback and examples have great power in influencing student achievement because they clearly show how to meet an objective and perform a task effectively and successfully.

When work is returned, it may also be advantageous to engage the whole class in the feedback process. Take a common mistake and use it for discussion. Elicit correct responses and engage the class in assessing their own work. You may want to prompt with, "We have a learning target. Are we there yet? Why or why not? What do you think we can do to get closer to it?"

Feedback Should Be Specific

Feedback is only useful if it is understood and accepted by the student. Effective feedback contains information that individual students can use, which means that they have to understand how it pertains specifically to their work. If feedback is too vague or generic, no student will believe that it pertains to him or her.

---

[7] John Hattie, *Visible Learning for Teachers: Maximizing Impact on Learning* (New York: Routledge, 2012).

Learning Objectives and Feedback Questions

Photosynthesis

These objectives and questions are used by science teacher **Karen Rogers** in Kansas. She uses the questions to check for understanding and provide discussion on her lesson on photosynthesis.

Learning Objectives

- Explain how energy is transferred from the sun, to living organisms, to heat.
- Write and memorize the chemical equation for photosynthesis.
- Design an experiment that will test the process, or the rate, of photosynthesis.
- Evaluate the significance of photosynthesis to life on Earth.

Feedback Questions

1. Feel your forehead. Why is it warm? (Socratic questioning—why? Why? Why?)
2. You are eating a ham and cheese sandwich. Describe (or draw) how energy is transferred from the sun to the sandwich. What happens to the energy after you eat the sandwich?
3. Can you correctly write down the chemical formula for photosynthesis? Write it down now and we will discuss everyone's (yes, everyone's) answer.
4. What has to happen for photosynthesis to occur? How could we test to see if this is true?
5. How could we test to see what affects the rate of photosynthesis? (If we wanted plants to grow faster, what could we do?)
6. Do you think photosynthesis is the only way organisms get energy? Why or why not?
7. Do you think all life on the planet would die without sunlight? Why or why not?

Geography of the Early River Valley Civilizations

These objectives and questions are used by **Jeff Gulle** in Kentucky. Each question number corresponds to the number of the objective it assesses. The lower numbers address lower levels of Bloom's Taxonomy (that is, remembering and understanding) and they steadily scaffold to evaluation (number 5).

Learning Objectives

- List each of the ancient river valley civilizations and identify which river(s) supported each civilization.
- Locate each ancient river valley civilization on a map.
- Contrast architectural features of different early river valleys.
- Analyze the impact of irrigation on early river valley civilizations.
- Evaluate the impact of the annual floods on early river valley civilizations.

Feedback Questions

1. What were the four early river valley civilizations of the eastern hemisphere? Which river(s) supported which civilization?
2. Where were the four river valley civilizations located?

3. Why were the cities of some river valley civilizations surrounded by walls, while the cities of other civilizations were not?
4. What were the social and economic effects of irrigation on each of the early river valley civilizations?

Alternate questions:

4a. What impact did irrigation have on the (a) availability and (b) cost of agricultural products?
4b. You are a potter or an artisan or a priest. You could not have that job if it were not for irrigation. Why? (In other words, explain the relationship between irrigation and the development of specialization.)
4c. Choose a river valley civilization, such as Mesopotamia or Ancient Egypt. How do you think that culture would have developed differently if it had never developed irrigation?

5. Do you think the annual flooding had a helpful or a detrimental impact on the river valley civilizations? Defend your answer.

Use precise vocabulary in your written or oral feedback. "Great work!" is a nice comment, but it's too general and too vague to be useful. Comments like "Write more" at the top of the paper do not give students much guidance. More of what? "Try harder" is another vague comment. What should the student try to do more of or try to do more intensely? Other confusing classics include "Awkward," "Needs work," "Unclear," and the frowny face—whatever these mean. Students with good intentions may end up going in the wrong direction and doing something you do not want them to do.

Specific feedback is helpful input. "The way you describe how to bake a snickerdoodle cookie is clear and well organized! It makes me feel confident about trying the recipe." The student knows exactly why you thought their recipe was well presented.

Always bear in mind when giving feedback that your words have power. The words you choose when speaking to students have a tremendous influence on their productivity. Research evidence shows that teachers tend to talk with "good" students as if they are active self-learners. Average to poor students, on the other hand, are often simply told what to do, or to just "try to get it right," and the message conveyed is that they are expected to cope, but not excel. Even the tone you use will affect students' motivation and capacity for improvement.

Listen to yourself. Be very aware of what you are saying and the language and tone you use. Be very aware of how you are saying what you say.

Feedback Leads to Action

As has been repeatedly emphasized, feedback is most powerful when it is obvious, transparent, and visible to the student. It is most helpful when the information is understandable, actionable, simple, timely, and ongoing.

The ultimate purpose of assessment feedback is to give students the means to correct their own work to make progress. **Feedback must enable students to take action.** If a teacher over-corrects a paper and all

the student does is copy the corrections, nothing has really been learned. It can have a negative effect on the learning process. The student's only thought is, "Is this enough to get a good grade?"

Although teachers may want to step in and guide students through the feedback process, it may actually undermine students' efforts and deprive them of the opportunity to make sense of the learning process. At times it may be better to refrain from providing students with feedback instruction that is too detailed. Let them struggle, engage, ask questions, and figure things out on their own.

Feedback allows the student to see the path to success.

Feedback to Struggling Students

To help students meet learning goals, both the teacher and students must know immediately where they stand on the content being taught at that moment. There is no benefit to scoring papers after lessons are over and returning them days later. Achievement is directly linked to timely feedback. **Feedback is of most value while students are still thinking of and still working on the learning target.**

For underachieving students, or students in an early stage of learning a new topic or skill, **frequent and immediate feedback is imperative.** The best feedback occurs when it is conveyed to the student as soon as possible after work is reviewed or observed. When feedback is frequent and ongoing, students begin to hit learning targets and realize small successes. As a result, they become more confident learners and are more likely to persevere.[8]

As assessment is conducted, students who have difficulty engaging will discover

- ◆ if they are capable of succeeding or not. (They are.)
- ◆ if learning is worth the effort. (It is.)

- ◆ if they have the wherewithal to risk investing in the school experience. (Immediate, practical, and understandable feedback will give them confidence that they do indeed have what it takes.)

---

[8] Jan Chappius and Rick J. Stiggins, *Classroom Assessment for Student Learning: Doing It Right—Using It Well* (New York: Pearson, 2019).

Correction Keys

A feedback technique that uses a correction key requires students to find their errors, do the thinking, and make the corrections. The teacher provides the feedback in the margin with symbols, dots, or marks to alert the student that something is amiss.

Providing a key to the markings allows the student to become an active learner as corrections are made. Show students a sample of how you are going to provide this type of feedback and work through your expectations for corrected work.

Error Key	
C = Capitalization	P = Punctuation
S = Spelling	T = Tense
SF = Sentence Fragment	SS = Sentence Structure
WC = Word Choice	

Teacher Notes	Student Samples
C	I remember when i was little
S	and everytime my daddy came
C	home i would always tell him
C(2) – T – S	that i have been good. Becuse i'm usually doing something wrong.
C – WC	i believe she is very anxious
S	four the school year to end.
SS – S	Sleep all day is what she is going to due.
S(2)	She cant weight to start!

Error Key	
C = Capitalization	P = Punctuation
S = Spelling	T = Tense
SF = Sentence Fragment	SS = Sentence Structure
WC = Word Choice	

Teacher Notes	CORRECTED VERSION
C	I remember when I was little
S	and every time my daddy came
C	home I would always tell him
C(2) – T – S	that I had been good. ~~Becuse~~ Because I'm usually doing something wrong.
C – WC	I believe she is very ~~anxious~~ eager
S	~~four~~ for the school year to end.
SS – S	~~Sleep all day is what she is going to due~~ do. She is going to sleep all day.
S(2)	She ~~cant~~ can't ~~weight~~ wait to start!

The purpose of feedback is to help the student close the gap between what knowledge they have and what they need to know or what skill level they have and what they need to be able to do.

**Praise
does not close an achievement gap.
Specific information
helps close the achievement gap.**

One of the best ways to help students who are not achieving as well as they should be is to give frequent assessments or activities that focus on pinpointing where they need specific help. Examples of these can be seen in the assessment tools in Chapter 10 and Chapter 11 and the rubrics in Chapter 12.

Using tests and giving grades to evaluate what students have learned can too often just remind them again of what they have not learned. They then avoid investing effort in learning because they get another unsatisfactory, disheartening message about their academic ability. They come to believe that they lack ability and potential and have shortcomings that they themselves cannot overcome.

When the frequency of feedback goes up and evaluation goes down, students learn more.[9]

With assessment for learning, students are given a clear picture of the learning targets that are possible for them to attain. When feedback is practical and understandable, low-performing students are given the information they need to try again. Each achievement, no matter how modest, gives them the motivation they need to carry on.

Constructive feedback is a powerful method for transforming low achievers into successful students.

Effective teachers use assessment to prevent learners from losing hope. They use it to rebuild hope that has been eroded or destroyed. They use it to convince students that they are there to help, not judge or evaluate. They use it to create classrooms in which there are no surprises and no excuses. They use assessment to build trust and confidence.

Dollops of Feedback

Rather than give students a massive amount of feedback at one time, it is better to give shorter feedback more often. As **John Hattie** says, "Give dollops of feedback." A dollop is a lump or glob of some substance, such as a dollop of whipped cream on top of a sundae.

**The shorter and more targeted the feedback the better.
Too much feedback can be overwhelming and difficult to absorb.**

Giving Feedback with Respect

Students in a failure pattern may be defensive or feel embarrassed about the frequent presence of a teacher at their desk. If they need help, they may be hesitant about approaching the teacher, so they circle the room, hoping other students can be of assistance. They are reluctant to ask the teacher for fear of the subtle negative message they'll receive.

In fact, some struggling learners do not seek assistance at all but exhibit self-protection behaviors. This is because, as research points out, they have been traumatized by past teachers who have been demeaning

---

[9]Anne Davies, "Involving Students in the Classroom Assessment Process," in *Ahead of the Curve: The Power of Assessment to Transform Teaching and Learning*, ed. Douglas Reeves (Bloomington, IN: Solution Tree, 2007), 31–57.

in their mannerisms or choice of words.[10] Students are highly sensitive to the tone used when criticism is given. Sometimes what a teacher intends as helpful critical feedback turns to personal ego evaluation in the eyes of the receiver.

Like everyone, underperforming students want to maintain a sense of self-respect (looking good to peers and to the teacher). If the classroom environment makes them wary of dialogue and feedback from the teacher, underperforming students cannot know how they are actually doing, and the teacher cannot adjust instructional strategies to help them. This can further erode their emotional development and undermine their achievement.

As long as students feel there is more risk in seeking help than in making errors, they will remain passive, apathetic learners. Be attuned to their reactions and attitude, and find ways to gain their trust with high expectations and the belief you have in their potential to succeed.

Give students the respect they need so that they feel safe and comfortable seeking assistance.

Questions to Ask

When giving feedback to struggling students, be sure to consistently check for understanding. Feedback is of no use when there is no understanding of the observations, suggestions, or directions you have given.

Ask simple questions to provoke thought and discussion. For example, ask the student to tell you what is the most important point you made in your feedback. Or ask the student to tell you what is the next step, based on your feedback.

Be patient as small, gradual improvements are better for the student than being overwhelmed and giving up.

16

Corrective Feedback

See how English language learners struggle with corrective feedback.

Feedback Never Focuses on the Student

Feedback should always focus specifically on the work. It should never focus on the student. Focusing on the student rather than on progress related to

---

Whoa. Slow Down and Wait.

A common problem when teachers ask questions is that they do not wait long enough to allow students to think through their answers. This is called "wait time," and is the research of Mary Budd Rowe.[11] She found that the typical American teacher waits one to two seconds for a response. An Australian teacher waits half a second.

She also found that teachers will wait longer for a "smarter" student to respond. If there is no answer, teachers will typically answer their own question. With a short wait time, students learn to blurt out one word or one phrase answers or wait out the teacher. But when students see that the teacher is willing to wait a longer time, they will give longer responses, complete sentence responses, and even offer discussion responses.

Choose the question first, then the student. After a student responds, stay silent and give the class a body language look of "Anyone else?"

One way to increase wait time is to select a name stick from the container (page 118), hold it while you talk, and then ask the question. Students then know they must be prepared as they might be called upon. Or, give the class time to respond, and then ask them to discuss their thinking in pairs or in small groups, so that a respondent is speaking on behalf of others, giving all students time for thoughtful reflection and the opportunity to express their ideas.

---

[10] Hattie and Timperley, "The Power of Feedback," 81–112.

[11] Mary Budd Rowe, "Wait Time: Slowing Down May Be a Way of Speeding Up," *American Educator: The Professional Journal of the American Federation of Teachers* 11, no. 1 (Spring 1987): 8–43, 47.

the task can actually cause a decline in student performance. Don't belittle because something has been done incorrectly. Feedback has nothing to do with judgment or personal opinion. It does not involve comparisons with other students. When criticisms or comparisons are used, feedback makes underachieving students feel that they lack the necessary ability, causing them to believe that they are incapable of learning.

Feedback that is personal and negative will stop any motivation to continue working.

Any negative feedback is always problematic. Rarely does it accomplish anything. It doesn't help to say, "What's the matter? Can't you do better?" Students may feel the tasks set were unreasonable. They may believe the lesson was poorly taught or that the goal was not made clear. They may feel the expectation of them was being applied unfairly compared to other class members. They may even believe that the level of effort they put in was substantial, but it was not recognized for what it was.

Students want to know how to improve their work so that they can do better next time. They expect and accept mistakes, and they want mistakes corrected. They want helpful advice, not hurtful comments. **It will be necessary to repeatedly reassure your students that assessment is to help them achieve learning outcomes, not good grades.** Students will eventually understand this as you continue to assess and not grade. In time, they will work with you to produce work they can be proud of.

Feedback Is Not Praise

Teachers who give struggling students lavish praise could make them even less likely to succeed. Although teachers want to encourage underachieving students by giving them praise, this can have a negative impact on them.[12]

Robert Coe

Just as feedback is not about criticizing, nor is it about giving rewards. Do not confuse praise with the process of providing feedback. Praise does not provide

Feedback Sandwich

The "feedback sandwich" is a technique that can be used when assessing student work. If something critical needs to be said, say it pressed between two slices of positive feedback. In other words, describe two things the student did well according to the learning target then sandwich one suggestion for improvement in the middle. To determine if your feedback was of value, ask the student to explain or reflect on how they used the feedback and what they learned from it.

the specific information students need to enhance learning. Being praised repeatedly and excessively can cause them to become suspicious. They ask, "What is wrong with me that the teacher needs to praise me all the time?"

This is not to say never give praise. Minimal praise is fine, but use it to make students feel welcomed to class and worthwhile as learners. Students need to feel that they "belong" in learning, that there is a high level of trust between teacher, student, and peers, and that their work is appreciated, respected, and earned. The important thing is to establish a positive and friendly atmosphere—one of mutual respect and trust.

---

[12] Robert Coe et al., *What Makes Great Teaching? Review of the Underpinning Research* (London: Dunham University, Sutton Trust, 2014).

Students do not want to waste energy being worried about their standing on your approval index. Once praise is out of the way, the class can get down to the serious business of learning without having to worry about what you will approve or disapprove of.[13]

Limit generalized praise and do not make comparisons. Generalized praise ("Good job!" "Nice work!") or feedback about the person ("Smart girl!" "Bright boy!") does not contain information that can be used for further learning. Repeated, generalized praise can contribute to students believing that intelligence is

fixed. This removes or diminishes the connection between student effort—grit—and achievement.[15]

You want students to work hard and persevere. Encourage students to exhibit grit and succeed through their own efforts.

He Guarantees They Will Not Fail

There is no jostling for grades in **Brad Volkman's** class. He knows what the research says—**constant, ungraded quizzes significantly increase retention of learning.**[16]

Brad's students are eager to come to class, ready to participate, and willing to say, "I don't know." Wouldn't you if your teacher guaranteed you would not fail?

Brad's math class consists almost entirely of students who either failed math or were in a resource room pull-out program where they did a modified math of some kind. A quarter of the class is usually coded for severe or moderate special needs. These are students who are not university bound and aren't even sure they want their high school diploma. The only reason they come to school is because their parents make them or to see friends. In other words, Brad teaches the kind of students that many teachers dread or even fear.

Yet he guarantees his students they will not fail. He does not tell his students that they have to work harder than they've ever worked in their entire lives. He does not drown them in homework. And he certainly doesn't intimidate them by saying, "You better get busy! I grade everything in here!"

Give Feedback, Not Grades

Students were given an assignment with a quantitative task and a divergent-thinking task. Researchers investigated the effects of returning the assignment with

- evaluation grades,
- feedback comments, or
- neither grade nor feedback.

Their study revealed these findings.

- Students who received an evaluative grade performed well on the quantitative task but poorly on the divergent-thinking task and were less motivated.
- Students who received feedback comments performed better on both tasks and reported more motivation for them.
- Students who received no feedback performed poorly on both tasks and also were less motivated.[14]

Other studies, going back fifty years, have investigated the effects of grades versus comments on student performance. Research has confirmed that student achievement was higher for a group receiving feedback comments instead of letter grades.

If presented with both a grade and feedback, students will look at the grade and ignore most of the feedback.

---

[13] Edward L. Deci, Richard Koestner, and Richard M. Ryan, "Extrinsic Rewards and Intrinsic Motivation in Education: Reconsidered Once Again," *Review of Educational Research* 71, no. 1 (Spring 2001): 1–27.

[14] Ruth Butler and Mordecai Nisan, "Effects of No Feedback, Task-Related Comments, and Grades on Intrinsic Motivation and Performance," *Journal of Educational Psychology* 78, no. 3 (June 1986): 210–216.

[15] Carol S. Dweck, "The Perils and Promises of Praise," *Educational Leadership* 65, no. 2 (October 2007): 34–39.

[16] Henry L. Roediger III and Jeffrey D. Karpicke, "The Power of Testing Memory: Basic Research and Implications for Educational Practice," *Perspectives of Psychological Science* 1, no. 3 (September 1, 2006): 181–210.

Instead, each day, students are given a short quiz as bellwork to determine their understanding of yesterday's lesson. **The quiz is not graded. It's not a test; it's an assessment.** After the quiz, Brad goes over the solutions, often with student help, at the board. Then he asks students to tick either of these.

_____ I can do this.

_____ I'm still not too sure about this.

Problem 2: The cost of a cell phone is \$465.79. Mark makes \$16.55 per hour at his job. How many hours of work will Mark need to do in order to pay for the phone?

5. Define the variable:

6. Write the equation:

7. Solve the equation:

8. Answer the problem:

Name: _____

Please check one of the following **after we mark the quiz together**:

_____ I can do this.

_____ I'm still not too sure about this.

Brad says that at first his students are either shocked or suspicious of the two statements. They expect to be marked or graded and when asked to assess their own learning, they wonder, "Is this a trap? Do I get marked down if I check 'I'm still not too sure?'"

Brad is conscious that these students have been graded, scored, and ranked (always poorly) throughout their academic careers. They have been dismissed as "lazy" and "unmotivated" and humiliated by the ranking process. His priority is to convince them that he is on their side. Drawing on a sports analogy, he tells them that he is their coach. He is not the enemy—with tricks and surprises up his sleeve—trying to trap them. **He is their coach and the only way he feels like a winner is if they win.**

In the same way a coach needs feedback from the team to figure out a training strategy, the tick marks give Brad instant feedback on how well he has taught the class. They let him know if he needs to reteach the concept or if he just needs to meet with a few students to provide extra support or instruction.

But first, Brad goes over the quiz so that students can review the questions while they are fresh on their minds. He does not put the solutions on the board immediately but asks students to suggest possible answers. Brad says it's not uncommon to get several different answers to a question. "I ask the students who offered their solution to explain or justify it to the class. Sometimes, I ask the class to vote on which of the suggested answers they think is right. This may lead to further attempts by the students to justify or expand the answer, trying to win as many votes as possible. I thoroughly enjoy these kinds of discussions when they happen . . . I learn a lot from them!"

Once his students have had a chance to volunteer and discuss their answers, then, and only then, does Brad show the correct solution in detail.

The key to these daily quizzes is that they are NOT graded. When students see this, it relieves a major source of anxiety. Brad's students come to see that the quizzes are for them—a no-pressure opportunity to check their own understanding (self-assessment will be explained in Chapter 13) and to communicate any concerns to their teacher in a safe way.

Students are more willing to take risks in a safe learning environment than they would be if everything were to be graded.

What is amazing is that after the class discussions, even those students who got all the questions on the quiz wrong are able to check "I can do this." By having students discuss their answers, everyone is able to clarify their doubts and refine their understanding of the concepts. "It's like the lesson really got taught twice—once the day before when I taught it for the first time and again the next morning when I go over the quiz," says Brad.

Intriguingly, students are more motivated by a quiz that is not graded than a quiz that is scored. For Brad, it went against all his previous training and practice.

"It seemed that when the quiz was for their own personal feedback and to guide my instruction, the students relaxed and performed better on the quizzes. They actually tried harder. **The atmosphere in the classroom became less threatening and more collegial**," says Brad. "Plus, it is far more effective as I get one-on-one time connection with them to make sure they understand the concepts.

Brad capitalizes on the fact that all students want to succeed. No one wants to lose. "The students and I have a common goal—to be winners on game day!"

In the end, one hundred percent of Brad Volkman's students pass his class.

Build an atmosphere of trust in the classroom. When students see you are on their side and want them to succeed, you create a class of winners.

Mastering Instruction

 Feedback is always given against explicit objectives.

 Feedback is of most value while students are still working on the learning target.

 Feedback has great power in influencing student achievement because it is focused on how to perform a task more effectively.

 For underachieving students in particular, frequent and immediate feedback is imperative.

 Feedback should always focus specifically on the work, not the student.

 The most important feedback is that which the students give to the teacher.

...Produces Achievement!

How to Use Personal Assessment

> *Personal assessment tools enable teachers to check for understanding as they teach.*

Assessment Tools

Why do teachers need assessment tools? How do you know that your students have "caught what you have taught?" Sometimes, teachers think that saying something is the same as teaching something. But no matter how eloquently you may have stated or explained the lesson content, it could very well be that you have really only talked, and perhaps, unfortunately, not actually taught anything at all.

The assessment tools or techniques shared in this book are divided by use:

- **Tools used for personal assessment (Chapter 10)**
- Tools used with partners or in groups (Chapter 11)

The ideal assessment tool is one where students can self-assess their own learning and progress. Such personal assessment techniques give each individual learner the opportunity to communicate their progress during a lesson. They are used by students to affirm understanding, or lack of, during the course of instruction. They are used by teachers to check for understanding, or lack of, during the course of instruction.

A Tool for Every Task

> **Man is a Tool-using animal. Without tools he is nothing, with tools he is all.**
>
> Thomas Carlyle

When carpenters or plumbers go out on a job, they will have a toolbox with a variety of tools. Even with a screwdriver, there will be a variety of screwdrivers, each for a particular job.

There are many tools a teacher can use to assess for understanding and learning.

There are four personal assessment tools explained in detail in this chapter:

1. Whiteboards (page 106)
2. Exit Tickets (page 108)
3. Student Response Cards (page 110)
4. Guided Notes (page 113)

Additional personal assessment tools can be found by accessing the QR codes at the end of this chapter.

Personal assessment tools provide teachers with immediate feedback to determine student learning.

Personal assessment tools help teachers modify and improve their teaching during the course of a lesson.

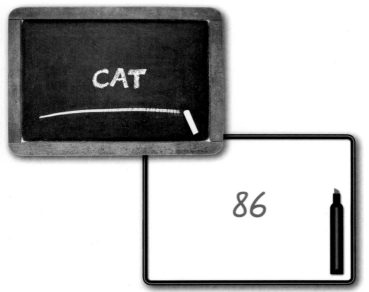

Teachers in the past and those in classrooms today know that personal boards make it possible to determine individual understanding and achievement quickly and quietly.

A Very Special Thank You

Region 13 Education Service Center in Austin, Texas, is one of twenty regional service centers serving educators in Texas. They have produced The Teacher Toolkit (www.theteachertoolkit.com) with a comprehensive listing and explanation of assessment tools. We thank them for their help in writing these chapters and sharing the work of so many from the school systems it serves.

Whiteboards

Whiteboards provide information about every student in the class at the same time.

If you have ever watched a movie or TV show set in the Old West, you have probably seen a teacher in a one-room schoolhouse instructing students to write something on their slates using a piece of chalk. In these settings, students used a slate to practice something, such as arithmetic or penmanship, when it wasn't practical or necessary to keep their work. In the same way, individual student Whiteboards are simply a modern adaptation of the slates used in classrooms in the 1800s.

With individual personal Whiteboards, students can write their responses to a prompt and have their responses looked at and assessed immediately. Teachers can quickly see the level of comprehension of concepts that were just taught and such timely feedback allows them to adjust how they move forward to keep students engaged and on task.

How to Use Whiteboards

Creating Whiteboards

To make your own set of Whiteboards, visit a home improvement store and buy a large sheet of white shower board. There may be a charge for having it cut into rectangles or squares, but if you go at a time when the store isn't busy, they are often willing to do it for free. A single four-by-eight-foot board will be enough for thirty-two, twelve-by-twelve-inch square boards. A parent may also be willing to do this for you.

There are also other ways to create Whiteboards:

- Plastic dinner plates
- Inserts such as a piece of card stock, a map, graph paper, or templates inside a clear sheet protector
- Plastic menu covers
- Laminated sheets of card stock

These are some recommendations from teachers who regularly use Whiteboards.

- Use brightly colored electrical tape to cover the edges and corners of each board to protect students' fingers from rough edges.
- Add dry erase markers to student school supply lists or wish lists for parent donations—they can be expensive.
- Ask students or parents to bring old (clean) athletic socks—they can be used for erasers and marker storage.
- A pom-pom glued to the end of a marker can also be used as an eraser.
- Keep a supply of extra Whiteboards to use for rainy day recess—students love to use them to draw or play games.
- Paint the back of each Whiteboard with chalkboard paint so that if markers dry out, students can use chalk to write on the back of their board.
- Remind students to clean boards after each use.

Reviewing Expectations

Next, review expectations for how to display Whiteboards properly. Before distributing markers and Whiteboards, model how to write an answer in a point size that is easy to see at a glance. Depending on the age of students, it may also be appropriate to remind them that only answers (not comments about their friends or other topics or doodles) should be written and displayed. Also, review the procedure for displaying Whiteboards. For example, waving Whiteboards wildly or thrusting them in front of other students is not inappropriate. Before beginning the response activity, model a question and response scenario and ask students to practice with you.

Asking for Responses

The next step will be to pose a question to the class regarding information just covered in the lesson. The question could be multiple choice, Yes or No, short answer, or a variety of other options. Once you have posed the question, it is important to incorporate wait time so that students will have a moment to think about and write their answer. Then it is helpful to provide a consistent series of cues for when it is time to respond.

For example, ask the question and say, "Thinking," pause, then say, "Boards up," and students hold up their Whiteboards with their answers. When you have had time to check the answers, say, "Boards down," and "Erase." To keep students interested, maintain a lively pace of questions and answers.

Assessing Responses

While students are displaying their Whiteboards, quickly scan the classroom to check students' answers. This will give you an immediate idea of who understands the information and who does not. Before moving on to the next question or signaling "Boards down," provide feedback to the class. If most answers are incorrect, display or say the correct answer, and immediately repeat the same question. Then, repeat this question again later in the cycle to be sure students have understood and now have the correct information.

Storing Materials

Because dry erase markers are expensive, teach the procedure for carefully replacing marker caps after the Whiteboard activity is completed, as well as quickly returning boards and markers to their storage location.

When to Use Whiteboards

Use Whiteboards in any number of ways:

- Multiple times during the input portion of a lesson to ensure students are following along
- As a closing activity so that students can review what was learned in the lesson
- As a review game or challenge for an upcoming test or assessment
- At the beginning of the lesson to activate prior knowledge or to review information from a previous lesson
- As a quick mood gauge to find out how your students are feeling, their attitude and expectations—ask them to draw a smiley face, a sad face or neutral (straight line for the mouth) face
- When students are sitting on the carpet or at a location away from their desk

◆ For any activity where it is not necessary to keep student work, such as handwriting practice, scratch paper, or when students are moving around the classroom collecting data that they will not need later

To specifically see how a teacher uses Whiteboards, go to Chapter 13, page 142.

Whiteboard Variations

Be the Teacher
Students can use Whiteboards to teach another student. They can write and draw on the boards to explain a concept or to review with a partner.

Group Wipe Out
In groups, students first discuss the question posed by the teacher, come to a consensus, and write their answer on the Whiteboard. The first group to hold up the correct answer scores a point (table point or game point).

Partner Practice
Students can practice spelling words in pairs, with one partner giving the word and the other writing it on their Whiteboard. They could also use the board to keep score when playing a game.

Electronic Options
As technology continues to be more common in the classroom environment, tools such as electronic tablets can act in a similar fashion to provide real-time demonstration of understanding of subject matter.

Value of Using Whiteboards

◆ Students love them because they're fun—mistakes made during guided practice can be easily brushed away so reluctant learners feel less threatened and frustrated.

◆ Students aren't waiting for their turn (and tuning out). It is a fast-paced activity that encourages student attention and engagement.

◆ Minute by minute, you can assess who is grasping the concepts and who is not.

◆ Students receive immediate response and feedback from the teacher.

◆ There is an opportunity for students to learn from each other.

◆ Whiteboards ensure increased on-task behavior.

◆ Using Whiteboards will save paper and significantly reduce the stack of work you take home to grade.

◆ They can be used in whole group instruction, small guided groups, and learning centers.

◆ Finally, there is no need to worry about technology failing when you need it most!

Whiteboards can be used to engage every student in every single lesson.

Exit Tickets

Exit Tickets let the teacher know what students are thinking and what they have learned at the end of a lesson.

Exit Tickets are student responses to questions that are answered when they exit the classroom.

At the conclusion of a lesson, students are required to focus on their accomplishment of the lesson objective or requirement. Exit Tickets provide a high

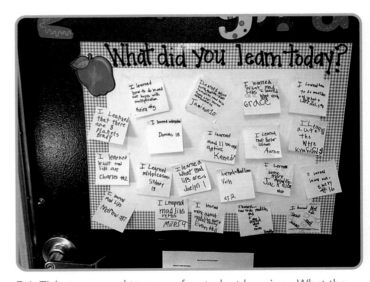

Exit Tickets are used to assess for student learning. What the student writes on the Exit Ticket allows the teacher to check for understanding. Exit Tickets can come in a variety of forms, each designed by the teacher to assess for what the teacher wants students to learn.

return of information for the amount of time invested and this information can be used to guide teaching decisions such as lesson pacing, quick clarification, and identification of student interests and questions. Exit Tickets provide real-time feedback on student performance so that the teacher knows exactly how every student is doing.

From highly-produced cards to blank three-by-five-inch cards to a simple sticky note, use the Exit Ticket that best suits your needs.

Before students leave—for recess, lunch, the end of the day, their next class, or transitioning to another subject area—they hand you or deposit their tickets filled out with an answer to a question, a solution to a problem, or a response to what they've learned. Exit Tickets help you plan for the next lesson or unit of instruction because they help you assess if students have "caught what you taught."

As with the other personal assessment tools described in this chapter, Exit Tickets are a formative assessment device, not a summative device. They are not graded—assessment is not evaluation.

Exit Tickets are beneficial for students and teachers.

For Students
- They foster a sense of ownership of learning.
- They can be used as a study aid to prepare for tests.

For Teachers
- They revisit concepts that are not clear to the students.
- They can be used to improve teaching the lesson the next time.

How to Use Exit Tickets

Creating Exit Tickets
Based on your lesson objectives, decide what you'd like to find out about students' learning at the end of the lesson. Write a question or pose a problem on the Exit Tickets, or post the question or problem for students to see. Use Exit Tickets for open-ended questions or give students a specific task to complete that goes with the lesson.

Exit Tickets are short prompts that can provide instructors with a quick student diagnostic.

- They verify that students can solve a problem, answer a significant question, or give a correct response based on the lesson.
- They emphasize the essential question for the day's lesson.
- They can be used to see if students can apply the content in a new way.

When creating Exit Tickets, it is best to use the same format, so students can complete the task without needing an explanation. Questions and answers can be written on three-by-five-inch cards, on sticky notes, on small pieces of paper, or online through a survey or a course management system. Consider allowing students to write their names on the Exit Ticket, giving them the freedom to express themselves.

An Exit Ticket can be this simple.

- Name one important thing you learned in class.
- What was accomplished by the small group activity we did today?

Or allow the students to express their frustration by asking these questions about the day's lesson.

- What in today's lesson left your puzzled?
- What questions do you still have?

Collecting Exit Tickets

The problem or question should require only a brief amount of time to answer, certainly no more than five minutes, and ideally only one or two minutes. Exit Tickets are not intended as a major task; they are a quick summarizer to provide useful feedback.

The Exit Ticket response is not graded. Its purpose is to provide valuable feedback to the teacher.

Set a specific amount of time for students to complete the Exit Ticket. Stand at the door to collect the tickets as students leave the classroom. Students could also deposit their Exit Tickets in a designated place in the room before leaving the classroom or transitioning to a new lesson.

Examine the tickets carefully. Depending on your purpose, it might be helpful to sort the tickets into piles—for example, tickets that demonstrate students have grasped the content, tickets that show that students don't understand, and tickets that you aren't sure about. You can have three baskets labeled for the Exit Tickets to be deposited.

- ◆ I've got this. I can teach someone else.
- ◆ I'm still learning. I need more review.
- ◆ I'm being challenged. I need some help.

When to Use Exit Tickets

At the beginning of a lesson, state the question or problem on the Exit Tickets to keep the concept of Exit Tickets at the forefront of students' minds. They will stay focused during the lesson as they search for the answer for their ticket out the door.

At the end of class, check students' understanding by having them summarize key points from the lesson.

Exit Tickets are an ideal way to end a class as they
- ◆ provide feedback to the teacher about the class,
- ◆ they require students to synthesize the day's content, and
- ◆ they challenge students with a question requiring some application of what was learned in the lesson.

Consider starting the next lesson with interesting ticket responses or with a graph or chart that highlights common responses. You can also formulate guided groups for students who did not demonstrate understanding after the lesson. Encourage them to ask questions they still have about the lesson. For students who demonstrate mastery of the lesson content, create extension of learning activities for them to pursue.

Exit Ticket Variations

Verbal Exit Ticket

Have students line up at the end of class while you stand at the door. As they reach the door, students must share an idea or concept they learned with you. Each student must give a different answer. As students stand in line, they can discuss different possible answers before they reach you.

Value of Using Exit Tickets

- ◆ They give you an indication of how well students understand the material.
- ◆ They allow teachers to assess what has been learned over a period of time.
- ◆ They provide a quick, informal assessment of where the students are in their understanding of the day's work.
- ◆ They require students to concentrate on the core content of the lesson.
- ◆ They communicate succinctly what has been learned during the lesson.
- ◆ They prompt students to begin to synthesize and integrate the information gained during a class period.

Exit Tickets collect feedback on students' understanding at the end of a class and provide them with an opportunity to reflect on what they have learned.

Student Response Cards

Student Response Cards provide information about every student in the class at the same time.

Student Response Cards are cards or signs that are held up by all students at the same time to display their responses to questions or problems presented by the teacher. Student Response Cards enable every student to respond to each question and provide the added benefit that the teacher can easily review the responses from individual students and determine overall trends in understanding for the entire class.

This strategy actively engages students while teachers perform a quick and easy check for understanding. At any point in the lesson, the teacher can pose a question to students, and rather than hearing from just one or two students, everyone answers.

How to Use Student Response Cards

Creating Student Response Cards

Create a set of Student Response Cards for each student using index cards, different colored pieces of paper, or cardstock. They can be labeled with answer choices, such as A, B, C, D, or color-coded, such as green for "Yes," red for "No," and yellow for "Not sure." Card sets may be put in envelopes or attached together with a ring through a hole punched in the top left corner.

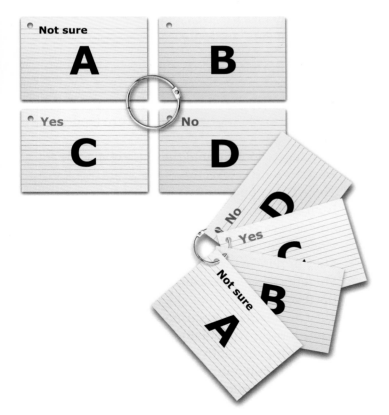

Reviewing Expectations

Next, review expectations for how to properly display response cards. For example, waving response cards wildly, or thrusting the cards in front of another student, would not be appropriate. The teacher should model how to display cards correctly, and review what each card means. This is especially important when working with younger students. Before beginning the response activity, model a question-response scenario for the students, and practice the procedure with them.

Asking for Responses

When students have demonstrated appropriate card response behavior, pose a question to the class regarding information covered in the lesson. These questions may be multiple choice, Yes or No, or a variety of other choices. Card packs should, of course, match the format of the question. Once the teacher has posed the question, students hold up their card with the corresponding answer.

Ensure you provide enough time for students to consider the question and determine their answer. Provide consistent verbal cues for students when it is time to respond. For example, ask the question, then say, "Thinking" while students consider the question and their responses, and, "Cards up" when it's time to show their answers. To keep students interested, maintain a lively pace of questions and answers.

Assessing Responses

While students are displaying their cards, quickly scan the answers across the classroom. This will give an idea of who has a grasp on the information presented, and who does not. Before moving on to the next question, or saying or signaling, "Cards down," provide feedback to the class. When all or most answers are correct, a quick and positive "[say the answer] is correct!" If most answers are incorrect, display or say the correct answer, explaining why if necessary, and immediately repeat the same question. Repeat this question again later in the cycle to be sure students have understood and have now learned the correct information.

When to Use Student Response Cards

Use Student Response Cards to assess student understanding at various points in the lesson:

- Periodically throughout the input section of the lesson to keep students engaged
- When playing a review game where students answer questions
- At the beginning of the lesson to activate prior knowledge or review material from previous day's lesson
- At the end of a class or lesson to check for overall understanding of important concepts

Student Response Card Variations

Paper Point-Out
As an alternative to cards, use a piece of paper with answer choice squares. With this template, students simply hold their paper in front of them with a finger on the square with their answer choice. Students can color the squares for color-coded responses or cut out the squares to make their own cards.

Assessments on a Stick
Instead of cards or paper, students hold up long craft sticks with their answer to the posed question.

Create the responses for your instructional needs. Words, numbers, or images provide quick personal responses in group settings to posed questions.

Thumbs Up, Thumbs Down
Students respond with thumbs up for "Yes," thumbs down for "No," and can point thumbs sideways for "I don't know."

Pinch or Clip Cards
Instead of having a separate card for multiple choice (ABCD) answers, print all letters on a single card. To indicate their answer, students "pinch" their answer by covering the letter with their thumb and placing their index finger behind the letter on the card. Or students can "clip" their answer choice using a clothespin.

Content Categories
Vary the words on the response cards based on the subject area or content being taught. The response choices could be words such as add and subtract, true and false, mammal and reptile, fact and opinion, period and question mark, and so on.

Picture Cards
For younger students, pictures or icons may be used instead of words. Use the ubiquitous happy face for "Yes," a frowny face for "No," and a slanted grin on a face for a "Not sure" response.

Value of Using Student Response Cards

- Every student practices the skill every time.
- Students aren't waiting for their turn (and tuning out).
- It is easy to look around the classroom and see who answered correctly.
- There is an opportunity for students to learn from each other.
- Students can't just repeat a response from the student who answers first.
- They provide increased on-task behavior.
- Students receive immediate feedback from the teacher.
- They are highly motivating and fun.
- It encourages student attention and engagement.
- It is a fast-paced activity.
- It is less threatening and frustrating for reluctant students.

Guided Notes

Guided Notes help students identify key concepts in a lesson.

Teachers are always looking for strategies to help students recognize and organize the important information in their lessons. Guided Notes are written outlines of a verbal presentation, with blanks or graphic organizers in designated spaces for students to complete. This strategy supports students on different levels, monitors student understanding, and keeps them engaged in lectures, videos, and direct instruction. These notes scaffold student learning in note-taking and critical listening skills.

Guided Notes can be used in large or small groups, as well as with individual students. For example, Guided Notes are useful as an accommodation in an inclusion setting for students with special needs to help them follow the lecture. Or they can be used as a classwide tool to help students organize notes from a science lab experiment.

Learning Has Become a Game

> *I have found great success when using the Student Response Cards. I typically utilize the response cards when analyzing multiple choice word problems.*
>
> *For example, when the STAAR (State of Texas Assessment of Academic Readiness) test is approaching, I begin review reading strategies with my students. After the strategy review, they independently practice reading and answering questions. Once everyone is finished, I pass out the Student Response Cards and have students show me their answers. This gave me a pulse check on how well students understood what was being asked.*
>
> *I noticed my students were much more excited to share their responses this way because it became a game for them. Student engagement increased, and the stigma of getting an answer wrong was virtually eliminated. I love the Student Response Cards because it is a quick and fun way to give a formative assessment to your students.*

Alex Melton
Austin, Texas

Physical Geography of North America

Name: _____   Date: _____

1. The North American continent includes the United States, _____, _____, and the islands of _____, _____, _____, and _____.

2. It is the _____ largest of the seven continents.

3. _____ is the largest island on the planet.

4. The United States and Canada are mostly located between the _____ Circle and the _____ of _____.

5. Mexico is located _____ of the United States.

6. The middle latitudes have a moderate climate because they are far from the _____ and _____ Poles.

7. _____ are features of Earth's surface, such as mountains, valleys, and plateaus.

8. A _____ is a thick sheet of ice that moves slowly across land.

9. Wind, rivers, and rain wear away soil and stone in a process called _____.

10. The longest rivers in the United States are the _____ and the _____ rivers.

11. The longest river in Canada is the _____ River.

12. The longest river in Mexico is the _____ River.

13. _____ maps show the natural features of Earth's surface.

14. North America is almost completely surrounded by _____.

During instruction, Guided Notes are used to point out important concepts, assist students in study skills, and monitor and assess student learning. Teachers prepare these handouts, which outline lectures, audiovisual presentations, or readings, leaving blank spaces for students to fill in key concepts, facts, and definitions. Guided Notes promote active engagement during lectures or independent reading, provide full and accurate notes for use as a study guide for test preparation, and help students to identify the most important information covered.

Use Guided Notes when introducing new material, or as a study guide for students to review the information learned. This strategy keeps students actively engaged in the lesson and structures a guide for efficient note-taking. Active note-taking helps students organize information and encourages increased retention. Teachers can create Guided Notes for a single lesson, or an entire unit of study.

How to Use Guided Notes

Creating Guided Notes
Decide what information is most important for students to understand in the presentation or reading for which they will be taking notes.

Prepare a set of notes containing the essential information from the presentation or reading. Underline or highlight the key concepts, facts, or information that students will be responsible for writing into the final version. Next, replace those concepts with blanks for students to fill in.

Explaining Guided Notes
Prior to handing out the Guided Notes, ensure that students understand their responsibility to fill in each of the blanks with the appropriate concepts, definitions, or other content to help them understand what they will be seeing, hearing, or reading.

Reviewing Guided Notes
Discuss the correct answers with the class as the presentation progresses, or after the reading.

When to Use Guided Notes

Use Guided Notes at any point in the lesson to structure meaningful conversation and appropriate note-taking. Guided Notes help in a number of other ways.

- They provide a framework that students can preview before a presentation or a reading.
- They accommodate diverse learning styles.
- They keep students focused and engaged.
- They serve as a recap after a lecture.
- They assess for student comprehension of key concepts.
- They serve as a study document for students.

Guided Notes assist ELLs with support in the structure of language, so they can focus on building vocabulary and understanding concepts. They are also useful for students who have difficulty with handwriting or spelling and cannot keep pace when taking notes and for those who find it challenging to process new information and identify critical concepts.

Guided Notes Variations

Student-Created Guided Notes
As a cooperative learning exercise, a group of students can be assigned to compose a set of Guided Notes for a text. The teacher reviews and edits the notes as needed before providing them to the class for use.

Context Clues Cloze Exercise
Prepare a paragraph with certain words blanked out. This cloze tool can be used to evaluate students' use of context clues when they fill in the blanks with appropriate responses to the assigned content. This can also be used as a diagnostic reading assessment.

Value of Using Guided Notes

- For students with disabilities included in a general education setting, Guided Notes can serve as accommodations allowing them to learn alongside their peers.
- They help teachers scaffold notes for learners on different levels.
- They model how to listen critically and carefully for key concepts.

Additional Personal Assessment Tools

Thank you to our colleagues at **Region 13 Education Service Center** in Austin, Texas, for allowing us to share with you the same information they share with their teachers for personal assessment tools. These are teacher-tested techniques that work!

21

K-W-L

This tool assesses what students already **K**now, what they **W**ant to know, and what they have **L**earned.

17

3.2.1

This tool collects specific, detailed information about what students understand to be the most important information about a topic.

22

One-Minute Note

This tool encourages students to form a concise summary of what they just learned at various points in the lesson.

18

Concept Map

This tool visualizes information so students can connect ideas, concepts, and terms.

23

Stop and Jot

This tool gives students the opportunity to record their perception of a key concept or idea about a lesson topic while it is still fresh in their minds.

19

Entry Ticket

This tool gathers information regarding previous learning and may help to prescribe changes for the day's lesson.

24

Study Cards

This tool creates personal note cards to use for study and review.

20

Graphic Organizers

This tool organizes and structures information to be readily recalled by students.

25

Triangle-Square-Circle

This tools accesses information that students feel is important, they agree with, or is still circling in their minds.

- They encourage students to actively engage in and respond to a lecture.
- They provide students with a standard set of notes for study and review.
- They give teachers a tool to informally assess and monitor student learning during a lesson.

Personal assessment tools give individual, immediate feedback in a classroom setting. Students and teachers benefit from knowing the impact of instruction and how to proceed for successful accomplishment of the lesson's objective.

U.S. History
GEORGE WASHINGTON

George Washington was the _____ President of the United States. He served for _____ years. His nickname is _____ of our _____.
He was born in _____. He led the _____ Army in victory over the _____ in the _____ _____.
The story of George Washington chopping down a _____ tree is likely _____. He died of a _____. In his will, he gave _____ to his _____.

We honor his contributions to the founding of our country in many ways:
1. _____
2. _____
3. _____

Guided Notes give students the opportunity to fill in the blanks with the information recalled during the course of study.

Mastering Instruction

 There are many tools a teacher can use to assess for learning.

 Personal assessment tools give teachers immediate feedback from all students at once during the course of a lesson.

 Personal assessment tools give students the opportunity to communicate what they have understood and what they have not.

 Personal assessment tools give teachers guidance when teaching a lesson and when developing future lesson plans.

 Personal assessment tools help create a lively, interactive classroom atmosphere where students are focused and engaged and teachers are responsive to their immediate needs.

...Produces Achievement.

How to Use Group and Partner Assessment

11

> *Group assessment strategies ensure the participation of all students and the opportunity for teachers to modify instruction as they teach.*

The assessment tools or techniques shared in this book are divided by use:

- Tools used for personal assessment (Chapter 10)
- **Tools used in groups or with partners (Chapter 11)**

There are four group or partner assessment tools explained in detail in this chapter:

1. Craft Sticks Random Calling (page 118)
2. Four Corners (page 120)
3. Inside-Outside Circles (page 121)
4. Whip Around (page 123)

Additional group and partner assessment tools and how to use them can be found by accessing the QR codes at the end of this chapter.

Group and partner assessments help create a lively classroom culture where every voice is given the opportunity to be heard.

They give teachers the opportunity to assess the effectiveness of instruction and lesson planning.

A Voice for Everyone

> **Tell me and I forget. Teach me and I remember. Involve me and I learn.**
>
> Adapted from a Chinese proverb

Peer collaboration is a valuable resource for teachers. Unresponsive and reluctant students are often more willing to participate in groups where they can benefit from peer support and the exchange of knowledge, or acknowledgment of confusion, that naturally occurs.

Group and partner assessments are dynamic and interactive. They keep students engaged and are especially effective when the assessment is designed as a puzzle or a game.

The exchanges, interactions, and connections among students make the effectiveness of teaching, or the need for further support or teaching modifications, immediately apparent.

Craft Sticks Random Calling

Craft Sticks Random Calling is a technique where teachers randomly call on all students ensuring fair participation.

One of the challenges every teacher faces is how to keep every student engaged in lessons. Teachers look for ways to motivate students to pay attention and to participate in discussions. One simple but extremely effective strategy is a random call method. It enlivens lessons by making the calling on students unpredictable, motivating students to be alert at all times.

The same principle is used in road safety. When we see a flashing speed sign while driving, we become much more alert and aware of our surroundings and our driving. The message on the speed sign influences our behavior. That effect is sustained over a period of time and can be reinforced at another point further down the road. This same concept can be used in the classroom to influence student attention.

Craft Sticks Random Calling can be used in both small and large groups, in any content area, and at any grade level. Students cannot anticipate when their name may be called, but they are always aware that it may be called at any point during the lesson or discussion. This results in all students paying attention and being prepared in case their name is selected.

Craft Sticks Random Calling allows for a quick evaluation of each and every student's learning and understanding of content because it prevents one or two eager students dominating the lesson or discussion by always volunteering to answer.

When their sticks are chosen and students are called on to answer questions or participate in discussions, they must process the newly-learned material into oral language. This begins the process of internalizing the learning and thinking at a higher level. It is then possible to assess if the student is accurately receiving and perceiving the information.

How to Use Craft Sticks Random Calling

Creating Craft Sticks
Write each student's name or number on a craft stick, and put the sticks in a cup or basket. If appropriate, in order to help with gender fairness, you can color code the tip of each stick with one color for girls and one for boys.

Randomly selecting a stick at various times ensures that all students are given an equal opportunity.

You could also involve students and have them make their own personalized craft sticks.

Selecting a Craft Stick
At various points during the course of a lesson or discussion, randomly pull sticks to call on students for responses to questions or contributions to discussions.

The name or number you've drawn is expected to articulate a response. If the student expresses confusion and requests more support or guidance, draw another stick and ask the same question of that student. If answered correctly by the second student, turn to the first student, repeat the question and give the student the opportunity to answer again to ensure that the correct answer is internalized.

As a variation, you could also draw a stick before asking the question. (Keep it hidden if the students have personalized their craft sticks.) The entire class will be on alert with a look of "I better pay attention as my name might be on that stick!"

When to Use Craft Sticks Random Calling

◆ Select a stick at any point during or after the lesson to increase engagement of all students and to show you value each person in the classroom.

- Randomly call on students to check for understanding during or after a lesson.
- Select a stick to ask interest questions as a pre-assessment before introducing new material to tap into prior knowledge.
- Select names to assign students to groups or tasks to ensure random combinations and prevent students from being in the same groupings or activities.
- Select a stick to choose who will receive a special privilege to eliminate bias and favorites.
- When reviewing homework, random selection encourages everyone to have their homework completed.
- When students are doing self-checks on correcting papers, use sticks to select who will provide answers.

Craft Sticks Random Calling Variations

Name Generator
An online name generator can create the same effect as craft sticks.

Stick Pick App
Apple has an app for the iPad called Stick Pick that functions like craft sticks in your classroom.

I'm Done Cup
Create an I'm Done Cup for students to choose from when they finish early. Instead of names on the sticks, sticks in this jar are labeled with a variety of tasks students can do.

Students can choose tasks from the jar like write a letter to a teacher, read a book, create a picture book, practice spelling words, work with math flash cards, study vocabulary, and so on.

Value of Using Craft Sticks Random Calling

- Every student in the classroom is motivated to stay engaged because the technique is random and unpredictable.
- It helps teachers solicit evidence of learning and understanding from every student.
- It solves the problem of calling on the persistent hand-raiser that dominates the class discussion.
- It eliminates favoritism and establishes the expectation that all students are valuable and worth hearing.
- Students are allowed to process learned information and share it orally using their own choice of words.
- It allows teachers to monitor and adjust lesson content in real time as they work with students.

Consistency Matters

Joanne Rodgers uses Craft Sticks Random Calling in her visually-impaired special needs class at the Texas School for the Blind and Visually Impaired.

During the first days of school, my class voted to be the "Bold Pandas" to represent a positive character trait and to differentiate my class from others at lunch, recess, and times when I need to call them together. So I created "Panda Sticks."

I put their names on the panda sticks in both bold marker and braille, using braille labels. I put them in a basket with a handle that I

can easily carry as I walk around the room teaching. On the first day, I passed them out to my students so they could feel them.

Sometimes, I'll also pass out the sticks and let students hold them. Then, when I'm doing an activity, I'll say, "Raise your panda if you know the answer."

One day, I felt my students were a bit chatty and not responding appropriately. I realized that I had not used the panda sticks that day. So the next day I was sure to use them. Sure enough, my students were attentive and on-task when I used them that day!

Every day we make choices and decisions. We base these on our likes, dislikes, knowledge, and opinions. Sometimes, we get help from others. And sometimes, we mumble our favorite nursery rhyme under our breath or resort to flipping coins to help us make our choice.

Four Corners

Four Corners provides a quick visual perspective of student understanding.

Students are offered a controversial statement or asked a question. An opinion about the statement or an answer to the question is posted in each of the four corners of the classroom. Students move to the corner that reflects their opinion or displays the answer that they think is correct. Then students must explain their reason for selecting that corner.

Effective teachers carefully observe and interpret the decisions and choices students make in order to determine their level of understanding of the topic or concept being taught. As students justify and talk to others about why they have chosen their corner, Four Corners facilitates discussions and dialogues.

How to Use Four Corners

Prepare a Statement or Question
Generate a controversial statement or a question related to your topic of study.

Provide four different opinions related to the statement—often teachers use Strongly Agree, Agree, Disagree, and Strongly Disagree—or four possible answers to the question.

For example, in a reading class, you can pose questions about an author's purpose in a novel; math students can debate if one process is better than others to solve problems; science students can consider the effects of different ecosystems; social studies students can debate political topics.

Present the Statement or Question
Begin by reading the statement or question to the class, but do not immediately reveal the choices you will provide. Allow time for students to independently think about and formulate an opinion or answer to the statement or question. Ask them to write down their response and the reason for their choice.

When they have finished, post the opinion and answer choices. Ask students to choose the option that most closely reflects their original response.

Commit to a Corner
Direct students to gather in the corner of the room that corresponds to their choice. When students are in their groups, have them discuss the reasons for their selection.

Discuss and Summarize Opinions
Allow two or three minutes of discussion, then call on students to present a group summary of their opinions. This can be done through an oral presentation or a written statement.

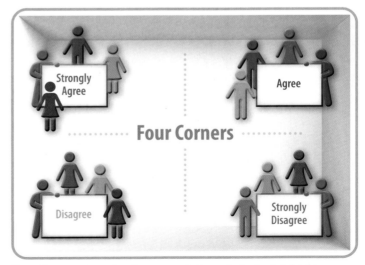

Four Corners is a visual representation of students' thinking.

When to Use Four Corners

The Four Corners technique can be designed to take only a few minutes of class or the entire period. It can be adapted for any subject area, at any grade level, from kindergarten to adult learning environments.

Use Four Corners at any point in the lesson to structure meaningful conversation:

- Before introducing new material to tap into prior knowledge
- After watching a debatable film clip to gauge a reaction
- After reading a short text to begin a discussion
- In the middle of direct teaching to help students process information
- When students need an activity that moves them around the classroom

Variations of Four Corners

ABCD
For a test review, place A, B, C, or D in each corner. Ask a multiple choice question, and have students move to the answer they would choose. Upon arrival at their corner, pairs or trios discuss why they have chosen their answer. Groups share their reasoning with the entire class. Then students are allowed to change their corner if they change their mind.

Content Comfort Corners
Students choose a corner based on their level of expertise. Pose a question like, "Based on your knowledge [of subject or topic], which corner would you choose?"

- Corner 1: The Dirt Road
  (There's so much dust, I can't see where I'm going! Help!!)
- Corner 2: The Paved Road
  (It's fairly smooth, but there are many potholes along the way.)
- Corner 3: The Highway
  (I feel fairly confident but have an occasional need to slow down.)

- Corner 4: The Interstate
  (I'm traveling along and could easily give directions to someone else.)

Value of Using Four Corners

- It quickly and effectively provides formative assessment to the teacher regarding the students' level of understanding on a topic.
- It provides an engaging format for students to present and defend thoughts and opinions.
- It encourages student discussion and dialogue about a specific topic or concept.
- It allows for visual opinion sharing.

Inside-Outside Circles

Inside-Outside Circles is a structured discussion technique that lets students respond to information with a variety of peers.

Inside-Outside Circles are an effective way of getting students who normally would be reluctant to participate to interact with others.

By using Inside-Outside Circles, teachers are able to listen to student conversations as the activity progresses to assess their level of knowledge and make note of any misconceptions they may have.

How to Use Inside-Outside Circles

Devise Questions or Problems for Activity
To prepare, choose what questions students will be discussing or what problems they will be solving. Inside-Outside Circles work best with discussion questions that are open ended, higher-level thinking questions, and problems that do not require lengthy paper-pencil solutions.

- For a history lesson, students could share their thoughts on the greatest discovery of all time.
- After reading a story or passage of literature, students could discuss a character's motivation or character traits.
- For a getting-to-know-you activity at the beginning of the year, students can share their favorite summer activity or a book they read.

◆ For a math lesson, students can list the steps to solve a problem or they can work through a math problem with a partner.

Split the Class

Divide students into two equal groups. If the number of students is uneven, join a group to even out the numbers or pair up two students to act as one person.

Decide which half of the students will form the inside circle and which half will form the outside circle.

Direct the first group of students to form the inside circle, facing out. They are called Partner B.

Ask the other group of students to form the outside circle by facing the students in the inside circle. They are called Partner A.

If necessary, adjust positions until all Partner A students and Partner B students are face to face with each other. The students facing each other are the first pair of partners for the activity.

Students can either stand on marks on the floor or sit in prearranged chairs to expedite the pairing process.

Rotating circles give students the chance to interact, communicate, and collaborate with multiple classmates on a random basis.

A variation to this arrangement of seating can be seen on page 255 in **THE First Days of School**.

Preview Questions

Write the question or statement to be discussed or the problem to be solved on the board.

Share Responses

First, Partner A shares her or his response to the question or problem with Partner B. Partner B listens actively. Then, Partner B shares his or her response to the question or problem with Partner A. Partner A listens actively. If students are working on a math problem or solving another type of problem instead of answering a question, students may be given time to work together on solving a problem with each partner.

Rotate

At a signal from the teacher, Partner B students in the inside circle move to their right and students in the Partner A outside circle move to their left. They are now standing in front of a new partner. Students share answers in the same way with their new partner. Partner rotation may be repeated several times.

You may want to mix up how students move to new partners each time, sometimes stopping at the next person or instructing students to skip three people just to make partner changing more interesting.

When to Use Inside-Outside Circles

Use Inside-Outside Circles at any point in the lesson to structure meaningful conversation:

◆ Before introducing new material to begin a discussion or highlight key issues in the presentation to come
◆ During a lesson to process important concepts or ideas before applying them in group or independent work
◆ After a reading to discuss key concepts

Variations of Inside-Outside Circles

Facing Desk Rows

Instead of having students form circles, have partners move desks to form two long rows facing one another. When it is time to change partners, students stand up and move one desk to their left or right. Students at the end of the row move to the desk they were facing.

Conga Line
Conga Line is very similar to Facing Desk Rows except that instead of sitting in desks facing each other in two rows, students stand in two rows facing each other. When it is time to change partners, students in each line move left or right, and students at the end of the row move to the opposite end of the row.

Secret Inside-Outside Circle
Students in one of the circles can be given information that students in the other circle are supposed to find out through questioning techniques.

Circumlocution Circle
To learn new vocabulary, students are given a word that they have to describe to their circle partners. Using the descriptions, the partner must guess the word that is being described.

Timed Circles
To add interest and variety, vary the amount of time with each partner. For example, students may spend one minute with their first partner, three minutes with their second partner, and two minutes with their third partner, and so on.

Value of Using Inside-Outside Circles

- Students can participate at their own level.
- It can be used with students who have minimal literacy in English.
- The activity involves authentic communication.
- It is fun and interactive, and it gets students moving, appealing to kinesthetic learners.
- Students are encouraged to teach each other, involving less teacher talk.
- It engages all students at the same time.
- Students are paired with classmates that they may not normally work with.
- It provides teachers with a quick assessment of student speaking and listening skills.
- It can be used to practice language previously taught.
- It can be adapted for any level.
- It provides students an equal opportunity to participate in the activity.

Whip Around

Whip Around actively engages students and encourages participation by all.

Whip Around is a strategy teachers can use to objectively assess the quantity and quality of the students' comprehension of the lesson. Though it does not allow for individual assessment, this is a quick and easy way to identify the presence of gaps in understanding. It also helps students and teacher find relationships and patterns in the content of the lessons they are discussing.

Students write down responses to a question or prompt and quickly share their responses with the class. Students have to pay attention and listen closely to their classmates' responses to compare them to their own.

How to Use Whip Around

Provide a Prompt or Question
Present a question, topic, or prompt that has several possible answers or responses. This will help ensure that you are offering students the opportunity to explore the topic. Depending on the topic or the age of the students, you may also want to provide guided examples to show them how to address the topic or question. Encourage students to write down as many responses as possible.

Fill-in-the-blank statements such as, "Justice is _____" are especially effective when used with this strategy. For a reading assignment, pose a question such as, "What word or phrases come to mind after seeing or reading this text?" Allow students time to think about their responses and write them down before they are asked to share.

These are sample questions to show the versatility of the Whip Around strategy.

- What are the parts of an insect?
- How did Ramona express her feelings about her family?
- How can a hurricane impact the economy of a city?

◆ Using the periodic table, name an element from the halogen family.

◆ If you could have any job for a day, what would it be?

◆ What are possible effects of climate change on the world?

Share Responses

After students have had sufficient thinking time and made a list of their answers, Whip Around the room, asking students to quickly and briefly share their responses. **It is important that there are no pauses or judgments during the answering process.**

If students hear an answer that they also have, they should cross it off their list. With Whip Around, students typically only share answers that have not already been given. Allow students to say "Pass" if all their responses have been covered. However, some teachers allow students to repeat answers already given, emphasizing that this is important information.

If possible, record each new answer as it is given so that students can see the full list once sharing time is completed.

Discuss

After the Whip Around has been completed and everyone has shared, ask students to report on common themes that have emerged or to comment on things that surprised them.

Listening skills are developed as students share responses and check their answers for the same response.

Give them the opportunity to ask for support. Clarify any misunderstandings. If a concept has been misunderstood by multiple students, take the opportunity to address the confusion and reteach the section.

When to Use Whip Around

Use Whip Around to encourage responses from all students in the class:

◆ During Guided Practice to get students talking about the material just covered

◆ As a closing activity so that students can review what was learned in the lesson

◆ As a review game for an upcoming test or evaluation

◆ At the beginning of the lesson to activate prior knowledge or to review material from a previous lesson

◆ To have students provide evidence from a text

◆ To help students uncover common themes in events in history or in a piece of literature

◆ As a brainstorming activity

◆ As a way to generate as many examples about a topic as possible

◆ During an icebreaker activity

Whip Around Variations

Whip Around, Sit Down

Have all students stand up. Start the Whip Around process. If students hear a response that they have on their sheet, they cross it off. If all of their responses have been said by classmates ahead of them, they sit down. Whip Around continues with those students who remain standing. This method facilitates the attentiveness of the class and allows the teacher to hear all ideas.

Alternately, instead of students standing up, have all students raise a hand. The Whip Around continues in the same way as if standing—if students hear a response that is on their sheet, they cross it off. Once all of their responses have been said, they lower their hands. The process continues with those whose hands are still up until all hands are down and all answers have been shared.

One-Word Whip Around

Using the same Whip Around process, students are only allowed to respond with one word. They do not write it ahead of time. For example, you could give the prompt, "Plants and animals in the desert" and students respond quickly with the first answer that comes to their minds. Do not stop and correct students if they are wrong; simply go over those incorrect answers when the process is completed.

Answer or Pass Whip Around

As you Whip Around, students are encouraged to answer or to say, "Pass" if they don't have an answer. Students with same answers are allowed to repeat the same and are encouraged to add something extra to the discussion. For students who previously said, "Pass," a few minutes is given to come up with something new and to present to the class.

Select-a-Sentence Whip Around

After reading a story or passage from a piece of literature, instruct students to select one sentence that is meaningful to them or one that they think is an important idea from the reading. Have students read that sentence aloud. Students should be instructed to listen for common themes.

Whip Around Ice Breaker

Use this strategy to build a welcoming classroom environment or to help students get to know each other at the beginning of the year. Choose questions that require students to share a non-threatening bit of personal information. For example, "If you could travel anywhere in the world, where would it be?"

Value of Using Whip Around

- It allows the teacher to quickly assess what students know, who is paying attention and following the lesson, and who is struggling.
- It can be used as an oral assessment of student learning.
- It provides an opportunity to hear common themes.
- It encourages all students to participate.

Additional Group and Partner Assessment Tools

Our thanks to our colleagues at **Region 13 Education Service Center** in Austin, Texas, for allowing us to share with you the same information they share with their teachers for group-partner assessment tools.

Card Sort

This tool engages students in activities of sorting and categorizing to help them analyze similarities and differences among concepts.

Back and Forth

This tool engages students in activities where they share ideas and discuss how each perceives the new information.

Quiz, Quiz, Trade

This tool allows students to assess the knowledge of their classmates in an engaging quiz-game format.

Buddy Journal

This tool pairs students and engages them in a back and forth written discussion about their writing and strategies to improve upon it.

Tableau

This tool asks students to physically manifest their understanding of a question or concept.

Group and partner assessment tools foster collaboration and communication. They are an engaging and dynamic way to check for understanding and progress during the trajectory of a lesson.

> It is important to use and experiment with a variety of assessment tools to keep students motivated and stimulated when they are in the classroom.

Mastering Instruction

 Group and partner assessment tools foster communication and collaboration among classmates.

 Group and partner assessment tools allow all voices to be heard.

 Group and partner assessment tools help reluctant participants who could benefit from peer support and interaction.

 Group and partner assessment tools help kinetic learners who are more likely to be engaged when learning activities are more dynamic.

 Group and partner assessment tools provide an efficient overview of all students in the classroom to measure the effectiveness of instruction.

...Produces Achievement!

How to Use Rubrics

Rubrics are guides that enable students to take responsibility for their progress throughout a lesson or assignment.

A Pizza Rubric

> **Shoot for the moon. Even if you miss, you'll land among the stars.**
>
> Norman Vincent Peale

There are three major ways to assess learning:

1. Asking questions and providing feedback (Chapter 9)
2. Monitoring with assessment tools (Chapter 10 and Chapter 11)
3. **Using rubrics to assess learning (Chapter 12)**

Discussing favorite pizza joints inevitably sparks debates. Creating a rubric can help clarify the criteria for judging and create a path for an unbiased outcome. A pizza rubric is a simple way to help students understand how levels of proficiency are scaffolded and achieved in an assignment. Even if you don't ultimately agree on the perfect slice of pizza, the experience of categorizing and identifying levels of excellence, from poor to superior, will be an instructive exercise. Students will benefit by gaining an insight into lesson planning and how they can take responsibility for their own accomplishments.

What Is a Rubric?

A rubric is a guide listing specific criteria used for assessing skill, knowledge, or understanding of content taught. A rubric tells

- where students are in their learning,
- where they need to go, and
- how best to get there.

A rubric is a tool that can be used by students to assess where they are in their work. It describes varying levels of performance or proficiency. A typical rubric is presented in a text box, chart, table, or spreadsheet that outlines a continuum of proficiency or performance. It shows students different levels of achievement and, most importantly, what they need to do to ultimately achieve. It defines the highest possible level of performance, what will be considered unsatisfactory, and several levels in between.

I ♥ Pizza Rubric

Restaurant _____

Taste Tester _____

Order Size and Price_____

QUALITIES \ SCORE	Excellent	Good	Average	Poor
Crust	Crispy, thin crust throughout	Crispy on edges, not crispy in middle	Crust too thick, not crispy	Soggy, falls apart
Pizza Combinations Offered	Numerous combinations, interesting and unique combinations	Many combinations offered	A few combinations offered, standard variety	Only single topping offered

Rubrics are not to be used for evaluation or grading. Rubrics are used as

- a tool for students to see a continuum of progress in their work, and
- a guide for student self-assessment and revision.

**The key word is continuum.
With a rubric, students can see where
they can go from where they are.**

The Purpose of a Rubric

The purpose of a rubric is to help students become aware of stages in learning performance. Rather than a teacher saying, "You can do better" or "That's not good enough," both of which are vague, undefined, and therefore meaningless assessments, a rubric gives students the concrete information they need to take responsibility for achieving different levels of performance. Rubrics define every step of the learning process so clearly that students can see where they are in accomplishing the objective of the lesson. In preparing a rubric, the teacher also determines how the lesson will be taught.

**Rubrics tell students specifically
what they need to check for and
what they can do to make progress.**

The value of rubrics is that students can see how the quality level of work is organized. Students can use the information a rubric provides to assess what they have already achieved and what they can do to move to a higher level of performance. The teacher can use the same information to help students make progress.

How Rubrics Are Used

- To measure student performance
- To provide information so teachers can adjust instruction
- To allow students to self-assess so they can make progress

Rubrics are valuable tools for every teacher and every student. When the teacher shares a rubric with students at the beginning of a task or lesson, students know what is expected of them and what to aim for in terms of quality of the completed task. When coherent criteria for success are spelled out, students know what to do. If students do not eventually show progress, the teacher can see that the lesson has not been taught well enough and must be retaught.

**Rubrics make it possible to assess
and guide students in every subject and every task.**

Students can also learn to identify levels of quality and performance when they are shown work examples. But if you are a new teacher, or have created a new assignment, or are teaching a class for the first time, you may not have examples to show students. Preparing a rubric is an effective way to show the stages involved in learning and mastering an objective.

**With rubrics, there are no surprises.
Teacher and students are
working together toward the same objectives.**

A Basic Recipe for Learning

Common sense tells you that students will learn easier, learn more, and take responsibility for their own learning if you follow this simple recipe when you create a lesson for them.

- What are the students to learn? **(Objectives)**
- How will they be assessed for learning? **(Feedback)**
- How will the quality of their learning be assessed? **(Rubrics)**
- How are they to demonstrate what they have learned? **(Application)**

When to Use Rubrics

**Rubrics are an integral part of
any task or lesson and should be shared
with students from the beginning.**

Rubrics outline expectations and are used by the teacher as students work to identify any gaps or misconceptions. As a lesson progresses, teacher and student work together to assess the student's knowledge, what the student needs to learn to improve, and how the student can best get to that point.

Rubrics should
- be given prior to the task or lesson,
- be used often during teaching as an assessment tool,
- monitor what students learn and how well they learn, and
- have clear directions of how students can improve.

**Rubrics give students the opportunity
to be active participants in learning.**

When using rubrics, explain their purpose and how they are constructed. Tell students that rubrics outline various stages of learning, ultimate goals for every lesson or task, and what they need to achieve to attain those goals. Rubrics eliminate the mysterious and uncertain ways in which students often feel they are judged by teachers. They ensure that teachers and students have the information they need to have a constructive dialogue about the shared teaching and learning experience.

Based upon **John Hattie's** research, there are three essential questions teachers and students should be asking to assess progress.[1]

- Rubrics ensure teachers and students know **the learning intentions** and the criteria for student success. Ask students, **"Where are you going?"** Encourage students to ask themselves, **"Where am I going?"**

- Rubrics ensure teachers and students know **how well students are attaining** these criteria. Ask

students, **"How are you doing?"** Encourage students to ask themselves, **"How am I doing?"**

- Rubrics ensure teachers and students know **where students need to go next** to make progress in reaching a goal or the next level of performance. Ask students, **"Where do you go next?"** Encourage students to ask themselves, **"Where am I going next?"**

Can Rubrics Be Used for Grading?

Rubrics are not recommended as a basis for grading. That's not the purpose of using a rubric. A rubric is used by teachers and students for assessment. A test is used for grading and evaluation. Rubrics help students see the value of working towards a goal that is worth achieving. They encourage students to keep trying. Tests do not encourage students to keep trying. For many students who are struggling, tests discourage them from learning or even coming to school.

Rubrics are equivalent to scoring guides that are used in gymnastics. The judges are not grading the contestants. Rather, they have  a predetermined guide that governs how points are deducted when gymnasts make errors of execution during their routines. The gymnasts are well aware of the scoring format and practice continuously to ensure they do not lose points.

The role of a teacher is not to grade students. The teacher's main role is to help every student reach the highest possible level of achievement.

---

[1] Hattie and Timperley, "Feedback," 88–90.

Rubrics Promote Self-Assessment

The ultimate goal of rubrics is to have students self-assess their work.

The most common form of self-assessment that is used every day is a checklist, such as a shopping or to-do list. As we work through the list, we assess the list constantly to see if everything has been done. When we finish checking off the list, we have this sense of accomplishment. That's a form of self-assessment.

The most important concept in assessment is self-assessment. Self-assessment is the process students use to monitor and take control of their own learning. The most powerful tool to promote self-assessment is a rubric. When students are given the means and opportunity to take responsibility for their own learning they no longer need to ask a teacher about their progress. Instead they can refer to a rubric and ask themselves the same questions.

- Where am I going?
- How am I doing?
- Where do I go next?

Rubrics give students control. They guide students to seek, accept, and act on feedback information. To foster high standards and creative and innovative work, the most important question students can ask themselves is, "Is this good enough to meet a performance level on the rubric?"

This does not mean that the teacher gives up responsibility. Rather, there is a gradual sharing of responsibility so that students gain greater ownership of the learning experience.

Once students see the value of using a rubric to self-assess their own work, they will rise to another level of academic achievement.

When students understand the value of rubrics, what to do and why, they are more willing to expend effort because they gain confidence in themselves as learners, called self-efficacy, and confidence that the information and guidance provided by the rubric is useful and worth the effort. When students use rubrics for self-assessment, their interest is increased because the feedback is "theirs." They feel in control of their learning.

Student self-assessment serves to
- increase students' responsibility for their own learning, and
- make the relationship between teachers and students more collaborative.

The Merits of Self-Assessment

Bert Johnson is the teacher of a very successful, award-winning marching band in Illinois. He has a rubric that students use each week to self-assess their contribution to the band as a whole. Each day, students aim to put an "x" for Yes after the criteria listed in the right column. The rubric is turned in each Friday and it is not graded. It is not used for disciplinary reasons. What Bert wants to know is who needs help to meet the performance levels as the success of the band on the field, in full sight of the fans, is dependent on everyone's contribution to the band's performance. As Bert works to help each band member to mark Yes, the quality of the band's performance excels.

When students know what is expected of them, the opportunity to excel and shine is offered to them as they march in the Rose Parade in Pasadena, California, shown on television throughout the world.

☒ yes ☐ no ☒ not applicable ☒ see note below	**Weekly Self-Assessment (Band)**		Name: _____ Hr:___			
For the week starting_____		**Mon**	**Tues**	**Wed**	**Thurs**	**Fri**
I am in my seat with my instrument and materials when the bell rings and until dismissed.						
I have a pencil.						
I have my instrument/reeds/mutes (in working condition).						
I have all my music.						
I was quiet and on task in rehearsal.						
I was focused on chorales/exercises/scales/rhythms.						
I tuned quickly and with precision.						
I always sit with great posture and am always ready to play.						
I have practiced my parts at home.						
I was productive and focused in rehearsal.						
I was absent *(remember to copy the objective from a neighbor)*.						
We did not have school.						
Notes:						

See the QR code on page 136 to download and use **Bert Johnson's** band rubric.

The students in Bert's band ask themselves three basic questions during self-assessment.

1. **Where am I going?**
   Students need to know where they are in order to do what is necessary to arrive where they want to go. Marking Yes or No lets the student think about their progress.

2. **How am I doing?**
   What students do, their work practices and procedures, indicates how well they are doing.

3. **Where do I go next?**
   If No was a response to one of the criteria, the student knows what needs to be modified and improved in order to answer Yes.

How to Create a Rubric

Rubrics focus on instructional quality—how to get the best of effective teaching for all students, especially those who need it most.

Rubrics are typically formatted in columns and rows and have three things in common:

1. A list of criteria
2. Several levels of proficiency
3. The performance expected at every level

The criteria of what is to be accomplished is in the left column. Next to it are several columns that define how well the criteria were performed. Students read from left to right, and it is suggested that the highest performance be the first column they read, as many do not read the whole page. You will want students to read the best first so that they strive to be the best they can be.

A Basic Rubric				
Levels Criteria	Exemplary	Proficient	Developing	Beginning
Criteria 1	Expectation	Expectation	Expectation	Expectation
Criteria 2	Expectation	Expectation	Expectation	Expectation

There are many ways to categorize levels of performance. A general rule of thumb is to use four to five levels of quality—three levels or less do not provide enough variation, while six or more may be too detailed, which makes it difficult to distinguish progression.

Here are three common examples used to express levels of proficiency:

◆ Excellent	◆ 4	◆ Exemplary
Above Average	3	Accomplished
Average	2	Developing
Below Average	1	Beginning

Using the basic rubric, write in the criteria and then a description of each level of performance.

Rubric Title				
Levels Criteria	Exemplary	Accomplished	Developing	Beginning
Stated Objective or Performance	Description of exceptional levels of performance	Description of sufficiently accomplished levels of performance	Description of emerging levels of performance	Description of inadequate levels of performance
Stated Objective or Performance	Description of exceptional levels of performance	Description of sufficiently accomplished levels of performance	Description of emerging levels of performance	Description of inadequate levels of performance

These are examples of descriptions of levels of performance for a report or other piece of writing:

- **Highly Proficient**
  The work is clear and focused. It holds the reader's attention. Relevant details and examples add to the work.
- **Proficient**
  The work is mostly interesting, and with more details and illustrations, it will hold the reader's attention.
- **Apprentice**
  The work struggles a bit and the development is still basic or general.
- **Novice**
  As yet, the work has no clear sense of purpose or central focus. The development is sketchy or missing details.

Rubrics can be presented in many ways for many different purposes. In this chapter, there are several examples of rubrics that can serve as guides as you create your own. The best way to understand the organization and value of a rubric is to design one yourself. You can approach this task in various ways.

- Adapt a rubric.
- Modify and combine existing rubrics.
- Reword parts of a rubric.
- Drop or change one or more levels of a rubric.
- Omit criteria that are not relevant to the outcome you are measuring.
- Mix and match scales from different rubrics.
- Change an existing rubric for use with a different grade.
- Create a new rubric from scratch.

Be flexible and reuse or modify the same rubric for various class assignments, differentiating for heterogeneous classes, and accommodating a range of learning levels, from gifted to challenged students.

In other words, there are an infinite number of ways to create and present rubrics and they can be used for an infinite number of purposes.

Introducing Rubrics

When you first use a rubric for a lesson or task, do not assume that students know how to use it. Show an example of one so they can see how it is organized by a continuum or range of performances that will be assessed. Explain how they can use the criteria to understand how they can improve from one level of performance to the next. As suggested, use something familiar like assessing pizzas. A pizza tasting rubric, or something along those lines, is a fun way to introduce rubrics to students.

Ask students to imagine being at a restaurant and the owner very graciously asks if they would help her with a survey about the pizza they have just been served. She asks that they taste the pizza and mark an "x" in one of the four boxes after "Crust" and "Pizza Combinations Offered."

I ♥ Pizza Rubric

Restaurant _____

Taste Tester _____

Order Size and Price_____

SCORE QUALITIES	Excellent	Good	Average	Poor
Crust	Crispy, thin crust throughout	Crispy on edges, not crispy in middle	Crust too thick, not crispy	Soggy, falls apart
Pizza Combinations Offered	Numerous combinations, interesting and unique combinations	Many combinations offered	A few combinations offered, standard variety	Only single topping offered
Quality and Variety of Toppings	All ingredients very fresh and very tasty, gourmet ingredients offered	Fresh ingredients, flavorful, good variety	Semi-fresh ingredients, appears to come from bag, not much variety	Toppings not fresh, little or no taste, few options
Quantity of Toppings	Generous toppings, entire pizza covered in toppings	Good amount of toppings, doesn't go to edges	Fair toppings	Skimpy toppings
Sauce	Flavorful, compliments the pizza perfectly, perfect amount	Tasty, would have liked a little more sauce	Adds a little flavor, sauce is a bit thin	No flavor or not enough sauce
Cheese	Quality cheese, full of flavor, perfect amount	Tasty cheese, wish there was a little more	Not bad, nothing special	Rubbery cheese, no taste
Temperature	Piping hot, right from oven	Hot, but could be better	Just barely warm	Served cold
Value	Excellent value for the money	Very good value for the money	Fair value for the money	Overpriced, low value

Additional Comments:

Total Score _____

Will you go back? _____

See the QR code on page 136 to download and use the pizza rubric created by **Cindy Wong**.

Explain that the survey does not ask if the crust and combinations offered are tasty or not, as that does not help the owner of the restaurant. Rather, the survey has a continuum or span of responses that indicate what can be done to improve the product. There is a range or scale of options that will tell the owner how to create a better pizza.

There are other similar exercises that can be done so students can see and understand the use of rubrics. Give them a blank rubric and ask these questions.

- What are the criteria of a good hamburger? (Or chocolate cake, or spaghetti, or stir fry)

- What words would you use to describe each level of performance?

Have students work in pairs or small groups to create their rubrics and then share them with the rest of the class. Let students be involved in improving each other's rubrics.

Involving Students

You can find out how well students comprehend what performance levels indicate by asking them to state them in their own words or share examples of their work. Better yet, to help students truly appreciate the value of a rubric and become active participants in learning, have them create their own.

Students can be asked to share suggestions on the things they think are important to include when assessing their learning. This makes them feel ownership for their learning. They can also help develop a scoring rubric, a process that can lead them to understand the effort required.

In order to heighten students' awareness of different levels of work, provide them with examples.

- Begin by providing them with a sample of an outstanding paper to read and analyze. The next day, have the class discuss what, in their opinion, made the sample outstanding.

- Next, give students samples to illustrate each level on the quality continuum. Analyze and evaluate their features in some detail. Write notes on the board to gradually develop and agree on the characteristics and proficiencies of a high-quality paper.

- Using the key proficiencies, engage students in the process of transforming them into a rubric— a set of rating scales depicting a continuum of quality for each level of proficiency.

More Rubric Examples

As demonstrated by the pizza tasting rubric, there are an infinite number of ways to create and present rubrics and they can be used for an infinite number of purposes.

Use of equipment	Presenting in class
Creating an object	Doing a project
Reading aloud	Drawing an idea
Writing an essay	Analyzing a process
Diagraming a concept	Charting behaviors
Speaking in a foreign language	

Use the following examples of rubrics as guides as you create your own.

Building Better Reading Skills Rubric

This rubric for reading activities shows four levels of a banana split. One is just the empty dish; one is with the banana and ice cream; one is with toppings; and one is the ultimate with a cherry on top.

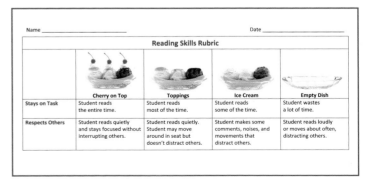

See the QR code on page 136 to download the reading skills rubric.

The teacher asks the class, "Which banana split would you like to have?" Of course, all the students say, "The one with the cherry on top."

The teacher then says, "If you want the banana split with the cherry on top, you need to be reading the entire time, do so quietly, and stay focused without interrupting others. If you read most of the time, you'll get just the toppings on your banana split. But if you only read some of the time, you'll get the banana and the ice cream. And if you waste time by not reading, you will get just the dish—waiting to be filled with better reading skills."

Because the rubric shows a span of examples, students can see
   ◆ where they are,
   ◆ how they are doing, and
   ◆ where they can go next.

Ask this to the class as a whole—or certain students in private who you suspect need to make progress.

   ◆ "To qualify for a banana split, what do you need to do?"
   ◆ "When will you check to see if this has been done?"
   ◆ "How can I help you do this?"

Writing Poetry Rubric

Oretha Ferguson of Fort Smith, Arkansas, coauthor of *THE Classroom Management Book*, gives students a scoring guide or rubric before each writing assignment to help them focus and to give them a sense of direction for their writing so that they know beforehand what they are to accomplish. The rubric is not only to assess students for learning, but also to assess how well she created the lesson.

For Oretha's lesson, she decided that five criteria were important to measure student performance. She divided each into four levels of proficiency—Advanced, Proficient, Basic, and Below Basic:

1. **Ideas:** How well can the student develop focus, interest, and involvement?

2. **Organization:** How logical and organized are the ideas?
3. **Sensory Images:** How vivid, detailed, and intense are the images?
4. **Use of Language:** Are the choice of words rich and imaginative?
5. **Presentation:** Does the presentation enhance and go beyond the assignment?

Name:		Period:	Date:	
🍎 Poetry Writing Rubric				
	Advanced	Proficient	Basic	Below Basic
Ideas	Captivates and involves reader deeply	Well-focused and keeps reader's interest throughout	Some focus, but lacks continuity	Unfocused; author seems unsure of direction
Organization	Poem uses a logical, effective organizational strategy. Poem uses form to interpret idea creatively and effectively.	Sequencing is logical. The poetry form has been followed with few errors.	Some sequencing is followed, but is not evident throughout the poem.	Sequencing is illogical, or not evident.
Sensory Images	Vivid, detailed images and	Clear use of sensory images to portray	Some use of image, idea, or emotion	Difficult to visualize image or

See the QR code on page 136 to download the full poetry writing rubric.

Project Proficiency Rubric

Here is an example of a rubric used to assess student progress on a project or report. Students are given a set of directions to guide them as they do their project. As they work, the teacher checks each student to assess what they have accomplished.

Make sure that students understand that the work they have done is considered "a work in progress." They must know they are not being evaluated. They are being helped to make progress.

The rubric consists for four criteria followed by four levels of performance, ranging from Highly Proficient to Not Proficient:

1. Content
2. Creativity/Neatness
3. Knowledge of Language and Convention
4. Directions Followed

Project Proficiency

CATEGORY	Highly Proficient	Very Proficient	Partially Proficient	Not Proficient
Content	Writing is descriptive, clear, concise and conveys tone and voice. Content is meaningful to writer and audience.	Writing is, for the most part, clear and concise. Conveys tone and voice that make content meaningful to writer and audience.	Writing is somewhat clear, but description may be wordy and simply "list." Meaning is not completely clear and may be distracting to the reader.	Writing is not descriptive, and meaning is not clear. Leaves audience without insight into author's life.
Creativity and Neatness	Project is creative, colorful, and neat. Effort is obvious.	Project is colorful, neat, and legible. Effort is clear; however, creativity is somewhat lacking.	Project is neat. Some effort is seen, but lacks creativity and color.	Project is clearly thrown together at last minute. Lacks effort, neatness, and creativity.
Directions Followed	Project is completed as instructed, and includes all	Most instructions have been followed as assigned.	Several errors were made in not following directions as	It is evident that no instructions were consulted when creating

See the QR code on page 136 to download the full project proficiency rubric.

Assume you sit down with a student named Gary. For the Content criteria, you both agree that he is only Partially Proficient because of where he lands on the rubric in that category.

> Writing is somewhat clear, but descriptions may be wordy and there is just a "list." Meaning is not completely clear and may be distracting the reader.

By using the rubric, you and he can see where he is and where he plans to go. When asked, Gary says, "I want to be Very Proficient." To do that, he can clearly see the work he needs to do to make progress.

> Writing is, for the most part, clear and concise. Conveys tone and voice that makes content meaningful to writer and audience.

When he achieves Very Proficient, Gary may want to reach for Highly Proficient. That can be done as the rubric spells out exactly what he needs to accomplish. He can self-assess.

Story Writing Rubric

Rubrics shared at the start of an assignment show the path to successful completion of the task. Instead of writing in the dark, students have a clear understanding of what makes a distinguished piece of writing.

Name: _____

Story Writing Rubric

CRITERIA	Excellent	Very Good	Average	Poor
Is my story creative and original?	Writing has many creative details that made the reader want to learn more.	Writing has three or more examples of creative ideas.	Writing has one to two creative details.	Writing is not creative and does not show imagination.
Is the plot of my story organized?	Has a coherent, logical plot that flows from one sentence to another	Has a nice plot that seemingly flows from beginning to the end	Has a plot that is not developed well	Has a questionable plot with no flow
Have I used descriptive words to express the story?	Uses many adjectives to show ideas and used excellent words to paint a clear picture	Uses many adjectives to show ideas, but some words that take away from the meaning	Uses few adjectives and descriptive words and many of the same words over and over	Does not have adjectives or descriptive words
Have I spelled words and	No spelling or capitalization	Less than five spelling and	Less than ten spelling and	Many spelling and

See the QR code on page 136 to download the full story writing rubric.

Picture Rubric

This rubric that can be used at any level where some students may have difficulty reading. It can be adapted for use in any content area.

	Am I done?	Excellent	Very Good	Good	Budding	Not Yet
	How did I do?	Excellent	Very Good	Good	Budding	Not Yet
	Was I creative?	Excellent	Very Good	Good	Budding	Not Yet
	Did I clean up?	Excellent	Very Good	Good	Budding	Not Yet

See the QR code on page 136 to download and use the picture rubric.

Teaching self-assessment is the highest form of teaching a teacher can hope to accomplish.

31

Rubrics on the Internet

No need to reinvent the wheel. The Internet is awash with websites for creating rubrics at all grade levels and all content areas.

32

Rubrics in This Chapter

The full version of all of the rubrics shared in this chapter are here for you to use or adapt to your curriculum needs.

Mastering Instruction

 A rubric is a tool that outlines a continuum of proficiency or performance.

 Rubrics are an integral part of any task or lesson and should be shared with students from the beginning.

 Rubrics give students the concrete information they need to take responsibility for achieving different levels of performance.

 Students can be active participants in learning by creating their own rubrics.

 The ultimate goal of rubrics is to have students self-assess their work.

 Once students see the value of using a rubric to self-assess their own work, they will rise to another level of academic achievement.

...Produces Achievement!

How to Teach Self-Assessment

> *The ultimate aim of effective teaching is enabling students to self-assess their own work.*

Self-Assessment Is a Life Skill

The most significant effects on student achievement occur when teachers become students of their own teaching and when students become their own teachers. When students achieve mastery over self-assessment and self-teaching, they are in possession of the most valuable attributes required for lifelong learning.

> *Self-assessment with its emphasis on student responsibility and making judgments is a necessary skill for lifelong learning.*[1]
>
> David Boud

The ability to self-assess is accomplished by practicing self-assessment skills. When students become adept at self-assessment, they can take responsibility and direct their own learning and progress. They know what direction to go towards, and they are able to set and achieve specific goals. They are resourceful and have the ways and means to adapt in a globalized and evolving technological society.

The Goal of Self-Assessment

> *The self-assessment process can help to prepare students not just to solve the problems we already know the answer to, but to solve problems we cannot at the moment even conceive.*[2]
>
> Angela Brew

Looking Within

> **I'm a huge advocate of student self-assessment.**
>
> Kristine Nugent-Ohls
> Lynden, Washington

It is the dream of every parent that their children will be productive adults able to cope with an ever-changing world. It's the expectation of every teacher, and articulated in many school mission statements, that their students will be resourceful thinkers who independently and creatively strive to solve complex problems through reflection, risk taking, and critical evaluation.

At the beginning of the year, I ask every student to write an essay. As a class we score exemplary papers as well as papers at various levels of writing. Once we have calibrated our scoring, they score their own writing to determine their baseline for the year. This provides me with a quick assessment of whether or not they understand the standards.

The ultimate purpose of self-assessment is to develop students' internal motivation to acquire the skills they need to continuously teach themselves. They are not only useful when students are completing a task or

---

[1] David Boud, *Enhancing Learning Through Self-Assessment* (Abington, UK: RoutledgeFalmer, 1995).

[2] Angela Brew, "What Is the Scope of Self-Assessment?" in David Boud, *Enhancing Learning Through Self-Assessment* (Abington, UK: RoutledgeFalmer, 1995).

solving problems assigned in class. Self-assessment makes immediate and lifelong learning attainable and ensures mastery in the classroom, careers, and other pursuits.

◆ Self-assessment promotes learner responsibility, independence, and initiative.
◆ Self-assessment inspires student ownership of learning.
◆ Self-assessment shifts the focus from depending on the teacher to students taking responsibility for learning.

During the process of self-assessment, students provide their own feedback and answer their own questions. They develop self-regulation skills as they monitor, evaluate, and make plans about their work. They figure out what information or strategies they need to enhance their performance without teachers, parents, or other authority figures directing them and telling them what to do.

Schools, teachers, and administrators also need to perfect the practice of self-assessment. Otherwise, they tend to resort to external factors. They ask, "What's available that I can buy or adopt to solve my problem?" When we give students the impression that we value outside sources more than critical thinking and personal initiative, we may drive them to take shortcuts and cheat.

Waves of Intelligence

First Wave:
Semiconductors (1970s)

Second Wave:
Personal Computers (1980s)

Third Wave:
Internet (1990s-2000s)

Fourth Wave:
Artificial Intelligence (Now)

Next Waves:
Machine Learning
Deep Learning
Liquid Learning

Student self-assessment stands alone as the preeminent strategy in closing the achievement gap.

Students who are taught self-assessment skills feel that they are in control of their learning. They are more likely to persist with difficult tasks, are motivated to improve partially correct answers, and take greater responsibility for their work. They are adept at using learning objectives and activities to extend their learning.

Skills for an Ever-Changing World

To succeed in today's ever-changing world, mastering the concept of self-assessment is an absolute requirement. The future appears before us every day in our homes, workplaces, cities, and schools, and we must have the internal resources to continuously learn and update, refresh, reset, and reboot ourselves. There are self-driving cars, robotic surgeons, devices that answer questions when we speak to them, portable translation gadgets—and so much more being created and discovered that we cannot even yet imagine. Already the next wave of transformative technology—artificial intelligence (AI)—is upon us.

Technology has gone through four waves of innovation—the semiconductor wave, the wave of personal computers, the worldwide web 1.0 wave, and now the AI wave. Each created new companies, industries, enterprises, and possibilities. The potential of AI technology is only just starting to be explored and exploited and machine learning will follow—the ability of artificial intelligence systems to analyze data, detect patterns, and make decisions with minimal human intervention.

One way of looking at AI is that it is concentrated brainpower transformed into software that can "learn" and "think." Technology does not decide FOR us or control us. We create it and use it because it can analyze data and information FASTER and more accurately than we can and so we use it to help us make decisions and reach conclusions.

AI in various forms is already doing complicated, dangerous, and boring tasks for us. For example, with software that is continually being developed, AI can train surgical robotic devices in hospital operating theaters by having them "watch" videos from hundreds of surgeries to learn what to do and how to make decisions. Artificially intelligent software can ingest all of a commercial company's customer data and offer solutions, such as predicting which sales leads are likely to pan out, which products to stock, and which products to develop years ahead.

Then there are chatbots, the most exciting thing since the smartphone. Instead of having to open an app and search with your zip code to see if it's raining, with a chatbot you can just say, "I wonder if it will rain today," and it will know your location and be able to answer conversationally whether you should bring an umbrella. Companies are creating chatbots to facilitate customer transactions by taking customer orders via smartphones. There will be systems that interact with humans using natural language. There is already text-to-speech software that can produce forty-seven different voices and convert twenty-four languages to create audio versions of text. And soon to come is AI that can perform tasks based on photo-identification.

AI will be embedded in everything. AI-based products will be able to take on several tasks at once, such as performing household chores, driving the car to the grocery store, and dropping off clothes at the dry cleaner. Tasks will be networked together with devices through "collective learning."

> **Keeping up with technological innovations in a complicated world requires inner skills, stamina, and resources so that we are able to constantly update ourselves.**

The Research on Self-Assessment

Over a period of eight months, twenty-five primary school teachers were taught how to use student self-assessment techniques. They then used these techniques while teaching math to their students. At the same time, twenty control teachers taught the same math lesson but did not use self-assessment techniques in their classroom.

Can a Person Beat Artificial Intelligence?

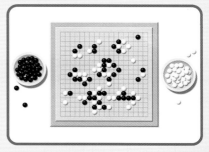

Go is a game for two. The players take turns putting black or white stones on a 19-by-19 grid and the winner is the player who surrounds more territory than his or her opponent. Go was invented two thousand five hundred years ago, and it is a game with more permutations than chess.

The Go world champion is **Lee Sedol**. In 2016, Lee played a five-game match, broadcast live, against an artificial intelligence program called AlphaGo, developed by Google DeepMind, for a one million dollar match prize. The AlphaGo program was developed by incorporating thirty million moves from world-class games of Go. Lee lost the first three games, won the fourth game, and was greeted by loud cheers and applause. But, he lost the fifth and last game.

Before we applaud the superiority of artificial intelligence, bear one major factor in mind. AlphaGo is not a mysterious alien invention from outer space. People who want to drive our intelligence beyond what we thought possible developed AlphaGo. As soon as Lee won the fourth match, the data from that match was fed into the program for it to "think" about—in other words, AlphaGo's winning performance was made possible by Lee Sedol being there to challenge it. AlphaGo learned from Lee Sedol. Artificial intelligent programs do not sleep; they study, learn, and improve 24/7.

33

Gaming Challenge

Read more about the challenge of computer gaming.

Results showed that students in those classes where they assessed their own learning scored higher than those who did not assess their own learning. In addition, those who used self-assessment were also found to be more autonomous and were able to predict their overall performance.[3]

In another study conducted in two third-grade classes, which included some special education students, students were provided with self-assessment tools to accompany their study and problem-solving strategies. The students were given reflection sheets and were asked to predict and graph their test scores on a weekly basis. When these were read, they showed that when teachers involved their students in monitoring their own progress, students were more autonomous and were able to accurately predict their performance on timed tests. In addition, the students enjoyed participating in self-assessment, as it allowed them to see and predict their progress.[4]

Self-Assessment Encourages Collaboration

Self-assessment does not mean that students are left alone to work by themselves. **Self-assessment is not an isolated activity. It should be an integral part of the curriculum and classroom community every day of the school year.** It is used during lessons when students organize what they know, where they need to be, and how they are going to get there. Just as teachers can teach more effectively if they check for student progress, students can learn more effectively if they understand what they're working towards and see what progress they are making. **The teacher does not give up responsibility; rather, there is a gradual release of responsibility in which the student gains greater ownership of the learning experience and uses the feedback for self-assessment.**

Student self-assessment serves to

◆ increase students' responsibility for their own learning, and

◆ make the relationship between teachers and students more collaborative.

In addition, getting students involved with each other in discussions and assessing work can help improve student learning. However, be very cautious of doing this, as the research shows that what students tell each other is often incorrect and misleading. Students should never be isolated from teacher monitoring. Be handy. Be ready to help. Be supportive. Learning how to assess one's self is a lifelong pursuit. After all, there are many adults who still find it difficult to analyze where they are, how they are doing, and where they are going.

Involving students in self-assessment invites them to be partners in the teaching and learning process.

Guiding Students to Self-Assessment

Guiding students to understand and internalize the process of self-assessment takes place in four stages:[5]

Stage 1: Students understand that assessment is based on lesson objectives, not on completing assignments.

Stage 2: Students understand that there are different levels of performance and that their goal is to produce work at the highest performance level. Showing examples of this will produce maximum performance.

Stage 3: While students are working at a particular performance level, help them by giving feedback and providing examples of what their performance could look like.

Stage 4: Help students create learning strategies they can use to improve their performance. This should involve setting goals so that students have a definite plan of how to self-assess their work.

[3] David Fontana and Margarida Fernandes, "Improvements in Mathematics Performance as a Consequence of Self-Assessment in Portuguese Primary School Pupils," *British Journal of Educational Psychology* 64, no. 3 (November 1994): 407–417.

[4] Susan Brookhart, Marissa Andolina, Megan Zuza, and Rosalie Furman, "Minute Math: An Action Research Study of Student Self-Assessment," *Educational Studies in Mathematics* 57, no. 2 (September 2004): 213–227.

[5] Carol Rolheiser, *Self-Evaluation: Helping Students Get Better at It! A Teacher's Resource Book* (Cheltenham, AUS: Hawker-Brownlow Education, 1998).

When students create a plan for self-assessment that they can internalize, they will acquire the confidence and motivation to learn. They will exhibit improved performance with all their future schoolwork, in their careers, and during their lives. Whether students are predicting how they will perform, setting goals before learning, or self-assessing as they learn, the key is that they are engaged in their own learning. They aren't just passive "receivers" of information.

Encourage student academic growth by having meaningful conversations about what students are expected to learn.

Here are some examples of questions that are effective in guiding students to assess their own learning, work, and progress. They are followed by questions for teachers to analyze the effectiveness of teaching strategies:[6]

Questions for Students
- ◆ Are you satisfied with your learning?
- ◆ Are you satisfied that you demonstrated your knowledge and skills?
- ◆ How does your work compare to the expectations on the rubric?
- ◆ With which parts of the assignment (project, performance, etc.) were you most satisfied?
- ◆ How closely does your work on this assignment reflect your learning?
- ◆ Why do you think this assignment worked for you?
- ◆ Were there any parts that didn't work?
- ◆ Were the strategies that you used effective in helping you reach your goals?
- ◆ If you were to do this over, how could it be improved?
- ◆ As a teacher, what can I do to help you?

Questions for Teachers
- ◆ What was the objective I wanted to teach?
- ◆ What assignment/prompt/project/activity did I choose to teach the objective/standard?
- ◆ How successful was the lesson?
- ◆ How do I know? What evidence do I have?
- ◆ What percentage of students reached the goal or standard?

- ◆ With which parts of the lesson am I most satisfied?
- ◆ With which parts am I not satisfied?
- ◆ How will I reteach and/or retest any unsuccessful students?
- ◆ How effective was the feedback that I gave to students? How do I know?
- ◆ What did I learn from this lesson that I can use in future lessons?

Self-Assessment Needs Transparency

How any times have you heard a young child say enthusiastically, "I can do it!" It's every teacher's dream to have a class full of students who know they will all get high grades because they know what to do and how to do it. Research says that this can be done. The first step is to establish clear learning targets so students understand what they should learn and then develop levels of performance they can work towards. (Teacher clarity is discussed in Chapter 20.)

We all want transparency in life. We want to know how to access useful information. We want clear rules and regulations that we can follow to maintain a safe and orderly society. We want to know what is expected of us so that we can do our best to carry out our duties and obligations and achieve success.

Imagine you are about to play soccer, basketball, football, or hockey. You and your team show up but there is no goal, hoop, goal post, or net. You can't play unless there is a way of knowing how your team scores. It's the same in a classroom. If there are no goals—no lesson objectives, learning targets, or essential questions—the teacher will not know what to teach, and the students will not know what to learn. There is no transparency. **Transparency begins with a goal.**

There is transparency when there are clear lesson objectives, feedback, and self-assessment.

Learning is no longer a mystery. Learning leads to mastery.

---

[6] Thanks to William Glasser for these questions captured in notes from his many lectures.

Checking for Understanding to Develop Self-Assessment Skills

It is crucial that teachers continuously check for understanding during lessons to find out what students have grasped or what areas may need to be re-taught. **Sarah Jondahl,** coauthor of **THE Classroom Management Book**, explains how this process develops students' self-assessment skills.

My aim is to create different ways to check for students' understanding. Putting a pencil to paper and correcting or commenting is one way to do this, but it can be somewhat monotonous for both teacher and students. I have tried to create new ways of assessing my students that are fun, quick, and effective. Ideally, my students really don't even realize they are being assessed, and I can obtain the information right away to know which students understand what has been taught, and which students don't. Getting those immediate results help dictate whether I move on with the lesson, slow down, or need to reteach. They also help me create small groups for intervention, if needed. Checking for understanding during a lesson is definitely an important part of the teaching process.

Mini Whiteboards. *One method of checking for understanding I often use is with whiteboards (page 106). Each of my students has one at their desk. Throughout a lesson, no matter the content area, students are asked to pull out their whiteboards and answer questions about the topic we are studying. They do the work quickly and independently. When finished, I tell them hold their boards in front of them but to wait before showing their answers. After I see that the majority of the class is finished, I say, "One, two, show me your boards" and they all turn their boards around so that I see their work. I can quickly spot check and see which students "have it"*

and who needs to try again. During this process, I carry a class list for quick anecdotal notes where I can log who needs reteaching and what errors might be happening. This method of checking for understanding can happen throughout a lesson or at the end. Students enjoy it and stay engaged, and I get the information I need to determine which direction I continue my teaching on that topic.

Peer to Peer. *Another method I use with my students is actually turning students into the teachers. I ask them to create their own problems. Again, this can be used when teaching any subject. For example, when teaching rounding in math, I will ask students to each write down in their math notebooks three numbers that have to be rounded to the nearest ten or hundred. I then ask them to hand their notebook to their seat partner and have their partner solve the problems. When their partner is finished, the notebook is handed back to the owner to be checked for accuracy. As this is going on, I walk around the classroom to observe students as they are working. I can see who is able to round numbers accurately and who may need more support. Students can also become peer tutors and assist their partners in correcting their work. When a student is helping teach a concept, it can reinforce their learning. This form of self-assessment can be a very powerful teaching tool. Students often have that "light bulb moment" and remember the concept being practiced.*

Collaborative Conversations. *Having students work together is a great way to make sure they are learning new concepts. My students have several opportunities every day to talk to one another about their learning. During this important conversation time, I can visit from group to group and listen in. That is then my opportunity to either stretch some of their learning by asking more challenging questions, which make them dig a bit deeper on the topic, or I can redirect what students are talking about so that they are grasping the concept better.*

Games. *My students love to work in teams to show off what they know. One fun way I like to check for understanding is to create a class game. Games like Jeopardy can be used to see if students have learned the elements of a lesson, and what a fun way to do this! Students encourage each other, push each other, learn from each other, and I can easily know if students understand the concepts. Another way my students can share what they know and have learned is by participating in our "What stuck with you today?" poster. This can be used as an Exit Ticket strategy (page 108), but can also be done during a lesson. I give a sticky note to each of my students and ask them to either write down something they have learned or ask them to show me what they've learned. This can be answering a problem, writing a sentence, spelling a word— the possibilities are endless on how this can be used. I can watch the answers being shared as they are posted to get a clear picture if my students are understanding what is being taught.*

Interactive Programs. *One more method I have to check for understanding is using a program like Google Forms or a website such as Kahoot! These are interactive programs where students access technology to answer questions about a topic. Their answers are shown right away, and I can also get all information inputted into a spreadsheet to see what answers have been stated and how students are doing. This is a unique way for students to self-assess, show what they have learned, and for quick results to be shared.*

Checking for understanding is a necessary element to include in all lessons. This can be done either formally or informally. By checking right away what students understand, a teacher can reteach, continue the lesson, or challenge students' learning. It is an area of the lesson that should not be skipped, and it is a way to continue the learning for your students in a fun and efficient way.

Sarah Jondahl
Georgetown, Texas

How to Teach Self-Assessment

Many students have no experience in self-assessment. They need to be taught how to do it and they need to be reassured that mistakes in learning are necessary and acceptable. Make it safe for students to self-assess. The more they practice self-assessment, the more they see how it becomes a growth process in their life.

Rubrics provide a solid foundation and good feedback because students can see a continuum of performance levels that tell them where they are in their learning and what to do next. Once they understand what to do and why, most students develop a feeling that they have control over their own learning and will eagerly practice self-assessment of their work.

John Hattie's findings in 2008, after fifteen years of research, established that the factor that had one of the greatest effect on student achievement was the expectation students set for themselves and the grades they predict they can achieve. Self-reported grades or student expectations, as Hattie says more clearly characterizes this strategy, had an effect-size of 1.33.

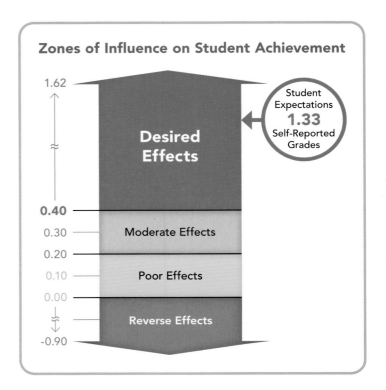

Zones of Influence on Student Achievement

1.62

Student Expectations **1.33** Self-Reported Grades

Desired Effects

0.40
0.30 — Moderate Effects
0.20
0.10 — Poor Effects
0.00

Reverse Effects

-0.90

To teach self-assessment, post our modified version of **John Hattie's** three questions for everyone to see each day.

1. Where am I going?
2. How am I doing?
3. Where do I go next?

Until students can answer these questions automatically, provide feedback to prompt responses. Teachers' feedback drives self-assessment. Students gain confidence as they discover that the information they receive on their progress is useful, and soon they are ready for a self-assessment tool that they themselves can use to set expectations and monitor and control their own learning.

The reason students can have expectations and make predictions is because they are fortunate enough to be in a classroom where they know what to do and how to get there. **Effective classrooms are structured and organized for student success.**

Students can succeed when
◆ there is clear justification for the purpose of the activity,
◆ there are explicit procedures that inform students what is expected of them, and
◆ there is the assurance of a safe environment where students can be honest about their own performance without fear that what they do will be used against them.

Best and Worst Days

A group of office workers was asked to keep a diary of their workdays. Then, they were asked which of the following factors contributed most to having a great day at the office.[7]

- Collaboration
- Instrumental support
- Interpersonal support
- Making progress
- Important work

Four of the five factors involve other people—collaboration with colleagues; instrumental support, such as technology, medical facilities, and a comfortable environment; interpersonal support, such as training, stress management, encouragement; and being given or having important work to do.

Only one factor doesn't involve others—progress—and it was the factor that resoundingly determined the highest percentage of best days at the office when the workers were able to get a project done. Those who felt that they had made progress were proud and satisfied with what they had accomplished on that day. This goes right back to the process of self-assessment.

What Makes a Great Workday?		
	Best Workday	Worst Workday
Progress	76%	25%
Instrumental Support	43%	12%
Interpersonal Support	25%	4%
Collaboration	53%	43%
Important Work	19%	15%

Making progress provides the greatest sense of accomplishment in a workday.

When students, and people in the workforce, know what to do and how to do it, and are able to complete a job or project through their own effort, they delight in the satisfaction of making progress and taking responsibility for their success.

[7] Teresa M. Amabile and Steve J. Kramer, "What Really Motivates Workers," *Harvard Business Review* 88, nos. 1/2 (January-February 2010): 44–45.

John Hattie has said that if he could rename his book *Visible Learning*, he would name it *Student Expectations*. This title would express more clearly that students can perform at a level beyond their own expectations when

- lessons have clear and specific objectives—students know where they are going,
- they receive feedback as they work—students know how they are doing, and
- there is a self-assessment tool that spells out the performance levels they can strive towards—students know where to go next and can even predict how well they will do in getting there.

Creating Their Own Self-Assessment

Once students feel they understand the value of rubrics, what to do and why, most students develop a feeling that they have control over their own learning, and they will practice self-assessment of their work.

To foster creative and innovative work, the most important self-assessment question a student must ask this.

Is this good enough to meet a performance level on the rubric?

Engagement with their learning increases even further when students help to develop an appropriate checklist or rubric and are involved in setting expectations and goals. It may be goals for a lesson, a paper, a project, a performance, or even for the semester. Research indicates that when students set goals for themselves, develop action steps to reach the goals, and monitor and evaluate their own progress, achievement increases. No matter what the endeavor, everyone loves to feel they are making progress.

However, **John Hattie** warns that, in general, students tend to set safe targets for themselves that require less work and effort. Therefore, **the primary goal for a teacher is to help students exceed, rather than just reach, their self-defined potential.** Discuss their checklists or rubrics and then challenge, encourage, and support them to do better than they think they can.

When students set their own goals, encourage them to go beyond and do even better.

Ask students to tell you how they plan to reach their goal, how they will assess their progress, and what grade they would like to earn. When they understand your expectations and how a class and a lesson are organized, they will have a better idea of how to predict their grade.

Golfers know this. They will study a golf course—play several rounds as practice—so that when a tournament starts, they can predict how to exceed their expectation. They play to win, not to lose. Students want to win, too.

Look at your students' goal plans and help them to assess their performance. Remind them periodically of the goals and grades they have set for themselves. Whether students are predicting how they will perform, setting goals before learning, or self-assessing as they learn, the key is that they are engaged in their own learning.

Helping Students Create Actionable Goals

Divide students into groups and ask each member to rewrite one of the lesson objectives in language they understand. Have them share the rewrites with each other and then agree on a final version they can all understand. Display this new objective for all to see.

This exercise lets students know that they have options for their own self-assessment. The more ownership students feel over goals and objectives, the more impact they will have and the more useful self-assessments will be to their learning.

Self-Assessment Tools

Checklists. The best way to introduce students to the process of self-assessment is to start by developing checklists before moving on to rubric development, as checklists are easier to construct and use. We use checklists every day. As we work through the list, we are constantly assessing to see if everything has been done. With a list, we can predict and foresee success. When we finish checking items off the list, we have a sense of accomplishment.

Must Do/Should Do/Could Do. A very simple self-assessment tool would be a three column or section to-do list using Must Do/Should Do/Could Do criteria. This is an effective tool when there are various tasks to accomplish.

◆ **Must Do** are the top priority things students must get done. They are important and contribute directly to a learning goal.

◆ **Should Do** are things that are important to do, but are not as urgent.

◆ **Could Do** are those things that are typically easiest for students to accomplish. They have the motivation and understanding to do the items on the list. They can see and predict how they can be successful. Learning and progress are visible.

Independent Reading Progress

Amy Groesbeck teaches in Garden Ridge, Texas. She uses her Stamina Chart to help students self-assess their independent reading progress. She discusses the importance of developing reading stamina, like cross country runners building stamina so they are able to run many miles without stopping to rest. She tells her students that they will practice every day, like a runner, to become thoughtful readers without getting tired or restless. Each day, their class goal is to read for thirty uninterrupted minutes.

To begin, Amy creates a list of expectations on a T-chart labeled Thoughtful Readers: With Stamina/Without Stamina. During this time, she invites students to share what they think they should/should not be doing; how they should/should not behave; and how they should/should not sound while reading independently.

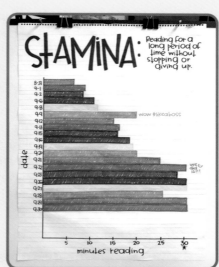

Using the desired expectations, the class writes a Reading Promise together. The students promise that they will stay in one spot, read the whole time, stay quiet, and so on. Amy records the promise on an anchor chart that each student signs. Then hand motions are created to accompany the reading promise chant that is recited every day before students read to help with engagement and reinforce expectations.

Here's where the Stamina Chart comes in. Amy sets a timer and monitors as students are reading. When she sees a student exhibiting behavior from the Thoughtful Readers Without Stamina, she provides individualized redirection. But if she notices a handful of students off task, she stops the timer and independent reading ends for the day. This is not a "gotcha" time, as she never indicates which individuals were off task. She records the date and time spent reading on the Stamina Chart and the class reflects on how they think they did that day. The chart keeps track of progress and allows the class to monitor where they need to make improvements. It's a great tool for establishing procedures and expectations.

Name _____

Language Arts for Week of March 8–12

★ Must Do	★ Should Do	★ Could Do
☆ Read "Leprechauns Never Lie"	☆ Explain why leprechauns never lie	Write a story that tells what happens to the family when they wake up the next day
☆ Define blathering and dawdled	☆ Practice reading the story aloud to a partner	Find another story about a leprechaun to share with the class
☆ List the things the leprechaun did to solve the family's problems	☆ Tell how the family got rich even without finding the pot of gold	Read about other Irish mythical creatures
☆ List ten words that expressed the emotions of the leprechaun		☆ Name the cat in the story and tell why you chose that name
☆ Write ten new sentences using your list of emotions words		☆ Play hangman with a partner using some of your favorite words from the story
☆ Create a timeline showing the sequence of the story		☆ Where do you think the next hiding place will be for the pot of gold?

A variety of activities are offered to students as they rotate through stations in their classroom. The Must Do list must be completed first, in the order presented, before moving on to the other items on the chart. Students may choose from any of the remaining items to stay engaged in learning. As students chart their progress, the teacher can see at a glance what the student has accomplished.

Photosynthesis

Must Do	Should Do	Could Do
Complete Photosynthesis quiz	Research the factors that affect the rate of photosynthesis	Create a mnemonic to help you remember the steps in photosynthesis
Complete model of a chloroplast	Explain why photosynthesis is one of the essential concepts in biology	Watch a video online about photosynthesis
Devise an experiment to test the effect of sunlight on the process of photosynthesis		"Paint" a picture using chlorophyll from leaves

∽ Sonnets ∽

Must Do	Should Do	Could Do
Define a Shakespearean sonnet	Identify the sonnets in *Romeo and Juliet* and explain how each fulfills the definition of a sonnet	Create an original sonnet

These are samples of checklists used by teachers with all levels of students.

Work Diary. Another simple self-assessment technique is to have students keep a work diary where they share what they are learning. Depending on the age of the students, you could provide the framework for diary entries, or you could allow students to create their own. The work diaries can also include students' perceptions of their degree of success.

Other simple tools for self-assessment include surveys, interest inventories, reader's notebooks, conferences, and sentence stems to guide reflection.

Good Examples

Rubrics for self-assessment are more powerful when used in conjunction with samples of student work or exemplary work.

Just as setting a good example is a tried and true way to maintain good standards of behavior, exemplary examples of student work are a very direct and practical way to help students self-assess and improve their own work.

Post examples of work from different grades and levels so that students can compare their work. (See page 51 for suggestions on how to post exemplary examples.) Ask which one most resembles their work and why. If possible, show student work from another class (with names removed) and have a group discussion about levels of performance and what needs to be done to improve them.

The expectation is that students will eventually apply what they've learned, develop and refine their powers of observation, and become proficient in being "constructively critical" with their own work.

- Display exemplary work that students can use as models.
- Have students sort the exemplary work into levels of performance to create a rubric.
- Have students compare and discuss their own work with the exemplars.
- Have students compare their work against the newly created rubric.

Good Pockets, Poor Pockets

Britta Hubbard teaches home and consumer science in Gunnison, Colorado. She has a large classroom with many kitchen and sewing stations, and a garden outside the classroom door where students harvest plants for cooking. When she walks around monitoring students, she wears an apron with various tools ready to use as needed.

Britta begins every lesson with an objective, for example, sewing a pocket. Britta is able to get students to achieve the objective because there are examples posted so they can compare and assess their work. The examples are a rubric to help them reach the highest possible level of performance.

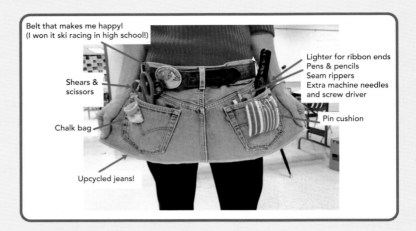

Belt that makes me happy!
(I won it ski racing in high school!)

Shears & scissors

Chalk bag

Upcycled jeans!

Lighter for ribbon ends
Pens & pencils
Seam rippers
Extra machine needles
and screw driver

Pin cushion

Britta's seventh-grade students see the value of using the examples to self-assess and monitor, evaluate, and improve their own work.

Britta displays a rubric that clearly shows different level of success to help her students self-assess their own pocket-sewing skills.

> *The example pockets help me because I can see why the unfinished edges in the "Nope" section don't look good and why pinning correctly will keep the fabric from bunching. I can also see how different stitch patterns can cause different effects which helps me decide what stitch pattern I want and where I want to make the stitch line.*
>
> — Kai

> *I can see which pockets look better and which are sewn better.*
>
> — Justice

> *This pocket sample helps me because it shows me how good pockets will hold stuff better than bad pockets and I can see the good pockets look nicer with no strings hanging off and the fabric will hold up better because it won't fray.*
>
> — Kevin

My Students Create Their Own Examples

Kristine Nugent-Ohls teaches in Lynden, Washington. She uses an assortment of rubrics for students to assess their writing skills.

- She intentionally teaches students how to self-assess using the lesson objective, posting examples to strive towards, and providing many opportunities to practice.
- She ensures students understand that self-assessments are formative, not evaluations, and are being used to help improve their overall performance.
- She involves students in constructing rubrics, so that they may deepen their understanding of the criteria they are using to self-assess.

After students write essays, she posts examples of exemplary essays. She guides students through a three-step process.

1. Students score the exemplary papers.
2. Students score their own work and compare it with the scores on the exemplary papers.
3. Students score their next assignment and compare it with their previous score.

Argumentative Paragraph Structure Rubric

Standards	Color Coding	I have mastered this	I think I understand.	I'm still working on this.
I have introduced my source in my own words.	purple			
I have used a high-quality source.	green			
I have cited my source.	blue			
I have explained why my source mattered	red			

Above the rubric, Kristine provides color coded guidance to successfully master the writing objective. Download the full rubric to see her example.

34

Argumentative Paragraph Structure Rubric

Download the full rubric to use with your students.

> *I am a huge advocate of student self-assessment.*
>
> *At the beginning of the year, I ask every student to write an essay. As a class we score exemplary papers as well as papers at various levels of writing. Once we have calibrated our scoring, they score their own writing to determine their baseline for the year. This provides me with a quick assessment of whether or not they understand the standards.*
>
> *From there, the students set writing goals and work towards those goals throughout the year, adjusting them as they master their writing. They continue to self-assess, using the same writing rubric the entire year.*
>
> *For every writing assignment, project, and presentation, the students self-assess and provide evidence of where they see themselves.*
>
> *For instance, when they provide evidence in a focused writing lesson, they will highlight the places in their writing where they feel they met standards. If we are working on incorporating quality sources, they highlight their source. If we are working on adding character description, they will highlight the places where they have included description. This provides them with a way to show me they understand the focus lesson and it gives me an efficient way to scan papers and assess the focused learning target.*
>
> *As the year progresses and we establish our community, we begin to peer assess one another's work and learn to provide feedback in a constructive manner. This takes me, the teacher, out of the equation and gives the power to the students to critically assess one another in meaningful ways. It puts the emphasis back on the student, rather than the teacher, being the expert.*

These are other ways to use examples in the classroom:

◆ **Writing Samples.** Create a series of writing samples and give students a rubric. Working in groups, students assess the samples and determine which level of performance they are at on the rubric. Have the group defend their ratings. Then, have each student use the rubric to assess his or her own writing.

◆ **Progress Graphs.** Have students create data tables with graphs showing their progress week by week or month by month on whatever they are working on. Involve them in discussions about their expectations and how they can improve.

◆ **Three Dimensional Displays.** These provide an easy-to-see example of your expectation for exemplary work.

Recognition, Not Rewards

It is wise, however, to block out the names of the students on the examples. **Recognize performance, not individuals,** as this could be embarrassing to the recipients and may even cause teasing and bullying. You can also, of course, go to the students and personally acknowledge the exemplary work. Knowing they have reached a goal or completed a task motivates them to continue doing well.

Rewards, such as the treasure box, raffles, gold stars, and pizzas, do not facilitate or motivate learning and certainly do not teach self-assessment. They are momentary perks for students that can deteriorate into entitlements.

It has also been shown that awards such as "Students of the week or month" do not motivate students either. They can even discourage those students who feel they will never achieve that status.

Instead, post examples of highly proficient work so other students can review their rubrics, assess their progress, and determine what they need to do to improve.

Recognition is simple, immediate, and powerfully reinforcing.

Teaching for the Future

Students who have been taught to use self-assessment are more likely to develop internal resources, a feeling of empowerment, and a sense of autonomy. Self-assessment is really smart-assessment because the better people are at assessing and predicting performance, the smarter they become, and the better they are at making decisions. These are the same attributes that serve us well as adults in our own work, so it makes sense that they would do the same for students in the classroom, when they start their careers, and move into the workforce.

As educators, we must challenge both our students and ourselves to push our intellectual performance even further and become ever more efficient, effective, and resourceful.

Mastering Instruction

 One of the greatest effects on influencing student achievement is the expectations students set for themselves.

 The ultimate aim of effective teaching is enabling students to self-assess their own work.

 Self-assessment is an ongoing life practice, for both students and teachers.

 Self-assessment is not an isolated activity. It is woven into the curriculum and classroom community.

 When students become adept at self-assessment, they can take responsibility and direct their own learning and progress.

 When students set their own goals, encourage them to do even better.

...Produces Achievement!

UNIT D Instructional Strategies

Chapter

How to Create and Use a Lesson Plan

A well-planned lesson ensures effective instruction in the classroom.

The Components of an Effective Lesson Plan

Players go into a game with a game plan; couples make wedding plans. Teachers who use effective practices have carefully planned lesson plans that guide teaching the minute they enter the classroom. The most effective lesson plans are shared with students so they can collaborate with the teacher—they know how the lesson will evolve, what is expected of them, and what they will accomplish.

THE Classroom Instruction Book is organized around The Learning Triangle. Unit D focuses on instruction. **The common definition of instruction is the action, practice, or profession of teaching.** Every teacher is an instructor. However, there is a subtle distinction that can be made between teacher and instructor for the purposes of this chapter. **Teachers impart knowledge and instructors impart skills.** A teacher teaches about a subject; an instructor gives instruction on how to accomplish a task. When you create a lesson plan, you are imparting the skills students need to reach learning objectives or targets.

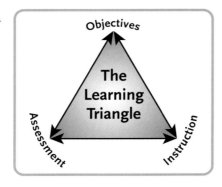

Objectives

The Learning Triangle

Assessment

Instruction

Working the Plan Every Day

"**The staff needs to see how dedicated <u>YOU</u> are to improving your school and helping students.**"

Karen Whitney
Sisseton Middle School

Three years after taking over a school in South Dakota on an Indian reservation, Principal **Karen Whitney** announced that she and the teachers at her school had made Adequate Yearly Progress (AYP), becoming the first public school on an Indian reservation to do so.[1]

The key to how this was accomplished is in one word—**Consistency.** Consistency built around consistent lesson plans. Consistency in classroom management. Consistency is what students—and teachers—need more than anything else for them to succeed in school and in life.

When planning a lesson, a teacher can begin anywhere on The Learning Triangle. The three components that make up the triangle are not sequential—there is no beginning, middle, or end. A teacher can start by devising the instruction, or the assessment, or the

---

[1] Adequate Yearly Progress (AYP) is a measurement that the U.S. Department of Education uses to determine how well a public school or district is performing on standardized tests as defined by the United States No Child Left Behind Act.

objectives because ultimately they are all related to each other, fit together, work together, and form a coherent instructional design model that works.

Every building has a foundation, but what is built on top of the foundation reflects the creativity of the architect. The foundation does not determine the design of the building. Every lesson has a foundation—the lesson or instructional plan based on The Learning Triangle. How the lesson plan is fleshed out reflects the creativity of the teacher, and the creativity and success of the lesson is based on the background knowledge and experience of the teacher.

- In Unit B, you learned that a lesson has learning objectives, targets, or essential questions.

  With a set of objectives, students know the goal of the lesson. They know what they are responsible for learning. Likewise, with a set of objectives, the teacher knows what to teach and what to do to keep the lesson moving towards achieving the learning objectives.

- In Unit C, you learned that assessment of student work must be done continuously and concurrently while students learn the objectives.

  By asking questions, providing feedback, and using assessment tools, the teacher can track what students have learned and provide additional instruction as needed to help them make progress.

- **In Unit D, you will learn how to organize a lesson plan so that you know how to teach, how to provide instruction, and every student knows how to proceed with learning.**

  There can be an increase in student achievement without extra cost if the components are performed effectively.

The Sisseton Lesson Framework

Educator **Madeline Cheek Hunter** was the creator of Instructional Theory into Practice. It is a summary of what she observed when watching effective teachers teach. **Karen Whitney** and her staff developed the lesson plan used at Sisseton Middle School based on Hunter's observations of effective lesson planning.

In an environment overwhelmed with problems where inconsistency was the norm, a structured educational program that ensured students experienced consistency and stability in a predictable, dependable environment led to the school achieving AYP—Academic Yearly Progress—after three years, becoming the first public school on an Indian reservation to do so.

Lesson Plan for the Week of:		Teacher:			Subject:	Grade:
	MONDAY	TUESDAY	WEDNESDAY	THURSDAY	FRIDAY	
Content Standard(s)						
Learning Target(s) (What students understand, know, or demonstrate at the end of the lesson)						
Instructional Strategies (What you do so students achieve the learning target)						
Assessment (How you use formative and summative tools to know if students met the learning target)						
Evaluation (How you use summative tools to test for reaching the learning target)						
Bellwork (What students do upon entering the classroom)						
Guided Practice (What students do with your assistance to boost the learning target)						
Independent Practice (What students do independently to reinforce the learning target)						

This "Lesson Plan Template" was created by Karen Whitney, Principal, Sisseton Middle School, Sisseton, South Dakota, and modified by Harry and Rosemary Wong.

The components of the Sisseton lesson plan are not sequential. There is constant jumping back and forth among the components to help students make progress in the most effective ways toward the lesson objectives. Sisseton's plan for success has two parts:

1. A consistent, schoolwide classroom management plan that makes it easy for everyone to know how the school and classrooms are organized and run

2. A consistent, schoolwide lesson plan format that makes it clear what teachers are to teach and what students will do in their assignments

The Basics of a Lesson Plan

In the classroom, lesson plans ultimately boil down to three stages—"I do, we do, then you do." The first step in the process is to explain the learning objectives and provide examples of the work required to achieve them. The next step is to do what's necessary with students until they understand what they need to accomplish. The last step is for students to have the motivation and wherewithal to do the work and employ the skills correctly by themselves. When this happens, students are ready to work independently and take responsibility for their learning. At this point they will also start to take pride in their accomplishments.

The Basics of a Lesson

Stage 1—I do. The teacher instructs and models to a goal.

Stage 2—We do. The students are engaged, usually cooperatively, in practicing what has been taught, while the teacher provides feedback.

Stage 3—You do. The student, independently, completes a piece of work that demonstrates learning of the goal.

As you plan each lesson, constantly ask yourself how these three stages can be used strategically. Ensure that ample time is provided for students to thoroughly connect with the ideas and practice the skills so that they have a sense of making progress. The positive reinforcement they experience when they do make progress will give them confidence that they can indeed achieve what is required of them.

To begin building a lesson plan, begin with content standards. Then turn your attention to planning and developing all the other essential components—the learning objectives, the instructional strategies, the assessments, and the evaluations.

The Content Standards

It's hard to imagine a world without standards. They certify that products you purchase and services you use are safe, effective, and reliable. When you buy food at a grocery store, you know it is safe to eat because you know it has passed the standards of the Food and Drug Administration (FDA) and the U. S. Department of Agriculture (USDA). You feel safe flying on a plane because you know the plane has passed Federal Aviation Administration (FAA) standards.

Standards are something we accept and expect in our everyday lives.

There are standards in education, too. Content standards define the parameters of success. What should students be able to do and know at each grade level? Students learn better when the teacher plans instruction using content standards. Clearly defined content standards ensure that everybody in the classroom is working towards the same goal. Content standards are usually organized by grade level and can also be called grade-level expectations.

These standards should be easy to find, as most all states and professional organizations have their own set of standards, such as the Texas Essential Knowledge and Skills (TEKS), the Standards of Learning (SOL) in Virginia, and Florida's B.E.S.T. standards.

35

Setting Standards

View the list of professional organizations to access their set of standards.

Content standards determine the results teachers and students aim to achieve. An effective lesson plan begins by considering the end results first.

Some schools and districts will provide a curriculum guide or map based on the adopted standards. The guide will set forth the content standards that are to be taught for the year. Some guides will sequence the content standards for each quarter, semester, or trimester.

Depending on the subject or subjects you teach, determining the sequence in which to teach each standard will depend on the content area and the ability and achievement of the students you are assigned to teach. For example, in first grade, reading instruction most effectively begins with phonemic awareness (sounds).

Planning lessons based on standards does not stifle your creativity. Standards do not tell you how to teach. They simply answer the question every teacher wants to know which is, "What am I supposed to teach?"

You can be as creative as you want in implementing a standard. However, mastery of content comes first and foremost.

The next step in lesson planning is to construct lesson objectives, or targets, based on the standards.

The Learning Objectives

What is the intention of the lesson? What are students to learn? When you plan a road trip, you need to identify exactly where you are headed, design the best route to get there, and monitor your progress along the way. Objectives steer your instruction and lead your students to their final destination—mastery of the content standards. It's common sense, actually.

When you take a road trip, it's a good idea to know where you're headed. You rely on signs to help guide you to your final destination.

The research is very specific about student achievement. In a classroom where teachers use effective instructional practices as identified by Hattie's influences, students know what they are to learn and the teacher knows what to teach.

Teach to the objectives and there will be a significant rise in levels of achievement.

It is important that you plan instruction by writing clearly defined objectives. Start your lesson plan with an objective that tells both you and your students what you are aiming for. **Identify the knowledge, tasks, and skills students must know and do to demonstrate mastery of the content standards.** The purpose of the lesson should be visible for all to see. When clear learning targets are communicated to students, there is effective teaching and meaningful student learning.

Lesson targets should be specific and concise. Keep them simple and easy to understand. The intention is to increase student performance. If students don't fully understand the lesson's objectives, it is less likely they will learn.

The Instructional Strategies

Instructional strategies are what the teacher does to instruct and deliver the content. We use strategies for everything—to accomplish a goal, to play games, to negotiate traffic, to save money, and even to meet the kind of people with whom we want to socialize.

Instructional strategies offer opportunities for teacher innovation and creativity. The more effective and engaging they are, the more likely students will be interested in the learning. But as you think of tasks and activities, always ask yourself, "Does this activity help teach the objective? Or is this activity just busywork with no goal in mind?"

These are things that you need to think about and choose as you prepare a lesson.

◆ What anticipatory set (motivator) will you use to engage and interest students in the lesson? Will it be an opening lecture, perhaps accompanied by showing a set of PowerPoint slides?

- What instructional strategies will you use? There are many possibilities—Socratic questions, reciprocal teaching, concept mapping, problem solving, Cornell Note-Taking, think-pair-share, field trips, worksheet, visualization, games, videos, inside/outside circles.

- Will you use chunking, scaffolding, and pacing?

- Will the students work in groups, at the computer, with a partner, at the carpet, or individually?

There are many instructional strategies that can be used to help enhance student learning. For example, in Chapter 16, you will learn how to chunk, scaffold, and pace a lesson to maximize learning. You will also learn a technique called reciprocal teaching for instructing students how to read and interpret text.

The Assessment

Good lessons begin with a clear, standards-based objective, followed by multiple cycles of various types of instruction, guided practice, assessment or checks for understanding, and ongoing adjustments to instruction.

**To be effective,
determine your assessments (check-in points)
while planning instructional strategies
and learning activities.**

Once you have written clearly-defined learning targets, you are now ready to determine the assessment you will use. The assessment should measure how well the student is mastering the learning target. Assessment is used during the instructional unit to monitor progress. There is no grading—that's evaluation—during assessment. It is a mistake not to plan the assessment until the end of lesson planning. It should be an integral part of the planning from the outset.

**The assessments must be correlated to
the lesson objectives.
As soon as an activity is chosen to teach the objective,
write the assessment.**

How to Plan Teaching and Learning

1. Determine the content standards.
2. Write clear learning targets and objectives aligned to the content standards.
3. Plan the instruction around the learning targets and objectives.
4. Develop assessments to check for understanding of the learning targets and objectives.
5. Create an evaluation to determine how well students have mastered the objectives content standards.

Going back to our road trip analogy, the assessments you use are like check-in points along the way to ensure you and your students are headed in the right direction to reach the final destination. Some fun activities or personal projects may be fine, but it's important to ensure that such side trips don't distract from the route to learning or reaching the desired destination.

The Evaluation

As has been discussed in Chapter 8, evaluation is different from assessment. Assessment is conducted during the teaching and reteaching of the lesson. Evaluation tells you to what degree students have mastered the content at the end of the lesson. (See Chapter 19.)

But if you are wondering why evaluation is listed after assessment in the Sisseton Lesson Plan template, and not at the very end, it is because evaluation questions must also be written to correlate to the objectives.

Lesson objectives, instructional strategies, assessment, and evaluation are all written at the same time as they must all be correlated to each other.

Evaluations measure levels of mastery. Objectives tell students what is to be learned; evaluations tell how well the objectives were learned.

An Assignment to Begin the Day

Now that the lesson objectives, activities, assessment, and evaluation are all written, class can begin. A key component of planning a successful lesson is to have an assignment that students tackle immediately upon entering the classroom. This can be called "bellwork," "do nows," "fast starts," "welcome work," or simply, "opening assignment." It doesn't matter what you call it; the important thing is to plan and have an assignment ready for students every day as they enter the classroom. It is to be started before or at the sound of the signal to start class.

Post the assignment in the same, consistent location every day. As a teacher, you want students to be actively doing work the minute they step into the classroom. Having students immediately engaged gives the teacher time to perform any required administrative duties. But most importantly, it gets students on task right away.

Being on task the minute they enter the classroom is valuable because it is part of establishing a consistent structure for students. They know how class starts. They have a purpose. When they know what to expect and what is expected of them, students feel safe, comfortable, and ready to learn.

> **It costs no additional money or teacher training to have instruction from bell to bell.**

When planning these assignments, consider activities that are related to the day's objectives, or that review a concept already learned, or that provide motivation for what is to follow in the lesson.

The Guided Practice

Guided practice is a shared process between the teacher and students. It is part of "We do." You have experienced this when you take golf, tennis, dance, art, computer, or music lessons. Or consider when you learned to ride a bike. Someone explained and showed you what to do, then most likely held on while you pedaled until you were able to balance and ride by yourself. This is guided practice.

We know from life experience that we learn how to do things really well by practicing them over and over again. The well-known saying, "Practice makes perfect!" is especially true in the classroom. The teacher teaches, and then guides students as they practice what has been taught. **Guided, correct practice is essential for student academic growth.**

During instruction, the teacher directly explains, demonstrates, and models. Then students practice what has been taught, often in groups. The teacher is watching, ready to supply feedback assessment, if necessary, correcting errors or mistakes until students master the skill or concept. This is learning-by-doing, but only after the teacher has shown the right way to do something. (Additional information on guided practice is in Chapter 17.)

The Independent Practice

> **Independent practice is what students do by themselves to demonstrate that they have mastered the learning target.**

As the term states, this is when a student must independently show achievement of the objective. It is part of "You do." This is where teachers use an effective practice called "release of responsibility," but the release only takes place after the teacher has guided the class to this point. Examples of independent practice include giving a speech; completing a portfolio or presentation; a solo performance; completing homework, classroom assignments, or inquiry, problem-solving projects.

You want students to be able to apply new skills and information in many different ways and at many different times. With learning reinforced during independent practice, student confidence and achievement increases. Independent practice repeated several times helps cement the new knowledge or skill into the student's long-term memory. Practice makes it stick and produces real learning.

A Model to Follow

Here is a completed first grade lesson plan that can serve as a model for your lesson plans.

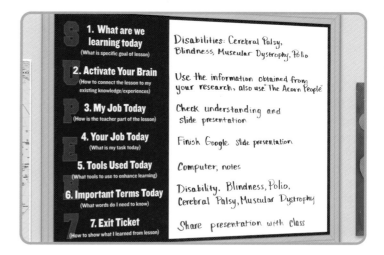

Lesson Plan for the Week of: Oct. 4–8		Teacher: S. Jackson		Subject: Reading	Grade: First Grade
					FRIDAY
Content Standard(s)	Demonstrate understanding of spoken words, syllables, and sounds.	Ask and answer questions about key details in a text.	With prompting and support, read prose and poetry of appropriate complexity for grade one.	See Monday and Tuesday	Identify basic similarities in and differences between two texts on the same topic.
Learning Target(s) (What students understand, know, or demonstrate at the end of the lesson)	I can correctly say and write words using oo, ou, and ew.	I can ask and answer questions about key details from the story *Visiting Butterflies.*	I can decode words in *A Butterfly Grows.* I can read *A Butterfly Grows* with fluency and expression.	I can correctly say and write more words using oo, ou, and ew.	I can tell how the stories *Visiting Butterflies* and *A Butterfly Grows* are the same and how they are different.
Instructional Strategies (What you do so students achieve the learning target)	I Do: Introduce sound of the week; show spelling patterns oo, ou, ew. Display sound and spelling words on Smart Board, give examples. **Read Moose's Tooth**	I Do: Teacher reads aloud *Visiting Butterflies* with students seated at the carpet. Introduce oral vocabulary: gentle, completely, settle, reflection, lonely, and recognize. Ask students to listen for the words.	I Do: Teacher reads *A Butterfly Grows.*	I Do: Teacher reviews sound of the week—oo, ou, ew. Display sound and additional spelling words on Smart Board, give examples. **Read Moon News**	I Do: On chart paper with students record the sequence, events, and key details from each story.
Assessment (How you use formative and summative tools to know if students met the learning target)	Monitor student independent practice. Give verbal feedback. Note student's progress.	Use Teacher Checklist for each student's responses during independent practice.	Teacher monitors and gives feedback as students practice with a partner.	Monitor student independent practice.	Give verbal feedback during guided practice.
Evaluation (How you use summative tools to test for reaching the learning target)	Write the following spelling words independently as the teacher dictates: soon, new, noon, zoo, boot, too, moon, blew, soup, you, grew, scoop.	None Today	Use expression and fluency rubric to evaluate each student's independent practice.	Spelling Test: room, spoon, tooth, drew, flew, group, soon, scoop, you, and broom	Students identify in writing two similarities and two differences in the two stories.
Bellwork (What students do upon entering the classroom)	Sight word worksheet review placed on the student's desk.	Write words with oo, ou, and ew on paper placed on student's desks.	Draw a picture of a gentle and lonely butterfly.	Spelling words matching worksheet review placed on the student's desk.	Draw three pictures of how *A Butterfly Grows.*
Guided Practice (What students do with your assistance to boost the learning target)	We Do: Blend words together that are written on the Smart Board. Practice with student leaders at the Smart Board. Then practice with a partner.	We Do: Ask students to turn and talk: why the author used the word *gentle* to describe the butterfly? Share with your rest of the vocab words. Continue to pair then share.	We Do: Echo Reading of *A Butterfly Grows.* Teacher reads a sentence. Then class rereads the sentence together. Students practice reading with students.	We Do: Review blending words routine from Monday, connect sounds to written words. Practice blending words with students. Model then practice.	We Do: Guide students in creating a class T chart recording from student responses how the two stories are the same on one side and on the other side how the stories are different.
Independent Practice (What students do independently to reinforce the learning target)	You Do: Practice writing spelling words: soon, new, noon, zoo, boot, too, moon, blew, soup, you, grew, and scoop on individual whiteboards as teacher says the word orally.	You Do: Teacher calls on each student to answer a question from the story. Teacher differentiates the question for each individual student.	You Do: Students take turns reading independently with expression in a small group while teacher listens.	You Do: Practice writing the spelling words: room, spoon, tooth, drew, flew, group, soon, scoop, you, and broom on white boards as teacher says the word orally.	You Do: Independently write two ways the stories are the same. Write two ways the stories are different.

This "Lesson Plan Template" was created by Karen Whitney, Principal, Sisseton Middle School, Sisseton, South Dakota, and modified by Harry and Rosemary Wong.

36

Lesson Plan Template

Download this lesson plan and **Karen Whitney's** lesson plan template to use as a guide when planning your instruction.

37

Middle and High School Lesson Plans

Access examples of completed lesson plans for middle and high school.

38

Consistency

See what Sisseton Middle School does to establish consistency in classroom management.

The Super 7 Plan

The Super 7 Plan is another example of a lesson plan. Principal **Bruce Hurford** of Kansas developed Super 7, a daily tool that the staff can use for planning lessons each day. It consists of seven instructional components with the corresponding objectives written next to each. Super 7 is a great tool for teaching and learning. The plan is posted in every classroom and it focuses on communication to students (teaching methods) and communication from students (formative data collection along the way).

When teachers and students come to class each day, the teachers know what to teach and the students know what to learn. Everyone at the school, even the paraprofessionals, cafeteria workers, custodians—and the parents—know what Super 7 means because it creates a consistent culture at the school in which everyone can participate. The program ensures that anyone walking into the classroom can see and understand the instruction. When paraprofessionals are in the room, they quickly refer to the Super 7 to know where the lesson is going without even needing to communicate with the teacher.

The Super 7 program is used as a "learning map." Students read it with the teacher at the beginning of each class period. Hurford says, "I know that students are more confident when they know what is coming and can mentally prepare for the lesson. This also helps keep all staff on track to provide a quality lesson for the students."

Super 7 is not used sequentially. Teachers and students will jump back and forth from component to component. Teachers are able to customize the components—some write full sentences; others outline the lesson through important connecting terms or supply every piece of information possible; some provide the information verbally. But the strategy is always to lay clearly visible breadcrumbs for students to follow.

Consistency in the Super 7 Plan

Located in a rural Kansas, this middle school in Osawatomie (pop. 4,293 in 2019) has a Super 7 lesson plan posted in every classroom so that there is consistency throughout the school. As the students go from class to class, they and the teachers know the plan for learning.

Jamie B., a sixth grade ELA teacher, says, "The Super 7 helps me think deeper into what I am doing in my teacher role and helps me visualize what exactly the kids should be doing. It also keeps me accountable to know what to do next."

Gara C., an eighth Grade ELA teacher, says, "The Super 7 keeps both students and teachers on track. Staying on track for the day is crucial when working with varying abilities. It remains as a visual aid the full hour and the complete day. The students can follow along and use reasoning skills by referring to the Super 7."

Grant K., a student, says, " The Super 7 is a good tool for helping us know what the teacher has planned for us each hour. I like that it is used in all classrooms."

Meghan S., a student says, "The Super 7 is very helpful. I also like that it is always in the same place every day so I can see what we need for class without asking."

With the Super 7 framework posted consistently each day, all a teacher has to do is "chunk" information into small blurbs on whiteboards so students know exactly how to proceed with their work. It is also a good way to communicate what is happening in the classroom to students' homes.

The Exit Ticket portion also helps teachers create a quality lesson for the next day based on the information they learn about what students got out of the day's lesson.

Hurford says, "It really is our formative assessment strategy, but Exit Ticket is more kid-friendly to use. As an example, to make sure the kids could easily identify what was happening, the Essential Question was changed to, 'What are we learning today?' This is more inviting to a middle school student."

This prompt is an efficient way to start every period, to keep both students and teachers on track. Every staff member uses the strategy daily and understands the importance of the consistency Super 7 provides to visually establish the concept of what is being taught on any given day. The teacher's job is to lead the class so that they reach and comprehend the goal of the lesson. When Super 7 is used schoolwide, the consistency makes it easier for the students to know what is going to happen in every classroom, every day.

The Sharing Out Lesson Plan

There are so many public schools in New York City—over 1,700—that they are allocated numbers. Staten Island, one of the five boroughs that make up New York City, is home to PS 861, a K–8 school. But PS 861 has another name—the Staten Island School of Civic Leadership (SISCL). Founded in 2009, one year it earned the distinction as the highest-rated school in New York City.

SISCL's principal was **Rose Kerr** (now Director of Education, Office of the Staten Island Borough President) at the time of its recognition, and SISCL is her brainchild. Its goal is to nurture students who are committed to the public good through personal achievement. As part of their lesson plan, they are asked and encouraged to make public presentations in the local community.

Sharing Out is the lesson plan template that is the basis of all lessons in every grade at SISCL. All lessons are organized in the same way:

- **Essential Questions:** The anticipatory set that motivates students about what is to come.

- **Lesson Focus, Learning Outcomes:** The lesson objectives or learning targets.

- **Teaching Point:** The statement that brings relevance to the lesson so students can identify a personal goal, and what they need to do to reach that goal.

- **Opening Activity:** The activity the teacher has chosen to start the lesson.

- **Mini-Lesson:** The activity, or several activities, used to teach and illustrate the lesson focus.

- **Small Group and Independent Work:** The activity or activities students will participate in to achieve the lesson focus. This could be small group work—guided practice—where students demonstrate that they have grasped the knowledge, skills, or concepts of the lesson focus.

  During this time, the teacher circulates and checks for understanding, as feedback and reteaching are important for helping students make progress.

- **Independent Practice:** After guided practice, there is independent practice where the students complete a task, perhaps as homework, on their own and away from teacher guidance.

- **Sharing Out:** Students gather to present their finished work, explain how they met the lesson focus, and discuss their goals and plans to reach those goals.

  Sharing Out is the main purpose of the SISCL lesson plan as they expect students to learn how

to make public presentations and become leaders in their community.

- **Final Summary:** A blend of all parts of the lesson, from the expected outcome to the tasks assigned, that results in the verification and celebration of mastery of the goal.

- **Follow-Up:** All lessons are sequential and coherent, so students keep personal data charts to record progress towards their goals.

A Purposeful Tomorrow

At SISCL, it is evident and essential that the school helps students develop into highly trained, highly motivated, and highly committed individuals and citizens.

What SISCL aspires to for its students is stated in its mission statement.

The Staten Island School of Civic Leadership
is founded on the principle that
our students will become disciplined,
diverse leaders
who are inspired to make a difference
in America's civic purpose.
We believe embracing civic responsibility,
as a pillar of learning,
creates a culture of proactive thinkers
who begin with the future in mind.

A Home School Lesson Plan

A former teacher, **Emily Floyd** of the Dallas-Fort Worth area, homeschools her two boys. During her first-year teacher orientation, the district provided her with a copy of *THE First Days of School*. The procedures she learned from it became the basis for how she structured and organized her homeschooling schedule and curriculum.

She began to homeschool her son, Levi, when he was four. Today Levi is twelve and is joined by his younger brother, Tait, who learns with the same structure and procedures.

Emily creates consistency in her home school environment. Each day begins with a task that she creates for each of her sons that sets the stage for the day's learning. The activity is checked, corrected, and discussed before moving on with the day.

The day begins with saying the pledge, getting seating, and beginning the Morning Message. In addition to checking for mechanical errors in grammar, phonics, and sight words, Morning Message poses a question that provides clues to an activity that will be part of the day's lesson.

Centers follow Morning Message. There is a small rolling cart with drawers, each labeled with a day of the week and containing tasks to focus on and complete that day: Marvelous Monday Math, Terrific Topic Tuesday, Word Power Wednesday, Thoughtful Thursday, Finish Up Friday.

The morning routine is consistent and predictable. When the work is finished, it is set aside to be corrected, discussed, or presented before moving to the next task. All the materials needed for the Centers are also in the cart, maximizing work time and minimizing time searching for materials.

Writing Workshop is next. The books to be used for the daily mini lessons in Writing Workshop are displayed in order on a large easel with a shelf. This provides a visual cue for what will be happening that week and sets the tone for the next day's mini lesson. A Writing Workshop notebook is kept in the same place.

When Emily started Writing Workshop with Levi, she spent the first two months learning, modeling, and practicing many new procedures. One wall in their home classroom has all of the strategies, steps, visual cues, writing processes, and published pieces. This helps them both to see where they are in Writing Workshop. The following year, only the first week was needed for reviewing procedures.

Reading Workshop follows Writing Workshop. The daily books used for these mini lessons are also displayed. All the procedures and strategies for Reading Workshop are posted on the wall with a visual reminder. For example, when the focus is on the strategy for Imagery and Visualization in reading, a short explanation is posted along with a picture of a picture frame. Emily reads aloud and models a comprehension strategy; they read together (with a purpose); then her son reads aloud on his own, practicing all the strategies that he has learned.

Math follows Calendar Time. After having explained, modeled, and practiced how to complete all the things in Calendar Time, her son is handed a marker, and he completes them on his own. He changes the day of the

The procedure for each step in the writing process is read and modeled. After a discussion on what Levi will be doing during writing time, he completes whatever tasks he needs to do in the writing process (get an idea, write, share, revise, edit, publish, illustrate).

week, updates the song of the week, and forecasts the weather for the day. Then, together, they work in the math books on number, money, time, and graphs and complete a daily story problem. Counters, dice, and manipulatives are displayed like the writing and reading books—visual cues of what will be used that week.

Lesson objectives are sometimes written in the Morning Message or in the lesson planner that they read together daily. A sample objective for Reading and Writing Workshop is, "Identify and include three transition words (time, location, or continuation of an idea) that would help with the organization of the paper." For math, an objective could be, "We will learn how to find the lateral area and surface area of different shapes."

The end of the day is focused on a weekly theme related to science or social studies. The weekly themed materials are displayed just like the writing and reading materials and can include activities such as art projects, games, recordings, field trips, and experiments.

While "her students" work, Emily prepares for the next week. During Finish Up Friday time, Emily changes the items in the daily drawers and the weekly pocket

chart, writes the new word wall sight word cards for each day of the next week, and arranges all the books for the mini lessons in each subject.

Emily's routine strives to be consistent, organized, and structured to include a variety of tasks. With a second child to homeschool, Emily's teaching day is a balancing act between the instructional needs of each. While one works independently, she instructs the other. When one child completes the mini-lesson with modeling and guided practice, he then completes an additional assignment as independent practice.

Emily goes back and forth between her two students about every twenty to thirty minutes to re-direct or instruct. If one child completes independent practice and she is occupied, he can choose from a variety of activities while he waits. The day flows in a similar fashion to a school classroom where the teacher balances between whole-group, small-group, and individual instruction.

Emily also enriches their studies with piano lessons taught by an outside teacher who comes in, along with art (in class and at museums), swim team, and travel.

39

Sample Elementary Lesson Plan

See how **Amanda Bivens** of Dyersburg, Tennessee, creates a lesson on abolitionist leaders.

Create Your Own Lesson Plan

The effective teacher understands the value of an organized, structured, and consistent lesson plan.

As you can see from the examples shown, there is no one correct way to design a lesson plan. What is essential is that you have your own plan—and that the plan is shared with your students so they can follow and be active participants in the instruction.

When creating your own lesson plan, start small. Four models have been shared. Each is different in design, yet remarkably similar in concept and purpose. Take the basic components of these models and implement your own lesson plan. Once you have the lesson plan done, all you need to do is tweak the basic plan "for life."

If you do not start with a plan, you will have nothing to tweak and improve—you will be muddling through for the rest of your career. Each year, make a resolution to research and add some more effective techniques to your plan. Discuss plans with your colleagues; read journals and magazines; search the Internet. New and interesting ideas will jump out at you. Why? **Because when you have a plan, you know what to look for, what you can add, and how to modify your plan to make it better and better until it's the very best plan for you and your students.**

> **Well-planned lessons increase the likelihood that teaching will be effective and students will receive quality instruction.**

Mastering Instruction

 For instruction to be effective, there needs to be an instructional plan, also commonly called a lesson plan.

 With a lesson plan, students can come to school each day and experience a consistent, stable, predictable, and safe environment.

 Since content standards define end results, an effective lesson plan begins by considering the standards.

 Instruction, assessment, and evaluation must be correlated to the lesson objectives.

 Once a basic lesson plan is created, the effective teacher continuously researches ways to enhance the plan.

...Produces Achievement!

How to Deliver the Instruction

> *Effective communication in the classroom is the key to teaching and learning success.*

The Basics of a Lesson

1. The teacher instructs and models to a goal. **I do.**
2. The students are engaged, usually cooperatively, in practicing what has been taught, while the teacher provides feedback. **We do.**
3. The student, independently, completes a piece of work that demonstrates learning of the goal. **You do.**

A Lesson in Three Stages

You now have the basics of a lesson plan. Your next step is to execute it. You have to present it to the students in such a way that they will be inspired to learn what you are going to teach. There are three stages in presenting a lesson plan:

1. **Direct or explicit instruction—I do.** The teacher instructs and models lesson objectives.

2. **Guided practice—We do.** The students are engaged, usually cooperatively, in practicing what has been taught, while the teacher assesses and provides feedback.

3. **Independent practice—You do.** The student, independently, completes a piece of work that demonstrates learning of the lesson objectives.

The Class Is Absolutely Quiet

> " **I do; We do; You do. This brings calm, respect, and equity to the classroom.** "

William Martinez

William Martinez is known from his many presentations to educators.[1] When he conducts his workshop to show how American Sign Language (ASL) can be used as an effective way to communicate with students, the room is absolutely quiet. Everyone is calmly focused, and they think, "I can run my classroom like this and not have to talk or yell all day long!"

Jennifer Varrato of the Clark County School District in Nevada says, "William's workshop addressed the importance of student engagement, classroom culture and climate, and student metacognition."

1. Direct or Explicit Instruction

> **Direct instruction is what the teacher does.**
> **I do.**

In direct instruction, the teacher's primary role is to teach the basic knowledge required by the district curriculum and content standards. This is done by

---

[1] www.william-martinez.com

explicitly presenting, telling, explaining, lecturing, describing, illustrating, and demonstrating the content, accompanied by supplemental readings, artifacts, and multimedia resources.

Direct or explicit instruction is directing the class as you would direct a show, a team, or a band. It is not necessarily lecturing and expecting students to take long, laborious notes, although there are times when that may be appropriate, as will be discussed later.

Direct instruction takes students through learning steps systematically, helping them see both the purpose and the result of each step. In this way, they are not only introduced to a lesson's content, but also to the methods for learning that content.

The basic components of direct instruction are
- ◆ setting clear objectives for students and making sure they understand those objectives,
- ◆ presenting a sequence of well-organized assignments,
- ◆ giving students clear, concise explanations and illustrations of the subject matter,

Influences with Positive Effects on Student Achievement[2]		
Influence	Effect Size	Page
Teacher estimation	1.62	18
Collaborative impact	1.57	250
Self-reported grades	1.33	143
Teacher clarity	0.75	239
Reciprocal teaching	0.74	201
Feedback	0.70	89
Direct instruction	**0.60**	**28**
Spaced vs. mass practice	0.60	192
Mastery learning	0.57	235

As can be seen from **John Hattie's** research, direct instruction has a significant effect-size of 0.60.

- ◆ giving students frequent opportunities for guided practice to enhance what they have learned, and
- ◆ asking questions frequently to assess if students understand the work.

2. Guided Practice

**Guided practice is
what the teacher and students do together.
We do.**

The teacher uses guided practice combined with assessment to help students make progress in learning the lesson objectives. Hands-on activities are provided to further explore the content-rich material that must be learned for the objectives.

As students are doing the hands-on activities, the teacher is moving from group to group asking questions, helping students to discover and explore for themselves, and scaffolding their experience. There is constant guidance and assessment of the learning to provide clarification, encouragement, and positive expectation.

As students are working, the teacher is gradually stepping away from explicit instruction so that students practice what has been taught. To expedite understanding, guided practice involves asking questions and providing feedback and explanations to foster understanding of the lesson objectives.

3. Independent Practice

**Independent practice is what students do.
You do.**

This is the stage where students can show that they can do, on their own, what they have been taught. At this point, the teacher releases the responsibility of guided practice and allows the move to independent practice where students are to demonstrate they have the knowledge, skills, and confidence they need to practice and perform what they have learned. This is where students can show creativity in projects and independent learning.

---

[2] *Visible Learning*, "Hattie Ranking: 256 Influences and Effect Sizes."

Teaching American Sign Language (ASL)

William Martinez can be seen in his many presentations to educators and on the DVD, *You Have Changed My Life*, included with *THE First Days of School*. After his more formal presentation, he is often asked to conduct a workshop to show how American Sign Language (ASL) can be used in the classroom as a strategy for classroom and instructional management.

With some basic ASL signs, a teacher can give instructions and commands, correct unwanted behavior, and offer praise without interrupting the flow of the lesson. By introducing students to another language and culture, they are learning a skill they can carry with them throughout their lives. More importantly, they will be taught to respect another way of communicating, how to honor it, and how to use it correctly.

During the workshop, William teaches these signs and many more for use in the classroom.

During the entire workshop he models the I do; We do; You do lesson stages.

- **I do.** From the front of the room William teaches and demonstrates each sign. Then he invites a couple of teachers to demonstrate or model how to do it.
- **We do.** The teachers (and administrators) model the sign in guided practice with each other while William circulates the room watching and giving assessment feedback suggestions. He selects people to come to the front of the room and share what they have learned while the entire class applauds—in silence, using the applause sign.
- **You do.** The teachers are then told to use what they have learned in independent practice by signing sentences that William shows on the screen.

  - It's assembly time. Please line up at the door and wait for the bell. Good job!
  - Class. No talking. Please quiet down. Thank you!

Again, he selects people to come to the front of the room and show what they have learned. The rest of the class gives them one of the affirmation signs he teaches.

While William conducts his workshop, the auditorium is absolutely quiet. For thirty minutes or more the room is void of sound. Yet ample praise and encouragement is given—silently, of course. Everyone is engaged in the learning process. What he teaches brings calm, respect, and equity to the classroom.

Every teacher thinks, "I could run a classroom like this, too, and not have to talk or yell all day long. I can instruct and then determine if the students have learned. I can bring calm and deliver instruction all day—and enjoy it."

Line Up

Quiet

| Awesome | Stop | Please |
| Read | No | Thank you |

> **I do; We do; You do—**
> **this is as basic as effective teaching gets.**

Sage on the Stage

Perhaps you have read that teachers should not stand in front of the classroom or to place their desk in the front of the room. Otherwise you may risk being ridiculed as a "Sage on the Stage."

A sage is the instructor of a hundred ages.

Ralph Waldo Emerson

A sage is a person who is wise and imparts wisdom. But "Sage on the Stage" is a disrespectful and derogatory expression used by some people in education to describe a teacher who stands in front of a room and talks to the class. The implication is that they are not actually wise and do not possess wisdom. No one will disagree that lengthy lectures and presentations can drone on and be tedious, but there is no need to sarcastically demean teachers with the word "sage." Many, if not most, teachers have the desire to positively affect the lives of their students and do indeed possess a great deal of intelligence, initiative, and wisdom. They cannot be glibly dismissed as sages on stages.

A sage is someone who is astute, learned, wise, perceptive, sagacious, and erudite
—an accurate description of many teachers.

Effective teachers are more like Oscar-award winning directors whose aim is to enable a diverse group of students to succeed in a complex and ever-changing world. They offer immeasurable support and do innumerable things for the students in their classrooms, and more.

Photo credit: Elizabeth Medwick

Mickey Smith Jr. taught band in Sulphur, Louisiana, when he received the 2020 Grammy Music Educator Award. In fifteen years, he increased the band enrollment from twenty-eight to one hundred forty-six students, half the student body.

Mickey not only teaches band with passion; he teaches with compassion, bad notes and all. His spirit transforms his students. He loves what he is doing. He exudes enthusiasm and humanity.

True learning takes place with
an effective teacher
leading, directing, and inspiring students.

One of our responsibilities as teachers is not only to teach the curriculum, but to also help nurture and establish within our students the foundations of how to be a decent human being. The teachers students remember for the rest of their lives are those whose simple humanity shines in the classroom. The way they work personifies generosity and wisdom.

- They give lectures, explanations, and directions.
- They devise interactive activities for learning.
- They create visual demonstrations and slide shows.
- They provide activities to reinforce learning during guided practice.
- They ask Socratic questions to stimulate thought.
- They engage in formative assessments to track student progress.
- They give constructive feedback.
- They bring the class together as a unit.
- They applaud performances.
- They provide empathy and encouragement.
- They create a learning environment that is stable and consistent so that every student is given the opportunity to excel.

In other words, an effective teacher is a dedicated professional who employs many techniques and methods to give students every opportunity to succeed.

Command respect with your presence,
intelligence, personality, and wisdom.
Students will see that you want them to learn.

Before the Lesson Begins

A teacher's primary role is to organize a lesson plan and then execute it in the classroom. But before that happens, the entire endeavor begins each day or each period when the teacher greets students.

Professor Douglas Brooks of Miami University in Ohio videotaped a series of teachers on their first day of school.[3] The way they began their classes was crucial in determining how the class would be conducted thereafter. In  the worst cases, teachers started abruptly covering the subject matter, without welcome or introduction—or they gave a busywork activity with little relation to the day's lesson. Students were left to wonder, "Am I in the right class? What's expected of us? What will we be doing? What are we going to learn? How is this class organized?" He noted that such teachers spent the rest of the school year chasing after students, wondering why there were behavior problems and little cooperation.

Conversely, those teachers who took the time to welcome students and introduce themselves; who explained how the class was organized, what students would be doing, and how they would be graded— the question they always want to know—were far more assured of a wonderful, constructive academic experience for the year. Those teachers made a point of creating a community in the classroom with shared expectations and the best atmosphere possible for getting work done.

The organized and effective teacher always begins with a welcome, establishes procedures, and has an opening assignment ready that reviews the previous day's lesson or introduces the lesson for the day. The agenda and lesson objectives are posted and the teacher explains what will happen in class. The class flows day after day, because each day has a sense of consistency and stability.

To begin class in a welcoming manner and increase interest and engagement, simply say, "Good morning. It's so nice to see you." Say it with presence and a genuine smile.

However, it is imperative that you never ask, "How are you?"

"How are you?" can be a very difficult, painful question to answer. Some of your students may have come from a homeless situation or a home in turmoil. They may have confronted bullying; they may not have had any breakfast; they may have walked through a metal detector and passed a security guard. They may be so numb or overwhelmed by their life experiences that they may not even know what to answer when asked, "How are you?"

So it is better to address the whole class with a positive greeting such as, "Good morning! I hope you are all doing well." This places no burden on individuals to respond if they feel shy or uncertain or upset. If you do notice that a student needs some special attention, find a moment later in the day to have a private conversation to express your care and concern.

> *Greeting increases classroom engagement by 27 percent.*[4, 5]
>
> Allan Allday
> University of Kentucky

The Human Voice

**What you say and how you say it
can change your class for the better or the worse.**

---

[3] Douglas Brooks, "The First Day of School," *Educational Leadership* 42, no. 8 (May 1985): 76–78.

[4] R. Allan Allday and Kerry Pakurar, "Effects of Teacher Greetings on Student On-task Behavior," *Journal of Applied Behavior Analysis* 40, no. 2 (Summer 2007): 317–320.

[5] R. Allan Allday, Miranda Bush, Nicole Ticknor, and Lindsay Walker, "Using Teacher Greetings to Increase Speed to Task Engagement," *Journal of Applied Behavior Analysis* 44, no. 2 (Summer 2011): 393–396.

Verbal communication is an essential part of teaching and learning. This is the way humans have always learned from their ancestors. For tens of thousands of years, individuals were almost never alone and people communicated by direct speech. From the moment they are born, children learn things, starting with their name, by listening to people speak. Speaking and listening have always been the most common forms of communication used in the classroom.

Teachers' verbal skills and their ability to communicate effectively with students predict academic gains.[6, 7]

It's only in recent history that we have begun to use and rely on technology to replace teaching by an actual, physical teacher. We direct students to "teach yourselves" and "think for yourselves" and "go work (by yourself) at the computer." It's so easy for a student to be distracted, apathetic, and, off course, lost when left alone.

Students do not want to learn this way. Humans are social animals and school is a social environment. Students come to school to see their friends. They come to interact, be stimulated, and challenged. They enjoy working with their teacher and classmates. It is easier for most students, especially those who are learning impaired or struggling, to learn conceptual information from spoken communications accompanied by graphics and sound, discussions, and in groups rather than alone. Without a responsive and communicative human being leading the classroom, it is difficult for true learning to take place.

The social context of a lecture taking place in real time makes it far easier for most students to focus attention and remember what is said, than when students are required to work alone.

Teachers share information, give instructions, explain ideas, and motivate students. The way this is done can be called by any number of names including lecture,

presentation, or led discussion. Whatever you call it, the intention is the same. Throughout any given day, the teacher will need to do these activities.

- ◆ Introduce new material.
- ◆ Explain safety procedures.
- ◆ Teach a procedure.
- ◆ Give instructions.
- ◆ Explain ideas.
- ◆ Generate interest in a topic.
- ◆ Emphasize key points.
- ◆ Tell a story to make a point.
- ◆ Help, encourage, and praise.

The more accomplished you are in speaking in front of a group, the better students will understand you and be motivated to move on to the lesson plan activities when the discourse ends.

Your success as a teacher is dependent, to a great extent, on how well you communicate with the class. The more teachers know about the techniques of effective speaking and presentation, the more impact they will have on their students.

Which is more effective? Learning from a caring, enthusiastic teacher in the company of friends or learning in isolation in front of a monitor?

[6] Linda Darling-Hammond, "Standard Setting in Teaching: Changes in Licensing, Certification, and Assessment," in *Handbook of Research on Teaching* (4th edition), ed. Virginia Richardson (Washington, DC: American Education Research Association, 2001), 751–776.

[7] Andrew J. Wayne and Peter Youngs, "Teacher Characteristics and Student Achievement Gains: A Review," *Review of Educational Research* 43, no. 1 (2003): 89–122.

How to Speak Effectively

Arguably, the most important skill a student must have when entering the workforce is the ability to speak effectively and who better than a teacher to model this skill.

Effective teachers know how to speak clearly and concisely. Teachers must know how to communicate well orally because when teachers speak in such a way that students listen, then students learn. The ability to speak well is an important skill for both teachers and students.

It is a skill that can be learned, practiced, and improved.

There is actually no need, in most cases, to give long-winded, boring lectures. You just need to help and guide your students.

- You speak to present information students cannot easily find on their own.
- You speak to provide an explanation of information that is complex and difficult to understand.
- You speak to present a concept in such a way that a novice or struggling student can understand.

When speaking, stand where students can see you. Presence helps the presentation. This is a time when you can shine, when you can show your enthusiasm for the topic you are teaching.

- Post the topic you plan to talk about and list three to five points you will share.
- Have a grabber that will pique students' attention. (page 184)
- Use images that illustrate the concepts and ideas (70 percent of the sensory cortex of the brain is made up of the visual cortex).
- Use analogies and stories that provide concrete examples to illustrate the topic.
- Pause and ask questions.
- Plan an activity, even in the middle of your talk, or allow for interaction and questions.
- Finish with a conclusion so students can see or can summarize what was said.

The Third Most Popular Class at Harvard

Lectures can be the best teaching method in many circumstances for many students, especially when communicating conceptual knowledge where there is a significant knowledge gap between the teacher and students.

At Harvard, the two most popular classes are, predictably, introductory economics and computer science. However, the third most popular class, with over seven hundred students, is an arcane subject: *The Path: What Chinese Philosophers Can Teach Us About the Good Life*.[8] The class is taught by **Michael Puett** from a theater stage with no notes and no slides—it's simply a lecture.

Entrevue de Confucius et de Lao-tse.

The students have no prior knowledge of or interest in Chinese history or philosophy, nor will they receive credit that is related to their major. Yet students come because of its reputation—"If you connect with these ideas, they can change your life"—that has circulated the campus.

Here is a prime example of an effective lecture. A teacher has gathered and organized information too difficult for students to gather themselves and presented it in a fashion that can make a difference in a person's life.

These college students, positioned to become future leaders in whatever career they might pursue, are stimulated by the idea of a lecture that contains the possibility that they can be awakened and transformed by what it offers.

---

[8] Michael Puett and Christine Gross-Loh, *The Path: What Chinese Philosophers Can Teach Us About the Good Life* (New York: Simon and Schuster, 2016).

How to Create an Effective Presentation

You create and execute a presentation the same way you teach how to write a paragraph. Just as there are three parts to writing a paragraph, there are three parts to presenting a lesson.

Part 1: Introduction

Determine the purpose and objective of the presentation. Write or post the topic so students know your focus.

Constantly ask yourself, "Who is my audience? How can I make my presentation clear, interesting, and easy to understand?" The way you introduce the purpose and objective is crucial. It should grab everyone's attention and spark curiosity so that they are eager to listen to what follows.

As part of the introduction, explain what task students will do during the presentation. It may be to just listen and enjoy, or to take notes, or to fill in the worksheet (graphic organizer), or to use a responsive clicker, or to participate in an interactive lecture-discussion.

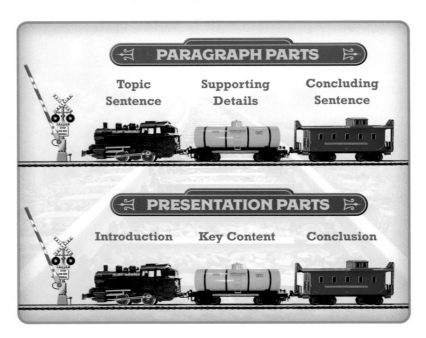

Consider the most effective methods that you have at your disposal to support your presentation:

- **Handouts.** Will they benefit your students? What is the procedure for distribution?
- **Technology.** Do you have the computers, projectors, remote controls, and sound ready and tested before class?

Part 2: Key Content

Write down the ideas and supporting details for the main body of the presentation. Try to use colorful, concise vocabulary.

The main body is the key content of the lesson. Make it clear, concise, and easy to follow.

- Explicitly state the main topic and key points of the presentation.
- Discuss each point and add the supporting information.
- Make it interactive, not a monologue, so that students feel free to ask questions or clarify issues.

Part 3: Conclusion

Summarize the body of the presentation in a few sentences to reinforce its purpose and objective.

Movies, novels, plays—we expect them to build to a satisfying ending that ties all the plot threads and characters together to bring understanding, closure, or material for reflection. Do likewise as you conclude your presentation by

- restating the purpose,
- restating the main ideas, and
- ensuring students know what is expected of them.

When you are finished, give the class something to do to process or follow up on the lecture. It should be short and quick, such as writing a summary, discussing the summary from the Cornell Note-Taking system page, or completing an exit slip. Students will quickly adapt to consistency in the classroom—they will know that there will be an assignment.

Speaking Techniques

There are specific speaking techniques that professional speakers use to deliver effective presentations. You can use them, too. Practice these techniques so that you can rely on them when you speak.

Voice. Project your voice (or adjust the microphone) so everyone can hear you. Vary the volume, pitch, inflection, and pace of your speech for emphasis and to make it interesting.

Conviction. Speak with confidence, passion, and enjoyment. You want students to know that you know what you are doing and are dedicated to their success.

Language. Use accessible, normal language, not slang, and do not try to impress the class with big words or long-winded sentences that will distract from meaning.

Pause. Find moments to pause when you speak. It is a powerful technique. When you pause, it adds impact to a statement; it gives the audience time to process information; it encourages the audience to laugh at a punchline; it gives you a measure of control—if you pause long enough, everyone will look up.

When students see that you love what you're doing and that you are doing the best you can, they will love how you're doing it and they will learn. You are not lecturing; you are communicating and inspiring. That is teaching.

Use the speaking techniques to make a presentation your own. Humor helps, but you do not have to be a comedian. Simply consider a combination of little things that you can do to make your content a little more engaging and enjoyable for your students.

- Add some pertinent humor.
- Add music or sound.
- Tell a story.
- Use an analogy.
- Use visual aids.
- Use repetition (or a chant) to make key points.
- Make it relevant to your students' circumstances and interests.

Cornell Note-Taking Method

If students are to take notes when you speak, lecture, or watch a video, review the Cornell Note-Taking Method with the class.

Background information can be found in **THE First Days of School**, page 190, and **THE Classroom Management Book**, pages 184–187.

How to Tell a Joke

Watch actors and comedians. It's not just what they say; it's their timing and delivery. They pause before delivering a significant line, or the punch line to a joke. Here's an example.

An elderly woman says to her husband, "Will you get me some ice cream? Write it down so you don't forget."

He says, "I won't forget. Ice cream."

She says, "Put some whipped cream on it. Write it down so you don't forget."

He says, "I won't forget. Ice cream with whipped cream."

She says, "Put a cherry on top. Write it down so you don't forget."

He says, "I won't forget. Ice cream with whipped cream and a cherry on top."

He leaves the room.

Some time goes by. He returns and says, "Here are your bacon and eggs."

PAUSE before delivering the punch line.

She says, "You forgot the toast."

Things to Avoid

When giving a presentation, consciously work to avoid doing things that will interfere with your intention to communicate and inspire.

- **Using vocal fillers** such as, "So, Uh, Um, Okay, Like, Y'know"—they distract and annoy listeners.

- **Acting arrogant or rude or complacent**—your audience will react negatively to negative attitudes.

- **Using unfriendly gestures** such as finger pointing or fist thumping—accusatory or commanding gestures will alienate listeners.

- **Using nervous gestures** such as fiddling with hair, clothing, jewelry, or change in your pocket—they distract and annoy listeners.

Non-verbal Communication

Non-verbal communication is as important when speaking and presenting as the words themselves. Your posture, body language, facial expression, gestures, and delivery convey that you believe what you say.

- **Posture** is an indicator of attitude and internal thoughts and feelings. Stand in an upright, relaxed manner to convey calm confidence. Smile to assure your students that you are prepared and capable of helping them achieve, and even exceed, expectations.

- **Eye contact** keeps students engaged. Try to have a few seconds of eye contact with as many students as possible as you speak rather than looking down or over them. However, do not make eye contact with individuals for too long. It will make them feel self-conscious and uncomfortable.

- **Facial expressions** add variety and convey meaning to express sadness, doubt, confidence, excitement, and happiness. The best expression is that sly smile that conveys, "I just surprised you with some new information, didn't I?"

- **Gestures** convey meaning, emphasis, and add variety. Use a gripped fist to show enthusiastic agreement. Point upwards to indicate a good idea. Spread palms outward to express inclusiveness.

Where to Stand in Class

Seating arrangements and where the teacher stands are determined by practicalities, the classroom layout, the subject matter, and the methods used to teach the lesson. Even though some are of the firm opinion that teachers should not stand or position their desks at the front of the room, this is a nonsensical, inflexible approach. The front of the room could be the most effective place to be. But there are many other possibilities that could be considered.

Nile Wilson, an orchestra teacher, stands in front of the classroom. That's where the conductor's podium is located. While Nile is conducting, she may have a student modeling the technique in front of the classroom as part of the "instructional strategy" and "guided practice" component of the lesson plan.

Keep the center of attention on you, in the front of the classroom, during instruction.

The front of the room is where the coach stands in the locker room. The science teacher stands behind the demonstration table in a science lab, the culinary arts teacher stands behind the cooking table, and the welding teacher stands in front of the room facing the students watching who are protected by fireproof gear. There are times when a PowerPoint presentation is being given—the teacher needs to stand next to the screen, not elsewhere in the room, as that would distract students from looking at the screen.

Then there are teachers who will sit on the rug or on a low chair as the students sit, "crisscross applesauce," facing the teacher. There are teachers who sit next to students when they are in accountable talk (page 205), in reciprocal instruction (page 201), or in an inside-outside circle configuration (page 121). There are teachers who walk among students and interact with groups and individuals as they work. When speaking to an autistic student, for example, you must face the student so he or she sees your face.

The effective teacher adapts the physical aspect of teaching to suit the needs of students, the subject matter, and the classroom activities.

Signs of Disinterest

No one enjoys a long, boring presentation. As you speak or lecture to your students, watch for signs of listlessness or disinterest:

- **Too long.** The average attention span is fifteen to twenty minutes, or less. Even if students are quiet or pretending to listen during a long lecture, it does not mean they are focusing and learning. Keep track of time as it is always better to end a little early. Do not go until the last second before the end of class. If you talk until dismissal, the students will rush out of class and forget everything that was said.

- **Too much writing.** It is hard to listen, write, and process information all at the same time. If students spend the whole time writing, they are probably not learning.

- **Ineffective speaking.** When a speaker goes too fast, uses complicated language, speaks with a monotone voice, or says, "Uh" before every statement, it takes away from the message.

- **Preaching to the audience.** This didactic style of lecturing is alienating. Good presenters interact and form connections with their students.

The Importance of Listening

When the teacher speaks, students need to be listening. If students are not listening, there is no possibility of learning. Quieting the class is one of the procedures in an effective, organized classroom.

When you want your students' attention, use your established procedure or signal. There is no need to yell at the class. Then say, "All eyes on me, please" and point to the topic of the presentation that has been posted. The signal and request are accompanied with a smile. A handout may be helpful. The main thing is to begin without wasting time.

Interactive Lectures

- **Think-Pair-Share.** Instead of asking, "Are there any questions?" have each student write one or two questions. Then have them pair up and discuss the question with their partners. Ask students to share their perspectives with the whole class.
- **Finding Illustrative Quotations.** Ask students to read the accompanying text and find quotations that support particular arguments from the lecture. Then have students share the same or different arguments.
- **Problem Solving.** Pause and give students a problem to work. After a few minutes, work through the problem, discussing it with the class.
- **Classroom Response Systems.** Hand out instructional "clickers" that allow instructors to collect and analyze student responses to multiple-choice (and sometimes free-response) questions during class.

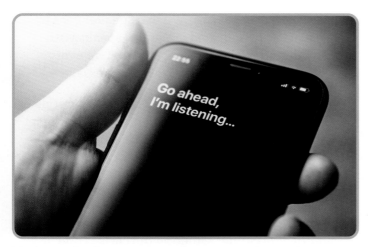

Modern technology integrates the concept of active listening to form a relationship with the user.

It is essential that students learn how to listen.

Businesses spend millions each year in teaching their people, especially their salespeople, how to listen to a customer. This is not surprising when you consider that good listening skills can lead to better customer satisfaction, greater productivity with fewer mistakes, and increased sharing of information that in turn can lead to more creative and innovative work.

We live in an interactive world. When a person does not listen, the mind is closed. In class and in life, listening requires receiving, understanding, evaluating, remembering, and responding. To do this, active listening is required.

When relationships go sour, it's often not about love or hate—it's, "He or she ignores me." This behavior of ignoring or retreating from human company begins when young people sit at the dinner table and stare into a phone. Scrolling through text messages is not listening. Enlightening, stimulating conversations at the dinner table are the result of active listening.

Listening is communication.
Communication is only possible when people listen.

Listening is not the same as hearing. We hear with our ears. **To really listen requires focus and concentrated mental effort, and sometimes physical effort as well.**

Three Steps to Active Listening

1. Look at the person who is speaking.
2. Wait until she or he is finished before you speak.
3. Respond with words or gestures that indicate you heard and understood what was said.

Listening means paying attention not only to the presentation or lecture, but how it is delivered, the use of language and voice, and how the presenter uses his or her body. In other words, it means being aware of both verbal and non-verbal messages. Our ability to be active listeners depends on our ability to perceive and understand these messages.

Listening creates shared consideration and provides us with an understanding into people's needs and desires so that we can bond with them.

◆ Tell students that the most basic and powerful way to connect to another person is to listen.
◆ Tell them to give the speaker their full attention and to listen with their entire body.
◆ Tell them it's like listening to a friend, a relative, or business associate.
◆ Tell them to listen for the main idea or thought and capture it in their mind.
◆ Tell them to respond and indicate that they are interested in what the speaker is saying.

The most important gift we give each other is our attention. Listen for the feeling being conveyed. It's not words, but feelings.

Changing the World

Abraham Lincoln spoke for two minutes, said two hundred and seventy words, and changed the world.

Martin Luther King fervently spoke just four words and changed the world.

Students want someone who can change their world. What you say in your lecture or presentation is one of the best ways to build relationships with students. It provides a time to share content information and to learn from each other. Instead of dreading a lecture, students will look forward to it. They need and deserve good speakers. **They even value sage advice.**

Teachers are revered and respected in almost every country and culture in the world, except in certain quarters of American education. Students whose ancestry is from Central and South America, Africa, Asia, Eastern Europe, and the Middle East are taught to respect and listen to teachers—members of the community who provide intelligence, wisdom, and inspiration. One of the finest museums in Washington, DC is the National Museum of the American Indian. They have exhibits that show how tribal elders use stories to transmit generations of sage advice to their young children.

Students attend class in front of a small building in a remote village near Ntchisi in Malawi. It is the teacher that makes the difference in the classroom.

> **When the way you teach is effective and compassionate, you will make a difference in the lives of your students. You will change the world.**

But in the United States, it is common to tell the current generation, "Ignore the past and learn from what you discover for yourself." Teachers are told not to lecture so that students can discover things for themselves. There are even teachers who announce, "I do not teach. I facilitate. I am not a sage on the stage; I am a guide by the side."

Build your capacity to be THE teacher all students long for and deserve.

Of course, autonomy should be encouraged, and students should be given every opportunity to discover, inquire, explore, and be creative. That, in essence, is what teachers encourage students to do during independent practice. But just because a teacher also chooses to talk and actively direct the class at various times is no a reason to degrade that style of teaching.

Effective teachers use many different strategies and techniques, while making hundreds of decisions every minute of the day.

The teacher's role
- **is to assess whether students have mastered the material,**
- **identify which students have not, and**
- **ensure that those students get additional time, instruction, and practice to master what the curriculum specifies.**

Be proud that you are a teacher. You teach a variety of grade levels and subjects and a great diversity of students. There are students with disabilities who value your loving, encouraging, direct teaching. There are students with exceptional abilities who value your creative and stimulating style of teaching. There is no one right way to teach. Whichever way you chose to present and execute your knowledge and wisdom, do it in a way that reflects your ideals and enthusiasm.

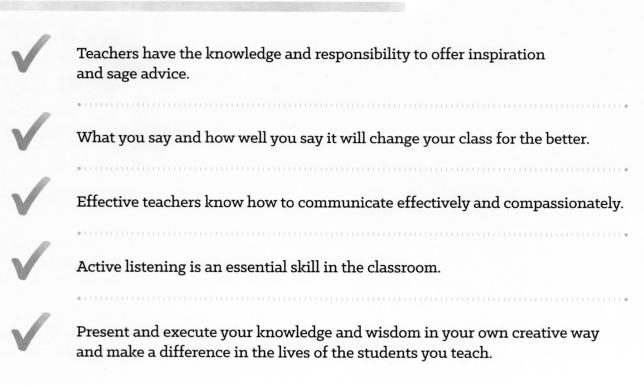

Mastering Instruction

✓ Teachers have the knowledge and responsibility to offer inspiration and sage advice.

✓ What you say and how well you say it will change your class for the better.

✓ Effective teachers know how to communicate effectively and compassionately.

✓ Active listening is an essential skill in the classroom.

✓ Present and execute your knowledge and wisdom in your own creative way and make a difference in the lives of the students you teach.

...Produces Achievement!

How to Use Instructional Strategies

> *The effective use of instructional strategies supports and enhances student learning.*

The Importance of Instructional Strategies

Students learn more when teachers use research-based instructional strategies.

You have a set of standards and objectives. You also have a lesson plan. But the lesson plan will just be a piece of paper unless you execute it in the classroom for the benefit of your students.

The purpose of this chapter is not to tell you what to teach, but how best to teach what you choose to teach. To maximize teaching effectiveness, you use what are called instructional strategies. The research-based instructional practices explained in this chapter will do two things for you.

1. You will more effectively implement the lessons you teach.
2. You will improve the effectiveness of your teaching.

Teachers make well over a thousand decisions each day or four decisions every minute of the day. Every decision that is made is of utmost importance because it affects the life and future prospects of a student. Effective teachers know to use tried and true, research-based instructional strategies to achieve the goal of student learning.

Instructional strategies are what you use to effectively teach a lesson to enhance student learning.

Seeing Is Believing

> **The most exciting phrase to hear in science, the one that heralds new discoveries, is not "Eureka!" but "That's funny . . ."**
>
> Isaac Asimov

David **Marasco**, physics instructor, is lying on a bed of nails, face up, with another bed of nails balanced on his stomach. A concrete block is placed on the top bed of nails. **Frank Cascarano**, his fellow physics instructor, will smash the concrete block with a sledgehammer.

How many nail holes will there be in David Marasco's body?

The purpose of an instructional strategy is not to replace what you are doing; rather, a strategy is what you use to improve the impact of your lesson. The effective teacher's goal is to be a more effective teacher each year. This is done by mastering a set of strategies.

Research-based instructional strategies enhance both student learning and teacher effectiveness. This is truly the creative part of teaching, where teachers can experiment and determine the best strategy they can use to help their students make progress.

Lesson Plan for the Week of:		Teacher:		Subject:	Grade:
	MONDAY	TUESDAY	WEDNESDAY	THURSDAY	FRIDAY
Content Standard(s)					
Learning Target(s) (What students understand, know, or demonstrate at the end of the lesson)					
Instructional Strategies (What you do so students achieve the learning target)					
Assessment (How you use formative and summative tools to know if students met the learning target)					
Evaluation (How you use summative tools to test for reaching the learning target)					
Bellwork (What students do upon entering the classroom)					
Guided Practice (What students do with your assistance to boost the learning target)					
Independent Practice (What students do independently to reinforce the learning target)					

This "Lesson Plan Template" was created by Karen Whitney, Principal, Sisseton Middle School, Sisseton, South Dakota, and modified by Harry and Rosemary Wong.

Strategies Make People Effective

Everyone uses strategies every day to negotiate, get what they want, improve their situation, and help others. When you drive a car, you steer it to a destination. As you drive, you constantly make decisions to be sure you reach your destination.

This is the same in teaching. Strategies in the classroom are a type of problem solving—a way of thinking through a sequence of possible solutions to determine the best way to achieve your objectives.

As a teacher you have the monumental task of increasing the probability of learning by making strategic instructional decisions.

A strategy is what a teacher uses to achieve a specific goal. There is a strategy for getting students to start working when they enter the classroom, a strategy for providing the best feedback, and a strategy for creating a clear and coherent lesson plan.

Techniques Are Used to Implement Strategies

Strategies and techniques go hand-in-hand.

A day does not go by that you are not strategizing, knowing what you want to accomplish, and then wondering what method or technique you can use to achieve your goal.

- ◆ How can I buy a new car? What technique will I use?
- ◆ What is the best way to reorganize the closet? What technique will I use?
- ◆ How can I stop the cat scratching the furniture? What technique will I use?
- ◆ How can I relax more when I have time off? What technique will I use?

During time out, the coach draws a play that represents the best strategy and technique to use against the opposing team.

A technique is a practice or procedure that a teacher does to carry out a strategy. When you have articulated a strategy, you then determine the best technique for executing the strategy. Posting an agenda with the opening assignment and the day's lesson objectives is the technique used to let students know what you expect them to accomplish and to ensure they start working the moment they enter the classroom.

Know Your Students

When you understand and know your students, and use that insight and information to design lessons that support them, you make it possible for those students to learn more.

Students have individual personalities, strengths, and weaknesses. They come from different backgrounds and cultures that influence the way they think and act. They come to school with a range of prior physical and cognitive abilities, skills, and beliefs that significantly influence how they will receive, organize, and interpret new knowledge. In addition, there are students with medical and physical fragilities, special-needs learners, and immigrants who are often at a disadvantage because they may be years behind in their preparation and academic skills, usually through no fault of their own.

Students can only read about, write about, and understand and absorb things that are somewhat familiar to them. A content-focused curriculum is of utmost importance as students do best in classes where the design of the lesson reinforces and furthers what they already know. The more teaching builds on previous learning and experience, the more possibilities there are for learning to take place.

Showing interest in a student says that you care. It makes constructive dialogue and meaningful interaction possible.

If we, as teachers, put more effort into who we are teaching, then the what would take care of itself. Paying attention to students' interests, desires, aspirations, and concerns allows teachers to build upon their strengths and successes, which is particularly important when students are acclimating to a new classroom and possibly a new country, culture, and language.

When students also get to know something about you, and about each other, they will feel more comfortable in the classroom and more willing to participate. It is far less likely that a student will act up or disengage when they know their teacher and their fellow classmates have a genuine interest in their wellbeing.

Get to know every student to make them feel like they matter. Then your efforts will matter to them and you'll achieve more together.

The Index Card Technique

The more you know about your students, the more you can gauge their needs and the best strategies and techniques to use to help them make progress. Get to know your students as efficiently as possible. On the first day of school, give each an index card. Post the information you want them to write on the front of the card—name, address, email address, contact person. On the back of the card, ask them to respond to questions like these.

- What one word would be a good description of you?
- If your house was on fire, what one thing would you try to save?
- What do you aspire to be in your adult life?

The information they share, perhaps in private, opens the door for you to have pleasant and constructive discussions with individual students. It gives you insight into the student as a person and a learner. Use the information positively to express your interest, care, and support.

Ten Effective Instructional Strategies

Using instructional strategies to create a lesson plan is an exciting and constructive task. It is when your creative inspiration kicks in as you look for better and more effective techniques and practices that ensure successful learning.

Ten strategies with accompanying techniques are explained and shown in this chapter:

These Are Not Strategies

Here are three common occurrences in classrooms that may be mistakenly considered instructional strategies. These are NOT instructional strategies.

1. **Cover the textbook.** Covering a textbook is not a strategy. The textbook is part of the lesson and is used to help students gather and summarize information. Simply turning the pages of a textbook is not considered a strategy for learning.

2. **Do lots of activities.** Activities and projects are fine but they must be correlated to lesson objectives. If there are no objectives, and no strategies and techniques to achieve those objectives, there is no instruction—activities, projects, reading, or computer work will be meaningless busywork.

3. **Adopt a program.** A program is not a strategy. A program is what a teacher blindly follows expecting it to instruct students and achieve academic results.

---

1. **Appropriate Level of Learning.** Students learn more when the lesson is tailored at the appropriate level.

2. **Continuity.** Students learn more when a lesson begins with a short review of previous learning to reinforce continuity.

3. **Discrepant Events.** Students are motivated by discrepant events—something that intrigues them and inspires them to enquire further and learn more.

4. **Chunking.** Students learn more when new material is presented in small, manageable steps with practice after each step.

5. **Scaffolding.** Students learn more when information or skills are constructed and presented in a logical order.

6. **Pacing.** Students learn more when the lesson is paced appropriately for their needs.

7. **Spaced Practice.** Students learn more when practice is spaced strategically over a period of time, not massed together at the same time.

8. **Interleaving.** Students' memory can be improved when random jumping from topic to topic is used rather than plodding along in sequence.

9. **Retrieval Practice.** Students recall and apply information previously learned.

10. **Combining Graphics with Words.** Students' learning is maximized when text is combined with graphics to add visual interest and support.

1. Strategy of Appropriate Level of Learning

New knowledge is built on existing knowledge.

The more students learn, the more they can learn and the more they want to learn. Instill confidence by beginning the lesson with what they know. When you provide a familiar foundation as a starting point, taking the next steps forward to learn more will be less intimidating.

There are some students who will enter your classroom without the prior knowledge or cultural background needed to be successful in meeting the standards and objectives in your classroom. For those students keep the standards and objectives structured (step-by-step, chunk-by-chunk) for guided practice and learning.

There will also be students—in the minority—who will be ready to move on, independently, from the lesson provided. Give these students autonomy when they do independent practice, but keep the standards and objectives posted as important reminders for learning.

When designing a lesson, it is important to determine what your students have learned in the past or are learning in other classrooms. This may be difficult in schools that subscribe to the ideology of personalized learning where students can determine their own curriculum, what they want to learn, when they want to learn, and at their own pace. (There is no research to authenticate the efficacy of this method.)

It is then your responsibility to gather what has been covered in the classes preceding yours by asking for a copy of the school's curriculum, if there is one, or finding out the course of study followed in the grade before yours—assignments, exams, lesson plans, and whatever else might be available. It is also important to talk to colleagues teaching classes that follow yours and ask what kinds of skills and knowledge they expect students to have when they leave your class. **This is done for one major reason—the continued success of students at the school.**

Whatever you do, do not test students to determine their prior knowledge or abilities. Testing causes anxiety for many students and to start the school year with a test is tantamount to losing your possibilities with them.

These are some techniques to find out the appropriate level for your lessons based on how much and what students know.

PowerPoint Inventory

- Prepare numbered PowerPoint slides showing pictures from a forthcoming unit with an accompanying question. For example, in a geography unit, show the Panama Canal and ask, "Why is the Panama Canal important?" Try to avoid asking a low-level factual, one-word answer question such as, "Where is the Panama Canal?" as surely someone will answer, "In Panama."
- Ask students to write their responses next to a number for the slide. Tell them not to put their names on the paper. Collect the responses and examine each to determine the class's general level of knowledge.

Whiteboard Inventory

- Make a list of statements related to course content, including misconceptions. Have students mark T or F next to each statement.
- Write questions on the board. Ask students to respond in two or three sentences to each question or circle a response.

- Prepare two or three open-ended or multiple-choice questions. Let students know these will not be graded and that their answers will help design the lesson for their learning.

Example: Mount Everest—I . . .
- have never heard of this place.
- have heard of it, but don't know where it is.
- have some idea where it is, but not exactly.
- have a clear idea where it is and can explain.

Gallery Walk

- Set up information stations or posters around the classroom, on the walls, or on tables.
- Place images, graphs, and excerpts from upcoming course content on poster paper.
- Hang the poster papers around the room. Point these out to the class.
- Create groups of two to four students and tell them their task is to write what they think is on each poster. Tell the class you want short sentences, a phrase, or a list. There is no need for a lengthy explanation. Place one group in front of each poster. Give them two minutes to discuss and then three minutes to write their observations on what they know or what they are wondering about the material.
- Explain to the class that how they answer will help you organize your lessons for their learning.

- ◆ If time permits, have the class rotate to the next poster and repeat the procedure. Collect the papers with their responses.
- ◆ The next day, or sooner if possible, give the students feedback and explain how this information will help with your lesson design.

One-minute Papers

- ◆ End class a few minutes early and ask one or two questions that students answer on index cards, paper, or electronically and submit. Questions often asked are, "What were the main points of today's class?" or "How did today's lesson help you make progress towards the objectives?"

2. Strategy of Continuity

Students will only learn when they see how each lesson relates to a previous lesson. It is incumbent that teachers design a curriculum where the units of study have coherence and continuity. Dressing in a coordinated manner, having a dinner party where each course complements the other, or moving in coordination during a dance sequence all involve the concepts of continuity and coherence. Effective teachers create classroom environments where teaching and learning flow meaningfully together from start to finish.

Planning a beautiful flower garden requires coordination with the season, the soil and light requirements of various plants, and the physical design of the flower bed to assure an aesthetically pleasing visual experience.

To determine what students have learned, and what your starting point for the lesson should be, begin with a short review of previous learning to establish a base of knowledge and to reinforce continuity.

Doing this every day is an excellent technique to build on what has been learned and what is to come. A good way to conduct a review is as an opening assignment, followed by discussion, and a smooth transition to the lesson or objective for the day.

Make a point of discussing homework and quizzes. If you don't, students will believe that homework is busywork and quizzes are a threat to their success. Use review to recall ideas, vocabulary, equations, formulas, concepts, and skills. The next step is to practice these until they become automatic.

Definitely review anything that is difficult to be assured that students have a firm grasp of the skills and concepts that are needed for the day's lesson.

Continuity can also be observed by using exit tickets as a transition to the next lesson. Young people, including those in high school, tend to see life as a series of isolated events. To encourage their intellectual growth, help them to become conscious and make connections to the knowledge and skills they have and the challenges that lie ahead of them.

3. Strategy of Discrepant Events

Every teacher wonders, "What can I do to motivate and inspire students?" There are many ways to excite, influence, and motivate students. Motivational tactics and techniques are used routinely in movie trailers, advertisements, and clothes displayed on store mannequins. They want to grab your attention with the intention of making you acquire or desire more.

In the classroom, one of the simplest ways to engage students is to ask a question. The right question at the beginning of a lesson can spark student interest and help them focus on what's important. Here are some examples of questions that will pique students' curiosity and help them think and learn.

- What's wrong with this picture?
- What do you think?
- What's happening?
- How do you think that happens?
- What do you think will happen next?
- If you could swap places, what would you do?
- What else can you use?
- How does that make you feel?
- How would you feel if . . . ?
- What can you do about it?
- What did you like about it?
- What would happen if . . . ?
- How can you find out?
- What did you do?
- How did you do that?
- What do you need to do next?
- What can you tell me about that?
- What do you think the problem is?
- How can you solve your problem?
- What should you be doing right now?
- What happened prior to this?
- Can you think of another way you can do this?

You may remember the term "anticipatory set" from your college days and wondered what it means exactly. A common term would be "the hook." You hook the class so that students can anticipate and are curious about what will happen next.

At the Physics Show that has been produced for fifteen years at Foothill College in Los Altos, California, **David Marasco**, physics instructor, is lying on a bed of nails, face up, with another bed of nails on top of him. A concrete block is placed on top and **Frank Cascarano**, his fellow physics instructor, smashes the concrete block with a sledgehammer.

The audience applauds and screams with delight when David stands up, brushes himself off, and there is not a single nail hole in this body. Why?

When the sledgehammer hits the block of concrete, the audience is hooked by the seemingly impossible result. Everyone wants to know why. When students are motivated to discover why, even the most disinterested student will suddenly be totally intrigued.

The answer? Because the nails are numerous, the weight is distributed among them. By distributing the weight as well as the force of the sledgehammer hit over many nails, the pressure under each one is not enough to pierce the skin. In addition, the breaking block absorbs much of the force of the sledgehammer and disperses it, generating heat and randomness in the pieces.

This kind of discrepant event is a powerful motivational technique. Discrepant events are occurrences which defy our understanding of the world by presenting unexpected outcomes. A discrepant event is something that doesn't make sense to the mind, even while staring at it in disbelief. They are often used to grab the attention of a class and engage visual learners, particularly young students.

Discrepant events do two things.

1. **They motivate students to anticipate the topic of the lesson.**
2. **They serve as the transition to the lesson.**

Discrepant events engender learning because the discrepancy causes students to think about, inquire, and problem-solve to determine what is causing the discrepancy. Learning evolves from the discrepancy between the presumed and the actual. **Always encourage students to predict what will happen BEFORE the activity takes place.** Allow them to convince themselves that they know what will happen before surprising them with an unexpected result.

An Air Pressure Mystery

The class enters the classroom and are greeted with a sign on the board that says, "$1 million offered today."

Place two books at the edge of a table, leaving a small space between them. Ask a student to place a piece of writing paper over the books. Then offer anyone in class one million dollars if they can blow between the books and blow the piece of paper off the books. It's impossible no matter how hard they try!

When they can't, they all demand to know why. And as effective teachers know, you never tell them why immediately because, once you have them engaged and involved, you can use any strategy with them.

If you want to lecture and explain what happened, they will listen. If you want them to watch a video related to the topic, they will watch. If you want them to break into groups and solve the problem themselves, they will work in groups.

You can use this discrepant event to set the class up to anticipate your lesson on air pressure.

Discrepant events cause students to have teacher-to-student and student-to-student communication—analyzing, comprehending, and evaluating their thoughts and questions.

Discrepant events create puzzling situations that result in cognitive disequilibrium. They challenge students to change prior ideas and think about unexpected results.

As a teacher, you can allow students to ask Yes or No questions; break the class into groups to formulate inquiry hypotheses; or focus their inquiries to conduct open-ended discussions. The research and problem

solving continues until the teacher reassembles the class to hear the various answers.

After the event, ask students for possible explanations for the discrepancy between what they thought would happen and what actually happened. It is important to bring closure to a discrepant event and guide students to a conclusion so they are not left confused by the unexplained. **Use the closure as a perfect transition to the lesson that follows.**

Creating discrepant events is fun and exciting. You will enjoy seeing students baffled—knowing you have their full attention. Discrepant events cause them to sit in absolute amazement and then go home with a great sense of pride knowing that their teacher is even better than the most astonishing magician in causing people to ponder and wonder—which are the seeds for learning.

4. Strategy of Chunking

Students learn more when new material is presented in small steps with practice after each step. Present only a small amount of material at any time, and then assist students as they practice this material. This strategy is called "chunking."

How do you eat an elephant? One small bite at a time. **With chunking, new material is presented in small digestible bites.** Effective teachers do not overwhelm their students, especially younger and struggling students, by presenting too much information at once. They teach by giving a series of short presentations using many examples. The examples provide concrete learning and give the opportunity for asking questions. Then, as the teacher assists and assesses, students do activities to practice the point being taught.

The important aspect of chunking is knowing when to stop so students can discuss and internalize the information. Chunking can be extremely effective when students are listening to a lecture, during reading, when watching a video, doing an activity, or watching a demonstration.

When information is chunked into related topics, it makes it easier for students to engage and remember

A Variety of Discrepant Events

Language Arts Discrepant Event

In language arts, a palindrome is an example of a discrepant event. These are words, phrases, and sentences that spell the same backward or forward, such as "mom" and "deed" and "name no one man."

- A man, a plan, a canal, Panama
- Was it a cat I saw
- A nut for a jar of tuna
- Don't nod
- Never odd or even

Ask students to answer these riddles with a palindrome.

- What did the right triangle trade with the hairdresser? (Answer: Leg for a jar of gel.)
- What did Nat notice about your day at the beach? (Answer: Nat saw I was tan)
- What did the clock say to the race driver in second place? (Answer: Now I won)
- What did the teacher trade with the lab researcher? (Answer: Star for a jar of rats)
- What did the person say who did not want cake? (Answer: I prefer pi.)

Math Discrepant Event

It is easy to create a palindrome with a string of numbers:

- 535
- 3773
- 59695
- 76067
- 374473
- 416614
- 87966978
- 246191642

Some numeric palindromes occur naturally. Depending on how a date is written, American style as month-day-year or British style as day-month-year, the third palindrome American date of the 21st century was November 2, 2011 or 11-02-2011—11022011. There was also Pi Day, March 14, 2013 written as 3-14-13—31413. A British style date in 2013 was 31 July 2013—31713.

Ask the class to add 47 + 74. Do they get a palindrome?

Social Studies Discrepant Event

An American history teacher tells the story that in 1837, a young boy named David lived on a farm in a beautiful, mountainous, wooded area in Georgia. His family planted crops and raised animals for food. His father participated in the legislative branch of government. His mother taught English in a local school. He had four brothers and three sisters. It was a happy and prosperous family.

In 1839, the family moved to a treeless, dry, flat prairie. Because they were barely able to raise enough food to feed the family, two of David's brothers and one of his sisters died. The father remained a member of the legislature. The mother helped publish the local newspaper, but David and his family missed their beautiful home in the mountains.

The teacher poses this puzzling question, "Why did David and his family leave their beautiful home in Georgia and take a hard journey to a hot and barren land?" (Answer: David and his family were Cherokees who were forcibly relocated during the Trail of Tears.)

Geography Discrepant Event

Tell the class that in 1000 CE, the Netherlands had 8,380 square miles of land. They farmed 5,866 square miles. Today, the Netherlands has 13,967 square miles of land, and they now farm 9,776 square miles, but the national boundary of the Netherlands has not changed since 1000 CE. How is this possible? (Answer: At the start of the eleventh century, the people of the Netherlands built dikes and dams to control the movement of seawater and created new land without expanding its boundaries.)

the information. Lessons need not be complicated or lengthy to be effective. **Lessons are effective when they are the right length for students to be able to do them and learn what they must know.**

Chunking is also a skill that can be taught to students at all grade levels to help them remember important information. Chunking helps overcome short-term memory to allow the brain to process more items into long-term memory, a process useful in real life. For instance, to understand the parts or chunks of a paragraph, the teacher identifies the

- topic or main idea of a paragraph,
- supporting sentences or details in a paragraph, and
- summary of the paragraph.

Making the Journey to Learning Easy and Enjoyable

It helps to break up long car drives by stopping every two to three hours for food, sightseeing, or simply to stretch your legs. By taking frequent breaks, the trip feels like a series of convenient drives instead of one endless one.

Effective teachers present only small amounts of new material at one time. They teach so that each point is mastered before the next point is introduced. They assess their students' understanding of each point and reteach material when necessary.

When chunking is incorporated with a strategy called "think aloud," students hear the teacher thinking through the construction of a paragraph. **By hearing a teacher analyzing and modeling problem solving out loud, students discover how to emulate this in their own minds.**

Students can use chunking techniques in textbook reading. This will be a very constructive learning experience for all involved. Chunking breaks down difficult text into more manageable pieces, which helps students to separate and identify key words, phrases, and illustration captions.

Several pages can be chunked into paragraphs or sections. When reading a sentence, teach by breaking it into key phrases, either verbally or by marking up the text. Draw vertical lines after each key phrase to set them apart. For some students with literacy deficiencies, this technique may also improve comprehension.

Processing small bits of information rather than a large chunk of content typically yields greater learning and understanding. To present a lecture or video, carefully examine the content to determine where to pause so students can interact with the teacher or one another about the new information. Consider the research of **Bob Wallace**, a middle school teacher in New Jersey. He divided his students into three groups and did the following experiment:

> **Group 1:** He showed the students a video and gave them a test.
> **Group 2:** He briefed the group on the video they were going to see, and then played the same video shown to Group 1 and gave the same test.
> **Group 3:** He briefed Group 3 exactly the same as he had Group 2 and then showed the same video. However, during the video, he stopped the show frequently. During each stop, he asked questions and held class discussion. He then gave the same test he had given to Group 1 and Group 2.

Guess which of the three groups scored the highest on the test? Group 3, of course. (The research basis for this strategy can be found on page 42 in *THE First Days of School*.)

We Use Chunking Every Day

Chunking helps break down difficult text into more manageable pieces. Look at this sequence of numbers: 8, 2, 3, 5, 4, 7, 9, 0, 0, 8.

Now close your eyes and repeat them out loud. You probably were only able to remember the first few numbers. It is much easier to remember the ten numbers if they are divided into smaller chunks: 823-547-9008. Now you only have to remember two groups of three digits and one group of four digits. Phone numbers, social security numbers, and credit card numbers are chunked for easy recall.

Remembering numbers grouped together—numbers that have been chunked—is far easier than remembering digits presented in a continuous sequence.

When attempting to remember non-numeric information, the same chunking concept applies. Think grouping to remember key pieces of information:

- States—think regions of the country
- Countries—think continents
- People—think field of endeavor
- Animals—think phylum
- Music—think music style

Organizing a shopping list will help you remember like items to purchase and save you time gathering the items from aisles of like grocery items.

Mnemonic Devices

A mnemonic device is a chunking technique that uses a pattern of letters, words, or ideas to assist in the retention of information.

Acronyms

- **HOMES**—The Great Lakes: Huron, Ontario, Michigan, Erie, Superior

- **ROY G. BIV**—The rainbow color spectrum: Red, Orange, Yellow, Green, Blue, Indigo, Violet

Catchy Sentences

- **Please Excuse My Dear Aunt Sally**—The order of operations for solving an equation: Parenthesis, Exponents, Multiplication, Division, Addition, Subtraction

- **King Philip Came Over For Great Spaghetti**—The order of taxonomic rank: Kingdom, Phylum, Class, Order, Family, Genus, Species

When you remember **My Very Elderly Mother Just Sat on Uncle Ned**, you will remember the order of the planets in the solar system.

5. Strategy of Scaffolding

Scaffolds are used to support a work crew and materials during construction, maintenance, and repair of buildings, bridges, and other structures. The concept of scaffolding is also used in education.

Chunking involves deconstructing new content into bite-size pieces.
Scaffolding involves the logical order of presenting the bites.

The Influence of Jerome Bruner

Harry Wong was influenced by **Jerome Bruner**, one of the great minds of education, with his book, *The Process of Education*, written in 1960. Bruner coined the word "scaffolding" and said every subject has great ideas that can be taught from a series of concepts. For instance, instead of trying to teach history chronologically since the beginning of time, teach it as a set of recurring ideas. **He taught that a set of related facts will form a concept and a set of related concepts will form an idea.**

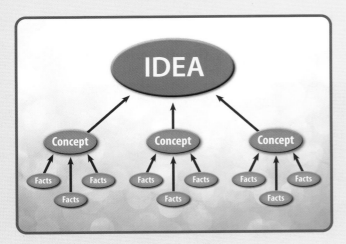

Bruner taught that structure in learning is crucial in teaching. Students must see how the knowledge they learn is organized in order for it to be transformed into understanding and stored for later learning.

Building on the concept of chunking, scaffolding is the construction of information or skills in a logical order. **Jerome Bruner** devised the term to describe the way students often build, step-by-step, one chunk after another, on the information they have already mastered to create a concept or major idea. That is, they can put pieces together and say, "Oh, I see it now."

To illustrate, let's say a teacher is showing students the structure of a sentence, starting with the basic subject, predicate, and object to show how the words of a sentence are put together.

In writing a sentence, each component is built upon the other—scaffolded—one at a time. When teaching the principles of writing, monitor carefully and assess for understanding before presenting the next chunk so students understand how all the pieces fit together in a logical way.

Scaffolding helps students to constantly build on prior knowledge so they can be successful before moving into the next phase of an unfamiliar lesson. This minimizes failure and is especially important for students with special learning needs.[1]

Scaffolds allow construction, repair, and maintenance to proceed in an orderly fashion. In the classroom, effective scaffolding helps students see a logical sequence where each part leads to the next.

[1] Rachel R. Van Der Stuyf, "Scaffolding as a Teaching Strategy," *Adolescent Learning and Development*, Section 0500A, Fall 2002, accessed March 20, 2020, http://ateachingpath1.weebly.com/uploads/1/7/8/9/17892507/stuyf_2002.pdf.

Scaffolding a Lesson

Select the skill you want students to practice or the content you want them to review and establish tasks at three (or more) levels of difficulty.

- **Level 1** should be a relatively easy task that all students can complete; however, the task should require full demonstration of the focus skill or grasp of the focus content.

- **Level 2** should be a challenge for most of your students, but not so difficult as to discourage them.

- **Level 3** should be a challenge for all students in your class. To complete a Level 3 task, students must exhibit what you consider to be the highest levels of competence or comprehension.

6. Strategy of Pacing

Pacing is the speed at which we move through a lesson—or, the rate of delivery for different parts of the lesson. Good pacing is how you bring students along the learning trajectory. There is a flow, a rhythm, and a beat that students can follow. There is no need to push the class as they can just go with the flow of the process.

- First, you have **chunks**, the bits of information you want students to learn.
- Second, you **scaffold** the chucks in a logical order.
- Third, you **pace** the chunks of information appropriately—not too fast and not too slow—so students are able to optimize their learning.

As in teaching the three parts of a paragraph, a teacher must monitor carefully to assess that students have learned each part, one at a time, to know when to present the next. That's pacing.

Pacing is the skill of creating a perception that a class is moving at "just the right speed" for students. Generally, this will mean that the lesson appears to unfold more quickly.

A good pace helps students feel like they are moving along and learning is effortless.

Pacing keeps students engaged in learning. One way to create the illusion of effortless learning is to change the pace by changing the type of work or activity, the method of presentation, or the way students are grouped. This creates interest and momentum.

Make the breaks between various activities crystal clear to students. Ensuring that activities begin and end clearly gives a positive sense of pace and progress. Give clear timelines for activities, for example five minutes, as this helps students focus on learning at a good pace. This technique is referred to as "bookending" because learning segments are clearly marked by the teacher.

The right pacing is something that gets easier with organization. With organization, lessons can be conducted at a brisk pace and students learn more. A brisk pace of instruction enhances student attention and increases the number of responses and interactions. To keep the classroom running smoothly throughout the year, continuously reflect, evaluate, and assess for flow and learning. If the flow is going well for the teacher, and if the learning is going well for students, then celebrate success.

These are the four elements to pacing effectively.

1. **Have materials ready.** Prepare supplies and materials ahead of time to ensure smooth transitions during the lesson.

2. **Share objectives and lesson plans.** At the beginning of a lesson, post the lesson objectives and outline the lesson plan so that students can independently transition from activity to activity. Pacing is made easy when both teacher and students can see the before, during, and after of a lesson.

3. **Check for understanding.** The key to effective instruction is the teacher's mastery of assessment feedback. If students are mastering concepts quickly, you should move along faster. If they're struggling with something, slow down and incorporate an additional activity to help students make progress. See Chapter 10 and 11 for an assortment of quick assessment tools.

Guided notes	Graphic organizer
Concept map	One-minute note
Exit ticket	Stop and jot
Four corners	Triangle-square-circle

You can use these assessments to speed up or slow down the pace of your lesson.

4. **Allow for downtime.** Allow students to have some time when they can relax and reflect. Structure downtime—it can be independent reading or writing—and make it a part of their routine for a smoother running school day.

When pacing is well executed, it is a valuable strategy for increasing student learning.

7. Strategy of Spaced Practice

As students acquire new skills or information, there can come a point where what they have learned can be easily forgotten unless there is a strategy used to improve retention and long-term memory. The strategy is called spaced practice which entails repeated exposures over several days. Key to this strategy is the repetition of concepts. The opposite of spaced practice is massed practice, which involves cramming study into one extended session.

Students learn more when practice is spaced out, not massed together.[2]

When studying for a test, are you better off tackling small bits spaced over a week or will you do better cramming the day before the test? Consider the research if you are a golfer and want to improve your putting. Two groups were given two hundred and forty trials. One group putted all the trials on one day,

with a short break after each block of ten. The other group did sixty trials each day over four consecutive days. Result—the group that spaced the trials was more successful and putted better.

To achieve better results in any discipline, the technique of spaced practice helps concentration and maintaining energy levels.

In a nutshell, spaced learning involves splitting up learning into lots of short sessions, rather than a few long ones. Key to this technique is the repetition of concepts. This improves long-term learning and memory as it prevents students from forgetting what was learned over time. This practice continues until concepts are crystallized in the minds of students.

When you teach something, you want students to remember what you taught them. That is where the strategy of spaced practice comes in. The concept of spaced practice is familiar to most teachers and students. Many of us first heard the advice from our mothers, "Honey, why not study an hour today and an hour tomorrow instead of doing it all the day before the test?"

Spaced practice or spaced learning involves splitting learning into lots of short practice sessions.

In the science class that **Harry Wong** designed for his vulnerable students, he chunked lessons into small

---

[2] Sean H. K. Kang, "Spaced Repetition Promotes Efficient and Effective Learning: Policy Implications for Instruction," *Policy Insights from the Behavioral and Brain Sciences* 3, no.1 (January 13, 2016): 12–19.

bits, paced each concept, and went back to review and practice each of the concepts so students could more readily store the learning. **Jerome Bruner's** research found students must see how knowledge is organized and then practice for more permanent learning. Building on Bruner's research, additional research comes from **John Hattie's** *Visible Learning*:

Students often need three to four exposures to the learnings—over several days—before there is reasonable probability they will learn.[3]

Influences with Positive Effects on Student Achievement[2]		
Influence	Effect Size	Page
Teacher estimation	1.62	18
Collaborative impact	1.57	250
Self-reported grades	1.33	143
Teacher clarity	0.75	239
Reciprocal teaching	0.74	201
Feedback	0.70	89
Direct instruction	0.60	28
Spaced vs. mass practice	0.60	192
Mastery learning	0.57	235

Spaced practice has an effect-size of 0.60, making it an effective strategy that produces results.

You know the old adage, "How do you get to Carnegie Hall?" You practice. But you space your practice. People who perform at Carnegie Hall, and athletes who succeed, all space their practice. They do not wait until the day before a performance to rehearse and practice and expect to perform well. **Spaced practice leads to better learning than does massed practice.**[5] The goal of spaced practice is to attain mastery and retain knowledge. Most everyone has crammed for a test only to forget most everything shortly thereafter. The "forgetting curve" shows how fast information is lost when it is acquired with massed practice.

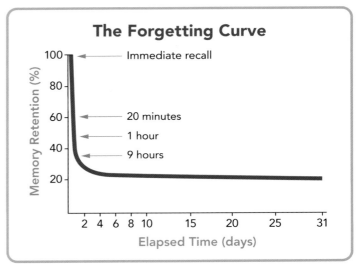

The forgetting curve is based on the research of German psychologist **Hermann Ebbinghaus**. In 1885 he published *Memory: A Contribution to Experimental Psychology* in which he showed that unless information is reinforced, there will be exponential loss of memory.

The purpose of spaced practice is to help students learn and retain learning.

In a study on spaced learning with eight seventh-grade pre-algebra classes, half of the classes studied linear equations and proportions using the spaced practice method, while the other half learned graphs and slopes using the mass practice method. At the end of the semester, the students who learned the material via the spaced practice method scored 72 percent, while the students who learned the material via the mass practice method only scored 38 percent.[6]

Most sports coaches know that spaced practice will get the same kind of results. It is better to have more frequent short practices than to have long practices; that is, two workouts a day is better than one. It's more

[3] Hattie, *Visible Learning.*

[4] *Visible Learning,* "Hattie Ranking: 256 Influences."

[5] John Dunlosky, Katherine A. Rawson, Elizabeth J. Marsh, Mitchell J. Nathan, and Daniel T. Willingham, "Improving Students' Learning with Effective Learning Techniques: Promising Directions from Cognitive and Educational Psychology," *Psychological Science in the Public Interest* 14, no. 1 (January 8, 2013): 4–58.

[6] Doug Rohrer, Robert F. Dedrick, and Sandra Stershic, "Interleaved Practice Improves Mathematics Learning," *Journal of Educational Psychology* 107, no. 3 (2015): 900–908.

effective to keep coming back to the information or skills rather than to prolong practice for a long period of time during one session.

Do not be concerned with the precise time spent teaching segments as this does not have a great impact on learning. Instead, these techniques will help students learn.

◆ Keep lessons short. Cover three to five skills, facts, or concepts per lesson. If there is more to be covered, all you need to do is split up your long lesson into a series of small lessons. This is the very essence of spaced practice.

Practice Makes Perfect

For students to be good at something, they need two things—instruction and practice. The only way for students to learn to write well is by writing, rewriting, and rewriting again. For students to learn how to read well, they need to read and read and read. They become better readers only if they read.

It's no different from how they learn to play a musical instrument, perform CPR, or make successful jump shots. They need teachers, coaches, parents, and mentors who will see that they practice consistently. It's practice, practice, practice. Practice makes perfect and leads to success.

◆ Expose students to the same content three or four times, usually over several days.[7]
◆ Stagger new learning between the practice.
◆ Give students three spaced, short review or practice assignments paired with a short quiz that is correlated to the lesson objectives. Ask the same questions from previous lessons to reinforce learning.

How to Use Spaced Practice

◆ Teach the subject matter.
◆ Wait (days, weeks, or months).
◆ Provide a review activity.
◆ Go over the results, correct errors.
◆ Reteach and review again as necessary.
◆ Give a comprehensive or cumulative test.

Examples

Homework Assignments
Give a review activity as a homework assignment. Go over the results and give feedback to correct any errors, otherwise students will continue to make the same mistakes on the cumulative test.

Quizzes
Give quizzes at spaced intervals to refresh key content and to give students practice in retrieving information.

Review Games and Contests
Make the review activity fun and engaging:

Review Game
◆ Divide the class into two teams.
◆ Ask a question to one team and pick a person to answer. If the person answers correctly, the team gets a point. If not, the other team gets a chance to answer.
◆ Ask the other team the next question. Alternate between teams.

---

[7] Graham A. Nuthall, "The Cultural Myths and Realities of Classroom Teaching and Learning: A Personal Journey," *Teachers College Record* 107, no. 5 (May 2005): 895–934.

- ◆ Simply keep score by tallying one point for each correct answer.
- ◆ Have students who seem to know all the answers read the questions or keep score so others participate more often.

Review Contest

- ◆ Divide the class into two teams.
- ◆ One member of each team goes to the board.
- ◆ Ask a review question and have students write the answer.
- ◆ The person who writes the correct answer first gets a point for their team.

Student Pair Reviews

Make the review an interactive, cooperative activity:

Student Pair Reviews

- ◆ Have one student ask another a set of questions.
- ◆ Record the number of correct answers.
- ◆ Switch roles. Use the same questions but the other person answers.
- ◆ Continue this process. The object is for students to improve their own score each time.
- ◆ Have students graph the results, if appropriate and meaningful.

Spaced Practice in Orchestra

Nile Wilson teaches orchestra in an organized way commonly used by many elementary, physical education, fine arts, culinary arts, and foreign language teachers.

- ▪ Nile explains the name (objective) of the piece of music and leads the orchestra in playing a small section of the music, making assessment comments as the students play the piece several times.

- ▪ Each section of the orchestra practices the same section and receives guided practice instruction, if necessary.

- ▪ For independent practice or homework, the students are assigned to play the same section by employing "mindful practicing" techniques—the use of strategies that allow our brain to work harder while doing repetitive tasks. In the same way that marathon runners train at higher elevations than the actual race course, expert "practicers" set themselves the task of using more brain power when practicing to avoid falling into the trap of mindless repetition. One strategy that is used on passages with many moving notes is varying the rhythms during each repetition of the passage. After several rhythmic variations, the musician then reverts to the original rhythm.

Because Nile's classes meet every other day, the students have a day in between the next rehearsal to fine tune their practicing. At the next rehearsal session, the orchestra plays the same section again, but this time an additional, or even a new piece, is introduced so students will not be bored with playing the same thing over again. She and the orchestra can sense improvement as the entire piece of music comes together, all because of spaced practice.

There are usually six to eight weeks between each concert. During the first week of rehearsals, Nile's priority is for students to read the whole piece and know its overall structure. During the second and third weeks, students learn notes and rhythms and work out any instrument technique issues. During the fourth and fifth week, Nile goes into more detail with phrasing, balance, and cleaning passages that are still not accurately performed. By weeks six and seven, students are ready to practice transitions within and between pieces and run the whole program before the concert.

8. Strategy of Interleaving

When students space their learning over a period of time, they will recall 10 percent more than if they studied the same information all at one time. However, there is another strategy of learning that is even more effective. Here the student jumps from related topics over a period of time, weaving the learning together. **This strategy is called interleaving.**

Instead of the traditional method of block learning, where students cover one topic at a time, interleaving works on the basis of mixing things up in smaller, randomized chunks, switching between and revisited at intervals throughout the year. When interleaving, it's not necessary to focus learning in an orderly sequence. The only stipulation is that what is studied must be related.

While cramming information the night before a test might help pass the test, there is a good chance that students will not retain what was crammed during that time. A study has shown that students who used interleaving practice were better at recalling information a few days later.[8]

Progress may seem slower initially, but long term retention is improved through interleaving a subject. How often have you had an "Aha" months or years after learning something?

How to Interleave Worked Examples

A powerful strategy to help students solve problems in math and science is to provide examples of worked problems for them. Alternate the worked examples with problems that students solve on their own. This five-step process of interleaving has been proven to produce better results on math tests.

1. Model an example problem (or problems) similar to the ones students will solve.
2. Include all the steps and the correct answer.
3. Provide copies for students.
4. Alternate, or interleave, the worked examples with problems that students solve on their own.
5. As students make progress and grasp the skill, provide fewer worked examples.

Homework Assignments

If the homework assignment is to find the solutions to the odd-numbered problems, provide worked examples of the even-numbered ones.

Story Problems

Lessen the worry associated with story problems by giving students worked examples of similar ones.

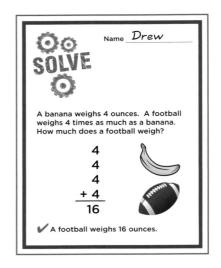

Beginning a Lesson

Show students a worked example at the start of a lesson. This gives them a model of what they will be doing and what it should look like in the end.

During Large Group Instruction

When teaching problem solving to a large group, occasionally put a worked example on the board and discuss the steps.

40

Kansas Teacher Examples

Karen Rogers shows how to use spaced learning and interleaving.

[8] Kelli Taylor and Doug Rohrer, "The Effects of Interleaved Practice," *Applied Cognitive Psychology* 24, no.6 (September 2010): 837–848.

9. Strategy of Retrieval Practice

Prior knowledge has long been considered the most important factor influencing learning and student achievement. Consequently, teachers and students alike can benefit from taking time before instruction to identify what is known or, more accurately, believed to be known about a topic.

Planning and instructional time is dedicated to accessing preexisting knowledge. If lack of prior knowledge is not retrieved, students may fail to correctly grasp new concepts or give up on a subject or task altogether.

Retrieval practice is not rote memory, or reviewing content that has just been covered in class, or rehearsal where you are repeating what you already know. Rather, it is becoming aware and remembering information that was previously learned, perhaps long ago. Retrieving information is enhanced if the information was spaced and interleaved with feedback to embed it in the mind.

Learning is influenced as much by students' prior knowledge as by the new instruction they receive.

Background knowledge is the basic building block of content and skill knowledge.

Connections to prior knowledge are the synapses that link old and new information. This relationship building can be brief or in-depth as long as it enhances continued learning. Learning ultimately begins with the known and proceeds to the unknown. Connecting everyday experiences with classroom topics and intentionally engaging preexisting knowledge with new classroom content can help promote a meaningful and lasting learning outcome.

These teacher techniques can be used to enhance retrieval practice.

♦ Simply asking students what they know about a topic before reading or instruction can raise achievement. See how **Brad Volkman** does this in his class every day (page 102).

♦ Exercise retrieval practice with mnemonics (page 189), flash cards, daily quizzes that are not graded, summarization, or a concept map (page 115) where key words are used to help remember something in its larger context.

10. Strategy of Combining Graphics with Words

Graphics are visual representations used to help students learn. Graphics include diagrams, pictures, graphs, charts, symbols, illustrations, animations, and videos. To maximize learning from visual aids, simply discuss them or use words to verbally describe them.

The strategy of combining graphics with words works better than just studying text, looking at a diagram, or verbally explaining a concept. The key to this strategy is the pairing of visual and auditory information.

It is a simple process. Select a good visual representation of the concept you wish to teach. Then take time to discuss it with your students. If there are written words or captions, read them out loud. If it is a video or animation, pause it and discuss the key points.

When visual aids are discussed, it gives teachers information on student learning and thinking. It provides an opportunity to clarify main points and promote deep thinking about key ideas.

Using a visual aid to show the development of a seed from planting to sprouting to maturation will help students recall the steps.

These are steps for combining graphics with words.

- Select a visual for the concept to teach.
- Verbally discuss it with students by asking them questions about it.
- Highlight relevant parts of the diagram while describing them.
- Listen to feedback from students.
- Clarify key points and correct any errors.

These are typical questions that promote thinking.

- What is in this picture?
- What does this diagram show?
- What does it mean?
- Is something happening or going to happen?
- Are there any captions or written explanations?
- What do they say?

Time, and Practice, Makes Perfect

Effective teachers will spend about twenty-three minutes of a forty-minute period demonstrating, modeling, questioning, working and giving many examples, checking for understanding, and providing sufficient instruction and practice so students can learn to work independently without difficulty. **Students in these classes are successful because they are told what they are to learn and then shown, modeled, and taught how to learn what is to be learned.**

41

Strategies for Instruction

Read about the ten, research-based strategies for instruction.

Mastering Instruction

 Effective teachers employ research-based instructional strategies and techniques to motivate and inspire students.

 Effective teachers get to know their students and create lessons that address their strengths and weaknesses.

 Students learn more when lessons are appropriate to their level of learning and have continuity to previous lessons.

 Students acquire knowledge and understanding when new material is chunked and scaffolded logically.

 Students learn more when teachers pace lessons and allow ample time for students to practice and master new material before more material is introduced.

...Produces Achievement!

How to Use Guided Practice

> *Guided practice encourages collaboration and gives students the support they need to reinforce learning.*

"We Do" Comes After "I Do"

- You have a set of standards and objectives. (Unit B)
- You have a lesson plan. (Chapter 14)
- You know how to deliver the lesson. (Chapter 15)
- You have a set of strategies to effectively teach the lesson. (Chapter 16)

Teaching begins with **I do**. The "I" is **you**, the teacher, and your task is to prepare the lesson and deliver it.

You research standards, become familiar with curriculum guidelines, and are aware of what classes in the year before and the year after yours are aiming to accomplish.

- **You** prepare objectives, assessment, and instruction that are aligned as per The Learning Triangle to create lesson plans that have integrity.
- **You** decide what strategies are most appropriate and effective for delivering the lessons.
- **You** present and explain what will be learned so students are active participants in your lesson plans from the outset.

Then, after you have taught the lesson, it is time for **We do**, when students and teachers work together to reinforce the learning. Students practice what they are learning, often in collaboration with their peers, while the teacher is present, ready to assess and assist. **This is guided practice, the subject of this chapter.**

Reinforce the Learning

> **"An ounce of practice is generally worth more than a ton of theory."**
>
> E. F. Schumacher

Kimberly Keesling teaches middle school in Lafayette, Indiana, and has a lesson where the objective is to make students wary and aware of loaded words and emotional responses. The guided practice activity she uses is based on a well-known hoax that started out as an April Fool's Day joke concocted by the *Durand Express* in Michigan.

She begins by distributing a fact sheet that lists the data about a mysterious substance called dihydrogen monoxide, or DHMO for short. She explains to students that they are going to have a debate about DHMO, and they have to use facts to support their arguments for or against banning it.

Is DHMO Dangerous or Not?
Ban the Chemical Dihydrogen Monoxide or Not?

- Prolonged exposure to solid DHMO causes severe tissue damage.
- Used in pesticide production and distribution.
- Contributes to soil erosion.
- Exposure decreases effectiveness of automobile brakes.
- Ingested by elite athletes to improve performance.
- Causes death when accidentally inhaled in small quantities.
- DHMO is a major component of acid rain.
- Gaseous DHMO can cause severe burns.
- Leads to corrosion and oxidation of many metals.
- Helpful as a spray-on fire suppressant and retardant.
- Used in the production of Styrofoam.
- Used in the production of baby food and beer.
- Found in biopsies of pre-cancerous tumors and lesions.
- When it contaminates electrical systems, it often causes short-circuits.
- Associated with killer cyclones, hurricanes, and blizzards.
- DHMO is a suspected contributor to the El Niño weather effect.

**Students learn by practicing the learning.
The learning is enhanced
if there is a teacher to guide the learning.**

Guided Practice

Guided practice is exactly what it says—students practice what has been taught while the teacher observes, assesses, and guides them to do it correctly.

Hands-On Is How to Teach

How often have you had someone try to teach you a computer technique while you stand and the person sits in front of the monitor, hands flying over the keyboard, and then says, "See how it's done?" Umm . . . not really.

If someone tries that on you, simply say, "I'll sit in front of the monitor. Now you tell me what to do and watch me do it, hands-on."

It's the same in class when you say to a student, "Carmen, can I show you some keyboard shortcuts?" Using guided practice, you instruct her how to bold words, italicize them, and underline them. And while the student actually does it, you guide and supervise.

Several weeks later, you'll notice that students don't need to refer to the table outlining shortcuts. They have been using them when necessary—spaced practice (Chapter 16)—and the shortcuts have become part of their long-term memory.

Whether it's studying algebra or painting a portrait, the more opportunity for practice there is, the better a student will learn the lesson objectives. Learning will be enhanced and reinforced, and practice will be even more effective, when there is a teacher guiding the process.

Guided practice is what coaches, conductors, and directors do. They do not teach simply by telling or giving the athletes or performers a set of instructions to follow. They train by helping them to perform the right motions and organize a sequence of actions in the precise manner. They correct faults again and again and insist on repetition until performances achieve a measure of perfection. This applies to any endeavor, whether it be physical, intellectual, or artistic. This is what skillful teachers do when teaching reading, writing, math, foreign languages, and all other subjects.

In guided practice, students practice what has been taught while the teacher observes, assesses, and guides them to do it correctly.

Lesson Plan for the Week of:		Teacher:		Subject:	Grade:
	MONDAY	TUESDAY	WEDNESDAY	THURSDAY	FRIDAY
Content Standard(s)					
Learning Target(s) (What students understand, know, or demonstrate at the end of the lesson)					
Instructional Strategies (What you do so students achieve the learning target)					
Assessment (How you use formative and summative tools to know if students met the learning target)					
Evaluation (How you use summative tools to test for reaching the learning target)					
Bellwork (What students do upon entering the classroom)					
Guided Practice (What students do with your assistance to boost the learning target)					
Independent Practice (What students do independently to reinforce the learning target)					

This "Lesson Plan Template" was created by Karen Whitney, Principal, Sisseton Middle School, Sisseton, South Dakota, and modified by Harry and Rosemary Wong.

It has been emphasized again and again that effective teachers don't simply tell or give students a set of instructions to follow, or a textbook, or random activities, and expect learning to happen automatically through some magical, mysterious process. Teaching and learning both require effort and collaboration. Teachers must learn to assess, explain further, and encourage. Students must be in an environment where they are willing to try and fail, ask questions, and try again until they achieve what is required so they can progress to the next stage.

It goes without saying that whether it's studying algebra or drawing a picture, the more practice students have, the better they will learn and the more adept they will become. **Practice cements new learning into long term memory.** Practice makes what has been learned "second nature." And what makes it all possible is a skillful teacher taking an active role guiding students so that each time they try, each time they practice, they will be better.

**Practice and teacher guidance
are the keys to learning.**

Reciprocal Teaching

Several different strategies and techniques involving guided practice were explored in Chapter 16. There is another very effective strategy you can introduce when students are starting to feel confident with lesson objectives and procedures. It takes guided

Influences with Positive Effects on Student Achievement[2]		
Influence	Effect Size	Page
Teacher estimation	1.62	18
Collaborative impact	1.57	250
Self-reported grades	1.33	143
Teacher clarity	0.75	239
Reciprocal teaching	**0.74**	**201**
Feedback	0.70	89
Direct instruction	0.60	28
Spaced vs. mass practice	0.60	192
Mastery learning	0.57	235

The effect size of reciprocal teaching is 0.74, making it a major strategy for learning.

practice to another level because you teach your students how to teach each other and learn together. It is truly collaborative learning. The strategy is called reciprocal teaching and has an effect size of 0.74.

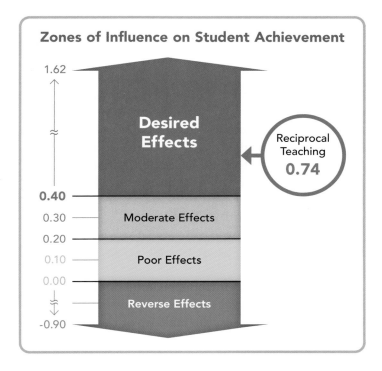

Reciprocal teaching is also called reciprocal learning. After all, that's what the word "reciprocal" means—something shared or done similarly on both sides. Thus, **reciprocal teaching is something we teach together and learn together**.

Reciprocal teaching is an instructional strategy in which students do some content area reading and then take responsibility for leading an academic conversation within a group. Within a reciprocal teaching group, each student is primarily responsible for the use of one strategy. There are four different strategies that students utilize in reciprocal teaching:

1. Predicting
2. Questioning
3. Clarifying
4. Summarizing

[1] *Visible Learning*, "Hattie Ranking: 256 Influences."

In reciprocal teaching, the role of students is reversed as they become teachers of reading strategies. They take turns coaching and guiding each other, doing the reading, answering questions, and solving problems, while helping their partners reach the correct answers on their own. **At the same time, the teacher is monitoring and guiding the strategy and even joining in, when necessary.**

Like other classroom activities and procedures, reciprocal teaching must itself be taught and practiced. **Predicting, questioning, clarifying, and summarizing are not typically intuitive to students. It is therefore incumbent on the teacher to ensure that students have ample opportunities to understand, learn, and rehearse the responsibilities of each role they will play and how they will collaborate.**

Implementing Reciprocal Teaching

After each strategy is introduced, explained, and modeled, opportunities must be provided for guided practice. Depending on the makeup of the class, learning each strategy might be done in one day, two days, or more. Each could become the "skill of the week." What is important is that students master each strategy—not the amount of time it takes to do so.

Here are the steps to implementing reciprocal teaching and learning in your classroom.

- Divide students into groups of four.
- Open a text or distribute copies of the reading selection to each group. Select a text that provides opportunities to practice each of the four skills—predicting, questioning, clarifying, and summarizing.
- Distribute a worksheet that shows and explains each of the four skills. They can also be shown using a Fab Four Dial.
- Explain and model each of the skills as you analyze a similar story.
- Assign one of the four roles—Predictor, Questioner, Clarifier, or Summarizer—to each student in the groups of four. Each student is

responsible for leading the discussion about the reading selection with his or her assigned skill.

- As you proceed, rotate students in their roles.

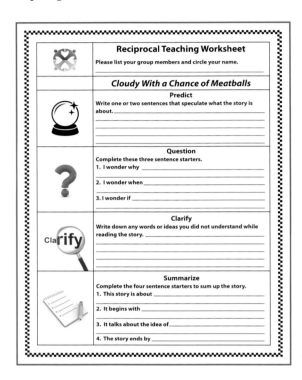

The Fab Four Dial can be used during whole-class discussion or guided reading groups. An enlarged version can serve as a wall chart. Or use the back of a paper plate to show the four skills. Insert a brad and a pointer in the center that is turned as the strategies are discussed.

42

Role Cards

Use these role cards to help students with the responsibilities of the Predictor, Questioner, Clarifier, and Summarizer.

1. Predicting

The predicting strategy greatly increases students' awareness of, and familiarity with, trends and cause-and-effect relationships. During the course of the school year, they can often see the same concepts repeated multiple times.

The act of predicting reinforces student learning and increases the rate at which content is learned as the school year progresses.

Predicting is done prior to and during reading. Observations are based on scanning subheads, charts, graphs, captions, and other supplemental material. Predictions should be based on what students have read and are reading, not random thoughts.

Students use this strategy to discern what will happen next; that is, what the short- and long-term outcomes will be of the events they are reading about. The student selected as the Predictor fills out a guide designed for this purpose prior to and during reading.

Another advantage of predicting is that it familiarizes students with the organization of a text. Learning these basic features is a skill which will serve students in their academic lives and into the future.

The Predictor opens the discussion with his or her observations on what the passage will be about. The group then reads the text, stopping when they have reached a specified point (perhaps a certain paragraph or the end of the section). The Predictor again facilitates a discussion (not a lecture) of predictions based on the content just read.

The process repeats until the entire text has been read.

2. Questioning

The use of questions broadens students' learning of the content. By asking and answering certain questions, opportunities are provided for students to see events in their context, rather than seeing them in isolation. They should use evidence contained in the reading as a basis for developing and defending positions taken as answers to questions.

Questioning is done as students read the text. As the reading is in progress, the Questioner writes down questions as he or she thinks of them. After the Predictor has concluded his or her discussion, it is the Questioner's turn to take the lead. There is no limit to the questions that can be asked.

Questioning also enables students to connect present learning with previous learning which, in turn, will make it easier for them to grasp concepts in the future. Finally, the questioning strategy can force students to examine to what extent the current content has an impact on their lives today. They may be surprised by what they discover.

3. Clarifying

Clarifying addresses any confusion or uncertainty students may have about the meaning of certain words, phrases, paragraphs, or even entire readings.

The Clarifier is responsible for recording not only anything that he or she doesn't quite understand, but any points that other members of the group might find tricky. Clarifying is done as needed during or after the reading.

When reading aloud within a reciprocal teaching group, it is useful for students to have a discreet signal, perhaps as simple as raising their hand, to signify that they have a need for clarification. Some teachers find that it is beneficial to allow the group to pause for immediate clarification, while others prefer to defer for later discussion. Whenever it is done, the Clarifier is responsible for facilitating a discussion—after the Predictor and the Questioner—to clarify whatever material was unclear.

Sentence Starters

Predicting
- I think that _____ will happen because . . .
- I don't think that _____ will happen because . . .
- I wonder if . . .
- Since this happened, then what if . . .

Questioning
- What did you mean when you said . . . ?
- Do you think that . . . ?
- Can you tell me more about . . . ?
- Why is that happening?
- What is happening?
- Why do you think that way?
- What is another way to look at this?
- Why doesn't the character do this instead?
- Why is this justified?
- How do these events impact the world?
- What if these events were to happen again?

Clarifying
- Now I understand _____ because . . .
- No, I think it means . . .
- I agree with _____ because . . .
- I disagree with _____ because . . .
- I want to go back to what _____ said.
- At first I thought _____, but now I think _____ because . . .
- That is confusing because . . .
- What I hear you saying is . . .
- I don't understand _____, but I do understand _____ because . . .
- Could you please repeat that for me?
- Could you please explain a bit more?
- Could you please say more about that?
- What's your evidence?
- How does that support our work or mission at . . . ?

Summarizing
- This reminds me of . . .
- This is like _____ when . . .
- This is like _____, but different because . . .
- That is a good idea because . . .
- I was thinking about what _____ said, and I was wondering what if . . .
- This makes me think . . .
- I want to know more about . . .
- Now I am wondering . . .

Once students have become proficient at identifying where clarification is needed, they can turn to the next step, strategies to achieve clarification. Each of the following skills are at the disposal of the Clarifier:

- Rereading the section they did not understand
- Continuing to read, while looking for context clues
- Reflection—what *could* this mean?
- Discussing with other students

4. Summarizing

Summarizing is an important strategy as it helps to promote student retention of the material. It helps them grasp the big ideas. It helps them "connect the dots" and evaluate and draw conclusions from what they have read.

Summarizing is an important strategy for concluding reading and discussion. Even while the Predictor, Questioner, and Clarifier are performing their duties, the Summarizer can begin to summarize the reading.

There is no need to wait until everyone is finished to summarize—the process can start as the discussion is progressing. The summary should be short, but to the point. There is no need to be lengthy.

Summaries don't have to be written statements. Students can create a reenactment of an event, draw a timeline of activities, or even make flashcards of terms that need clarification.

Each of these strategies involves a summarization of the content, and each, in its own way, can effectively promote student retention of the material. When the Summarizer creates a timeline, it can serve as a useful visual aid. Flashcards, too, are summary aids that foster memory.

Reciprocal Teaching

Kentucky teacher **Jeff Gulle** reports how he uses reciprocal teaching in his history lesson.

Accountable Talk

Accountable talk is a strategy used to teach students how to communicate respectfully.

Accountable talk is a structured discussion that builds conversational skills—speaking and listening skills—in the classroom. It teaches students to be "accountable" for what they say—to take responsibility for what they say—and to be able to support what they say with evidence. Accountable talk helps students reflect on their learning and communicate their knowledge and understanding. It creates a collaborative learning environment in which students feel confident in expressing their ideas and opinions.

Research shows there is a strong correlation between talk and learning in school. However, just having students speak in class does not necessarily result in learning, or in the constructive exchange of ideas, or in expanding verbal and intellectual capabilities. For classroom talk to truly promote new learning, teachers need a procedure to teach students to talk and participate in discussions in a respectful manner.

Guiding *how* students talk and *what* they talk about is key to creating an accountable talk classroom. To help do this, place prompts around the classroom as anchors or visible reminders for students to always use appropriate language and helpful forms of discussion when in class. Over time, with teacher support, students will incorporate these prompts as norms in peer discussions.

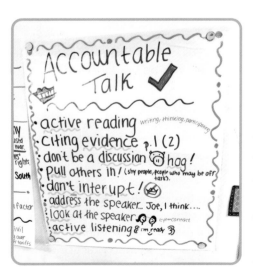

Amanda Bivens of Dyersburg, Tennessee, created Accountable Talk posters to help remind her students to use appropriate language and behavior in discussions.

An ideal way to model accountable talk is during Read Aloud Time. During accountable talk, the teacher selects the reading, but the students discuss the reading with minimal interference from the teacher, except when guided practice advice is needed. Through accountable talk, students are active members of their learning community, learning to agree and disagree with one another's thoughts and points of view about a text. Accountable talk promotes both active reading and listening, and the teacher becomes a guide for discussion when guidelines for students to follow are in place.

Implementing Accountable Talk

Accountable talk is taught by using a series of sentence starters. Provide students with a selection of sentence starters that are appropriate for your class and for the reading you will give them. There is an extensive list of suggestions that you could consider, with far too many of them to use at one time.

Amanda Bivens only uses five to start teaching the strategy of accountable talk.

- I disagree with that because . . .
- I agree with that because . . .
- I still have questions about . . .
- I want to add to what (student's name) said about . . .
- Based on my evidence, I think . . .

To provide a basis for accountable talk, Amanda uses a strategy in her classroom called "Noticings and Wonderings."

Noticings are facts students notice from the text. Emphasize that non-fiction noticings will be different from fiction, but they are still to be noticed. Encourage students to include the big ideas in their noticings, pull in text features, and try to tie in whatever weekly skill they are working on.

Pro or Con DHMO?
A Fishbowl Debate

During guided practice, another procedure for engaging students in a structured conversation is called the Fishbowl Debate. This is an activity where students teach each other and learn together.

Kimberly Keesling teaches middle school in Lafayette, Indiana, and has a lesson where the objective is to make students wary and aware of loaded words and emotional responses. The guided practice activity she uses is based on a well-known hoax that started out as an April Fool's Day joke concocted by the *Durand Express* in Michigan.

She begins by distributing a fact sheet that lists the data about a mysterious substance called dihydrogen monoxide, or DHMO for short. She explains to students that they are going to have a debate about DHMO, and they have to use facts to support their arguments for or against banning it.

Students are given five minutes to ask questions, study the fact sheet, and write out talking points supporting one side or the other. Those in favor of banning DHMO go to one side of the classroom; those against banning it go to the other. The Undecideds sit in the middle.

These are the ground rules for the Fishbowl Debate.

- Three people—volunteers, one from each group— go to the front of the room—the fishbowl. Using their notes and fact sheets, students take turns presenting their point of view about DHMO.

- When a speaker finishes, if another student wants to support that point of view, he or she taps the speaker on the shoulder and the first speaker sits down. In that way, only three students at a time are at the front of the room. The teacher doesn't take a position during the debate, being present only to see that the procedure is being done properly.

Middle schoolers love to talk, love to debate, and Kimberly's students did so brilliantly. Their arguments for and against banning the mysterious substance were cogent and fact-filled. Some students were direct and succinct; others became quite animated. Within fifteen minutes, just about everyone in the room had spoken. Impassioned and powerful statements were heard.

- Although it is used to generate power . . .
- It's a risk, but life is about risk.
- Bottom line, it kills people!

Sophisticated stuff for seventh graders. At the end, Kimberly asked how many students had switched sides because of the arguments they heard. Some had.

Then she made the "big reveal"—DHMO is water.

Can you imagine the class smacking their forehead and having a big laugh because they had been fooled? She broke the scientific words down into their roots and prefixes: di—(2); hydrogen; mono—(1); oxide. Students caught on—H_2O.

Why, she asked students, had they come down on the side they had? What followed were insightful responses that boiled down to the persuasive influence of strong, emotional words such as "kill, severe tissue damage, found in tumors." It was easy to be led to a conclusion. And that was Kimberly's teaching point. **Scientists have to investigate dispassionately. Scientists have to examine the facts. Scientists have to ask questions. They can't be swayed by emotional language.** Everyone needs to think before they jump to a conclusion about something they know nothing about.

The Fishbowl strategy had the students out of their seats moving and talking. They took ownership of the lesson. It was a life lesson that will remain in their memory of school activities, a great **"We do"** guided practice activity.

Wonderings are questions students have about the text. Encourage students to ask both strong questions (higher level thinking questions from Bloom's Taxonomy) and weak questions (questions with answers found directly in the text). To encourage this, provide students with question stems to use as they learn to ask strong questions.

◆ To model the structure for writing noticings and wonderings, have students divide a sheet of paper into two columns and write "N" on one side and "W" on the other.

◆ Have students practice noticings first, and then follow with wonderings. You want to spend several days to teach them the importance of each before combining them.

◆ Practice sharing with sentence stems using noticings. Amanda's students sit in a circle and each shares a noticing. This gets them familiar with sharing and allows Amanda to do some modeling with "adding on." For example, a student's noticing may be "Abraham Lincoln was the sixteenth president." Amanda will say, "I'd like to add on to Anna's noticing. Abraham Lincoln was the sixteenth president and was president during the Civil War."

◆ Once you have spent several days and weeks practicing, provide students with a text and have them record their own noticings and wonderings. Amanda starts off by giving students the task of finding two noticings and two wonderings.

Although accountable talk is not a process that yields immediate results, it is most worthwhile because you start to hear students using accountable talk language outside of class. You can see it in action in the hallway, at recess, and in the cafeteria.

Accountable talk is a maturing process. When students learn how to listen and talk respectfully; when they learn how to articulate what they notice and wonder; when they learn how to have meaningful conversations and constructive dialogues, they will be prepared to meet the challenges presented by life and any future career.

Accountable talk prepares students for success in the adult world.

> *I can't emphasize enough how much my students enjoy it, and everyone who comes in to watch it does as well. It encompasses so many different things. It makes students say, "Yay!" about reading. It is golden!*
>
> Amanda Bivens
> Dyersburg, Tennessee

The Value of Communication and Collaboration

When employers are asked about the skills they value in potential employees, most often they will say, "The ability to communicate verbally with people inside and outside the organization." It is our responsibility to help students *grow as talkers*. All of our students—especially the quiet ones—must learn how to communicate, collaborate, and present their ideas effectively. Accountable talk and reciprocal teaching are structured—even the most reluctant students will be encouraged or forced to speak. They will be supported as they learn the conventions and etiquette they need to progress and achieve.

Everyone must learn to express themselves. To be successful in this world, a person must be able to communicate, articulate, and have the ability to approach a stranger and ask for directions, make a request, or seek information.

If you can't speak up for yourself; if you can't muster the courage to tell people in a meeting that equity and civility are important; if you can't advocate for your own safety; if you can't express your thoughts and feelings, the world will be a very overwhelming and frightening place.

The strategies and activities discussed in this chapter are an excellent way to teach your students not to be intimidated by the people they interact with and the situations they encounter. They will light up as they learn to engage in constructive, stimulating conversations that will empower them to make an impact with their words and ideas.

Mastering Instruction

 The strategy of guided practice is based on "We do."

 In guided practice, students practice what has been taught while the teacher observes, assesses, and guides students to do it correctly.

 Reciprocal teaching gives students the skills to collaborate and help each other learn.

 Accountable talk is a strategy used to teach students how to participate in discussions in a respectful manner.

 Students who are given the opportunity to master communication and collaboration skills will be prepared for success.

...Produces Achievement !

How to Use Independent Practice

The end goal of teaching is to guide and support students so that they are able to take responsibility for their own learning.

Seeking Independence

One could say that throughout most of our lives, we are all at various stages of trying to achieve and maintain independence of one sort or another. We learn to eat on our own with a spoon, then we learn to prepare the food we eat; we learn to walk, and then we can go wherever we want to go; we acquire language, and then we are able to say whatever we need to say.

It is our nature as human beings to need a lot of guidance as we mature and prepare for adulthood. Teachers are actively involved as guides during some of the most essential times in students' development. Every teacher wants to give their students the skills, knowledge, and assurance they need to face a very complicated world. Every teacher wants to unlock their students' talents and imagination so that they can lead fulfilling lives.

Every teacher wants to nurture independence and initiative so their students have control over their futures.

Independent practice is when students are given the opportunity to practice and demonstrate what they have just learned. It is when they acquire the confidence and ability to produce work that shows their mastery. It follows direct instruction—**I do**—and guided instruction and practice—**We do**.

Independent practice is "You do."

Turning Learning into Action

> **Learning is creation, not consumption. Knowledge is not something a learner absorbs, but something a learner creates.**
>
> George Couros

Americans toss about 25 percent of the food they bring home from the store amounting to approximately $165 billion worth of waste a year. At the same time, up to fifty million Americans are "food insecure"—they don't always know when, where, or how they will source their next meal.

The Community Assistance & Resource Effort (CARE) Closet[1] is an on-site, high school food pantry program that was established by sixteen-year-old twins **Lauren** and **Grant Seroyer**. After a classmate asked for some of her breakfast one morning, he confided to Lauren that he did not have enough food to eat at home and that he and his siblings had to take turns eating dinner each night.

Lauren shared this information with her brother. They asked the school administration if they could have a food pantry in the counseling office so that students could discreetly fill backpacks with food for students in need to take home to their families. All agreed to their plan and the CARE Closet was born.

---

[1] www.carecloset.org

Gradual Release of Responsibility

The gradual release of responsibility is a research-based instructional model where the responsibility for learning and task completion shifts gradually over time from teacher to student.[2]

After guiding students through a lesson to meet learning objectives, and then showing them strategies for collaborating with their peers, the next stage is having them tackle work independently. This is when students truly internalize learning and use what they have learned in their own unique way. It is the ultimate goal of attending school—to prepare students to leave the nest and fly.

There comes a time when the teacher can gradually release students so they become responsible for their own learning.

Independence Needs Guidance

Gradual release of responsibility is not the same as personalized or individualized learning. In personalized learning, students determine their own curriculum, where and when to learn, and at their own pace. In gradual release of responsibility, students are responsible for completing the curriculum tasks and objectives that have been determined by the school or teacher.

Lesson Plan for the Week of:		Teacher:		Subject:	Grade:
	MONDAY	TUESDAY	WEDNESDAY	THURSDAY	FRIDAY
Content Standard(s)					
Learning Target(s) (What students understand, know, or demonstrate at the end of the lesson)					
Instructional Strategies (What you do so students achieve the learning target)					
Assessment (How you use formative and summative tools to know if students met the learning target)					
Evaluation (How you use summative tools to test for reaching the learning target)					
Bellwork (What students do upon entering the classroom)					
Guided Practice (What students do with your assistance to boost the learning target)					
Independent Practice (What students do independently to reinforce the learning target)					

This "Lesson Plan Template" was created by Karen Whitney, Principal, Sisseton Middle School, Sisseton, South Dakota, and modified by Harry and Rosemary Wong.

Gradual Release of Responsibility

I Do
Teacher Mode

The teacher provides background information and vocabulary.

The teacher states the objectives of the lesson.

The teacher shows models and examples.

The teacher generates interest with questions or an anticipatory set.

We Do
Class Mode

The teacher provides hands-on experience and practice.

Students are working in guided practice.

The teacher checks for understanding and provides feedback if necessary.

Students begin to learn how to self-assess.

You Do
Student Mode

Students work together or in independent practice.

Students use rubrics to self-assess their progress.

Students produce an outcome to show mastery of the objective.

Students collaborate with classmates to share outcomes.

Guiding to Independence

When your child plays in a piano recital, you know that what you are finally hearing is a result of months or even years of guided practice coupled with disciplined independent practice. Students who

[2] P. David Pearson and Margaret C. Gallagher, "The Instruction of Reading Comprehension," *Contemporary Educational Psychology* 8, no. 3 (July 1983): 317–344.

want to remember and cement what they learn must continuously practice, and they need teachers who help them refine their practice.

So do not be misled by the word independent. Independent practice doesn't mean that students are working in isolation with no external input. They still need an effective teacher as much as ever. They still need correction, encouragement, assessment, collaboration. They still need guidance. Humans don't go from being a chrysalis to a butterfly in one magical moment. Becoming an efficient, independent learner so that one is able to achieve one's goals and aspirations is a lifetime endeavor.

As has been emphasized throughout this book, the components of a lesson plan based on The Learning Triangle—objectives, assessment, and instruction—are not a sequential list. They are not taught singly and in a certain order. They are all related to each other and have coherence. They are equally essential components of a whole. They fit together, work together, and form an instructional design model with integrity.

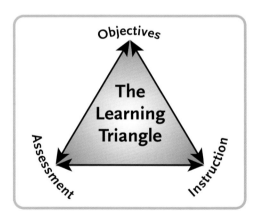

Effective teachers manipulate the lesson plan framework as needed. When teacher and students are engaged in independent practice, it does not mean that the teacher's job is done—that is, students can be ignored and left to their own devices. The teacher still steps in, as often as necessary, to modify instruction and offer assessment and guided practice help—always keeping the focus on the lesson objectives.

Practice Makes Progress

Doctors and dentists practice medicine and dentistry, and they will jokingly say that they practice what they do so as to do it better and better.

When **Pablo Casals,** the preeminent cellist of his time, was asked when he was over ninety years old why he still practiced every day, he said, "Because I am making progress."

Stephen Curry of the Golden State Warriors has been voted twice as the Most Valuable Player by the National Basketball Association and the only player to be selected unanimously the second time. His practice sessions are legendary. He says, "I can get better. I haven't reached my ceiling yet on how well I can shoot the basketball."

Those who are very good at what they do know that they can always be better.

During guided practice, and then independent practice, students learn to be more and more proficient with self-assessment techniques. (Chapter 13) Gradually, eventually, they refine their awareness so they no longer need be dependent on the teacher's assessment and can take responsibility for learning into their own hands—and minds.

> **Students need to learn from teachers and be informed about their progress, but eventually they need to be challenged to work independently and collaboratively.**

The Importance of Independent Practice

For learning to be retained, it must be practiced. Practiced, repeated, and rehearsed, over and over again—however long it takes—until it is transferred from short-term memory to long-term memory and made available for lifetime use. Practice leads to proficiency. In planning each day's lesson, the bulk of class time should be devoted to guided and independent practice for students to take possession of and retain the learning.

Effective teachers create independent learners.

Who is doing all the practice and work in class? **John Hattie** says that, in many schools, students come and watch the teachers work. In an effective teacher's classroom, the stage has been set so that it is students who are doing most of the work. Students are provided with the stability and consistency they need to fully engage in independent practice.

Practice Makes Perfect Projects

Class books	Letters to resources
Architectural plans	Mock trials
Art objects	Models
Community service projects	Podcasts
Documentaries	Portfolios
Essays	Photo albums
Films or plays	Poster presentations
Instruction manuals	Research projects
Simulations	TV or radio programs
TED Talks	Word clouds

The effective teacher creates a classroom where
- objectives are clear,
- procedures are in process, and
- instruction is strategic.

As stated, however, students still need your expert guidance. When time is given to students to "freely" and independently produce results, some will be distracted, or uncertain, or find other things to do. The teacher needs to be fully present and alert, ready to support individuals as they work.

- Monitor students by walking around the classroom, pausing to observe individuals at work.
- Use specific praise when you see effort (perfection is not the goal).
- Post examples on the document camera to show what is being achieved.
- Remind students that what they are doing is preparation for college and adult careers, where independent practice, confidence, and responsibility are rewarded and essential.

Examples of Independent Practice

Just as independent practice is what students do to demonstrate mastery of lesson objectives, it is also the time when effective teachers demonstrate their ability to create challenging, purposeful activities that foster and nurture student independence.

The ideal form of independent practice is an activity or work that has been specifically created with the intention of furthering lesson objectives and what has been done in guided practice. There are many types of independent practice activities that can be considered, depending on the lesson and age appropriateness of the students.

The time it takes for independent practice should be as flexible as possible because projects and activities can take differing amounts of time. This is why independent practice is often called "open work time" to allow students to spend several days if needed. Students learn at varying rates, but it is best to make independent practice as thorough, purposeful, and meaningful as it can be for everyone. This approach will help ensure students improve thinking, organizational, and practical skills over time.

Devise, suggest, and offer a multitude of ways to practice what has been taught. Be ready to provide proper modeling, materials, and high expectations so that all students can participate with confidence and enthusiasm and experience successful learning.

The most beneficial aspect of independent practice, even more important than the outcome of the project itself, is when students are encouraged to articulate and analyze these four aspects of the process when the work is done.

1. What was the goal of the project?
2. What were the challenges as the project proceeded?
3. Is there still work to be done?
4. What did you learn and what did you accomplish?

Centers in the Classroom

Projects and activities can take many forms and this chapter will present a few examples of independent practice that you can use to create your own. But before students begin independent practice, you need to start by creating the best learning environment possible for projects and activities to take place.

In the 1960s, the fad in education was the open classroom and open schools, but the concept failed.[3] Then, there was talk over thirty-five years ago that schools should be deconstructed and designed like shopping malls so that students could participate in whatever classes that took their fancy.[4] That was another untenable idea.

However, you can use the concept of a shopping mall within the confines of your own classroom by creating centers. The Internet is full of ideas for different kinds of centers for all grade levels and all subject matter.

Learning centers are defined areas within a classroom where students focus, enrich their learning, and practice their skills.

They can be called centers, corners, stations, or hubs. Whatever the name, they are areas where students can go, alone or with a partner, to do their own work, create what they desire, do research, experiment with ideas, and invent and make things. They are stimulating places in the room that have been designed in purposeful ways with resources available for students to use their initiative and further their learning.

The Reading Center is one of the most common centers found in classrooms. From Book Corner to Literature Lounge, it goes by many names. The important thing is that it be a calm, comfortable area of the classroom dedicated to books and reading.

---

[3] Geoffrey James, "9 Reasons That Open-Space Offices Are Insanely Stupid," *Inc.com*, February 25, 2016.

[4] Larry Cuban, "The Myth of 'Failed' School Reform, (Part 1)" [Blog Post], *Larry Cuban on School Reform and Classroom Practice*, January 10, 2017, https://larrycuban.wordpress.com/2017/01/10/the-myth-of-failed-school-reform-part-1-2/.

Learning centers tend to evolve based on the needs of the teacher and students. Some teachers have an area set aside for art projects. Others have a space reserved for students to work on computer skills. Sometimes, a learning center is used to store supplies for certain tasks. The types of centers in your classroom should provide whatever is needed to engage your students in meaningful independent practice.

Assorted Working Centers

Whiteboard Center	Writing Center
Science Center	Math Center
Computer Center	Art Center
Independent Reading Center	Puzzles and Game Center
Fluency Center	Dance and Drama Center
Vocabulary Center	Finding/Inquiry Center

Centers can be created in large or small spaces. You can create them with something as simple as a small table and chairs, or with a shelf and a few tubs or boxes. Some teachers place kits, or baskets, of learning materials on student desks rather than in a designated area in the classroom. Be creative and set them up however it works best for you.

Learning centers save time and give students a sense of ownership. They make learning and working in your classroom much more organized and enjoyable. They send a message that you want your students to excel. Teachers in your school may already have some form of learning centers in their classrooms. Use their ideas as examples and create your own. Here are some suggestions for types of centers:

- **Art and Crafts.** For students working on creative projects, set up an area that has construction paper, glue, scissors, markers, crayons, string, yarn, pipe cleaners, cotton balls, Popsicle sticks, duct tape, and wiggly eyes. You may want to avoid glitter.

- **Nature Center.** Students love a class pet. A hamster, goldfish, or a betta fish are easy to maintain. Class pets provide a shared bond among students regardless of their cultural background. Plants do the same thing—have a cactus or succulent or grow something from a bulb. If you don't want any living things in your classroom, you could still make an interesting nature center with shells, feathers, gemstones, crystals, dried leaves and flowers, bones, pine cones, acorns, eucalyptus pods, and the like.

- **Hands-on Area.** Students like touching things. Provide a shelf or an area with content related items (nothing valuable) that they can touch. If you are teaching a lesson about oceans, for example, get a jar of sand, several different shells, a sand dollar, a crab claw, dried seaweed, driftwood, a seahorse, and other types of objects from the ocean.

- **Project Display Area.** Maybe a student wrote a great poem, or drew a beautiful picture, or made a wonderful model of DNA. Put their work on display for others to appreciate.

- **Photo Board.** Use a bulletin board or other designated area and decorate it with photographs of students working on projects in your classroom. Or, ask them to bring in pictures related to the current lesson. Use their pictures to add interest and spark discussion.

- **Presentation Center.** Create a place that looks like a newsroom studio. Provide a desk, two chairs, and maybe a background. Students can give presentations, conduct interviews, host talk shows, or make videos related to lesson content.

- **Drama and Film Center.** Create a place with a box of unusual pieces of clothing, hats, glasses, gloves, belts, costume jewelry, and other accessories. Students can create, present, and film skits related to lesson content.

- **Model Station.** Provide a designated area with materials for students to create models such as balsa wood bridges, aluminum foil boats, craft stick buildings, or nuts and bolts robots.

Students like being innovative in an experiential space where they can focus on and show mastery of lesson objectives.

Managing Learning Centers

Learning centers need structure and organization. Create procedures for students to follow while participating in the centers. Explain the purpose of the center and teach the procedures for each one when students are first using them. Monitor activity until you feel secure that they know the routines and how to maintain order.

1. **Explain the purpose of the learning center.**
   This is the Arts and Crafts Area. When you are working on creative projects, making and designing things, you might need supplies like glue, scissors, construction paper, markers, and tape. This is where you can work and create.

2. **Explain the procedure.**
   You may use any of the items in the center when you need them. Make sure to return the supplies exactly where and how you found them stored because they are shared. If you run out of glue or if something breaks, please let me know.

3. **Practice the procedure.**
   We are going to make a poster. We will use supplies from the Arts and Crafts Area. You are welcome to help yourself to whatever you need. Remember to follow the procedure and put everything away exactly where you found it when you finish working. I will check at the end of the class period.

4. **Rehearse the procedure as needed.**
   You normally do a great job taking care of the Arts and Crafts Area, but I noticed that scissors were put into the box of markers, and I found garbage in some of the kits. There is a procedure that everything is put away properly and garbage goes into the trash can. Please remember to follow the procedures so we can all work efficiently.

Allow time for students to clean up. Give feedback and specific praise for keeping it neat, clean, and well organized. If you don't allow time for cleanup, the bell will ring and students will rush out the door leaving things in disarray. A good closure activity is to stop early and ask, "What did you learn today?"

More Strategies and Techniques

Aside from what students do in learning centers, there are myriads of other ways that can be used to effect independent practice.

Graphic organizers can be used for total class direct instruction, as guided practice, or, for the purposes of this chapter, as independent practice. The effective teacher knows how to use an organizer in all content areas and with students who are at different levels of reading comprehension.

A graphic organizer incorporates both text and pictures to visually represent concepts, knowledge, or information. Examples include calendars, maps, Venn diagrams, and flow charts. Graphic organizers allow students to see important relationships and patterns:

- ◆ **Alike and Different Diagram.** This makes use of a Venn diagram so students can see similarities and differences in defined spaces when comparing items.

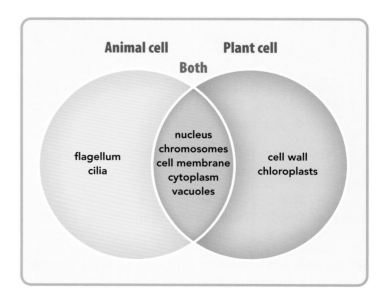

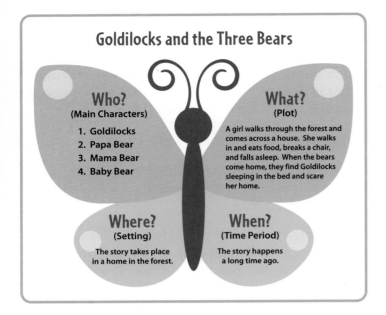

- **Story-Elements Butterfly.** A butterfly-shaped graphic organizer is intended to make identifying the four elements of a story—setting, time period, main characters, and basic plot—easy, likeable, and unintimidating.

- **Student Books.** Students writing and publishing their own books demonstrate mastery of the writing process. As a hook, show some books students have created and published in the past. There are companies that publish student-created books. The process is free and parents can purchase the published books with no obligation, but you can also do it easily in your own class at no cost.

Discuss the differences between fiction and non-fiction books. Then let students work alone or in pairs to produce a book of their choice.

Model the creation of a book by walking them through the process:

- Step 1: Pre-write
- Step 2: Write a draft
- Step 3: Revise
- Step 4: Edit
- Step 5: Illustrate
- Step 6: Publish

When the books are finished, organize a book-signing party. It's a gratifying example of independent practice.

- **Cycle Illustrations.** Translating words into pictures becomes a visual representation of a student's understanding of a concept and can oftentimes lead to deeper investigations into the topic, if so desired. Change one step in the cycle and that becomes a point of inquiry with the ramifications. Students become the investigators, the creators, the discoverers of new information.

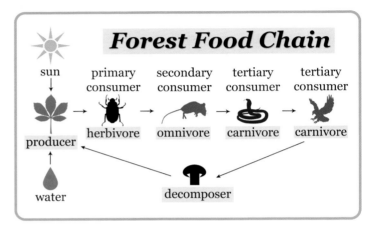

What would happen to our forests if there were no herbivores to eat the plant matter? Cycle illustrations show how everything is interconnected.

- **Genius Hour.** The purpose of independent practice is for students to individually demonstrate knowledge and proficiency of lesson objectives. This independent work can be extended using an activity called Genius Hour. Genius Hour is appealing to students because the title refers to them as geniuses. It gives them the autonomy and inspiration to pursue a genius idea of their own.

The concept of Genius Hour can be traced to tech companies such as Google where employees are encouraged to spend up to 20 percent of their time working on projects they are personally passionate about. Company management learned that by allowing people to work on things that interest them, productivity and creativity go up. This can happen in the classroom, too.

During Genius Hour, students are in control. They choose what they study, how they study it, and what they do, produce, or create through self-directed learning. They have the freedom to explore their own curiosity while still having the support systems of teacher and classmates. They often begin by articulating an essential question related to lesson objectives that they are interested in pursuing. They can spend several weeks researching the topic before they start creating a product that will be shared with the class. The products they create are personally meaningful and can even be inspirational for others.

The teacher provides a set amount of time for students to design their own learning and work on their projects. The time allotted should follow the 80/20 rule and be no more than 20 percent of the time set aside for the lesson. Deadlines are limited and creativity is encouraged. Throughout the process the teacher facilitates the projects to ensure that students are on task.

Time is then allocated for students to share what they have been working on with the entire class. Students benefit from seeing what others have done and having their projects discussed and validated by their peers. Grading of the project should be based on the process of the research rather than the end product. A rubric could be designed for this purpose.

Research Projects as Practice

Oretha Ferguson, English teacher in Fort Smith, Arkansas, and coauthor of ***THE Classroom Management Book***, transforms independent practice into independent research projects. She posts the content standards and learning objectives so students can see how they relate to the project they are about to undertake.

- ◆ I can research answers to a set of questions.
- ◆ I can gather relevant information and synthesize multiple sources on a subject to demonstrate understanding of the subject.
- ◆ I can assess the usefulness of each source in answering research questions.

Cycles, Phases, and Rhythms

Edward **Russel Dewey** was an economist who devoted his life to the study of cycles, claiming that, "Everything that has been studied has been found to have cycles present." He studied more than five hundred different phenomena in thirty-six different areas of knowledge and he found a rhythm to the many cycles.[5] This partial listing of topics lends itself to cycle illustrations, but also opens the door for further investigations.

Human development	Agricultural cycles
Butterflies	Photosynthesis
Lunar phases	Food chains
Animal migrations	Water cycle
Circadian rhythms	Business life cycle
Sleep cycle	Musical interval cycle

44

Extending the Learning

See how a teacher uses the food chain to extend students' learning beyond independent practice.

- ◆ I can write the results of my research, and avoid plagiarism. (It may be appropriate to explain what plagiarism is and how to avoid it.)
- ◆ I can create visual displays and use digital media to enhance understanding of presentations.
- ◆ I can present information so that listeners can follow my line of reasoning.

There are an infinite number of possibilities when it comes to independent practice research projects to teach content standards. Oretha uses one about

---

[5] Edward R. Dewey, "The Case for Cycles," *Cycles,* July 1967.

Independent Practice in Action

The Community Assistance & Resource Effort (CARE) Closet started as an independent practice school activity. CARE Closet is an on-site, high school food pantry program that was established by sixteen-year-old twins **Lauren** and **Grant Seroyer**. After a classmate asked for some of her breakfast one morning, he confided to Lauren that he did not have enough food to eat at home and that he and his siblings had to take turns eating dinner each night.

Lauren shared this information with her brother and they decided to ask the school administration if they could have a food pantry in the counseling office so that students could discreetly fill the backpacks with food for students in need to take home for their families. All agreed to allow them to do so and the CARE Closet was born.

It occurred to Lauren and Grant that there were probably students in other schools that were struggling as well. They contacted the counseling departments at various high schools and found out that every school had a percentage of homeless students. With this discovery, they requested and received permission to create CARE Closets in these schools with the understanding that the food distribution would be completely confidential. Their efforts have resulted in the national expansion of the CARE Closet concept.

Most importantly, other young people have been inspired to give back to their communities in creative and meaningful ways.

leadership called The Power of Voice. She begins by having students discuss and answer these essential questions to frame their research.

- ◆ Who are the people who have a positive influence in today's world?
- ◆ How do their voices and opinions impact the society in which we live?
- ◆ What is a leader?
- ◆ What does it take to be a leader?
- ◆ What are the qualities of a leader?
- ◆ What makes some leaders more successful than others?

From this discussion, a student or a group of students choose an influential leader to research and demonstrate how that person's voice and opinions impact the society in which we live. This person can be a political leader, a religious

leader, a well-known author, a speaker, or an activist. She steers students away from entertainers unless they can seriously justify their choice.

Students can create a presentation using PowerPoint or Google Slides. In whatever way it is done, the presentation needs to include the following information:

- ◆ Name, birthdate, and nationality of the leader
- ◆ A picture of the person
- ◆ The person's accomplishments
- ◆ How this person contributes to humanity
- ◆ The personal sacrifice this person makes for his or her cause
- ◆ Quotes that reflect the mission and character of the leader

This lesson can be divided into two parts: research and technology. Students need time to decide on a leader, research facts, and create the presentation. Allow approximately one week to complete the assignment, or more time if an area of research, or assimilating information, or avoiding plagiarism needs additional focus or practice.

Each student must contribute to researching and presenting the information. The presentation should be smooth, organized, thoughtfully planned, and enthusiastically presented. Oretha distributes the rubric to help them self-assess their work. She explains the categories and how to interpret them to arrive at their level of progress:

- Picture of person
- Quote
- Music option
    - Delivery of presentation
- Art option
- Originality
- Content

45

Independent Study Rubric

Download **Oretha Ferguson's** The Power of Voice rubric to use with your students.

For students who want to go beyond the expected outcomes, Oretha offers them optional opportunities and research extensions to enhance their work:

- **Music option.** Incorporating music in projects gives band, orchestra, choir, and musically-inclined students the opportunity to use their talents across the curriculum. Students find or create an appropriate tune or melody and write original lyrics from researched information. The song should include two verses and a chorus to express factual information explaining who the leader is and his or her benefit to humanity. An easy-to-use music creation tool for this optional extension is UJAM, but students can use any tool or app to assist them. The music may be performed live, burned to a CD, or saved to a flash drive.

- **Art option.** Students use artworks, other than photos of the person, that portray the person's mission. Art expresses important ideas—students can include, for example, a painting by a well-

known artist and describe how the artwork reflects the leader's voice in society. Students should include the title of the artwork as well as the artist's name, and where it can be found in a museum of art (more practice in research). For example, show students famous paintings such as *The Problem We All Live With* by Norman Rockwell, *The Starry Night* by Vincent van Gogh, or *Landscape With the Fall of Icarus* by Pieter Bruegel and discuss lives that could be reflected in these paintings.

- **Extension Research Activity 1.** In this related, extension activity, students work independently or in small groups to research, keep a journal of their work, write a collaborative report, and present their findings on this essential question— What is a leader?

    - What influential events and personal qualities are significant in a leader's life?
    - Are these qualities similar across different times and cultures?
    - Is there a correlation between being an influential leader and possessing all or part of these qualities?
    - What guidelines can you offer for becoming an influential leader?

- **Extension Research Activity 2.** In this extension activity, students create the questions, design the rubric, and determine the criteria to be included in the project. For The Power of Voice activity, this is the essential question, "What is the role of leaders in today's society?"

Effective Learners

You have now brought your students to the point where they have the necessary skills to take responsibility for their own work and assess their own progress. You have prepared them for a fulfilling future because independent practice, which gradually becomes more and more independent, is the art of teaching your students how to learn. It's when they muster and coalesce the learning they have to further their learning and to find their voice, their talents, and their strengths.

In today's world, people do not have careers where they do one thing again and again year after year. People nowadays are expected to continuously learn, change, and adapt.

When you impart learning how to learn to your students through focused, constructive independent practice, you give them the ability to access possibilities and opportunities for the rest of their lives.

> **When students learn how to learn, they have the power to take control of their lives.**

However, the stress of grades still haunts most students. All of the good you achieve by involving students in lesson planning, reinforcing and extending their learning through guided and independent practice, can be eliminated during the evaluation phase of your lesson.

The process you use for providing grades for lessons is extremely important. Students are affected by what grades they achieve because that's how they feel rewarded and validated, and judged and humiliated. They are concerned that their livelihoods and future possibilities are determined by grades. Grades can motivate them. They can also severely discourage them.

It is possible for evaluation to be a positive experience. Learn how to do it in Chapter 19.

Mastering Instruction

 The end goal of effective teaching is for students to take responsibility for learning.

 Independent practice is when students have the opportunity to coalesce what they have learned to complete and produce a product that shows mastery of lesson objectives.

 The classroom should be designed to be a place that promotes independent practice.

 Teaching independent practice is teaching students how to learn.

...Produces Achievement!

> *To ensure student success, align tests to learning objectives and grading to mastery of the objectives.*

Evaluation Versus Assessment

There is great confusion in educational circles between assessment and evaluation. Many people misuse the word assessment thinking it means testing. It does not. As has been stressed in Chapter 8, assessment is what a teacher does to monitor and provide feedback to assist a student in making progress towards the learning objectives.

Assessment is for learning.
Evaluation is for testing and grading.

Evaluation is testing. It is listed after objectives, instructional strategies, and assessment, but this does

Lesson Plan for the Week of:		Teacher:		Subject:	Grade:
	MONDAY	TUESDAY	WEDNESDAY	THURSDAY	FRIDAY
Content Standard(s)					
Learning Target(s) (What students understand, know, or demonstrate at the end of the lesson)					
Instructional Strategies (What you do so students achieve the learning target)					
Assessment (How you use formative and summative tools to know if students met the learning target)					
Evaluation (How you use summative tools to test for reaching the learning target)					
Bellwork (What students do upon entering the classroom)					
Guided Practice (What students do with your assistance to boost the learning target)					
Independent Practice (What students do independently to reinforce the learning target)					

This "Lesson Plan Template" was created by Karen Whitney, Principal, Sisseton Middle School, Sisseton, South Dakota, and modified by Harry and Rosemary Wong.

She Uses *Informances* to Evaluate Her Students

> **Because my students know what is expected of them, they are free to imagine and explore in an environment of trust and equity.**
>
> Laurie Kash
> Rainier, Oregon

Laurie Kash is not only the Student Services Director for her district in Oregon, she also teaches English, writing, world literature, basic theater, advanced theater, and alternative education arts classes at the high school.

Each year, she typically directs two mainstage productions and two showcases—over the years, she has directed over fifty theatrical productions and showcases.

How can Laurie have students eagerly come and work show after show, year after year?

It is because she teaches her students how to consider the feedback they are receiving without becoming defensive. This allows the evaluation to run smoothly and in a safe environment where everyone grows.

She calls her evaluations "informances"—informal, informed performances.

not mean, in any way, that evaluation is the last thing that a teacher does or thinks about. In fact, **determining the evaluation component must be done early while planning a lesson because every test question must be aligned to a learning objective.** The test should be written soon after the objectives are written or soon after guided practice. **Tests are used to determine if students have or have not accomplished and comprehended the stated objectives of the lesson.**

Don't Test What You Didn't Teach

Lesson objectives tell students what they will learn, what will be taught, and how they will be tested. Don't test what you didn't teach, and don't teach what you won't test.

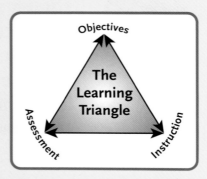

Objectives

The Learning Triangle

Assessment

Instruction

As you write lesson objectives, think about the test that will follow to ensure that every test question you write is aligned to an objective.

Tests and objectives are inseparable. Effective teachers use learning objectives to guide their teaching; they frequently check to see if students are mastering the objectives; they assess student work and provide feedback to assist students in the learning. When students are ready, they give a test. After the test, they give students opportunities to correct (or enrich) their knowledge of the objectives.

Students should be told at the beginning of an assignment, lesson, or unit that the test has already been written and that every test question is correlated to lesson objectives. **There is one main reason for giving a test—to monitor and evaluate if students have mastered the learning objectives.** If there are

no objectives, do not test students. If there are no learning objectives, there is nothing to test, measure, assess, or evaluate. That would be like the Department of Motor Vehicles (DMV) not telling you what you need to know before you take your driving test. A test is simply a tool that gives students an opportunity to demonstrate whether they have, or have not, met the learning criteria.

If it was not taught or experienced,
do not test students.
If it is to be tested,
it needs to be taught or experienced.

In a classroom, the effects of incorrectly writing and administering tests are serious and potentially devastating. When students do not have a clear idea of the evaluation criteria, this hinders not only their motivation and love of learning, but also their potential and future success. Tests should not be mysteries or nasty surprises. A test should never be given to punish, humiliate, rank, label, sort, segregate, confuse, or assert power over students. These practices harm relationships, endanger futures, and they do absolutely nothing to promote student learning.

Formative Versus Summative Tests

There are two forms of tests that can be administered to students—formative and summative. As with evaluation and assessment, the differences between formative and summative tests are important to clarify. It is important to understand the purposes of both and essential that students understand how they are used.

Formative tests are aligned with assessment. **The purpose of a formative test is to check and correct, check and correct, check and correct.** Formative tests are practice tests or low-stake quizzes. Formative tests give students an opportunity to practice using new knowledge and skills in a risk-free environment. They are the dress rehearsals, not the opening night.

Formative tests are given to students
while their knowledge is *forming* or developing.
They are used for checking, not grading.

A practice quiz, a run-through of a performance, a practice problem, a review activity, and a rough draft are examples of formative tests. Use them to determine what remediation is needed to help students master the objectives. Tell students when they are taking a formative test that they are used to help them achieve success on the final evaluation or summative tests.

Summative tests are given at the end of a unit to sum up what the student has learned and then used to determine a grade.

Summative tests are aligned with evaluation. They can be chapter tests, unit tests, or comprehensive exams. A summative test is like a final essay; it is not the rough draft. With the results of a summative test, you will know how well you taught your students to have or have not mastered the learning objectives.

Testing for the Wrong Reasons

Teachers who use ineffective teaching practices will cover the material, give a test, give grades, and then move on to teach the next topic. They use tests to sort, punish, reward, rank, label, and even hoodwink students. Students have to guess what the most important points of the lesson are, what they are supposed to know and do and, worse yet, how they will tested or evaluated. They spend time being confused, anxious, and overwhelmed—not learning.

Avoid these four pointless testing practices that are commonly used by ineffective teachers:

1. The passage of time. Do not write and schedule a test because progress reports are due in a few days or because "Oh, two weeks have gone by; it's time for a test." Time intervals have nothing to do with student learning. Students need time to learn, practice, and master the learning objectives before they take a test. If grades have been scheduled, create assignments and tests to fall within the pre-determined grading period.

Not: You will be tested this Friday. Why?

The Value of Daily Quizzes

A group of memory researchers at Washington University in St. Louis conducted a study that validated the findings from earlier research in the 1930s. The study concluded that quizzes given at the end of every class session are the best way to help students retain what they've learned.[1]

Called the "testing effect," the daily quiz method, if done correctly, is very effective at implanting learning in students' minds. Quizzing forces students to retrieve and apply facts from their memories and enables them to become more fluent and confident with the material. **Brad Volkman,** described in Chapter 9, uses this method.

2. Material covered. Do not write a test because you covered the material. Tests should not be given because a certain volume or amount of content has been presented. The specific criteria found in the learning objectives determine when students are to be tested. There are several ways to check for student learning to determine when they are ready.

Not: You will be tested on everything that has been covered. Why?

3. Grading on a curve. Do not write a test to rank or compare students. There has never been anyone who has ever recommended grading on the curve. Grading on a curve hinders cooperation and harms relationships. A test is written for students to demonstrate individual mastery of the learning objectives, not for them to be sorted, labeled, and pitted against each other.

Not: You will be graded in comparison to the entire class. Why?

[1] Henry L. Roediger, III and Jeffrey D. Karpicke, "Test-Enhanced Learning: Taking Memory Tests Improves Long-Term Retention," *Psychological Science* 17, no. 3 (March 2006): 249–255.

4. Class period to kill. Do not write a test to take up the whole class period. The length of the test and the number of questions should be determined by the learning objectives. A well-designed test is written for students to complete tasks and questions related to the objectives. It is not determined by the length of a class period.

Not: The test will take up the entire period. Why?

Testing for the Right Reasons

Every student wants to earn good grades. Just as you want to know where you are going before beginning a trip, students want to know what to expect when it comes to being evaluated and earning a grade at the end of the lesson. It is extremely important to have the right approach when testing to ensure it is a beneficial and constructive experience for both teacher and students.

Tests are diagnostic. They are not tools of terror. They tell the teacher how well the subject was taught, and they tell the student how well they learned the subject.

Tests evaluate instruction. There are many ways to teach. Some strategies are more effective than others. Tests help teachers determine which strategies are the most effective. They help teachers make modifications to their instruction.

Tests correct and remediate problem areas. A well-designed test specifically measures and determines whether students have met the learning objectives. Very few people learned to ride a bike without falling a few times. Every good cook has burned a meal. Students need time to practice using a new skill. Sometimes they need more than one opportunity to demonstrate mastery.

The Importance of *Earning* Grades

In the recent past, one of the main purposes of schooling was to prepare students for the discipline and standards required in an increasingly industrialized world. Grades were a seemingly efficient system to sort and select the best workers of the future.

Today it is different. Many people are more likely to work in a digital world where thinking, flexibility, initiative, and creativity are valued. There is no justification for using grading to sort and label students.

This is what we know about grades.

◆ **Grading is not essential for teaching and learning; checking for learning is.** Grading can mean labels and judgment. Checking for understanding is diagnostic.

◆ **Grades have very little value as rewards and no value as punishments.** Giving low grades does nothing to motivate students to work harder.

◆ **Grades should be determined in reference to the learning criteria.** Establish the student's mastery of the learning objectives, and then provide a grade or score that is earned.

Proper and professional grading is serious business that must be done correctly. Students and their families live and die based on the grades they receive. Their future entrance into a university may well depend on the grades they receive in class. Grades are meant to report student progress toward learning goals—giving students, teachers, and families useful information on what modifications need to be made to achieve these goals.

> Ineffective teachers GIVE grades.
> Effective teachers have students EARN grades based on learning the objectives.

Some teachers assign grades based on their own beliefs and experiences, such as, "This looks like a B- paper," "This looks like it can be done better," "This is a great A paper to me," or "Your score is average compared to the rest of the class." Personal opinions are not consistent with good evaluation research, effective classroom practices, or school grading policies. Grades can affect relationships and future options for students. Nearly every person can tell a story (or several) about a time when they felt they were graded unfairly.

With well-defined learning objectives, students become responsible for mastering the objectives. They have power and control over their grade because they know what they are to achieve and how they will be evaluated. They should no longer have to worry about teacher bias or subjectivity. Students can earn good grades and have positive relationships with their teachers. For this to happen, learning objectives and grading criteria must be well-defined. The evaluation criteria are based on an earned grade which makes things easier for students, parents, and administrators to understand. A teacher's teaching is for mastery, not test scores.

Nobody is judging you;
you have the means to judge yourself.
This is the message an effective teacher
conveys to students.

Do Not Give Zeros

This statement might come as a surprise, but never give a student a zero, especially if you use a 100-point grading scale. Why not?

A zero distorts the average. To recover from a single zero, a student must get a perfect score on nine more assignments to mitigate the effect of one zero. Do the math and you will see how it is almost impossible

The Perils of Averaging

Why do students get low grades? Failure to know what they are responsible for learning— no objectives, no guided practice, and nothing to assess.

Since a teacher's responsibility is to bring students along in their learning, only a student's work in the final quarter should count towards passing a class. For instance, when you ask a doctor, "How am I?" you are not asking for an average since you began treatment. You are interested in hearing the result of the progress you have made.

Grading should reflect mastery at the point of the grading period, not an average of the student's work since the beginning of the school year.

It is time to get rid of averaging because averaging does not give you an accurate picture of the most recent learning. It does not give an indication of what students have managed to achieve despite the challenges they may have faced at the outset. Some schools score harder with percentages than others, and a student shouldn't be punished for not learning a certain skill during the first few weeks of school. Nationwide, a score of 92 in one class is not a 92 in another teacher's class. Students should be graded on whether or not they have met the required skill by the end of the year. If we report

to parents or guardians that their child is meeting the standard, that means the same to every parent of a fourth-grade child.

Unfortunately, some teachers tend to look at grading as a "One shot—either you know it or you don't" event. This fixed outlook results in unfair punitive measures that distort our understanding of what students know and are able to do at a current moment or achieve in the future. Again—**we need to focus less on grades and more on mastery of knowledge and skills.**

Give your students opportunities to learn over a period of time through assessment and formative testing. Don't limit them to one-shot tests that could condemn them to being classified as an average or inferior student.

to recover from one zero, even for the most talented students, much less those who struggle with learning. A single zero can doom a student to failure, regardless of what dedicated, Herculean effort or level of performance might follow.

Students need to know that there are consequences for what they do and do not do in school, of course. Laziness should be penalized, but should the penalty be so severe that students have no chance of recovery regarding their grade?

In a percentage grading system, a zero is the most extreme score a teacher can assign. To move from a B to an A in most schools, for example, requires an improvement of only 10 percent at most, say from 80 percent to 90 percent. But to move from a zero to a minimum passing grade requires six or seven times that improvement, usually from zero to 60 percent or 70 percent.

Teachers Who Fail

"I am a tough teacher; my tests are always hard and I rarely give an A."

Giving an F is not a symbol of rigor and "tough teaching." **Giving an F is a symbol of failure— the failure of the teacher** to be clear and coherent; **the failure of the teacher** to assess and assist; **the failure of the teacher** to support, encourage, and ensure student success.

The purpose of grading is, or should be, to communicate information about students' learning and achievement in school. It is not to punish students in ways that make recovery from a lapse in an assignment impossible.

A zero tells nothing about learning. Why didn't they complete the assignment? Maybe they didn't understand how to do it. Maybe they were absent from class. Maybe they were defiant and refused to complete it. Maybe they did it, but they didn't turn it in. Maybe they were going through some personal trauma. Students must be responsible for doing the work and there should be consequences for not doing it, but there is no justification for punishing harshly with a zero.

A zero is not an effective form of punishment. Giving students a zero generally means there is no hope for completing the assignment, and it gives them no reason to keep trying. How beneficial is it to give them a zero or an F? Not at all. It is damaging, absolutely no learning occurs, and it does not change their behavior. It just demeans them.

A zero is an easy way out. The students don't have to do the work. Teachers don't have to help them complete the assignment. **Giving a zero represents giving up on teaching and learning.**

Grading Fairly and Effectively

What can be done to make grading fairer and more effective so that students are assured that it is always possible for them to make progress? One alternative is to make the lowest grade a 50 on a 100-point scale. On a 100-point scale, if A = 90–100; B = 80–89; C = 70–79; and D = 60–69; F should be 50–59. The lowest grade should be 50, not zero. How can it be justified that an F is 60 points of the scale when all the other grade categories are no more than 10 points each?

These are alternatives for students instead of using a zero or F for fail.

- ◆ Give them an incomplete, or a not yet complete.
- ◆ Provide a time for students to complete missing work.

- Make it a priority to help them get their work done.
- Modify the assignment or break it down into smaller steps.
- Provide resources to help them get it done.

Or, as suggested, it may be best to do away with percentages in grading and use integers or words that indicate proficiency levels instead. In an integer system, students can improve from a zero to a one, rather than from zero to 60 percent or 70 percent. This makes recovery possible. This way a zero won't destroy a grade. It also helps make grades more accurate reflections of what students have learned and accomplished in school.

Another consideration, especially if the rubric is used for formative feedback, is to omit the numbers from the rubric entirely and focus instead on the proficiency. Once students see a score, no matter how temporary it might be, some will internalize that score as final. By omitting the grade from the feedback, students can focus on what needs to be done so that their attempts meet more sophisticated criteria.

Percentage grades are the foundation of many state grading policies. Nearly every online grading program available to educators calculates percentage grades. Yet despite their popularity, percentage grades are difficult to defend from a procedural, practical, or ethical perspective. It is time to abandon grading scales that distort the accuracy, objectivity, and reliability of students' grades.[2]

Thomas R. Guskey

The Rubric Integer System

It cannot be overemphasized that we need to move from a grading culture to a mastery-based evaluation culture. What does a letter grade or a percentage really tell you about student achievement? Not much. Most tests generated in school, often the night before, are taken one time and only provide a snapshot of what students have learned. If a student fails to learn a skill, he or she is forced to accept that result and move on to the next topic with the rest of the class. Students are marched forward, falling further and further behind. A student cannot correct mistakes or relearn the subject matter. Some call it "autopsy testing."

What's the Real Grade?

In 1912, a study by two Wisconsin researchers, **Daniel Starch** and **Edward Charles Elliott**, found that 147 high school English teachers in different schools assigned widely different percentage grades to two identical student papers. Scores on the first paper ranged from 64 to 98, and scores on the second paper ranged from 50 to 97. One paper was given a failing mark by 15 percent of the teachers, yet 12 percent of the teachers gave the same paper a grade of over 90.[3]

The study was highly criticized by those who claimed that judging good writing is, after all, highly subjective. But when the researchers repeated their study using geometry papers graded by 128 math teachers, they found even greater variation. Scores assigned by teachers to one of the math papers ranged from 28 to 95 percent!

In 2011, **Hunter Brimi** replicated Starch and Elliott's 1912 study and attained almost identical results.[4] Brimi asked ninety high school teachers—who had received nearly twenty hours of training in a writing assessment program—to grade the same student paper on a 100-point percentage scale. Among the seventy-three teachers who responded, scores ranged from 50 to 96. And that's among teachers who received specific professional development in writing assessment.

The conclusion? Testing and grading can be highly problematic. But there can be no objections to test scores that are carefully aligned to objectives.

---

[2] Thomas R. Guskey, "The Case Against Percentage Grades," *Educational Leadership* 71, no. 1 (September 2013): 68–72.

[3] Daniel Starch and Edward Charles Elliott, "Reliability of the Grading of High School Work in English," *The School Review* 20, no. 7 (September 1912): 442–457.

[4] Hunter M. Brimi, "Reliability of Grading High School Work in English," *Practical Assessment, Research, and Evaluation* 16, no. 17 (November 2011).

Instead of letter grades, consider moving to an integer or numbered system based on rubrics. Rubrics are an ideal way to show progress in learning because they articulate clear learning targets and levels of proficiency. They make scoring meaningful by telling students exactly why they attained the grade they did and how they can improve. They eliminate punitive grading practices.

Rubrics also give parents concrete information on how their children are actually doing in class. Instead of an obscure letter grade, a proficiency level tells how close a first-grader is to reading sixty-five words per minute or how well a fifth-grader can add and subtract decimals.

Rubrics typically have four proficiencies, each accompanied by a description:
- ◆ 4 = Highly proficient
- ◆ 3 = Very proficient
- ◆ 2 = Partially proficient
- ◆ 1 = Not proficient

Here is another way to describe proficiencies:
- ◆ 4 = Mastered standard—the student can apply a certain skill or concept independently and correctly, showing a higher level of thinking.
- ◆ 3 = Meets standard—the student understands the skill or concept and shows a clear thought process.
- ◆ 2 = In progress—the student cannot completely apply the skill or concept, but has some understanding.
- ◆ 1 = Does not meet standard—the student has no understanding of the skill or concept.

Norm-Referenced Versus Criterion-Referenced Tests

There is no doubt that testing and grading can be highly problematic. However, the crucial factor when testing for mastery of learning objectives is HOW summative tests are graded and how students are evaluated. There are two methods—norm-referenced

A General Scoring Guide				
Criteria \ Score	4	3	2	1
Complete	Assignment is 100% complete. It meets all the criteria on checklist.	Assignment is missing something, but not much. It is not 100% complete.	Assignment is a start. But it misses some of the major criteria on the checklist.	Assignment does not meet the criteria.
Correct	Assignment is correct. There are no errors.	Assignment has one or two errors. Overall, it is mostly correct.	Assignment has several major errors or several minor errors.	Assignment is incorrect.
Quality	Assignment looks good. It shows effort and attention to details. You cared about the quality.	Assignment looks good. It would have been better with a little more effort and attention to details.	Assignment was done quickly. Not much attention to neatness, spelling, or making it look good is shown.	Assignment is sloppy and embarrassing.

Karen Rogers uses this guide to help her students understand how to master the content and improve their scores.

and criterion-referenced. The difference between them is not only significant but can determine whether students are encouraged to achieve and succeed or whether they will feel doomed to a trajectory of failure.

A norm-referenced test is commonly known as grading on the curve. It is designed to rank or sort students in comparison to other students using a normal distribution (bell-shaped) curve. Standardized tests, like a basic skills test, the ACT, and the SAT are norm-referenced tests. If students take a test and are placed in the eightieth percentile, it means they performed as well or better than 80 percent of the students in a previously tested norm group. When teachers grade on a curve, students are ranked, sorted, and labeled. There are a few As (the highest scores), a few Fs (the lowest scores), but most students fall into the B, C, D range, which is considered average.

The grading used for a norm-referenced test divides students into groups of winners, losers, and the mediocre. It tells us nothing about what individual students have actually learned.

When handing back a graded assignment, a teacher who uses ineffective practices may even decide to show the grade distribution to the class—for example, three As, ten Bs, twelve Cs, five Ds, two Fs. Imagine the faces of students looking at the grades and their anguish as they try to figure out where they landed. Norm-referencing can have a very damaging effects on learners' motivation, especially for struggling students. They lose interest and hope. Educational research has shown that when students are tested, ranked, and placed on a curve in third grade, they will typically fall into that same spot on the curve in the seventh and eleventh grades.[5]

> Norm-referenced tests play into a fatalistic mindset that says "natural" student ability, not deliberate effort, determines success.

The purpose of a norm-referenced test is not content knowledge. Norm-referenced testing is of no value in determining mastery of a subject. Such tests actually eliminate important content questions—if there is a question on the test that a majority of students answer correctly, it will get dropped from the test even if it is a key content question. Most norm-referenced tests are developed for large-scale use. Publishers have test banks from which teachers can take questions (for those who do not know how to write test questions). These types of questions fail to consider differences in the curriculum, such as what you taught in your classroom.

Norm-referenced tests don't give opportunities for correction and remediation. They are one-shot tests—given, scored, and the class moves on. The teacher does nothing to evaluate the success of the teaching and learning so as to provide correction and

remediation. Also, if something happens to a student on the day of the test, something beyond his or her control, the test score does not indicate the student's actual ability or knowledge.

Norm-referenced tests results are typically linked to SES—socio-economic status. Students in higher socio-economic groups perform better on norm-referenced tests. Those students have had substantially more resources and opportunities provided to them since birth. How accurately norm-referenced tests measure classroom teaching and learning is debatable.

A criterion-referenced test is based on a set of standards or learning objectives. These tests give students an opportunity to demonstrate mastery of lesson criteria. Students in an effective teacher's

Grades Reflect Lesson Objectives

" *Grades should **always** be based on clearly articulated learning criteria, **not** norm-based criteria. Grades derived from norm-based criteria that indicate students' relative standing among classmates communicate nothing about what students have learned or are able to do. Instead, they compel students to compete against their classmates for the few high grades the teacher will distribute. Such competition is detrimental to relationships between students and has profound negative effects on the motivation of low-ranked students.*[6, 7] "

Thomas R. Guskey

---

[5] Benjamin S. Bloom, "New Views of the Learner: Implications for Instruction and Curriculum," *Educational Leadership*, April 1978 (paper presented as a General Session address 1978 Annual ASCD Conference, San Francisco).

[6] Thomas R. Guskey, "Grades Versus Comments: Research on Student Feedback," *Phi Delta Kappan* 101, no. 3 (October 2019): 42–47.

[7] Thomas R. Guskey, *Get Set, Go: Creating Successful Grading and Reporting System* (Bloomington, IN: Solution Tree Press, 2020).

classroom are well prepared to take the test. There has been continuous feedback and constructive assessment during the teaching of lesson objectives. The concept of criterion-referenced testing has often been regarded as the most appropriate strategy for educators who focus more on teaching students than on comparing them.[8]

My class always has the highest test scores in the school because I have learned to correlate my test questions to the lesson objectives.

A Texas teacher

A criterion-referenced test is used to grade students based on individual mastery of the learning objectives.

Effective teachers write criterion-referenced tests because
  ◆ they are based on specific learning objectives,
  ◆ they have prepared students, through feedback and assessment, for testing, and
  ◆ such tests give all students the opportunity to succeed.

Constructing a Criterion-Referenced Test

There is a standard method of test construction that will make the process crystal clear to students and eliminate much of the anxiety that many students suffer at the thought of being tested. Post the steps in the classroom alongside a sample test as an example so students understand exactly how a test is written, how exactly they are to study, and exactly what it is they are to master.

  ◆ When students understand how the test is written, they know how and what to study.
  ◆ When students know how and what to study, there is less test anxiety.

Know how to construct a test before giving a test. Writing a criterion-referenced test can be broken down to three parts.

First, keep telling students that tests will be aligned to the learning objectives they have been working on

Testing for Success

Are you critic or a coach? Ask yourself to determine which type of test to use.

  ◆ **Do I give a test to determine placement on a team or in a group?** If yes, give a **norm-referenced test**. In a regular classroom, they force students to compete against their classmates for the few high grades the teacher—the critic—will distribute.

  ◆ **Do I give a test to determine mastery of the lesson objectives?** If yes, give a **criterion-referenced test**. There is no competition for grades, only the positive effect to do the best on known objectives, a motivation for low-ranked students who have confidence in their coach.

Use these steps to lead all students to a successful learning experience.

  ◆ Tell students what you want them to know and do.
  ◆ Teach them so they know how to do it.
  ◆ Let them practice and correct.
  ◆ Reteach how to know and do it.
  ◆ Let them practice, and practice again.
  ◆ Give them a criterion-referenced test for mastery of the lesson objectives.

throughout the lessons. As you assess and assist, give students the opportunity to ask questions, to express confusion, to ask for clarification, to express doubt and insecurity. Reteach and reteach, as necessary. Let them know that you want them to succeed, and it is your job to support them so they do succeed. Student anxiety is lessened.

Second, provide students with an assessment device—a rubric, which need be no more than a

---

[8] W. James Popham, "Criterion-Referenced Measurement: Half a Century Wasted?" *Educational Leadership* 71, no. 6 (March 2014): 62–66.

checklist—that they can use to stay on task and keep track of their own progress. With informative guidelines that they can use to self-assess, they will feel more in control of their learning—another anxiety lessened.

Third, post a model test showing how each test question has been correlated to an objective. Have students study the objectives, the rubric, and the questions to assure themselves that there will be no surprise format to the test. Reiterate that they will be tested on what they have been told they are responsible for learning.

> **When students are assured of the clarity of criterion test construction, it greatly lessens and can even eliminate test anxiety. They are prepared for challenges.**

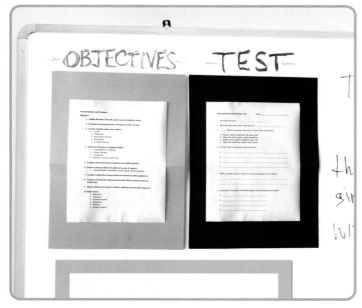

Karen Rogers, a science teacher in Kansas, posts her lesson objectives and then an example of the correlated test questions so students can see how the test has been written.

Things to Consider When Writing Tests

Writing Objectives. The first step in creating effective lessons and evaluations is having quality objectives to begin with. Excellent objectives not only detail what it is that you expect students to learn, but also indicate how you will evaluate what they learned:

- ◆ **Bad Example of an Objective**
  Upon completion of the lesson, the student will know the Preamble to the Constitution of the United States.

- ◆ **Good Example of an Objective**
  Upon completion of the lesson, the student will be able to (any or all of the following)
  - identify who was referred to by the phrase "We the People."
  - describe why a "more perfect union" was needed at the time the Constitution was written.
  - explain how the Constitution established justice.
  - evaluate whether the "blessings of liberty" were established by the Constitution's ratification.
  - cite clauses in the Constitution that
    - promoted "domestic tranquility."
    - provided for the "common defense."
    - promoted the "general welfare."

Number of Questions. There is no rule to the number of questions per learning objective. However, write more than one test question for each objective to make sure students have mastered it and didn't just guess correctly on one question.

> **When test questions are written aligned to the objectives, you are not teaching to the test; you are teaching to the lesson objectives.**

Different Test Options. There is no rule about the format of test you should use. The main priority is the type of test you choose allows students to show mastery of the objectives. There are many options to choose from.

- ◆ **Written tests.** Multiple choice, true/false, fill-in-the-blank, short written answers, essay
- ◆ **Problem solving tests.** Math and science problems, scenarios
- ◆ **Products.** Journals, notebooks, portfolios, reports, projects
- ◆ **Performance tests.** Presentations, speeches, skits, songs, demonstrations

Grading and Evaluation. Students need to know how they will be graded and evaluated. A scoring guide or a rubric gives them a list of the criteria needed to demonstrate mastery in advance. Go over the criteria on the scoring guide so students know exactly what each category means and how they can get the best score.

Examples and Models. Show students an example of assignments, test questions, and even similar tests. Just as you have objectives posted, post an example of a test and explain how it was written and how to study for the test so students are able to clearly see what they are expected to produce or achieve. It clarifies expectations, saves time, and eases anxiety for everyone (students and teachers) because students know exactly what to do.

When the evaluation expectations are crystal clear, students can achieve success.
Write a <u>mastery</u> test, not a mystery test!

Test Tips

- ◆ Use a variety of testing forms—written tests, performance tests, and projects.

- ◆ Establish criteria for scoring and grading in advance.

- ◆ Post or provide examples or models of the final product or test.

- ◆ Prepare more than one test for correction and remediation purposes.

- ◆ Divide the test into sections based on the objectives so students can retake sections.

- ◆ For written tests, mix up formats—use multiple choice, true/false, short written answers, essay.

- ◆ Make sure directions are clear.

- ◆ Consider open note or open book tests.

- ◆ Revise tests as needed.

Correction and Remediation

The learning objectives are posted and you have worked through the instructional strategies with your students. They have used guided and independent activities to practice what they are learning. You have given the test to see if they have mastered the learning objectives. Now what?

If the learning objectives were mastered, students can feel a sense of pride, accomplishment, and success.

But, students may still need to correct any minor errors they might have made on the test so they don't keep making them, and other students now need enrichment or other activities to do while the other students work on correction and remediation. Give students who have mastered the objectives a task related to the objectives or another enjoyable activity. Don't punish them by assigning more work just to keep them busy. There are many options. Examples of enrichment activities can include puzzles, games, independent research, creative projects, helping other students, helping the teacher, extra computer time, and leisure reading.

If learning objectives were not mastered, do not label students as failures and move on. They must be shown how to correct errors and be given opportunities for remediation. Do not leave them with a zero or an F. That is the easy way out for both the students and the teacher. It benefits no one.

Correction and remediation are a part of life. If you don't correct a minor health problem, a minor car problem, or any other kind of minor problem, you know what happens—it gets worse. Minor problems become major problems, which are much more difficult to correct.

Learning is the same way. If students do not correct and remediate, they will continue to make the same mistakes and fall further behind as the year progresses. They give up, act out, and get sent to the office. Or they completely stop trying. It becomes a painful and stressful situation for everyone.

Don't let minor learning problems get worse! Correction and remediation are nothing to be ashamed of. The most beautiful gardens in the world need to be weeded.

There is no need to panic or give up. Simply correct the situation by pulling the weeds and move on to remediation. Work together to find solutions.

- Be prepared—students will need correction and remediation.
- Find out what the problem is or was and fix it.
- If they don't understand something, break it down into smaller pieces, go step-by-step.
- Provide resources, time, and support for them to correct and remediate.
- Do not let them give up!

Correction is part of the learning process. **Everyone learns by making mistakes and correcting them.** Your job is to help students. When the learning objectives and the evaluation criteria are clear, students can take control of their learning. Together you can identify what went wrong and fix it.

Some teachers say, "In the real world, you can't retake tests." This isn't true. In the real world, people can and do retake tests. You can retake a driving test. Lawyers, doctors, dentists, and many other professionals can retake tests. The reason for testing in the classroom is for students to demonstrate mastery of the objectives. Retaking tests holds them more accountable for learning the information. Letting them fail or take a low grade is the easy way out of teaching and learning.

Objectives, Evaluations, Correction and Remediation

The following example shows how to take a learning objective and write an evaluation to match. It is a simple and flexible process. The key is to look at the learning objectives for the lesson and then write a set of questions or tasks that are directly linked to the objectives and will provide evidence that students have mastered the objectives. Be prepared to offer correction and remediation, as necessary.

Elementary Math Lesson

Step 1. Start with the learning objective
I can solve long division problems with 100% accuracy.

Step 2. Write a set of test questions to match
Criteria for mastery—written, problem-solving test

Step 3. Correction and remediation

- Ask students to correct the ones they did incorrectly; sometimes, "Aha moments" come during this process.

- Ask them to show you how they worked an incorrect problem and have them talk through the steps.

Long Division Test	
Please solve each problem. Show your work.	**Points Possible** 2 = work shown, correct answer 1 = something is missing or incorrect 0 = no attempt was made
1. $3\overline{)63}$	
2. $4\overline{)64}$	
3. $7\overline{)735}$	
4. $9\overline{)551}$	
5. $10\overline{)890}$	
	Your Score _____ (10 possible)

- Find the error in their thinking, discuss and fix it, then let them try another problem until they get it.

- Give them another test with different problems.

There are many worthwhile and rewarding ways to support students who need more help and guidance.

- Break a large assignment into smaller steps.
- Take it one step at a time.
- Shorten the length of the assignment—give them five questions instead of ten.
- Provide more time to complete an assignment.
- Modify the difficulty—use an easier version of the same material.
- Provide page numbers or show students where to find information.
- Provide examples and models.
- Let another student explain how they did an assignment or worked a problem.
- Let them use notes on a test.
- Let them correct and retake tests.

Grades Are Temporary

*"Students and their families must understand that grades do not reflect **who** you are as a learner, but **where** you are in your learning journey—and **where is always temporary**.*

*Grades help enhance achievement and foster learning progress **only** when they are paired with individualized comments that offer guidance and direction for improvement. Comments that identify what students did well, what improvements they need to make, and how to make those improvements can guide students to mastery of important learning goals.[9]"*

Thomas R. Guskey

The Positive Power of *Informances*

Laurie Kash is not only the Student Services Director for her district in Oregon, she also teaches English, writing, world literature, basic theater, advanced theater, and alternative education arts classes at the high school. Each year, she typically directs two mainstage productions and two showcases—over the years, she has directed over fifty theatrical productions and student showcases.

How she can juggle so many roles and shows is quite simple—she's organized, and her cast members are organized, too. There are, of course, procedures and routines, but she can quickly and explicitly teach students what they are to do, assess and guide the practice, evaluate their work, and then turn them loose to be responsible for their task—while working collaboratively to put on a production.

Laurie does not scare her classes with tests and evaluations. She calls her evaluations "informances"—informal, informed performances. After rehearsing a scene, students are asked to give a performance to the class to demonstrate their progress.

Before informances begin, students are given a copy of the scoring guide or rubric that is correlated to the state performing arts standards. With these qualitative statements, students understand their critiques are focused on the art and not on the artist.

Students may share their informances with each other in small performance groups or in front of the whole class in very short, very informal reviews. At the time of the informance, the only critique is to ascertain if the students met the two to three lesson objectives for the day. Students can ask this of themselves, or Laurie

---

[9] Guskey, "Grades Versus Comments."

Teaching for Competency

THE *Classroom Instruction Book* emphasizes **mastery-based learning**, or as it is sometimes called, **competency-based learning.**

Competency-based learning focuses on students who may need more help and time. It is a teaching method that promotes equity. The core of competency-based learning allows students to compare their work to the competencies described on a rubric and be empowered as learners. Competency-based learning can be a group or class mode activity.

A typical class may begin with the teacher in "instructor mode," going over the day's assignment, but much of the time in class is spent in "student mode." The teacher engages directly with students as they work, providing feedback. Here's a teacher's process to support students to revise, correct, and grow.

- Write specific learning targets or objectives.
- Teach the subject matter.
- Use a rubric that will show students where they are in an assignment.
- Check for understanding frequently to allow students to make improvements to reach proficiency.
- Give a criterion-referenced test to measure proficiency.

The competency approach puts the focus on students and their personal growth. It empowers a student to change the conversation from, "I'm not successful at this," to "This is where I am on the ladder of growth." Students will say things like, "I can add and subtract decimals." "I can identify, understand, and describe unit rate." Or in English class, "I can identify story elements." "I can retell what is important in a text."

In competency-based learning, letter grades can be jettisoned in favor of feedback that students use to revise their work as they progress toward mastery of clearly defined skills. Instead of receiving a C grade on an essay, for example, a student's assessment can be based on a numerical scale from 1 to 4 of described proficiencies. When students can clearly see what is expected of them and what they can ultimately accomplish, they have the opportunity to submit additional drafts to make continued improvements.

Or, instead of numbers, students could watch their progress on a color-coded scale. Green means meeting the standard, yellow is approaching it, orange is missing many details, and red means the standard has not been met. The scale is designed to be visually appealing and to encourage students to think of learning as a process.

In competency-based learning, the goal is to provide students with every opportunity to take control of their own learning.

asks it of the larger group. The goal of the informance is to heighten outcome expectations and to clarify lesson objectives.

Unlike subjects like science and math where specific responses are required to master the objectives, fulfillment of objectives in the fine arts requires more subjective and creative interpretation. In drama, visual interest, expression, and stage movement are important to get across a message or feeling to the audience. When asked about the just completed scene, the students might respond with, "Yes, when the performers used both sitting and standing, upstage and downstage, they varied the levels and planes to create visual interest."

At the end of the performance, Laurie leads the class in a group evaluation. Having procedures for critiquing allows students to feel safe and creates trust. With a group evaluation, students learn suitable terminology to discuss theater. They also learn the appropriate way to give criticism and praise to their classmates.

Laurie has even developed a procedure for clapping. So that every student gets the same amount of applause for their informance, she uses the "One, Two, Three, CLAP!" procedure. After each informance, Laurie calls out, "One, two, three," and everyone claps once. This is introduced and rehearsed when students audition for their roles and then reviewed again at the start of class.

Laurie also uses the Roses and Thorns procedure as another form of evaluation. After the individual or group receives the one-clap applause, they sit on the edge of the stage for their critiques. Laurie first reminds the class of the lesson objectives for the day. The performers then choose whether they would first like to hear Roses, positive feedback, or Thorns, constructive criticism.

Laurie calls on students in the audience to share their thoughts. She teaches the performers to respond only with "Thank you." (You may not realize, but contestants on competitive television shows have also been rehearsed to respond graciously with a simple "Thank you" after receiving comments.)

Laurie teaches her students how to consider the feedback they are receiving without becoming defensive. **This allows the evaluation to run smoothly and in a safe environment where everyone grows.**

Laurie ends every class with a review of the objectives for the day. She uses a modified version of the business management tool Fist to Five to assess student understanding. Students are asked to show on a scale of zero to five how well they thought they achieved the day's objective—a fist (zero) being total confusion and five fingers being complete understanding.

To end the class on a happy and positive note, Laurie uses a group exercise—the Hand Slap Game.

Students lie on their stomachs in a circle so that their arms overlap with the right arm on top of the left arm of the student next to them. The exercise starts with a designated student slapping the floor with one hand. This slap is passed around the circle to the right as fast as it can go. Once this slap is going, Laurie adds another hand slap that creates more pulses of multiple hand-slapping going around the circle. Students are reunited, reconnected, and jump up with great energy to end the period.

46

Limitless Possibilities Through Structure

Learn how **Laurie Kash** organizes her class to bring out the potential creativity of all her students.

It's the Teacher, Not the Test

An abundance of books and articles have been written giving advice on how students, or anyone, can overcome test anxiety. The advice they provide boils down to these techniques.

- Use a relaxation technique, such as stretching or meditation.
- Take deep, slow breaths.
- Avoid cramming.
- Dress comfortably and in layers.
- Take care of yourself—sleep, eat well, and drink lots of water.
- Get some exercise or physical activity.

These suggestions are useful. But they only address the person who is taking the test. They don't offer advice to the person creating the test who may be the real culprit and cause of test anxiety. Too often, the test is written the night before from vaporized air and students are left anxiously waiting and wondering, guessing what the questions on the test will be and trying to study appropriately.

It does little good to teach how to breathe, how to study, or reminding students to sleep and eat well, when the problem is with ill-constructed tests that have been manufactured in mysterious ways. Test anxiety is a perfectly normal, and warranted, reaction to such circumstances.

**Student success
is related to the quality
of the teaching that students experience.**

Students who are taught well and provided with ample opportunities to practice and demonstrate what they have learned typically perform much better when tested than do students who are taught poorly and given questions that are not aligned to learning objectives. Attaining high scores is possible for well-taught students, whereas attaining even an average score might prove difficult for students who are poorly taught. Final grades reflect what students have learned.

In essence, it's not the test; it's the teacher. Those teachers who know their subject well (teacher clarity with an effect size of 0.75) and know how to write tests, will have students who can predict their achievement levels (self-reported grades with an effect size of 1.33). When the evaluation organization, explanation, and expectations are crystal clear, students can and will achieve success.

Teacher Clarity = Student Success

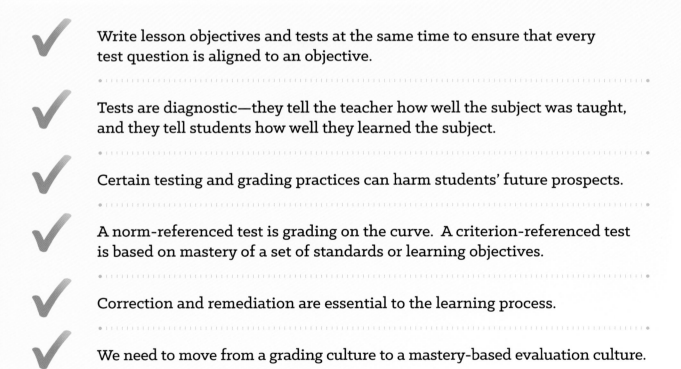

Mastering Instruction

✓ Write lesson objectives and tests at the same time to ensure that every test question is aligned to an objective.

✓ Tests are diagnostic—they tell the teacher how well the subject was taught, and they tell students how well they learned the subject.

✓ Certain testing and grading practices can harm students' future prospects.

✓ A norm-referenced test is grading on the curve. A criterion-referenced test is based on mastery of a set of standards or learning objectives.

✓ Correction and remediation are essential to the learning process.

✓ We need to move from a grading culture to a mastery-based evaluation culture.

...Produces Achievement!

UNIT E Implementation

Chapter

How to Use Teacher Clarity

Teacher clarity guarantees student success.

The Power of Teacher Clarity

If you are hired as a wedding coordinator, your job is to organize the wedding. You have to be very clear about what you and the wedding party want to achieve. You have to communicate, coordinate, schedule, and ensure everything is planned so meticulously that it all seems to take place effortlessly and naturally.

If you are hired as a teacher, your job is to organize instruction so that it is clear to students what they are to do and what they are to learn. You have to communicate, coordinate, schedule, and plan. With a well-organized instructional plan, students know exactly what they have to accomplish. Design lessons that let students know how they can succeed. That is teacher clarity.

**Teacher clarity makes instruction appear effortless.
It ensures student achievement.
It makes their success a natural outcome.**

Unit D guided you to focus on these essential questions when developing a lesson or unit.

- How will the material be introduced?
- How will new information be presented?
- How will students practice and apply what they are learning?
- How will student learning and progress be assessed?
- How will students reflect on what they learn and their own learning process?

A Lesson in Teacher Clarity

> **It's not enough to be busy, so are the ants. The question is, what are we busy about?**
>
> Henry David Thoreau

Stephanie Stoebe teaches in Round Rock, Texas. When you walk into her classroom, you will see her students actively engaged in their work. They will be working collaboratively, sharing knowledge, and learning from each other. Students love her class, and she is constantly pushing them to the next level. **There is instructional quality—a direct result of teacher clarity.**

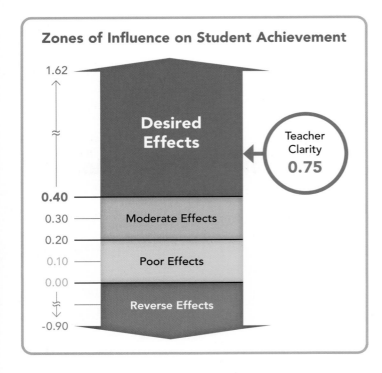

Zones of Influence on Student Achievement

Desired Effects

Teacher Clarity **0.75**

Moderate Effects

Poor Effects

Reverse Effects

1.62
0.40
0.30
0.20
0.10
0.00
-0.90

Teacher clarity has an effect-size of 0.75.

Use the guidelines as presented in previous chapters when planning lessons to ensure clarity, lesson integrity, and the ability of students to take responsibility for learning.

◆ Lesson objectives state what is to be taught and what is to be learned.

◆ Activities are related to lesson objectives and create a clear path to learning success.

◆ Monitoring, feedback, assessing, and assisting provide support to improve learning.

◆ Guided practice with chunked, scaffolded, and paced activities gives practice time to improve mastery of the objectives.

◆ Independent practice gives the opportunity to apply learning to think, create, and invent independently.

◆ All final test questions are correlated to the objectives so there is transparency in the evaluation.

Display the lesson planning and instruction process in the classroom. Put examples of finished products where students can examine them. Take the time to show, explain, and model what you expect the outcome of an activity to look like. Then give every opportunity for students to take ownership of their own learning.

Teacher clarity transforms students from passive recipients into active participants.

What Is Teacher Clarity?

Teacher clarity tells students what you'll teach. It also tells students what they'll learn.

Student Obsession

Students go to school for two reasons—learning and success. To make these ambitions a reality, effective teachers are driven by a strategy that could be called "student obsession."

Amazon, America's second largest company, operates with a business strategy they call "customer obsession."[1] Customer obsession is not the usual customer service—it is predicting what customers will want before they even know what it is they want. And what they *now* want is the convenience of shopping from home via the Internet and speedy delivery to the front door.

As founder and CEO of Amazon, **Jeff Bezos** says, "Customers are always dissatisfied even if they don't know it, even when they think they're happy. They always want a better way, yet they don't know what that will be. Therefore, we are always inventing on their behalf."

Many parents in the United States are dissatisfied with their child's progress in school even if they don't know what it is they want or should expect from the teacher or the curriculum. The same can be said for

[1] Brian Dumaine, "Amazon Was Built for the Pandemic," *Fortune* (June/July 2020).

students—they are dissatisfied with their progress in school even if they don't know what it is they want or should expect. Students have been failing in school for what seems to be forever to the point where failure has become an acceptable outcome for education. (Yet, retention has a negative effect of -0.32 on academic achievement.) So many have failed in school for so long that they do not even know what it is like to learn and succeed. Achievement is beyond their comprehension.

Every year, more than a million students drop out of high school in the United States alone. That's a student every twenty-six seconds—or approximately seven thousand a day. If student desks were set out to represent each dropout each day, it would stretch four miles. In a year it would stretch from New York to Chicago.

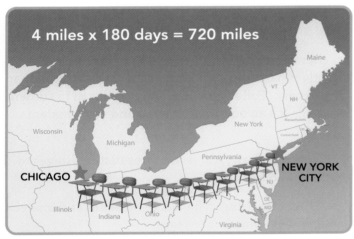

4 miles x 180 days = 720 miles

Approximately seven thousand students drop out of high school daily in the United States. With desks representing the students, the line would stretch for four miles in one day. Over the course of one school year, desks would stretch from New York City to Chicago. The loss of livelihood and human potential is staggering.

Students want to learn and succeed. They don't want failure—they want to have fulfilling futures. They want there to be better systems and practices in classrooms, but they don't know what that could be. So they just plod along, apathetic and discouraged.

Unless they are fortunate enough to be in a classroom led by a teacher with student obsession. Such a teacher knows exactly what they want and what they should have the right to expect.

Student Obsession Means Teacher Clarity

A teacher with student obsession has only one goal—ensuring students have the knowledge and skills they need to successfully negotiate the challenges and complexities of life.

Effective teachers are obsessed with creating and inventing lessons on behalf of their students so they will succeed.

When teachers use their experience and expertise to organize and explain learning targets, and to continuously support, encourage, and guide student efforts, they are teaching with clarity.

Teacher clarity is best viewed from the standpoint of the student. Clarity eliminates mystery, uncertainty, and confusion. It gives students purpose and lights their path forward. With an effect size of 0.75, teacher clarity is so powerful that it could potentially lead to up to two years' worth of growth.

> *I knew I had found the right teacher. He was focused and organized and proposed a precise lesson plan that I understood for my success. He showed me the parts of the plan, like a game plan, and laid out a precise timetable for me. It not only made sense to me, it made sense to my parents.*
>
> A student

In life, we all want clarity and transparency. You read the nutritional information on the food package to find out whether the contents are healthy. When you buy an airplane ticket, you want to know what the total price is and not get charged with add-ons after you purchase the ticket or at the airport before you can board the plane. You feel more secure when the dentist shows you an image of your mouth and explains what is going to happen before the drill starts whirring away.

Clarity Is a Win-Win

Students want to learn. Teacher clarity is very reassuring for students. It motivates and convinces them that they can succeed because it has been clearly explained to them how they can. They know how
- ◆ the classroom is organized,
- ◆ how the instruction is organized, and
- ◆ how they will be assessed and evaluated.

Teachers want to teach successfully. For this to happen, they must teach with clarity. Clarity gives students control over what happens in the classroom. When students are given the means to exert control, they perform better on cognitive tasks. And when students take control and succeed in school, they are more likely to view school performance as a controllable outcome.[2]

**When you make clarity
your mission and methodology,
you know how to teach and
your students know how to learn.**

Effective teachers are clearly focused on what they want students to accomplish. They employ every possible strategy and technique to ensure students understand what is required of them. They assure students that they will assist and support them so they are given every opportunity to succeed.

It can't be simpler to implement effective instruction in a classroom. If it were more complex, there would be no clarity in the process. Piano teachers know how to do it. Golf instructors know how to do it. Coaches know how to do it. Career tech teachers know how to do it.

**Effective teachers are effective because
they explain to students
how instruction is organized.**

When both students and teacher are clear about what is to be learned, you get student learning. This can't be stated more clearly.

Implementing Teacher Clarity

Teacher clarity begins when there is a curriculum with objectives based on standards. This creates a road map for teachers. Follow the map and it will lead to student learning. It's an environment you and your students can trust.

With teacher clarity, there are three distinct stages to teaching and learning:

1. **Direct teaching.** The teacher teaches and models what students are to learn.
2. **Guided practice.** Students practice what has been taught while the teacher provides feedback to help students make progress.
3. **Independent practice.** Students produce a product that demonstrates what they have learned.

Students want lessons where the work is stated clearly and in detail, leaving no room for confusion or doubt. The intentions are plain, straightforward, crystal clear, and easily understandable. There is no mystery about what learners are to achieve or what success looks like.

Mandie Ballman teaches in Owingsville, Kentucky. She relies on a management binder she has developed to ensure her classroom is organized for success so she can focus her attention on the academic success of her students.

[2] Ellen A. Skinner, James G. Wellborn, and James P. Connell, "What It Takes to Do Well in School and Whether I've Got It: A Process Model of Perceived Control and Children's Engagement and Achievement in School," *Journal of Educational Psychology* 82, no. 1 (March 1990): 22–32.

If we expect mastery or proficient performance, the learner must know what proficient performance looks like.

No Need for Superheroes

We need to demystify leadership. We don't need super men or women to lead a successful school. We need teacher clarity, ceaseless repetition, and practice.[3]

Mike Schmoker

Students, especially struggling learners, will succeed in these classrooms because they know the learning goals they are expected to attain, the ways in which their learning will be assessed, the instructional methods by which their learning will be supported, and their role as a learner in the process. **Teacher clarity enhances student motivation and achievement.**

Effective coaches make the "invisible visible" through countless models and examples. Basketball coaches shows film clips of effective skills so players can see proficiency in action. The yearbook sponsor has students review award-winning yearbooks from previous years and challenges them to produce a better one for their graduating class.

For clarity, show models and examples of all goals. Show examples of expertly written essays, laboratory reports, pronunciation guides, or paintings before students begin their work. Model the process for achieving excellence so that students can emulate you. Students benefit from paying close attention to models before they begin independent practice.

Teachers to Emulate

There have been many stories of teachers throughout this book to illustrate effective teaching. The teachers are a disparate group, all different, but they all have

There Was No Clarity

Almost everyone can remember getting back an assignment—an essay, a project, a worksheet—and the teacher saying, "I took points off for this and this and this." The teacher had not told the class how points would be assigned—or deducted—ahead of time. You may have felt betrayed. You may have thought the teacher was unfair. If you had known what "counted," you would have made sure to complete the assignment to specifications. But you didn't know. There was no clarity. It was a wasted school day.

---

[3] From an email communication between Harry Wong and Mike Schmoker, May 6, 2021.

After Action Review

Use the practice of an After Action Review (AAR) to get quick feedback on how effective your teaching is. This deceptively simple practice is used by the military and corporations and is powerful when done properly. An After Action Review can apply to just about anything at any time. If you have just completed a lesson and want to know the results or how effective an implemented program is, use an AAR. It's driven by four core questions.

1. What did I set out to do?
2. What actually happened?
3. Why is there a difference between the first two?
4. What should I continue and what should I change?

The key to making the review successful is to start asking the four questions as soon after the learning event as possible, so that your memory is clear. In asking and reflecting upon the questions, spend roughly 25 percent on the first two combined, 25 percent on the third, and 50 percent on the fourth.

It is critical not to skip the first two questions. When considering educational programs, people tend to immediately defend their approach and will jump to the third question without establishing "what could I have done differently" or "what went wrong." The goal of AAR is not to assign credit or blame, but rather to build a shared mental model that can be applied to future work.

This exercise in problem solving could also be beneficial for students to ascertain if there is a difference between what happened and what they had expected or hoped would happen. Then you can see what improvements should be considered, that is, what needs to be fixed. **This is how to sustain going forward with teacher clarity.**

one thing in common—you can follow and emulate what they do because the quality of the instruction is a direct outcome of teacher clarity.

As we expect and demand transparency in all aspects of our lives, students should receive nothing less when they come to school.

When **Amanda Bivens** talks to her class, this is what she says.

- *I will post a lesson objective so we both know what you are to learn.*
- *I will give you some background information to get you started.*
- *We will do a series of activities—lectures, videos, labs, field trips, discussions, and so on—that will give you hands-on knowledge of the objectives.*
- *While you are working, I will check on your learning to help you make progress, sometimes telling you how to do something better or just make suggestions.*
- *I will have you work in groups or teams because when you enter the adult work world, your success will depend on how well you can work and contribute to a group.*
- *I will then have you work alone to practice what you have learned to internalize it. Then, I want you to create, invent, and synthesize a product to demonstrate that you can do something with what you have learned.*
- *And don't worry about the test, as every test question will be related to the lesson objectives.*

High school teacher **Chelonnda Seroyer** has highly organized lesson plans that exemplify teacher clarity. The lessons are coherent, consistent, and continuous and are explicitly explained to her students.

- She has clear and specific objectives—students know where they are going.
- Students do the assignment based on the objectives—they know what they are doing.
- She provides feedback to help students make progress—they know how well they are doing.
- She adjusts instruction based on assessment—students know where to go next.

- Students are given opportunities to practice further—they gain confidence and master the objectives.
- She writes the evaluation based on the lesson objectives—students know how they will be tested and have positive expectations for good grades.

Chelonnda explains, "There is no secret as to what is expected of them. They all succeed because there is clarity about what they are to accomplish. When I do this, they can all predict their success."

Teaching is a precise skill. When you have learning objectives, quality instruction aligned to the objectives, and assessment to match, you have fewer confused students and fewer arguments and disappointment about grades. This is because there is clarity in what students are to do and learn. Together, you and your students can focus on accomplishing the lesson goals and achieving learning success.

Plan lessons with a clear goal and use questioning activities that lead students to learn, develop, and master a new topic every day. As you devise and implement lesson plans, ask yourself these questions.

- Are the learning outcomes clearly identified and exemplified in the work or simply things that are "nice to know?"
- Do students know the intended learning objectives and spend time performing the activities in terms of the objectives?
- Can students explain the purpose behind the various activities?
- Have students shown that they understand and can transfer what they have learned in meaningful ways?
- Were the time and energy devoted to the activities equal to the resultant learning?

Students who are actively focused on lesson criteria, matched learning activities, and aligned tests, do best in mastering the subject matter.[4]

Gordon Cawelti

Clarity Is the Key

Teacher clarity is the key to student success.

She goes in-depth and gives us all the information we need beforehand so we are prepared. She always tells us what we will be doing so there are never any surprises.[5]

A middle school student

Think about band directors, drama coaches, and fine arts teachers. Think about how they teach; how their teaching strategies and techniques unfold over time; how they plan, organize, and schedule. What is remarkable is how they work effectively with large numbers of learners, such as an orchestra or a company of students in a theater production. Everyone has a different role to play—working backstage, acting, playing percussion, violin, singing—and yet they all somehow coordinate and work together to create a piece of music or a production worthy of presentation. It is not a chaotic three-ring circus during the rehearsal process because these teachers know how to use direct instruction, guided practice, and independent practice to achieve a satisfactory end result.

[4] Gordon Cawelti, ed., *Handbook of Research on Improving Student Achievement*, 3rd edition (Bethesda, MD: Editorial Projects in Education, 2004).

[5] Mary Poplin and Claudia Bermúdez, eds., *Highly Effective Teachers of Vulnerable Students: Practice Transcending Theory* (New York: Peter Lang Publishing, Inc., 2019).

A Lesson in Teacher Clarity

Stephanie Stoebe is a Teacher-of-the-Year in Round Rock, Texas. When you walk into her classroom, you will see her students actively engaged in their work. They will be working collaboratively, sharing knowledge, and learning from each other. Students love her class, and she is constantly pushing them to the next level. There is instructional quality—a direct result of teacher clarity.

1. She sets up the purpose of the lesson, spelling out the objective, and modeling what the objective looks like. **Direct instruction.**

2. She invites students to practice the lesson with the teacher's help. **Guided practice.**

3. Students do the work independently to show they have mastered the purpose of the lesson. **Independent practice.**

This is a lesson that Stephanie teaches that incorporates the three distinct stages to teaching and learning to achieve teacher clarity.

Fifth Grade Language Arts (Reading and Social Studies)
How to Read a Biography to Gather Information

Materials and Technology
- John Adams biography (for example)
- Selection of leveled biographies aligned with guided reading level
- Graphic organizers
- Computers

State Standards
Students will
- (19A) establish purposes for reading selected texts based upon own or others' desired outcome to enhance comprehension.
- (19B) ask literal, interpretive, evaluative, and universal questions of text.
- (19C) monitor and adjust comprehension (e.g., using background knowledge, creating sensory images, rereading a portion aloud, generating questions).
- (19E) summarize and paraphrase texts in ways that maintain meaning and logical order within a text and across texts.

Lesson Objectives
Students will
- learn to ask relevant questions before and during reading.
- learn to take notes and categorize information.
- monitor comprehension as they read and skim text for main ideas and details.

Instructional Strategies
- By using graphic organizers, students write or draw meanings and relationships of underlying ideas. This has been shown to improve students' ability to recall content.
- By summarizing information, students improve by including ideas related to the main idea, generalizing, and removing redundancy.
- By working in cooperative groups, students may increase their learning of reading strategies through peer discussion. This may also lead to better comprehension.

Direct Instruction

Survey students' background knowledge
Ask students what a biography is and show an example of one. Ask them what sort of things they would expect to find out about a person's life in a biography. Write ideas on the white board.

Capture students' interest

Have students brainstorm famous people who might have biographies written about them. Designate a student leader for this if possible. Continue to collect ideas for display.

Show a sample of appropriate questions

Ask students for ideas of how biographical information might be categorized (such as childhood events, turning points, famous deeds). Share a biography of, for example, John Adams and ask students to work in pairs to generate questions about his life. Add the sample questions to the ideas and then categorize the questions so students understand the process of classification.

Guided Practice Activities

Distribute the graphic organizer(s)

Review the organizer and discuss how categories and subcategories can be used to summarize a person's life achievements. In the example of John Adams, categories in the story should include "A Congressional Honor," "A Historic Controversy," and "What Did John Adams Do?" Explain that under these headings, students will categorize the information pertaining to that particular aspect of John Adams' life.

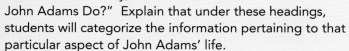

Divide students into small groups with leveled texts

For example, there could be a group for George Washington, Thomas Jefferson, Dolley Madison, or Abigail Adams. Allow students five minutes or so to examine the biographies, then have each student choose one to read independently. Instruct students to flip through their books and jot down headings to use in their graphic organizers.

Independent Practice

Create list of questions

Have students generate a list of questions that they hope to find the answer to in the biographies they have chosen. Students then read the biographies on their own and answer their questions.

Share information learned

After fifteen minutes or so of independent reading—adjust timing as needed—assemble students together based on the subject of their biography. Ask students to share the relevant information from their readings and to reflect on the knowledge they have gained during the process.

Assessment

Focusing student investigations

In a class discussion, ask students to reflect upon "big idea" conceptual questions to encourage and focus students' investigations.

Readers and writers use a flexible range of strategies and skills to monitor and construct meaning across a variety of genres.

- What strategies did you use to understand the text?

Authors use literary devices and language to convey a message in biographies and autobiographies.

- What are examples of literary language and devices used in biographies and autobiographies?
- How does an author's use of literary language and devices contribute to biographies and autobiographies?

Biographies and autobiographies tell stories about an individual's contributions to society.

- How does reading a biography or autobiography of a person's life impact you?
- What is the author's view of the person represented in the text?

Note: A rubric can be used to conduct formative assessment before moving to the final evaluation. Criteria would include ability to

- ask appropriate questions prior to reading,
- identify important information,
- categorize facts, and
- identify literary elements.

Evaluation

Completing the graphic organizers

As students work in pairs or in small groups, circle the room and check for understanding and participation from all students. As students break down the text into categories for gathering information, ensure that all students write on their own organizer. The completed graphic organizer will serve as a summative assessment or evaluation.

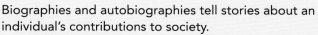

Effective fine arts teachers know, as most teachers know, that creativity is enhanced when there is a sense of order and clarity. Structure makes it possible for students to be creative and exceed expectations.

When there is teacher clarity, students have the structure they need to progress and realize their potential. Both teachers and students want good results and good grades. The reason students can work on getting good grades and good results is because they know clearly what to do, what to learn, and how to prepare for the test or performance. As a student says, "I like this school more (than my former school) because you learn more things."

Finally, when it comes to improving student achievement, all the research agrees on one very important finding—what is taught and what is tested must be in alignment.

When there is clarity in classroom management, lesson planning, assessing, and evaluating, there will be increased learning and a marked growth in student performance—a result every student, parent, teacher, and administrator wants.

> **Effective teachers strive to be paragons of clarity so that their students are paragons of success.**

Mastering Instruction

 Teacher clarity tells what is to be taught and what is to be learned.

 Effective teachers manage the classroom and instruct with clarity and consistency.

 Effective teachers are clearly focused on what they want students to accomplish.

 Instructional quality is directly linked to teacher clarity.

 Clarity gives students control over what happens with learning so they can achieve and succeed.

 Clarity and structure make it possible for students to realize their potential and exceed expectations.

...Produces Achievement!

How to Teach with Collaboration

> *Teachers who collaborate with colleagues give themselves and their students the best chance of success.*

Professional Isolation

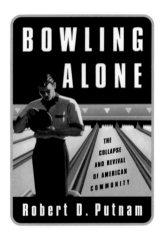

In 1995, **Robert D. Putnam** wrote *Bowling Alone: The Collapse and Revival of American Community.* Based on five hundred thousand interviews over twenty-five years, he showed that we belong to fewer organizations, know our neighbors less, meet with friends less frequently, and even socialize with our families less often than previous generations. Years ago, he wrote, thousands of people belonged to bowling leagues. Today, they're more likely to bowl alone.

Teachers, too, are often left to teach alone. The American education system typically views teachers as independent operators. With the present day's emphasis on personalization and individualization, teachers—and especially new teachers—are almost never given any adequate, formal induction into their school community or their district's curriculum. New teachers seldom even see another teacher in action. They are isolated in their classrooms, behind closed doors, never to interact with their colleagues. They are expected to do a good job even though they are not empowered to work cooperatively, opportunities for communication are scarce, and collaboration is rare.

> **Collaboration allows teachers to capture each other's fund of collective intelligence.**
>
> Mike Schmoker

I work with the best teachers and staff that I could ever ask for! When I needed help, I knew I had countless support behind me.

A Moberly induction program teacher

Do you want to be part of a collaborative effort to help students succeed? Look to "Mission Moberly: Designing the Future—The Strategic Plan of Moberly Public Schools." But wait, you say, Moberly is a small town in Missouri (population 13,615 in 2019) in a rural school district. How can what they do support me? It's because Moberly's strategic plan would make any and every teacher S.H.I.N.E.!

The **Moberly School District** has a teacher induction program called S.H.I.N.E—**S**upporting, **H**elping, and **I**nspiring **N**ew **E**ducators. Working alone is not done in Moberly, especially for a new teacher. Moberly's goal is to produce happy and effective teachers.

Loneliness and lack of support further exacerbate the usual frustrations of beginning teachers. To ask an enthusiastic, caring, dedicated teacher to go solo in a networked world is akin to writing that teacher's epitaph, and it might as well read, "Doomed from the start."

There are two major conclusions to be drawn from **John Hattie's** research in *Visible Learning for Teachers*:[1]

1. The power of teachers working together, assessing and critiquing their planning
2. The power of teachers designing and assessing lessons together

A Very Effective Effect Size

One of the strongest influences on student achievements occurs when teachers work together and purposefully focus on instruction that will make an impact.

With an effect size of 1.57, collaborative impact is ranked as the second highest factor influencing student achievement. Collaborative impact is more than three times more powerful and predictive of student achievement than socio-economic status.

Influences with Positive Effects on Student Achievement[2]		
Influence	Effect Size	Page
Teacher estimation	1.62	18
Collaborative impact	1.57	250
Self-reported grades	1.33	143
Teacher clarity	0.75	239
Reciprocal teaching	0.74	201
Feedback	0.70	89
Direct instruction	0.60	28
Spaced vs. mass practice	0.60	192
Mastery learning	0.57	235

The effect size of collaborative impact is 1.57, making it a significant strategy for improvements in teaching and learning.

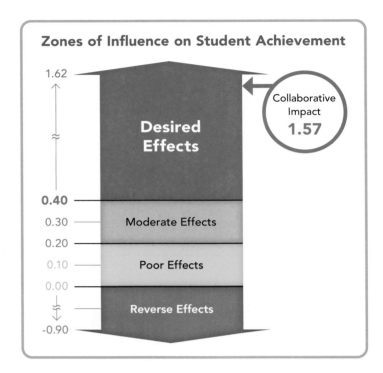

Zones of Influence on Student Achievement

1.62

Desired Effects

Collaborative Impact **1.57**

0.40

0.30 — Moderate Effects

0.20

0.10 — Poor Effects

0.00

Reverse Effects

-0.90

It is more than double the effect of prior achievement and more than triple the effect of home environment and parental involvement.

Collaborative impact is sometimes referred to as "collective efficacy." No matter the term used, with an effect size of 1.57, it is an extremely potent strategy for teachers because it guides their actions and results in positive outcomes.

If teachers blame their shortcomings and failures on not having smaller class sizes, or enough counselors and social workers, they won't be inclined to take responsibility and make constructive changes to influence student achievement.

However, when teachers are committed to working together to organize and improve instruction, assessing results when it is delivered to students and making adjustments as necessary, the positive effects reverberate throughout the classroom, the school, and the district. The impact is significant and far-reaching.

[1] Hattie, *Visible Learning for Teachers*.

[2] *Visible Learning*, "Hattie Ranking: 256 Influences."

When teachers share the belief that by working together they can positively influence teaching and learning, it makes a profound difference in the education and future possibilities of their students.

Collaborative impact is how teachers organize and execute the course of action required to have a positive effect on students.

Where there is a shared awareness of the impact that professional collaboration can have, student achievement improves because teachers

- have a more positive attitude toward professional development,
- commit to the implementation of evidence-based instructional strategies, and
- have a stronger focus on academic achievement.

Last, but not least, in schools where professional collaboration is present and making an impact, students are less likely to be suspended or be removed from classrooms as a result of misbehavior.[3]

The Failings of Individualism

Teams are at the heart of every successful organization. Employers say that one of the main things they look for in a new hire is a willingness and ability to work with other people—a trait that is contrary to the way teaching is conducted in many schools. In the workplace, everyone is working in a team of some sort.

Every successful sports team will tell you that every player is an individual with their own talents and foibles, but they play together as a team. The best teamwork is a group of people working together for the greater good—meaning that each person is willing to forgo their own ego, their own agenda, and make decisions that are in the best interests of everyone. **Phil Jackson**, one of the great coaches in NBA history, said, "The strength of the team is each individual member. The strength of each member is the team."

I Left at the End of the School Year

"I was hired by the district human resources office and assigned to a school. There was no preschool meeting for the newly hired teachers. I showed up on the first day for teachers with all the other teachers.

There were over three hundred teachers in the auditorium for the first day meeting at which the superintendent welcomed all the new teachers and asked us to stand. We received the obligatory round of applause. Then we sat.

After the meeting, I went to my classroom. There was no induction program, and I did not see my principal until two weeks after school began as we passed in the hall. He did not provide any kind of a guide as to how the school functions or whoever taught at the school.

I never saw another teacher's classroom. I survived in isolation. I had no idea if what I was doing was right or wrong. **I left at the end of the school year.**"

A new teacher

[3] Simon Gibbs and Ben Powell, "Teacher Efficacy and Pupil Behaviour: The Structure of Teachers' Individual and Collective Beliefs and Their Relationship with Numbers of Pupils Excluded from School," *British Journal of Educational Psychology* 82, no. 4 (December 2012): 564–584.

Food for Thought: Mealtime, Culture, and Connectedness

As will be seen in this chapter and Chapter 22, there is much to be learned in a professional sense from collaborative practices and communal traditions in other parts of the world.

Let's consider the food culture in different countries. The dinner table is a universal symbol of connection, communication, and hospitality. People feel a sense of inclusion as they satisfy their hunger, and they demonstrate gratitude and respect through manners.

The family dinner table is a forum for the transmission of ideals and values. In Chinese and Italian families, for example, meals are where children learn social graces, respect for others, and how to listen and partake in civil discussions.

In Morocco, a common dish is *shakshuka*, eggs in tomato sauce poached in a large communal pan and served with pita bread. Everyone clusters around the table, dipping pieces of bread into the pan, sharing and communicating.

In Ethiopia, people share food from common plates and food is picked up with a spongy pancake-like flatbread called *injera*.

This same sharing concept is practiced at certain meals in Japan, where everyone cooks their meat and vegetables in a communal hot pot of soup—*shabu-shabu*. In Korea, meals are grilled over a common barbeque at the table—*gogi-gui*.

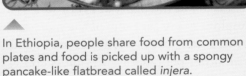

After a day's work in some places, such as Mexico, the community gathers outside—strolling, doing errands, and interacting with each other—as vendors prepare and serve street food. During the time of the Yucatec Mayan civilization, one would greet others by saying, "In lak'ech" (I am you), to which the response was, "A la k'in" (You are me), an exchange affirming relationship, coexistence, and interdependence.

The food culture in the United States is generally quite different. It is not uncommon for Americans to eat separated from one another. Notice that at a fast-food restaurant, a table for more than four is rare. Often there is a single person reading a book or looking at a phone so as not to have to acknowledge anyone else. It's frequently difficult for families to coordinate busy schedules and communal meals are not given priority. It's no wonder that so many of the students we encounter in our classrooms have no idea how to affirm relationships or carry on a conversation.

But times are changing. There are now restaurants that provide communal tables for seating guests not familiar with each

other, and there are dishes on menus made for sharing. Strangers, at times, become friends at the end of a meal. Millennials, in particular, do not feel comfortable being isolated. Social media is part of most people's daily lives. Offices are now designed to encourage interaction and communication.

In schools, however, the trend is still to favor individualized, personalized, differentiated learning. For most teachers in the United States, each day is pretty much the same—instructing students in isolation from other teachers and then telling students to personalize their own learning from other students. Students often work alone on what they want to learn at their own rate of speed.

Hattie's research reveals that individualized instruction has an effect size of 0.23, a low figure which shows the negative effects of individualizing teaching.

Individualized instruction deprives students of the opportunity to build collaboration in the classroom, a model that will almost certainly be required in their future workplace. One of the purposes of schooling is to socialize students. To their shock, students quickly discover when they get to college or into the workplace that they are required to coordinate and cooperate with other people and groups.

Learning is inherently social. It is as much social as it is academic.

In Japan and South Korea, people commonly believe they have a civic obligation to take care of one another. There are words for this sense of responsibility. In Japan, it relates to the concept of *giri*, or duties toward others. Koreans refer to *inhwa*, a culture of harmony between people. These are important social values to foster in the classroom.

Face-to-face interaction with peers is critical if students are to develop the interpersonal problem-solving skills that will be required of them as adults.

> **Classrooms around the world are collaborative environments where students are learning and growing together.**

The Science of Talking in Class[4]

Instead of students sitting at computer stations or working on their own in individualized instruction, research says that students learn more when they are involved in peer discussion and group work.

Students tend to learn better by interacting with each other rather than wrestling with an assignment on their own. And interacting with a teacher one-to-one is even better than peer-to-peer interaction, but given class size and the time needed for the process, it is not a feasible teaching strategy.

Instruction is important. The strongest learning gains for peer interaction were those where teachers gave students clear instructions for what to do in their groups. Explicit instructions to "arrive at a consensus" or "make sure you understand your partner's perspective" forced students to keep on track to debate, negotiate, and deepen their knowledge.

The Benefits of Collaboration

Building the group's collective capacity to achieve schoolwide goals must become a higher priority than the individual's independent learning.[5]

Rick DuFour

In schools, the era of isolated teaching is over. It is increasingly recognized that good teaching thrives in a collaborative learning environment created by teachers and school leaders in strong, professional communities working together to improve achievement.

High performing school systems throughout the world believe that when teachers collaborate they are capable of developing students' critical thinking skills, creativity, and mastery of complex content. (See Chapter 22.)

When teachers work together they produce the highest results in student learning and achievement.

What develops—and keeps—effective teachers is a structured, focused, and sustained professional development program that allows new teachers to be part of networks or study groups where all teachers share together, grow together, and learn to respect each other's work.

Teachers learn more in sustained teacher networks and study groups than with individual mentors. In high-performing schools, teachers are more likely to work with a collegial approach to decision-making and are willing to share with one another the knowledge and skills needed to help their students reach high academic standards.

- ◆ **Collaboration is the most effective way for teachers to learn their profession.**
- ◆ **Collaboration is the most effective way to train and retain good teachers.**
- ◆ **Collaborative practices make an impact on student achievement.**

[4] Jill Barshay, "The Science of Talking in Class," *The Hechinger Report*, February 3, 2020, accessed April 2, 2020, https://www.hechingerreport.org/the-science-of-talking-in-class.

[5] Rick DuFour, "In the Right Context," *Journal of Staff Development: The Principal* 22, no. 1 (Winter 2001): 14–17.

When teachers meet in teams and are laser-focused on student results, they ultimately create an impact that has positive outcomes throughout the school. Schools who value collaboration understand that their students' success is tied to how well their team members work together to achieve overall goals. The emphasis on making an impact is what energizes a staff of teachers to be even more effective and productive.

A Culture of Collaboration

Collaborative culture is the key to success. When you look at all the high-ranking countries, their schools have a collaborative culture where teachers have a history of teamwork and cooperation. They form networks and share resources and work together to create innovative practices that produce student achievement.[6]

Andreas Schleicher

There are many ways that a culture of collaboration, camaraderie, and cooperation can be instituted at a school. The first step is, of course, commitment. Teachers, administrators, and principals all have to agree to dedicate themselves to schoolwide systems and procedures—and students will ultimately be active participants.

Since the teacher is the most significant influence on student achievement, it is obvious that teachers must be trained to be effective from the start. After all, this is what happens when a new employee is hired at a company or small business. They are trained to be effective employees from the day they join and ongoing until the day they leave.

Teachers don't practice their profession as independent contractors. The principal manages the school, as a CEO or COO manages a business. Research has shown that there are learning gains in schools with a strong principal who exercises inclusive leadership with a well-aligned curriculum and a strong professional community of teachers. When teachers and administrators fail to work cooperatively, there is little or no improvement in student learning.[7]

They Had Never Seen Katie Teach

Three teachers had been teaching next door to each other for seven to nine years, Katie in the middle, and the other two on either side of her, yet not once had the two teachers ever been in Katie's classroom while she was teaching. Katie was an exceptional teacher, but the structure of the school was such that they were being excluded from the knowledge that Katie could have shared and that might have helped make them all better teachers.[8]

48

Katie's Outcome

Find out what happens to Katie by scanning the QR code.

> *Professional learning cannot thrive . . . in a silo. Strategic alignment and collaboration are core to achieving the vision of excellence for education organizations.*[9]
>
> Denise Glyn Borders, President and CEO
> Learning Forward

Collaboration is not just about teachers working together; it requires the entire staff to come together for one cause—student learning gains.

---

[6] Andreas Schleicher, "Collaborative Culture Is the Key to Success," *Times Educational Supplement*, March 8, 2013, accessed April 2, 2020, https://www.tes.com/news/collaborative-culture-key-success.

[7] Anthony S. Bryk, Penny Bender Sebring, Elaine Allensworth, Stuart Luppescu, and John Q. Easton, *Organizing Schools for Improvement: Lessons from Chicago* (Chicago: University of Chicago Press, 2010).

[8] Joan Richardson, "The Editor's Note: Getting Better at Learning," *Phi Delta Kappan* 98, no. 3 (October 31, 2016): 4.

[9] Denise Glyn Borders, "Strategic Alignment Is Ongoing, Challenging—And Necessary," *The Learning Professional* 40, no. 5 (October 2019): 8.

**The key to collaborative impact is that it is purposeful collaboration.
The purpose of the collaboration is to make an impact on student learning and achievement.**

The Academy of Singapore Teachers

The **Academy of Singapore Teachers** (AST) is a fraternity of teachers that works in synergy to foster a strong, teacher-led culture of professional collaboration and excellence. It is an organization set up by the teachers, with their own building, where they develop a common language to collaborate and learn from one another, intent on continuously furthering their capacity as teachers.

In most American educational systems there are no fraternities of teachers. There is no concentrated process to develop the instructional capacity of teachers; there is little or no collaboration; there is no common language. There is a serious lack of professional development organizations and therefore a disheartening lack of direction, or focus, within the entire educational system.

The **Academy of Singapore Teachers** aspires to be world-renowned for its professional excellence. It is. Mission accomplished!

Collaboration in Action

Imagine that on your first day as a new teacher, you are ushered into a curriculum group. It's not a group where people argue over their beliefs, ideology, and opinionated agenda. It's a group called "lesson study." As the name implies, the group studies lessons. Its function is to design and perfect lessons that make an impact on student learning.

Lesson study is a simple idea. If you want to improve instruction, what could be more obvious than collaborating with fellow teachers to plan, observe, and reflect on lessons?[10] During lesson study, teachers research and design a lesson, and then present it to other teachers, who give feedback. It's not about an individual teacher, but about teamwork.

Shota Matsumoto, as a first-year teacher in Tokyo, Japan, was immediately immersed in the culture of collaboration at his school. He became a member of a lesson study group in his first days as a teacher and will continue to be part of various groups throughout his career.

49

Lesson Study Process

Read the process that **Shota Matsumoto** and his colleagues engage in as they go through the details of a lesson.

Here is another example of collaboration in action. Picture a small group of teachers who bring a set of common assignments from their students to a meeting, and these are placed in one pile.

Then, subjectively, the assignments are divided into three groups—above average, average, and below average. One paper is pulled from the below average pile and the collaborative discussion is based on the student work (not the teacher's teaching methods).

---

[10] Catherine Lewis, "Does Lesson Study Have a Future in the United States?" *Nagoya Journal of Education and Human Development*, no. 1 (January 2002).

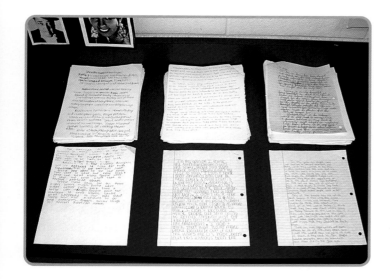

A Common Language

Building clarity around a common, foundational language is a prerequisite to collaborative impact. The process of identifying common instructional strategies is the pivotal step in bringing a faculty together with specific terminology. The expectation set in bringing the terminology to life sets the stage for common expectations.

Ruby Zickafoose, Principal
Manatee County, Florida

◆ Why is the paper considered below average?
◆ What feedback advice can be shared that will help the student to produce a higher performing or higher quality paper next time?

Then a paper is pulled from the average pile, and after that the above average pile, with the same two questions discussed. The teachers take notes that they will take back to class.

Back in class, the teacher is able to clearly and confidently explain to students the characteristics of the three levels, perhaps showing examples from a previous class or assignments from a prior year.

This process of constructive feedback is repeated and repeated until students understand the different levels of achievement and how maximum progress can be made.

The Power of Induction Programs

Just think of the impact that could be made on student achievement if every teacher had access to a simple induction process.

Once again—since the teacher is the most significant influence on student achievement, it makes total sense to train teachers to be effective from the very beginning of their employment with a district-wide, new teacher induction program.

Teachers want training, they want to fit in, and they want their students to achieve. For the most part, education has failed to recognize what other industries have recognized almost from the start—formalized, sustained training matters.

Effective induction programs have these three terms in common:

1. **Comprehensive**—The structure of the program is organized to include many activities and many people, not just a mentor.
2. **Coherent**—The various activities and people are logically connected to each other.
3. **Sustained**—The comprehensive and coherent program lasts for many years as continuing professional development.

It's the teacher. It's teaching.

Education experts will tell you that of all the things that go into improving a school, nothing—not class size, not technology, not length of the school day—pays off more than giving teachers the time for peer review and constructive feedback, exposure to the best teaching, and time to deepen their knowledge of what they're teaching.[11]

Thomas Friedman

[11] Thomas L. Friedman, "The Shanghai Secret," *The New York Times*, October 22, 2013.

Three New Teacher Induction Models

1. The Islip School District New Teacher Induction Program

One hundred percent of teachers who have gone through the three years of the **Islip Public Schools** new teacher induction program are still teaching and teaching well.

Linda Lippman is the assistant superintendent in the **Islip Public Schools** in Long Island, New York. She has been director of the district's induction program since its inception twenty years ago.

Linda says that she hires them, wires them, and, if necessary, fires them. The good news is that she has never had to fire anyone, because after three years of the Islip induction program, 100 percent of teachers receive tenure and stay to teach in a happy-to-teach-in school district. Since 2000, every teacher and administrator has gone through the induction program.

Because the induction program is so successful, new teacher attrition does not exist. Thus, each year only a small number of teachers need to be hired to replace experienced teachers who have moved or retired. As a result, Linda can be every new teacher's teacher, tutor, coach, and collaborative colleague. A consistent, trusting culture has been developed.

As Linda walks through different buildings each day, she has a connection with each teacher because she knows each teacher's journey. She is a resource, a coach, and always approachable.

Linda says, "What I do is unique, but it should not be, because every school district can do the same. I feel honored to be the architect of the induction program, to have my research on the need for new teachers to be supported realized, and to continue to work with such talent."

Islip's three-year induction prepares the newest educators for a career supporting the district's curriculum and possibilities for the future. It prepares teachers for the first day and every day of school thereafter. **The induction process builds relationships and trust.** A sense of belonging is cultivated among teachers that they replicate in the classroom. The results are the retention of highly qualified and invested teachers.

Everyone at Islip is well-trained and understands the need for an effective instructional program.

Islip's new teacher induction program begins with Orientation—three days of workshops, *before school begins,* to establish a learning environment and a sense of family. Workshops combine basic procedural information, introductions, a bus tour through the community, team building activities, food, first day advice, ice breakers, organizational strategies, meetings with various central office administrators, a welcome by the union president, and more food!

Year One teachers are presented with the book, ***THE First Days of School***, and begin the school year having completed ***THE Classroom Management Course*** online. This provides the classroom management skills necessary to ensure that they are successful from the very first minute of the very first day. Year One is used to tutor and coach the new teachers with Linda as the "I do" teacher.

Monthly meetings are held for three years, up until tenure. Meetings are framed around classroom management and instructional routines. The group

Active collaboration is part of the success of Islip's induction program.

Natalie Hamilton, an Islip teacher, teaches middle school family and consumer science. She has learned how to organize her instructional practices for maximum student success. Her classroom is organized with consistent procedures and her instruction reflects effective instruction practices.

- Natalie greets students at the door.
- Upon entering the room, students check the job assignment board for daily rotating lab responsibilities.
- Students sit with their cooking lab group and together review the Do Now assignment and the lesson objective.
- A demonstration sheet and recipe are on the desks for review.
- Natalie circulates the room as students work in a guided practice exercise and she provides assessment feedback.
- Natalie goes over review questions, safety precautions, and clarifies student questions in regard to the day's lab.
- Students begin lab procedures—putting on aprons, tying hair back, washing hands, and gathering ingredients and equipment.
- Students who did not complete the YouTube homework assignment watch the video during class time and answer questions while the lab group begins working. Once they have viewed the video assignment, they rejoin their respective lab groups.
- Students share various duties to complete the lab.
- Once the lab is complete, students fill out an evaluation sheet documenting taste, cooperation, and teamwork.

Because of Natalie's consistent classroom management plan and effective instructional practices, students and their families are engaged and student performance has soared.

proceeds through their three-year tenure track program as a cohort, building relationships and support groups. Collegial circles are held between the formal monthly meetings. Additionally, workshops are given on parent-teacher conferencing strategies, open school night, and an introduction to the essential elements of instruction.

Year Two teachers have a two-day orientation where management procedures are reviewed, and they are introduced to the essential elements of classroom instruction and The Learning Triangle. This is when they learn about lesson objectives, lesson targets, formative assessment, feedback, guided practice, independent practice, chunking, spaced practice, scaffolding, pacing, teacher clarity, and other tenets of effective instruction. These research-based strategies are used to deliver instruction in a culture of consistency. The teachers work together in cohort groups in "We do" projects and activities as they learn instructional practices.

Year Three teachers are asked to take what they have learned and apply it as independent practice to create classroom lessons. They learn questioning techniques, participate in instructional rounds, and increase their depth of content knowledge. Team building

A standing ovation is given to every teacher who has completed the Islip induction program and is prepared for a brilliant, satisfying career.

activities continue to promote the sense of cohesion and belonging. The cohort continues to grow together toward tenure. This is the "You do" phase.

After three years, teachers eligible for tenure are required to present a portfolio illustrating their three-year journey. The portfolio is designed to showcase their knowledge and skills and to chronicle their professional growth. The portfolio must include goals, strategies, evidence of student learning, and a statement entitled "I Believe." After a successful portfolio presentation, their tenure appointment is recommended to the Board of Education.

Year Four, on the first day of school, Linda presents a PowerPoint that showcases each newly-tenured teacher. After her introductory remarks, each teacher's baby picture is projected, then their "I Believe" statements, followed by their official teacher picture.

They are then introduced to the staff and receive a standing ovation to a cacophony of applause welcoming them to the Islip family of teachers.

What a magnificent and heartwarming welcome to the teaching profession by your colleagues!

The **Islip Public Schools** new teacher induction program is successful in creating effective teachers who produce student achievement.

- ◆ The student graduation rate is in the 98 to 99 percentile range.
- ◆ The number of students who receive the New York State Regents diploma is among the highest in the state.
- ◆ There is retention of highly qualified teachers in a career-long, developmental process.

The Islip induction program works because they spend their professional time and money developing human capital, and they do it consistently.

Study after study has shown that most new teachers would forego more money in favor of a good principal, the chance to work collaboratively with other highly motivated teachers, and an orderly, focused school atmosphere. An induction program provides these components.

The Islip induction program has shown that effective and successful teachers do not leave. They not only stay, but they are also the most significant factor in determining student learning and achievement.

What keeps good teachers are structured, sustained, intensive professional development programs that allow new teachers to observe others, to be observed by others, and to be part of learning teams or study groups where the focus is on student achievement.

2. **The Moberly New Teacher Induction Program**

If a rural school district says that it has difficulty attracting, hiring, and retaining new teachers, it should look at the induction model used in Moberly, Missouri.

The **Moberly School District** is located in a small town (population

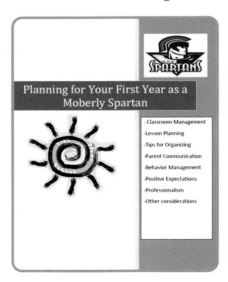

13,615 in 2019). It has a new teacher induction program called S.H.I.N.E—**S**upporting, **H**elping, and **I**nspiring **N**ew **E**ducators. Upon hiring, a new teacher is contacted by the S.H.I.N.E. Coordinator, **Tara Link**, and welcomed to the district.

The Moberly induction program structures its teachers to work collaboratively. Each new teacher is also put in contact with a retired teacher who provides positive encouragement. Working alone is not done in Moberly, especially for a new teacher.

The induction program is a multi-year process that produces happy and effective teachers.

Year One begins before the start of the school year and extends throughout the year.

- Induction begins upon hiring. New hires are contacted via email and encouraged to come visit their school. Resources are shared for finding housing, learning about the community, as well as school-specific resources.
- Two days of induction before school begins includes classroom time with a collaborative tutor, technology training, elementary and secondary model classroom experience, and learning district expectations.
- A bus tour is conducted by the leadership team to familiarize new teachers with the culture and community of the district.
- Teachers study resource books on classroom management and successful teaching components.
- Using **THE Classroom Management Book** as reference, teachers complete a classroom management plan prior to day one of teaching.
- There is a show of community business support to familiarize teachers with the local community.
- Moberly Spartan shirt and business promotional items are given as a welcoming gift.

- There are six professional development workshops held throughout the school year—one full-day workshop, three after-school sessions, and two half-day workshops. (During the day, workshops are held in off-campus locations to expose teachers to community resources and assets.) The focus of the workshops is on lesson planning, student learning, instruction, and classroom management.
- A coach for each teacher is provided from the same grade level or content area.
- There are weekly classroom visits and observations from the S.H.I.N.E. director, and weekly reflection opportunities, including watching a video of themselves instructing.
- There is weekly collaboration in the Professional Learning Community with cohorts in the same grade level/subject area.
- There are classroom release opportunities to observe other teachers.
- An end-of-year recognition celebration is held with the induction team, administrators, and school board members.

Year Two teachers continue in the same cohort and work to further develop lesson planning, instruction, and classroom management strategies. They meet quarterly for professional development and continue to meet regularly with their coaches. They observe other classrooms, as well as participate in self-video reflection opportunities. They also have access to online professional development resources, organized social events, continued help from a retired teacher to provide positive encouragement, and updates and invitations to attend local events or special activities in the community.

The S.H.I.N.E. program has been in existence for over ten years. New teacher support through both tutoring and coaching is now embedded in the culture of the Moberly School District. It is the expectation that the entire learning community supports one another. There is a common language, and all teachers model the foundations that have been established with the beginning teachers.

The most telling comments come from the first- and second-year teachers who talk to their college friends in education and learn the support they are receiving exceeds that of most of their counterparts in other districts. The Moberly retention rate for beginning teachers is above 83 percent, which exceeds the state average of 60 percent over the past ten years. As Moberly is a rural school district, teachers do sometimes leave for larger metropolitan districts near their homes or for family reasons. But when they leave, they are confident professionals, ready, willing, and able to tackle any challenges they may face elsewhere.

> **A trained teacher is always an asset wherever they are and wherever they go.**

3. The Clark County New Teacher Onboarding and Development Program

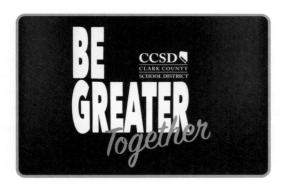

The **Clark County School District** in Las Vegas is the fifth largest school district in the United States. It hires hundreds and even thousands of new teachers every year and has been able to show a retention rate higher than the national average.

Clark County provides its new teachers with a customized, multi-year, induction program known as the Beginning Teacher Induction Program (BTIP). The BTIP consists of a series of professional learning opportunities that are specifically designed to support new teachers throughout their first two years of hire with the goal of retaining them for a life-long career.

Many of the professional learning opportunities focus on classroom management, instructional engagement, and building a positive, common culture.

The induction process is focused on organizing collaborative team opportunities with the theme, "We are centered on the idea that as a larger collective, we can all be greater together."

In a typical year, the induction program provides approximately ninety-nine large-scale, professional development opportunities to provide learning experience. During each professional learning session, instructors demonstrate multiple instructional strategies that new teachers can take back to their classrooms. Through these on-going induction events, relationships are built that positively impact the new teachers throughout their career to as they strive to "Be Greater Together."

Collaborative Impact

Teachers hold the potential of their students and their futures in their heads, hearts, and hands.

It's an enormous responsibility and it is no wonder that they crave connection and support. Induction and professional development programs are essential. A commitment to developing teachers the moment they are hired makes them feel valued. It gives them assurance that they have made the right choice professionally and the confidence to continuously improve as they practice their craft.

Learn. Anticipate. Plan for an effective career.

Leaving a Legacy of Love

There are administrators and policy makers whose high expectations for teaching and learning have made a significant impact on the whole school culture.

In almost thirty years as a public school superintendent, I have worked with some of the most extraordinary people in the world. Many of them are teachers. These extraordinary individuals consistently display the finest qualities of our profession, and I believe for them teaching is a calling.

There are other dedicated educators effectively teaching our children, and I believe they fall into several other categories.

There are those few that see teaching as a job. It is a means to earn an income. It may be an interim step on a career path or a second occupation leading to retirement. These individuals are competent, begin their duties on time, end them on time, and have fulfilling lives outside of their classrooms.

Most individuals see teaching as a profession. These individuals believe that teaching is their career and are proud of their profession and their contribution to their students and community. These teachers will spend the time necessary to support their students and continue to grow in their profession. They will use their personal resources to support their students. They are the hard-working, dedicated educators that give honor to our profession.

At the far end of the distribution are those special teachers that are an inspiration to their students, community, and their peers. These are the individuals that see teaching as a calling. It is part of their DNA.

They are the role models every adult remembers as a student and every parent wants for their child. These are the educators that see teaching opportunities for their students in every setting, every event, and every garage sale. No weekend, vacation, holiday, or family event is safe from their passion to serve their students. They will worry, sacrifice, and innovate so each child in their classroom will have every opportunity to succeed. Their passion for teaching and learning is unbounded and infectious.

Those unique educators who believe that their chosen profession is a calling are rewarded with a lifetime of experiences and memories that reinforce the significance their role. Photos, mementos, gifts, Bar Mitzvahs, Quinceañeras, graduations, weddings, phone calls, and letters from students past and present are among the treasures that accrue in the heart of these educators. In speaking with gifted teachers about their lives, I found a common theme unites their experiences. LOVE. Love of their profession, love of their students and their students' greatest gift to them—Love.

Kelvin Lee, Superintendent, retired
Dry Creek Joint ESD, California

One looks back with appreciation to the brilliant teachers, but with gratitude to those who touched our human feelings. The curriculum is so much necessary raw material, but warmth is the vital element for the growing plant and for the soul of the child.

Carl Jung

People are social creatures—we are motivated by relationships. Teachers are more likely to succeed if they feel connected to their school community and each other. Teachers thrive when they are able to collaborate constructively with colleagues. Teachers want and need to belong. If they do not belong in a positive way, they will belong in an apathetic, negative way.

> **Coming together is a beginning;**
> **keeping together is progress;**
> **working together is success.**

Teachers remain with a district when they feel supported by administrators and have formed strong bonds with colleagues. Research has shown that teachers in high-performing schools are more likely to work in a collegial culture of decision-making and are willing to share with one another the needed knowledge and skills to help their students reach high academic standards.[12]

> **It is imperative that administrators and policy makers create schools with a culture where collaborative impact is focused on pursuing a common vision for student learning and achievement.**

[12] Madiha Shah, "The Importance and Benefits of Teacher Collegiality in Schools—A Literature Review," *Procedia - Social and Behavioral Sciences* 46 (September 2012): 1242-1246.

Mastering Instruction

 Effective teaching thrives in a collaborative learning environment created by teachers and school leaders.

 Collaborative practices make a significant impact on student achievement.

 Professional development and induction programs foster collaborative practices.

 Collaboration is the most effective way to train and retain good teachers.

...Produces Achievement.

> *Effective teachers attain Mastery. Empowered teachers achieve Impact.*

Your Journey to Impact

As a result of what you have learned from chapters 1–21 and incorporated into your classroom teaching, you will have arrived at the Mastery stage of your professional life. Working with your colleagues, you can all make a collaborative impact on student learning and achievement.

You know to focus on each student's potential to succeed—Student Obsession—and to address these questions when designing instruction.

- ◆ What should my students know?
- ◆ How will I know when they know?
- ◆ What do I do if they do not know?
- ◆ What do I do if they already know?

You know what good instruction is. Effective instructional practices are foundational strategies that cost nothing to implement, are not controversial, and do not require the school day to be altered. Implement the strategies and practices and use them over and over again until they become second nature—a routine—in your instructional management plan.

Decades' worth of research has consistently found that teacher effectiveness is the most important school-based input into student achievement.[1]

---

[1] Raj Chetty, John N. Friedman, and Jonah E. Rockoff, "Measuring the Impacts of Teachers II: Teacher Value-Added and Student Outcomes in Adulthood," *American Economic Review* 104, no. 9 (September 2014): 2633–2679.

Surviving Survival

> **My mission in life is not merely to survive, but to thrive; and to do so with some passion, some compassion, some humor, and some style.**
>
> Maya Angelou

In Chapter 1, we presented the four stages of teaching with the hope that the information you have gleaned from studying this book will accelerate your growth and move you to the next stage in your career:

1. Fantasy—when the teacher has illusions of improbable success
2. Survival—when the teacher is trying to cope in the classroom
3. Mastery—when the teacher employs effective instruction practices
4. Impact—when the teacher is making a significant difference in students' lives

*This year I am teaching a course I have never taught before. I'm constantly reminded what it is like to be a beginning teacher. Giant of education, **Harry Wong**, reminds us that even experienced teachers can enter that lowest rung he calls "Survival mode" at any point in their career. However, I think he is wrong about one thing. There is a mode lower than Survival.*

Bobbie Cavnar
North Carolina Teacher-of-the-Year

This book has shared all the strategies, techniques, research-based effect-sizes, and teacher stories—everything teachers need to know—to reach Mastery, and eventually, we hope, Impact.

So why are so many teachers still stuck in the Survival stage of their professional journey when the road map is so clear?

To journey from Survival to Mastery to Impact requires tenacity and dedication—and faith and confidence that you have the skillset and capacity to continuously improve.

Can Technology Deliver?

Technology is by far the most over-rated classroom resource. There is absolutely no assurance that spending money on technology will benefit students and what they will achieve.

Education technology software spending alone totals $8.4 billion with over $5.6 billion wasted each year from non or underutilization. Two-thirds of software license purchases go unused.[2] When these resources and related activities are not fully harnessed, two unfortunate things occur—money is wasted, and most importantly, student achievement suffers.

Just think how much student achievement could be improved if a fraction of the wasted $5.6 billion was spent on professional development to train confident, skilled teachers; foster effective instructional practices; and pay teachers the salaries they deserve!

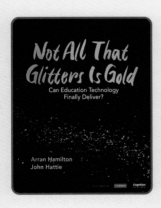

> *Sixty years of evaluation data show no major quantum leap in the impact of technology on learner outcomes. Most of the current technological interventions in schooling remain average or below their ability to enhance student learning when the technology is in schools and classrooms.*[3]

Arran Hamilton and John Hattie

Unlike countries that score high on international ranking tests, in the United States—most unfortunately—we do not prioritize student learning, effective teacher instruction, professional development for teachers, and collaboration among teachers. Instead, we put the latest fad first. It's *fad du jour* from year to year. Teachers are forced to jump from one program to the next, from one tech fad to another, on the road to who knows where—never being given the opportunity to ask and analyze where they are going and how they will know if they have arrived there.

Billions of dollars have been spent over the past seventy-five years chasing silver bullet programs shot randomly at incoherent reform targets hoping our education system will be revitalized and brought up to international norms.

Eric Hanushek, Stanford University, points out that among all the countless reforms tried over the years—smaller schools, smaller class sizes, beautiful new buildings—the one that correlates most reliably with good student outcomes is the presence of good teachers and principals who stick around.[4]

[2] "Glimpse K12 Analysis of School Spending Shows that Two-Thirds of Software License Purchases Go Unused," *Glimpse K12*, May 15, 2019, https://www.glimpsek12.com/blog-posts/glimpse-k12-analysis-of-school-spending-shows-that-two-thirds-of-software-license-purchases-go-unused.

[3] Arran Hamilton and John Hattie, *Not All That Glitters Is Gold: Can Education Technology Finally Deliver?* (Thousand Oaks, CA: Corwin; Auckland: Cognition Education Group, 2021), https://www.visiblelearning.com/sites/default/files/not-all-that-glitters-is-gold.pdf.

[4] Daniel Duane, "How the Startup Mentality Failed Kids in San Francisco," *Wired*, June 28, 2018, https://www.wired.com/story/willie-brown-middle-school-startup-mentality-failed/.

Repeating the Same Programs, Fads, and Issues Decade After Decade

In the January 2000 issue of the *Phi Delta Kappan*, **Wade Carpenter** wrote an article where he counted three hundred sixty-one ideas promoted to enhance education in the pages of the journal during a ten-year period beginning in 1987.[5] The programs listed were all created by caring and well-meaning people, but few made a dent in improving student learning.

Fighting for Change in Your School: How to Avoid Fads and Focus on Substance by **Harvey Alvy** listed two hundred forty practices and trends from the past thirty-plus years.[6]

The focus of the American education system is on the current fad or program when it should be on training for effective teaching practices and student learning. Scan through this list of some of the ideas tried through the years.

21st Century curriculum
Academy-based learning
Accomplishment-based learning
Achievement-based assessment
Adaptive assessment
Adaptive learning
Adaptive technology
After-school programs
Alignment of assessment
Alternative assessment
Argument Driven Inquiry
Art-centered learning
Assessment-based achievement
Assertive discipline
Audio Lingual Method
Blended learning
Block scheduling
Brain compatibility
Care-based practices
Case-based learning
Challenge-based learning
Clerestory learning
Community-based learning
Computer-based reading
Concerns-based improvement

Constructivism
Culturally responsive teaching
Curriculum-based measurements
Customized instruction
Data driven instruction
Deficit/Abundance Model
Design-based learning
Detracking
Differentiated instruction
Digital-based learning
Discovery method
Diversity-based curriculum
Dual-enrollment program
Earth-bound education
Embodied learning
Emotional intelligence
Evidence-based education
Experiential education
Flipped classroom
Four-day school week
Game-based learning
Games-based curriculum
Garden-based learning
Goals 2000
Hemisphericity

High-leveraged content
High-stakes testing
Hybrid learning
Inquiry-based learning
Interdisciplinary teaching
Land-based learning
Learning ecosystems
Learning to learn
Linked learning
Longer school day/year
Looping
Magnet schools
Maker movement
Mass customized learning
Micro-schools
Modular scheduling
Multi-age classrooms
Multi-classroom teachers
Multicultural education
Multi-dimensional assessment
Multiple intelligence
Nature-based learning
Needs-based education
Open classroom
Open-source learning
Outcomes-based education
Paradigm shift
Passion-based learning
PBIS
Performance assessment
Personal learning environment
Personalized instruction
Personalized, blended learning
Phenomenon-based learning
Picting
Play-based learning
Portfolio assessment
Practice-focused curriculum

Principle-based education
Problem-based learning
Proficiency-based learning
Project-based learning
Reality therapy
Reciprocal accountability
Reggio Emilia approach
Relationship-centered approach
Renaissance science
Restorative justice
Revolutionary learning
School choice
Self-directed learning
Self-esteem
Self-regulated education
Service-based learning
Shared decision making
Single-gender classes
Small class/school size
Social-emotional learning
Start school day later
Strength-based learning
Student-led learning
Studio-based learning
Systems thinking skills
Teaching for social justice
Team-based learning
Technology-based learning
Thematic-integrated instruction
Theme-based learning
Three-dimensional teaching
Total Quality Management (TQM)
Virtual learning
Whole language
Work-based learning
Year-around schools
Zero tolerance
Zombie-based learning

[5] Wade Carpenter, "Ten Years of Silver Bullets: Dissenting Thoughts on Education Reform," *Phi Delta Kappan* 81, no. 5 (January 2000): 383-389.

[6] Harvey Aly, *Fighting for Change in Your School: How to Avoid Fads and Focus on Substance*, (Alexandria, VA: ASCD, 2017).

Lower Than Survival

Bobbie Cavnar knows that there is a level lower than Survival. Survival has many levels and some of them are the lowest of the low. There are ways to recover from this stage. It is not a level to be mired in the rest of your professional career. You are the difference in the classroom and in the lives of your students. Strive for Mastery and Impact.

I have entered a mode that comes after you have already died, crossed through the threshold of hell, and are scouring the ground for change to pay the boatman on the river Styx because you spent your last few coins on construction paper. I call this Eighth Circle mode because so much of it makes me feel like a fraud.

Bobbie realized that what he had been trapped to do in his classroom made him feel like a phony.

I find myself Googling phrases like
- *What is AP Language and Composition?*
- *How do you teach AP Language and Composition?*
- *Why is one of my eyelids twitching?*

Quickly I discovered that, no matter what the topic, there is a teacher, somewhere, who has already broken it down into a video, made an activity, written a worksheet, and created all of the PowerPoint slides as well. Like the God of the Sistine Chapel proffering the divine touch to Adam, so John Green offered me a video lecture on the entire history of the 1920s in just fifteen minutes. I then knew that with teacherspayteachers.com at my side I could crawl from the primordial ooze. No longer would I be the Neanderthal teacher bent over my research notes. I would stand tall at my interactive whiteboard while Ken Burns answered their questions, as nature intended.

One day, a student asked if I ever read the comments on the videos. Now, I usually avoid Internet comments because of a little-known rule of the Internet called "Godwin's Law." It states that the longer an Internet discussion goes on, the likelihood of one of the participants comparing the other to Hitler approaches 100 percent. But I was curious, so I scrolled down and scanned the comments.

- *Hahaha my English teacher shows us vids all class, every class, and calls it teaching.*
- *Who else wishes that history teachers would, you know, actually teach like he does?*
- *My app world teacher uses this guy to teach our class while he sleeps, smh.*

It was like walking out of a darkened theater and suddenly discovering it is broad daylight outside. The teacher I imagined myself to be was ripped away and I was forced to look at the blinding reality that I had become a mechanical teacher. I had allowed technology to replace too much of my own labor and with it to replace the soul of my teaching.

Bobbie then discovered empowerment and joy by creating his own curriculum and his own lessons, using his own creativity and his own passion, in his own classroom for his students.

John Philip Sousa, in his article, "The Menace of Mechanical Music," warned of the consequences of becoming reliant on technology in our lives. "When a mother can turn on the phonograph with the same ease that she applies to the electric light, will she croon her baby to slumber with sweet lullabies, or will the infant be put to sleep by machinery?

"Children are naturally imitative and if, in their infancy, they hear only phonographs will they not sing, or if they sing at all, will they, in imitation, simply become human phonographs without soul or expression?"

Such is the state of too many teachers, including myself. We have become divorced from the labor of creating. The slow, methodical process of making a worksheet or of designing an activity can easily be avoided with a quick Google search. Ready-made curriculum units and "creative techniques" are packaged for sale at every workshop and districts often create websites where teachers can download pre-made units for instruction.

Sousa worried that when people could hear any kind of music they wish with the flip of a switch, they would avoid the labor of acquiring the skill to play and sing for themselves, but, more importantly, they would lose that human bond that comes with shared expression.

We must never allow ourselves to be separated from the process of content creation.

Creating our own assessments allows us to picture our students in every aspect of creation and thus to design something that is truly responsive to our class. By creating our own activities, we are forced to think deeply about the outcomes we wish to see and how best to design an exercise for that outcome. In my delivering the background information rather than John Green, my students see my passion, not someone else's, and I model for them the struggle and labor of academic study. How can we scold students for Googling answers rather than thinking for themselves when they are simply mimicking the behavior we used to create the question in the first place?

When we create our own curriculum, we express our creativity, our passions, and ourselves. We are using a piece of ourselves as professionals to connect with our students. That is the soul of teaching and that is what we lose when we rely on ready-made lessons or programs.

Good teaching has always been about building relationships. This is the dangerous side of "best practice" centered curriculum development. Often what is best for our students is not the "best" lesson or the "best" activity, but the lesson or activity that is uniquely ours. The activity I make for my students is uniquely ours. The relationship built when I look them in the eyes as I deliver the lesson is uniquely ours. It may not always be the "best" practice, but it is always authentic practice.

Like a mother who sings her child to sleep, you may not always be the "best" singer, but there is no substitute for you in the eyes of your children. **"**

Bobbie Cavnar is the 2016–2017 North Carolina Teacher-of-the-Year and the 2018 NEA Foundation's Top Public School Teacher. He teaches Advanced Placement Literature and heads the English Department at South Point High School in Gaston County, North Carolina.

Committing to Curriculum

Oretha Ferguson, a high school teacher in Fort Smith, Arkansas, is familiar with the **Bobbie Cavnar** story. She shares, "I thrive over creating something new that comes straight from my heart and into the heads, hands, and, hopefully, hearts of my students." (See her lesson in Chapter 18.)

If you have not been provided with a curriculum guide for your district, ask for it. It is essential that teachers in a school have access to one to ensure their lessons are aligned to the district's curriculum and student progress is measured and steady.

In high-performing schools and districts, a cohesive curriculum has been formulated and teachers continuously collaborate to refine and perfect it. Effective teachers put their heart and soul into finding creative ways to teach the curriculum.

> **The curriculum content drives instruction and effective instruction drives student achievement.**

All high-performing school systems have a content-rich curriculum. Teachers are hired to instruct the content specified by the curriculum. Throughout instruction there is constant assessment to evaluate if the content is being learned and taught effectively according to The Learning Triangle. Not to have a curriculum is like a store with no merchandise to sell, a stage play without a script, and a sports team without plays to run.

Ask classroom teachers in the United States what they teach, and you will typically get these responses.

- ◆ I am doing personalized instruction.
- ◆ I teach project-based learning.
- ◆ I use technology in a blended approach.
- ◆ I am into social-emotional learning.
- ◆ I do inquiry learning.
- ◆ I do not teach; I facilitate.

These responses center on themselves and what they are doing.

Ask classroom teachers in high performing countries like Finland, Singapore, Germany, Australia, Poland, and Estonia the same question, and you will get this type of response.

- ◆ I teach history.
- ◆ I teach music.
- ◆ I teach language.
- ◆ I teach math.
- ◆ I teach science.
- ◆ I teach the ministry's curriculum.
- ◆ I teach students to use the knowledge learned and apply it to life.

These responses clearly state what they teach and what their students are learning. These teachers are supported by a carefully constructed curriculum that gradually, consistently, and coherently imparts the skills and knowledge students need to be successful academically and professionally.

Students do best when the design of the lesson furthers what they already know. Students can only read about, write about, and work with what they have been introduced to and have internalized—even if only partially. If they have had no previous exposure to concepts, they tend to flounder and become discouraged. Knowledge builds on knowledge. **Thus, a structured, content-focused curriculum is of utmost importance.**

> *We in the education establishment in America have treated curriculum as ancillary, as if it's like the drapes on your walls and windows rather than a fundamental piece of the framework of your home. In every other functional education system in the world, the curriculum is thought of as a foundational piece.*
>
> *This is not the time for bunches of new ideas. This is the time for following through on our commitments.*[7]
>
> John White, former Superintendent
> Louisiana Department of Education

[7] Beth Hawkins, "The 74 Interview: Outgoing Louisiana Chief John White on the New Orleans Experiment, His Longevity and What It Means to Be Well Educated," February 18, 2020, https://www.the74million.org/article/the-74-interview-outgoing-louisiana-chief-john-white-on-the-new-orleans-experiment-his-longevity-and-what-it-means-to-be-well-educated/.

It's the Teacher

Absolutely no educational system in the world, except in the United States, is run on the endless, repetitive, futile cycle of chasing one program or fad after another. (See page 267.) A program is not an instructional strategy. A program is what a teacher is asked to follow blindly, expecting it to instruct students and achieve academic results. Teachers are hostages of the next miracle cure or technological innovation that has been imposed on their school.

It can't be emphasized enough that one of the saddest stories of the past seventy years is that money spent on fads, programs, and so-called innovations has a dishearteningly small effect on student achievement. Education in the United States has a junkyard of used programs. We even recycle unsuccessful programs, give them a fresh coat of paint, and try to pass them off as new.

> **Students do not learn from programs, structural changes, or fads, and there is no research evidence of the effectiveness for most of them.**

The Internet is full of agencies that report the top stories of the day, week, and year, and rarely is there substantial discussion about providing the necessary infrastructure to train teachers to be effective. The stories, once again, focus on the latest programs and interventions that epitomize the directionless, hodgepodge of decisions that govern the American education system.

It is a source of continuing amazement to me that almost all the discourse regarding restructuring and reforming schools over the last decade has emphasized every conceivable form of change and virtually ignored the obvious: getting better teachers. It's the teacher, stupid![8]

Martin Haberman
University of Wisconsin-Milwaukee

There are so many immediate priorities in education, but we are mired in ideological battles.

- **Linda Darling-Hammond**, Stanford University, says, "In the United States, we pour energy into a potpourri of innovations and then change course every few years."[9]

- **Marc Tucker**, Harvard University, determined that, "In the U.S., we don't have a system per se, but rather a series of 'random acts of intervention.'"[10]

Every few years, organizations such as the Program for International Student Assessment (PISA); Trends in International Mathematics and Science Study (TIMSS); and the Organization for Economic Co-operation and Development (OECD) publish their rankings of the world's educational systems. The United States is buried low on the list, bested by countries such as Estonia, Poland, Kazakhstan, New Zealand, Australia, South Korea, Finland, Singapore, Germany, Japan, Canada (Ontario), Netherlands, Belgium, Switzerland, and Ireland. There is a very good reason so many countries surpass us.

Research tells us that when teachers receive well-designed professional development, an average of forty-nine hours spread over six to twelve months, they can increase student achievement by as much as twenty-one percentile points. Workshops that are considered as "one-shot, "drive-by," or obligatory meetings lasting fourteen hours or less show no statistically significant effect on student learning. The most effective professional development programs are job-embedded and provide teachers with collaborative learning, active learning, and sustained learning.[11]

[8] Martin Haberman, "Preparing Teachers for the Real World of Urban Schools," *The Educational Forum* 58, no. 2 (Winter 1994).

[9] Linda Darling-Hammond, "Soaring Systems: High Flyers All Have Equitable Funding, Shared Curriculum, and Quality Teaching," *American Educator* 34, no. 4 (Winter 2010-2011).

[10] JD Solomon, "Why American Education Pales—and Fails—on the Global Stage," *District Administration* (June 2019).

[11] Vanessa Vega, "Teacher Development Research Review: Keys to Educator Success," *Edutopia*, November 1, 2015, https://www.edutopia.org/teacher-development-research-keys-success..

**High-performing countries stress
a content-rich curriculum taught by effective teachers
who are high-performing instructors.**

Empower Teachers

In the high-performing schools of the world, every teacher is trained to develop mastery in their instructional effectiveness day after day. High-performing school systems have achieved their status by focusing on three factors:[12]

1. **Recruit:** School systems selectively recruit the right people. In Singapore and Finland, only one person out of ten who applies is admitted to a teacher training university.

2. **Train:** They extensively train teachers and administrators for life. In Singapore, teachers and administrators receive one hundred hours of training each year until they retire.

3. **Empower:** Trained teachers in high-performing countries are given authority and permission to exercise their knowledge and skills in whatever ways they deem best for their students.

> **Create an effective teacher and that teacher will make an impact on students' lives and futures.**

To improve the educational system, a school, a district, a state, a country must improve the proficiency of its teachers. High-performing countries know this. They improve their education systems by investing in their teachers' professional development. The highest achieving countries by international measures are particularly intent on developing teachers' expertise before they enter the profession and throughout their careers. They empower teachers.

Empowered teachers have the capacity to attain Impact. Empowered teachers know what they are doing. They have a skill set. They know how to teach

for achievement. They make a difference in their school; they transform and empower their students.

When thinking of student learning and achievement, the future is not in technology or another program. The future is the teacher—the empowered, effective teacher.

Students need skilled, caring teachers who provide them with essential knowledge, as well as a moral compass that will guide them and help them cope with life's difficulties and uncertainties. Students want to be connected to a nurturing, trustworthy school community that instills hope for the future.

In many countries around the world, teachers are recognized as so essential to the economic, political, and social well-being of their nations that leaders have built entire systems to foster their recruitment, development, retention, advancement, and empowerment.

Good teachers can teach anywhere and with no more than a chalkboard or even pencil and paper—even under the shade of an Acacia tree.

In every high-performing country
- ◆ teachers are trained in their content area, pedagogical skills, and research procedures.
- ◆ teachers have a cultural affinity and professional obligation to work together in groups.
- ◆ teachers are empowered and expected to design and create the best education for their students.

[12] Linda Darling-Hammond, Ruth Chung Wei, and Alethea Andree, *How High-Achieving Countries Develop Great Teachers* (Stanford: SCOPE—Stanford Center for Opportunity Policy in Education, August 2010).

In high-performing countries, a new teacher is immediately introduced and inducted into the staff with which they will be working. The cycle of collaborative professional development begins and continues for the duration of their professional career. Equity is enhanced and instruction is improved.

High-performing countries emphasize curriculum and teachers are empowered to create curriculum together, teach the curriculum, and assess the curriculum school by school, district by district. The existing curriculum is continuously improved. In Finland, with one of the highest performing school systems in the world, teachers determine what needs to be taught in their schools and how it should be taught. Influences from elsewhere are seen as a distraction.

High-performing school systems succeed because their systems are understandable, transparent, and coherent. Teachers are treated as highly competent professionals who strive to ensure the best learning conditions for their students. These are systems where teachers collaboratively empower each other to provide greater impact.

Based on a half-century of research on student achievement, this single statement should be the beacon for **EVERY** education institution worldwide.

Teacher quality is the most significant factor affecting student performance.[13]

Empower Yourself

As has been shown in this chapter and Chapter 21, there are also education systems, school leaders, and policy makers that fail to provide teachers with the support and training they need and deserve. What can be done in these circumstances?

In Chapter 1, we shared this research finding.

The single greatest effect on student achievement is the teacher to whom a student gets assigned.

> *While technology strives to build first-class robots, as teachers we must strive to build first-class humans. Values such as compassion and empathy as well as human relationships cannot be automated. A machine can give you the facts and information, but human communication and social relationships are a different kind of connection.*[14]

Chua-Lim Yen Ching
Deputy Director-General of Education
Executive Director, Academy of Singapore Teachers

Throughout the book, we've shared the importance of the lessons you teach.

To make an impact on student learning, a coherent, knowledge-rich, well-rounded curriculum is the key to student achievement.

And now, in conclusion, we come back to how we began.

The single greatest impact on student achievement is the effectiveness of the teacher.

This is the key to making an impact.

When you make an impact, it's not what has happened to you, but what you have done for others.

You, the teacher, are the person who has the greatest impact on the success of your students. Knowing

---

[13] Goldhaber, "In Schools."

[14] Yen Ching Chua-Lim, "Teachers as Transformative Agents of Change," *Research Within Reach* 69, June 2019, https://singteach.nie.edu.sg/2019/07/23/issue69-bigidea/.

Beyond the Trailer Park[15]

At seven years old, I held onto the rusted chains of the trailer park's playground swing, pumping my legs ferociously, hoping my toes would eventually touch the top of the swing set. Little did I know that if I had made it high enough to reach the top of the swing bar, I would have seen what was on the other side of the singlewide mobile homes. I had no idea that a university was sitting in my backyard. At that age, neither did any other golden-blond, blue-eyed, freckle-faced boys in my neighborhood.

I was destined to stay in that trailer park forever, just like the rest of my friends, and never see what was beyond the playground. But my destiny changed when I met Mrs. Puryea, my second-grade teacher. She spoke a different truth into my soul that year, and it has followed me throughout my life. She believed I was smart. She believed I was kind. She believed I was responsible. She let me join the Self-Starters Club, a prestigious group of children in the class who got to walk to the lunchroom on their own and who wore a special button denoting utmost responsibility.

Mrs. Puryea called on me to sit on her special barstool at the front of the class, hold her teacher's edition, and give the spelling test to the rest of my peers because I consistently earned 100 percent correct on the pretest earlier in the week. She instilled in me a love of learning that year and, consequently, from holding the teacher's edition, sparked a love of teaching.

Nearly thirty years later, as I sat at my desk at that very university just on the other side of the trailer park, I received an e-mail from Mrs. Puryea. She addressed me as Dr. Zugelder, proud that I had earned such a credential, and invited me to spend her last day of teaching with her, as she had finally reached retirement.

Elated and humbled, I eagerly showed up to her classroom, where I was greeted with the warmest hug and most infectious smile. She handed me a torn, nearly battered photo album and insisted I take it with me. Because I didn't hold on to it securely, the cover—attached by only its last dab of glue—nearly fell to the floor. The cover was decorated with the handwritten words, "Mrs. Puryea's Book of Smiles, 1984–1985." It was filled with photographic memories from that year my classmates and I spent with her in second grade.

I sat next to Mrs. Puryea as she flipped through, page by page, telling me stories about all my classmates. Near the middle of the album, I spotted a photo of a golden-blond, blue-eyed, freckle-faced boy. I was sitting on a barstool, reading from a teacher's edition, giving the spelling test to my peers. Next to the photo, she had written "Professor Zugelder."

It is quite serendipitous that my trailer park was named University Village. Not only did Mrs. Puryea help me see what was beyond that playground, but she also believed that I would be a professor at a university. Second grade foreshadowed the career I have now, as a university professor.

Inspiring teachers believe in their students. They show them places they never thought they could go. They speak greatness into them, and they do not settle for mediocrity. It took a "village" of wonderful teachers and mentors to help me see beyond the trailer park . . . and Mrs. Puryea took the lead.

Bryan S. Zugelder
Associate Dean and Associate Professor of Education
James Madison University

---

[15]Bryan S. Zugelder, "Beyond the Trailer Park," *Kappa Delta Pi Record* 56, no. 3 (July 2020). Story shared with permission.

that, you have a choice to make. If you are in Survival mode, will you passively accept staying there at the detriment of your students and yourself? Or will you seek to empower yourself to make a positive impact in the lives of your students—and in your own life?

The focus of this book has been on improving student learning. To do this, take responsibility for your career and develop your skill set and competencies. Surround yourself with exceptional people who have a similar moral compass to your own and who share your vision. Gather together a cohort of teachers and work collaboratively to create the most effective curriculum possible. Support, inspire, and nourish each other.

It's a fact that either you shape the future or the future shapes you. If your school lacks the leadership necessary to promote and support what you now know is the most efficient and effective way to achieve success with students, **you will have to empower yourself to be your own leader, your own hero**.

It takes courage to empower yourself. You have to have a dream and be dedicated to pursuing that dream. You have to consciously take responsibility for creating a personal system that is organized, consistent, and coherent and can be adjusted for continuous improvement. There are numerous examples in this book of schools and teachers who have done just that. They are inspiring islands of stability and success in a sea of confusion and uncertainty.

If you are not moving forward, you are stagnating. If you are stagnating, you may even regress.

> *There's one investment that supersedes all others.*
>
> *Invest in yourself.*
>
> *Nobody can take away what you've got in yourself, and everybody has potential they haven't used yet.*[16]
>
> Warren Buffett

Choose Impact

> **Aim for Impact and fulfill your fantasy of making a difference in the lives of all of your students.**

The greatest ability a person possesses is the power to choose.

- We are free to choose to be the person we want to become.
- We are free to choose our values.
- We are free to choose how much we want to learn.
- We are free to choose what we want to accomplish in life.
- We are free to choose what we want to choose.

Only when you build your own capacity and empower yourself can you have an impact on your students. Attend workshops, conferences, and virtual learning opportunities. Discover what is happening around the world in education. Learn from it. Choose to enhance the quality of your life and the competence of your profession.

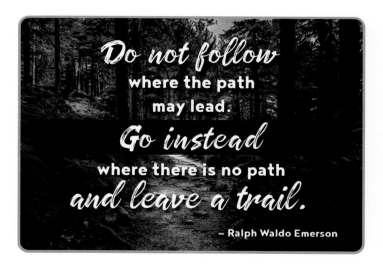

Do not follow where the path may lead. Go instead where there is no path and leave a trail.
– Ralph Waldo Emerson

[16]Carmine Gallo, "The One Investment Warren Buffett Says Will Change Your Life (And It's Not A Stock)," *Forbes* (November 30, 2017).

Twenty years from now you will be more disappointed by the things that you didn't do than by the ones you did do. So throw off the bowlines. Sail away from the safe harbor. Catch the trade winds in your sails. Explore. Dream. Discover.[17]

H. Jackson Brown Jr.
P.S. I Love You

The greatest quality a person can have is the desire to make other people's lives better. Review what it takes to be a master, effective teacher and then, each day, each year, build your own life, step-by-step, skill set-by-skill set, so that you will make an impact on your students' lives.

The Effective Teacher

bibiphoto / Shutterstock.com

In April 2018, an aircraft was flying from New York to Dallas near cruising altitude when one of the engines blew out. The pilot descended the aircraft quickly and landed safely in Philadelphia. As reported, the pilot did a textbook job of getting the aircraft on to the ground safely. She (**Tammie Jo Shults**) knew what she was doing.

As a result of chapters 1 through 22, you have received a textbook thesis, from objective to evaluation on how to teach effectively. Just as the pilot knew how to fly a plane, you should be able to land your students safely with the knowledge of how you want them to learn. You know what you are doing.

**Good people do good things for themselves.
Great people do good things for others.**

The greatest joy of a teacher is when a former student comes back to visit, years later. Even if you have moved, the student somehow finds you. During the visit, the student never talks about what program was used in your class. The student shares the impact you had on that individual's life.

**"You made a difference in my life."
"Because of you, I am what and who I am today."
"You lit my candle and showed me the path to take."**

Then, your former student says, "Thank you," and leaves, never to return but leaving you with the satisfaction of knowing that you were a very significant person in someone's life. You know you have made an impact and left a legacy. Isn't that what being a teacher is all about?

Every book has a protagonist, a leading character, a hero, a heroine. **The protagonist in *THE Classroom Instruction Book* is the teacher—YOU.** Nobody will believe in you unless you believe in yourself.

We need to celebrate the nobility of teaching as the most completely constructive force in our nation. Teaching is a journey of the heart, an opportunity to touch a life forever.

It is an unselfish investment in the dignity and potential of one's students. The life of the master teacher honors all that is good and noble in mankind.

The beauty and power of the loving teacher— that is the greatest instrument for good in our society.[18]

E. Grady Bogue
Former Chancellor
Louisiana State University, Shreveport

[17] H. Jackson Brown Jr., *P.S. I Love You* (Nashville, TN: Rutledge Hill Press, 1990).

[18] E. Grady Bogue, *A Journey of the Heart: The Call to Teaching* (Bloomington, IN: Phi Delta Kappa Educational Foundation, 1991).

You may think your light is small, but it can make a huge difference in other people's lives.

And if every teacher would light just one candle, the whole world will shine brighter.

The single greatest impact on student achievement is an empowered teacher.

Unleash your potential and live your dream to attain Mastery and make an Impact.

<u>YOU</u> are that empowered, effective teacher every student desires and deserves.

Mastering Instruction

 Effective teachers rely on structured curriculums, not fads, programs, or technology.

 The single greatest impact on student achievement is an empowered teacher.

 Empowered teachers make choices to continuously improve their professional skills.

 The greatest quality a person can have is the desire to make other people's lives better.

...Produces Achievement!

QR Code Summary

There are fifty-one unique QR codes in **THE Classroom Instruction Book**.

QR Code #	Page in Book		Text in Book
1	UNIT A 8		**Research on Effective Teaching** Scan the QR code for the complete citations for these studies. Additionally, access this information and all QR code files at www.EffectiveTeaching.com on the QR code tab for **THE Classroom Instruction Book**.
2	12		**Binder Covers** Download covers for your Classroom Instruction Plan binder.
3	16		**Ranking of Effect Sizes** See **John Hattie's** complete list of influences on student achievement.
4	16		**Effect Size** Read more information on effect size and the statistical implications for learning.
5	18		**Rising to the Top** See the list of countries and how to move to the top of the list.
6	28		**Don't Teach in Panic Mode** See if you're teaching in panic mode and how to get out of it!
7	UNIT B 39		**Bloom's Taxonomy** Access the code to see Bloom's Taxonomy.
8	46		**For the Love of a Closing Couplet** If you are curious, scan the code to see a correct response for the Shakespearean sonnet objective.
9	48		**From Paragraphs to Essay** See an example of how a student can convert paragraphs into an essay, bit-by-bit and step-by-step.

10	**UNIT B** (continued) 50		**WALT and WILF** Use these and other ready-made WALT and WILF graphics to bring clarity to your instruction.
11	57		**Note This Essential Question** See an example of how a single essential question can be utilized in a year-long general music class.
12	60		**Sources for Essential Questions** See this listing of websites for additional essential questions.
13	73		**How to Design an Efficient and Effective Emergency Room** This blog essay is a great example of Career and Technical Education where high school students work in teams.
14	74		**Study Guidelines Define Lesson Objectives** See an example of a study guide or find it in *THE First Days of School* on page 240.
15	**UNIT C** 84		**Outperform 98 Percent of Regular Students** Read and learn from studies that show that assessment for learning is comparable to individual tutoring in its effectiveness.
16	100		**Corrective Feedback** See how English language learners struggle with corrective feedback.
17	115		**3.2.1** This tool collects specific, detailed information about what students understand to be the most important information about a topic.
18	115		**Concept Map** This tool visualizes information so students can connect ideas, concepts, and terms.
19	115		**Entry Ticket** This tool gathers information regarding previous learning and may help to prescribe changes for the day's lesson.
20	115		**Graphic Organizers** This tool organizes and structures information to be readily recalled by students.

	UNIT C (continued)			
21	115		**K-W-L**	This tool assesses what students already <u>K</u>now, what they <u>W</u>ant to know, and what they have <u>L</u>earned.
22	115		**One-Minute Note**	This tool encourages students to form a concise summary of what they just learned at various points in the lesson.
23	115		**Stop and Jot**	This tool gives students the opportunity to record their perception of a key concept or idea about a lesson topic while it is still fresh in their minds.
24	115		**Study Cards**	This tool creates personal note cards to use for study and review.
25	115		**Triangle-Square-Circle**	This tools accesses information that students feel is important, they agree with, or is still circling in their minds.
26	125		**Back and Forth**	This tool engages students in activities where they share ideas and discuss how each perceives the new information.
27	125		**Buddy Journal**	This tool pairs students and engages them in a back and forth written discussion about their writing and strategies to improve upon it.
28	125		**Card Sort**	This tool engages students in activities of sorting and categorizing to help them analyze similarities and differences among concepts.
29	125		**Quiz, Quiz, Trade**	This tool allows students to assess the knowledge of their classmates in an engaging quiz-game format.
30	125		**Tableau**	This tool asks students to physically manifest their understanding of a question or concept.
31	136		**Rubrics on the Internet**	No need to reinvent the wheel. The Internet is awash with websites for creating rubrics at all grade levels and all content areas.

32	**UNIT C** (continued) 136		**Rubrics in This Chapter** The full version of all of the rubrics shared in this chapter are here for you to use or adapt to your curriculum needs.
33	139		**Gaming Challenge** Read more about the challenge of computer gaming.
34	149		**Argumentative Paragraph Structure Rubric** Download the full rubric to use with your students.
35	**UNIT D** 155		**Setting Standards** View the list of professional organizations to access their set of standards.
36	159		**Lesson Plan Template** Download this lesson plan and **Karen Whitney's** lesson plan template to use as a guide when planning your instruction.
37	159		**Middle and High School Lesson Plans** Access examples of completed lesson plans for middle and high school.
38	159		**Consistency** See what Sisseton Middle School does to establish consistency in classroom management.
39	163		**Sample Elementary Lesson Plan** See how **Amanda Bivens** of Dyersburg, Tennessee, creates a lesson on abolitionist leaders.
40	196		**Kansas Teacher Examples** **Karen Rogers** shows how to use spaced learning and interleaving.
41	198		**Strategies for Instruction** Read about the ten, research-based strategies for instruction.
42	203		**Role Cards** Use these role cards to help students with the responsibilities of the Predictor, Questioner, Clarifier, and Summarizer.

43	**UNIT D** (continued) 204		**Reciprocal Teaching** Kentucky teacher **Jeff Gulle** reports how he uses reciprocal teaching in his history lesson.
44	217		**Extending the Learning** See how a teacher uses the food chain to extend students' learning beyond independent practice.
45	219		**Independent Study Rubric** Download **Oretha Ferguson's** The Power of Voice rubric to use with your students.
46	236		**Limitless Possibilities Through Structure** Learn how **Laurie Kash** organizes her class to bring out the potential creativity of all her students.
47	**UNIT E** 239		**Ants** Ants. What are they busy about?
48	255		**Katie's Outcome** Find out what happens to Katie by scanning the QR code.
49	256		**Lesson Study Process** Read the process that **Shota Matsumoto** and his colleagues engage in as they go through the details of a lesson.
50	297		**Implementation Guide** A free, in-depth Professional Development Implementation Guide for **THE Classroom Instruction Book** is available at www.EffectiveTeaching.com or scan the QR code.
Front Cover			Harry and Rosemary have a special message for you.

Bibliography

Allday, R. Allan, and Kerry Pakurar. "Effects of Teacher Greetings on Student On-task Behavior." *Journal of Applied Behavior Analysis* 40, no. 2 (Summer 2007): 317–320.

Allday, R. Allan, Miranda Bush, Nicole Ticknor, and Lindsay Walker. "Using Teacher Greetings to Increase Speed to Task Engagement." *Journal of Applied Behavior Analysis* 44, no. 2 (Summer 2011): 393–396.

Allington, Richard L. "What I've Learned from Effective Reading Instruction." *Phi Delta Kappan* 83, no. 10 (June 1, 2002): 740–747.

Aly, Harvey. *Fighting for Change in Your School: How to Avoid Fads and Focus on Substance.* Alexandria, VA: Association for Supervision and Curriculum Development, 2017.

Amabile, Teresa M., and Steve J. Kramer. "What Really Motivates Workers." *Harvard Business Review* 88, nos. 1/2 (January-February 2010): 44–45.

Arnett, Autumn A. "Kentucky's First Black Superintendent Reflects on Her Journey and 'Mastery for Every Child' Education Philosophy." *Education Dive* (February 26, 2018).

Barshay, Jill. "The Science of Talking in Class." *The Hechinger Report* (February 3, 2020). https://hechingerreport.org/the-science-of-talking-in-class/.

Black, Paul, and Dylan Wiliam. "Assessment and Classroom Learning." *Assessment in Education: Principles, Policy, & Practice* 5, no. 1 (1998): 7–74.

Black, Paul and Dylan Wiliam. "Inside the Black Box: Raising Standards Through Classroom Assessment." *Phi Delta Kappan* 92, no.1 (September 2010): 81–90.

Bloom, Benjamin S. "New Views of the Learner: Implications for Instruction and Curriculum." Paper presented as a General Session address 1978 Annual ASCD Conference, San Francisco, California. *Educational Leadership* 35, no. 7 (April 1978).

Bloom, Benjamin S., and David R Krathwohl, eds. *Taxonomy of Educational Objectives Handbook 1: Cognitive Domain.* London: Longmans, Green, and Co. Ltd., 1956.

Bogue, E. Grady. *A Journey of the Heart: The Call to Teaching.* Bloomington, IN: Phi Delta Kappa Educational Foundation, 1991.

Borders, Denise Glyn. "Strategic Alignment Is Ongoing, Challenging—And Necessary." *The Learning Professional* 40, no. 5 (October 15, 2014): 8.

Boud, David. *Enhancing Learning Through Self-Assessment.* Abington, UK: RoutledgeFalmer, 1995.

Branch, Gregory F., Eric A. Hanushek, and Steven G. Rivkin. "School Leaders Matter." *Education Next* 13, no. 1 (Winter 2013).

Brew, Angela. "What Is the Scope of Self-Assessment?" In *Enhancing Learning Through Self-Assessment*, by David Boud, 48–62. Abington, UK: RoutledgeFalmer, 1995.

Brimi, Hunter M. "Reliability of Grading High School Work in English." *Practical Assessment, Research, and Evaluation* 16, no. 17 (November 2011).

Brookhart, Susan, Marissa Andolina, Megan Zuza, and Rosalie Furman. "Minute Math: An Action Research Study of Student Self-Assessment." *Educational Studies in Mathematics* 57, no. 2 (September 2004): 213–227.

Brooks, Douglas. "The First Day of School." *Educational Leadership* 42, no. 8 (May 1985): 76–78.

Brown, H. Jackson, Jr. *P.S. I Love You.* Nashville, TN: Rutledge Hill Press, 1990.

Bryk, Anthony S., Penny Bender Sebring, Elaine Allensworth, Stuart Luppescu, and John Q. Easton. *Organizing Schools for Improvement: Lessons from Chicago.* Chicago: University of Chicago Press, 2010.

Butler, Ruth, and Mordecai Nisan. "Effects of No Feedback, Task-Related Comments, and Grades on Intrinsic Motivation and Performance." *Journal of Educational Psychology* 78, no. 3 (June 1986): 210–216.

Carnegie Mellon University Eberly Center for Teaching Excellence & Educational Innovation. "Teaching Principles." Accessed October 1, 2021. https://www.cmu.edu/teaching/principles/teaching.html.

Carpenter, Wade. "Ten Years of Silver Bullets: Dissenting Thoughts on Education Reform." *Phi Delta Kappan* 81, no. 5 (January 2000): 383–389.

Carroll, Lewis. *Alice's Adventures in Wonderland.* London: Macmillan & Co., 1865.

Cawelti, Gordon, ed. *Handbook of Research on Improving Student Achievement* (3rd edition). Bethesda, MD: Editorial Projects in Education, 2004.

Chappius, Jan, and Rick J. Stiggins. *Classroom Assessment for Student Learning: Doing It Right—Using It Well.* New York: Pearson, 2019.

Chetty, Raj, John N. Friedman, and Jonah E. Rockoff. "Measuring the Impacts of Teachers II: Teacher Value-Added and Student Outcomes in Adulthood." *American Economic Review* 104, no. 9 (September 2014): 2633–2679.

Chua-Lim, Yen Ching. "Teachers as Transformative Agents of Change." *Research Within Reach* 69 (June 2019). https://singteach.nie.edu.sg/2019/07/23/issue69-bigidea/.

Coe, Robert, Cesare Aloisi, Steve Higgins, and Lee Elliot Major. *What Makes Great Teaching? Review of the Underpinning Research.* London: Dunham University, Sutton Trust, 2014.

Covey, Steven. *The 7 Habits of Highly Effective People.* New York: Free Press, 1989, 2004.

Cuban, Larry. "The Myth of 'Failed' School Reform, (Part 1)." *Larry Cuban on School Reform and Classroom Practice* (blog). January 10, 2017. https://larrycuban.wordpress.com/2017/01/10/the-myth-of-failed-school-reform-part-1-2/.

Darling-Hammond, Linda. "Soaring Systems: High Flyers All Have Equitable Funding, Shared Curriculum, and Quality Teaching." *American Educator* 34, no. 4 (Winter 2010-2011).

Darling-Hammond, Linda. "Standard Setting in Teaching: Changes in Licensing, Certification, and Assessment." In *Handbook of Research on Teaching* (4th edition), edited by Virginia Richardson. Washington, DC: American Education Research Association, 2001.

Darling-Hammond, Linda, Ruth Chung Wei, and Alethea Andree. *How High-Achieving Countries Develop Great Teachers.* Stanford: SCOPE—Stanford Center for Opportunity Policy in Education, August 2010.

Davies, Anne. "Involving Students in the Classroom Assessment Process." In *Ahead of the Curve: The Power of Assessment to Transform Teaching and Learning*, edited by Douglas Reeves, 31–57. Bloomington, IN: Solution Tree, 2007.

Deci, Edward L., Richard Koestner, and Richard M. Ryan. "Extrinsic Rewards and Intrinsic Motivation in Education: Reconsidered Once Again." *Review of Educational Research* 71, no. 1 (Spring 2001): 1–27.

Dewey, Edward R. "The Case for Cycles." *Cycles*, July 1967.

Diener, C.I., and Carol Dweck. "An Analysis of Learned Helplessness: II." *Journal of Personality and Social Psychology* 39, no. 5 (December 1980): 940–952.

Duane, Daniel. "How the Startup Mentality Failed Kids in San Francisco." *Wired* (June 28, 2018). https://wired.com/story/willie-brown-middle-school-startup-mentality-failed/.

Dufour, Rick. "In the Right Context." *Journal of Staff Development: The Principal* (Winter 2001): 14–17.

Dumaine, Brian. "Amazon Was Built for the Pandemic." *Fortune* (June/July 2020).

Dunlosky, John, Katherine A. Rawson, Elizabeth J. Marsh, Mitchell J. Nathan, and Daniel T. Willingham. "Improving Students' Learning with Effective Learning Techniques: Promising Directions from Cognitive and Educational Psychology." *Psychological Science in the Public Interest* 14, no. 1 (January 8, 2013): 4–58.

Dweck, Carol S. "The Perils and Promises of Praise." *Educational Leadership* 65, no. 2 (October 2007): 34–39.

Elmore, Richard. "The Limits of 'Change.'" *Harvard Education Letter* 18, no. 1 (January/February 2002).

Fendick, Frank. "The Correlation Between Teacher Clarity of Communication and Student Achievement Gain: A Meta-Analysis." PhD diss., University of Florida, 1990.

Ferguson, Ronald F. "Paying for Public Education: New Evidence on How and Why Money Matters." *Harvard Journal of Legislation* 28 (Summer 1991): 465–98.

Fontana, David, and Margarida Fernandes. "Improvements in Mathematics Performance as a Consequence of Self-Assessment in Portuguese Primary School Pupils." *British Journal of Educational Psychology* 64, no. 3 (November 1994): 407–417.

Friedman, Thomas L. "The Shanghai Secret." *The New York Times* (October 22, 2013).

Gallo, Carmine. "The One Investment Warren Buffett Says Will Change Your Life (And It's Not A Stock)." *Forbes* (November 30, 2017).

Gibbs, Simon, and Ben Powell. "Teacher Efficacy and Pupil Behaviour: The Structure of Teachers' Individual and Collective Beliefs and Their Relationship with Numbers of Pupils Excluded from School." *British Journal of Educational Psychology* 82, no. 4 (December 2012): 564–584.

"Glimpse K12 Analysis of School Spending Shows that Two-Thirds of Software License Purchases Go Unused." *Glimpse K12* (May 15, 2019). https://www.glimpsek12.com/blog-posts/glimpse-k12-analysis-of-school-spending-shows-that-two-thirds-of-software-license-purchases-go-unused.

Goldhaber, Dan. "In Schools, Teacher Quality Matters Most." *Education Next* 16, no. 2 (Spring 2016).

Goldhaber, Dan. "Teacher Pay Reforms: The Political Implications of Recent Research." *CEDR Working Paper*, no. 2010-4.0 (2010).

Guskey, Thomas R. "The Case Against Percentage Grades." *Educational Leadership* 71, no. 1 (September 2013): 68–72.

Guskey, Thomas R. *Get Set, Go: Creating Successful Grading and Reporting System*. Bloomington, IN: Solution Tree Press, 2020.

Guskey, Thomas R. "Grades Versus Comments: Research on Student Feedback." *Phi Delta Kappan* 101, no. 3 (October 2019): 42–47.

Haberman, Martin. "Preparing Teachers for the Real World of Urban Schools." *The Educational Forum* 58, no. 2 (Winter 1994).

Hamilton, Arran, and John Hattie. *Not All That Glitters Is Gold: Can Education Technology Finally Deliver?* Thousand Oaks, CA: Corwin; Auckland: Cognition Education Group, 2021. https://www.visiblelearning.com/sites/default/files/not-all-that-glitters-is-gold.pdf.

Hattie, John. *Visible Learning: A Synthesis of Over 800 Meta-Analyses Relating to Achievement*. New York: Routledge, 2009.

Hattie, John. *Visible Learning for Teachers: Maximizing Impact on Learning*. New York: Routledge, 2012.

Hattie, John, and Helen Timperley. "The Power of Feedback." *Review of Educational Research* 77, no. 1 (March 2007): 81–112.

Hattie, John, and Gregory C. R. Yates. *Visible Learning and the Science of How We Learn*. New York: Routledge, 2014.

Hawkins, Beth. "The 74 Interview: Outgoing Louisiana Chief John White on the New Orleans Experiment, His Longevity and What It Means to Be Well Educated." (February 18, 2020). https://www.the74million.org/article/the-74-interview-outgoing-louisiana-chief-john-white-on-the-new-orleans-experiment-his-longevity-and-what-it-means-to-be-well-educated/.

Hershberg, Theodore. "Value-Added Assessment and Systemic Reform: A Response to the Challenge of Human Capital Development." *Phi Delta Kappan* 87, no. 4 (December 1, 2005): 276–283.

Hodge, Winston. "Singapore Basic Education Curriculum Revisited: A Look at the Current Content and Reform." *Multilingual Philippines* (June 28, 2012).

James, Geoffrey. "9 Reasons That Open-Space Offices Are Insanely Stupid." *Inc.com* (February 25, 2016).

Jerald, Craig D. *Dispelling the Myth Revisited: Preliminary Findings from a Nationwide Analysis of "High Flying" Schools*. Washington, DC: Education Trust, 2001.

Kang, Sean H. K. "Spaced Repetition Promotes Efficient and Effective Learning: Policy Implications for Instruction." *Policy Insights from the Behavioral and Brain Sciences* 3, no.1 (January 13, 2016): 12–19.

Killian, Shaun. "Teacher Clarity: A Potent Yet Misunderstood and Often Abused Teaching Strategy." Australian Society for Evidence Based Teaching, June 16, 2017. https://www.evidencebasedteaching.org.au/teacher-clarity/.

Leahy, Siobhan, Christine Lyon, Marnie Thompson, and Dylan Wiliam. "Classroom Assessment: Minute by Minute, Day by Day." *Educational Leadership* 63, no. 3 (November 2005): 19–24.

Lewis, Catherine. "Does Lesson Study Have a Future in the United States?" *Nagoya Journal of Education and Human Development*, no. 1 (January 2002).

Louis, Karen Seashore, Kenneth Leithwood, Kyla Walhstrom, and Stephen Anderson et al. *Learning from Leadership Project: Investigating the Links to Improved Student Learning*. University of Minnesota, University of Toronto, Wallace Foundation, 2010.

Marzano, Robert J., Jana S. Marzano, and Debra J. Pickering. *Classroom Management That Works: Research-based Strategies for Every Teacher*. Alexandria, VA: Association for Supervision and Curriculum Development, 2003.

Marzano, Robert J., Debra J. Pickering, and Jane Pollock. *Classroom Instruction That Works*. Alexandria, VA: Association for Supervision and Curriculum Development, 2001, 2012.

Marzano, Robert J., Timothy Waters, and Brian McNulty. *School Leadership that Works: From Research to Results*. Alexandria, VA: Association for Supervision and Curriculum Development, 2005.

Mendro, Robert L., Heather R. Jordan, Elvia Gomez, Mark C. Anderson, and Karen L. Bembry. "An Application of Multiple Linear Regression Determining Longitudinal Teacher Effectiveness." Paper presented at the April 1998 Annual Meeting of AERA, San Diego, California.

Moss, Connie M., and Susan M. Brookhart. *Learning Targets: Helping Students Aim for Understanding in Today's Lesson*. Alexandria, VA: Association for Supervision and Curriculum Development, 2012.

Nelson, Howard. "Testing More, Teaching Less: What America's Obsession with Student Testing Costs in Money and Lost Instructional Time." *American Federation of Teachers* (2013). https://www.aft.org/pdfs/teachers/testingmore2013.pdf.

Nuthall, Graham A. "The Cultural Myths and Realities of Classroom Teaching and Learning: A Personal Journey." *Teachers College Record* 107, no. 5 (May 2005): 895–934.

Pearson, P. David, and Margaret C. Gallagher. "The Instruction of Reading Comprehension." *Contemporary Educational Psychology* 8, no. 3 (July 1983): 317–344.

Popham, W. James. "Criterion-Referenced Measurement: Half a Century Wasted?" *Educational Leadership* 71, no. 6 (March 2014): 62–66.

Popham, W. James. "Formative Assessment—A Process, Not a Test." *Education Week* 30, no. 21 (February 22, 2011): 35.

Poplin, Mary, and Claudia Bermúdez, eds. *Highly Effective Teachers of Vulnerable Students: Practice Transcending Theory.* New York: Peter Lang Publishing, Inc., 2019.

Puett, Michael, and Christine Gross-Loh. *The Path: What Chinese Philosophers Can Teach Us About the Good Life.* New York: Simon and Schuster, 2016.

Richardson, Joan. "The Editor's Note: Getting Better at Learning." *Phi Delta Kappan* 98, no. 3 (November 1, 2016): 4.

Rivkin, Steven G., Eric A. Hanushek, and John F. Kain. "Teachers, Schools, and Academic Achievement." *Econometrica* 73, no. 2 (March 2005): 417–458.

Roediger, Henry L. III, and Jeffrey D. Karpicke. "Test-Enhanced Learning: Taking Memory Tests Improves Long-Term Retention." *Psychological Science* 17, no. 3 (March 2006): 249–255.

Roediger, Henry L. III, and Jeffrey D. Karpicke. "The Power of Testing Memory: Basic Research and Implications for Educational Practice." *Perspectives of Psychological Science* 1, no. 3 (September 1, 2006): 181–210.

Rohrer, Doug, Robert F. Dedrick, and Sandra Stershic. "Interleaved Practice Improves Mathematics Learning." *Journal of Educational Psychology* 107, no. 3 (2015): 900–908.

Rolheiser, Carol. *Self-Evaluation: Helping Students Get Better at It! A Teacher's Resource Book.* Cheltenham, AUS: Hawker-Brownlow Education, 1998.

Rowe, Mary Budd. "Wait Time: Slowing Down May Be a Way of Speeding Up." *American Educator: The Professional Journal of the American Federation of Teachers* 11, no. 1 (Spring 1987): 8–43, 47.

Ryan, Kevin. *The Induction of New Teachers.* Bloomington, IN: Phi Delta Kappa Educational Foundation, 1986.

Sanders, William L., and June C. Rivers. *Cumulative and Residual Effects of Teachers on Future Student Academic Achievement.* Knoxville, TN: University of Tennessee Value-Added Research and Assessment Center, 1996.

Schleicher, Andreas. "Collaborative Culture Is the Key to Success." *Times Educational Supplement* (March 8, 2013). https://www.tes.com/news/collaborative-culture-key-success.

Schmoker, Mike. Abridged from "The Crayola Curriculum." *Education Week* 21, no. 8 (October 24, 2001).

Schmoker, Mike. *Results: The Key to Continuous School Improvement.* Alexandria, VA: Association for Supervision and Curriculum Development, 1996, 2007.

Scriven, Michael. "Beyond Formative and Summative Evaluation." In *Evaluation and Education: At Quarter Century,* edited by M.W. McLaughlin and D.C. Phillips. Chicago: University of Chicago Press, 1991.

Shah, Madiha. "The Importance and Benefits of Teacher Collegiality in Schools—A Literature Review." *Procedia—Social and Behavioral Sciences* 46 (2012): 1242–1246.

Sizer, Theodore R. *Horace's Compromise: The Dilemma of the American High School.* New York: Houghton Mifflin, 2004.

Skinner, Ellen A., James G. Wellborn, and James P. Connell. "What It Takes to Do Well in School and Whether I've Got It: A Process Model of Perceived Control and Children's Engagement and Achievement in School." *Journal of Educational Psychology* 82, no. 1 (March 1990): 22–32.

Solomon, JD. "Why American Education Pales—and Fails—on the Global Stage." *District Administration* (June 2019).

Starch, Daniel, and Edward Charles Elliott. "Reliability of the Grading of High School Work in English." *The School Review* 20, no. 7 (September 1912): 442–457.

Stronge, James H., Thomas J. Ward, and Leslie W. Grant. "What Makes Good Teachers Good? A Cross-Case Analysis of the Connection Between Teacher Effectiveness and Student Achievement." *Journal of Teacher Education* 62, no. 4 (September 1, 2011): 339–355.

Stronge, James. *Qualities of Effective Teachers.* Alexandria, VA: Association for Supervision and Curriculum Development, 2018.

Taylor, Kelli, and Doug Rohrer. "The Effects of Interleaved Practice." *Applied Cognitive Psychology* 24, no.6 (September 2010): 837–848.

U.S. Department of Education. *What Works: Research About Teaching and Learning.* Washington, DC: U.S. Department of Education, Office of Educational Research and Improvement, 1986.

Van Der Stuyf, Rachel R. "Scaffolding as a Teaching Strategy." *Adolescent Learning and Development,* Section 0500A, Fall 2002. http://ateachingpath1.weebly.com/uploads/1/7/8/9/17892507/stuyf_2002.pdf.

Vega, Vanessa. "Teacher Development Research Review: Keys to Educator Success." *Edutopia* (November 1, 2015). https://www.edutopia.org/teacher-development-research-keys-success.

Visible Learning. "Hattie Ranking: 256 Influences and Effect Sizes Related to Student Achievement." Accessed November 1, 2021. https://visible-learning.org/backup-hattie-ranking-256-effects-2017/.

Waters, Timothy, and Robert J. Marzano. *School District Leadership that Works: The Effect of Superintendent Leadership on Student Achievement.* Denver, CO: Mid-continent Research for Education and Learning, 2006.

Waters, Timothy, Robert J. Marzano, and Brian McNulty. *Balanced Leadership: What 30 Years of Research Tells Us About the Effect of Leadership on Student Achievement. A Working Paper.* Denver, CO: Mid-continent Research for Education and Learning, 2003.

Wayne, Andrew J., and Peter Youngs. "Teacher Characteristics and Student Achievement Gains: A Review." *Review of Educational Research* 43, no. 1 (2003): 89–122.

Wiggins, Grant, and Jay McTighe. *Understanding by Design.* Alexandria, VA: Association for Supervision and Curriculum Development, 2005.

Wiliam, Dylan. "Content Then Process: Teacher Learning Communities in the Service of Formative Assessment." In *Ahead of the Curve: The Power of Assessment to Transform Teaching and Learning,* edited by Douglas Reeves, 182–204. Bloomington, IN: Solution Tree Press, 2007.

Willingham, Daniel T. "Ask the Cognitive Scientist: Do Visual, Auditory, and Kinesthetic Learners Need Visual, Auditory, and Kinesthetic Instruction?" *American Educator* 29, no. 2 (2005): 31.

Willingham, Daniel T. "It Speeds and Strengthens Reading Comprehension, Learning—and Thinking." *American Educator* (Spring 2006).

Wright, S. Paul, Sandra P, Horn, and William L. Sanders. "Teacher and Classroom Context Effects on Student Achievement: Implications for Teacher Evaluation." *Journal of Personnel Evaluation in Education* 11, no. 1 (1997): 57–67.

Zugelder, Bryan S. "Beyond the Trailer Park." *Kappa Delta Pi Record* 56, no. 3 (July 2020). Story shared with permission.

Index

About the Authors

Harry K. Wong and Rosemary T. Wong

Harry and Rosemary are new teacher advocates, motivational speakers, and inspirational leaders. Colleagues have described them as connectors, angels, gurus, encouragers, cheerleaders, and rock stars who are enthusiastic, down-to-earth, patient, kind, giving, and real. Above all else, they are teachers—always have been, always will be. They have devoted their lives to creating effective teachers for the students of the world. Their complete bios can be accessed at www.HarryWong.com.

Sarah Powley

Sarah shares her years of successful classroom experience as a full-time Instructional Coach for middle school and secondary teachers in Lafayette, Indiana. She is an expert in instructional strategies and leads professional development for educators in her district. Her exceptional talent has been recognized with the Milken Educator Award and by Purdue University as a Distinguished Education Alumna. A fellow teacher said of her, "Her dedication and devotion to teaching sets an example for teachers everywhere." She blogs *In an American Classroom: Reflections on Teaching* at www.SarahPowley.com.

With Our Thanks

Our grateful acknowledgment to these people and organizations for the permission to include their pictures, classrooms, ideas, stories, and work in this book.

Mimi Allred
Stacey Allred
Cristina Andrews
Mandie Ballman
Aundrea Beck
Amanda Bivens
Joann Brewer
Douglas Brooks
Bobbie Cavnar
Clark County School District
Elaine Farris
Oretha Ferguson
Emily Floyd
Gaston County Schools
Amy Groesbeck
Jeff Gulle
Natalie Hamilton
John Hattie
Kara Howard
Britta Hubbard
Bruce Hurford

Bert Johnson
Sarah Jondahl
Laurie Kash
Kimberly Keesling
Rose Kerr
Kelvin Lee
Tara Link
Linda Lippman
David Marasco
William Martinez
Shoto Matsumoto
Alex Melton
Moberly Public Schools
Kristine Nugent-Ohls
Kasey Oetting
Juanita Radden
Region 13 Education Service Center
Joan Richardson
Joanne Rodgers
Karen Rogers
Noah Roseman

Maria Sanchez
Mike Schmoker
Chelonnda Seroyer
Grant Seroyer
Lauren Seroyer
Terah Slawnikowski
Mickey Smith Jr.
Janet Stearns
Stephanie Stoebe
Stonefields School
Deb Thompson
Katie Kitani Tokushige
Jennifer Varrato
Brad Volkman
Karan Wester
Karen Whitney
Nile Wilson
Cindy Wong
Ruby Zickafoose

You're Awesome!

A Basic Professional Development Implementation Guide
THE Classroom Instruction Book

The research is very specific. People learn best in the company of peers and colleagues. Collaboration is the most effective way for teachers to make progress professionally and achieve results in their classrooms.

- A school's collaborative culture is the key to success. Schools in all high-ranking countries foster teamwork and cooperation.

- When teachers work together, they are capable of producing extraordinary results in student learning and achievement.

- The most powerful influence on student achievement occurs when teachers purposefully focus on developing effective instruction using proven techniques and strategies.

- Building the group's collective impact to achieve schoolwide goals must be the highest priority for teachers and administrators.

- It is incumbent that schools create a culture where collaborative impact is focused on pursuing a common vision for student learning.

Effective schools develop and sustain a collaborative culture where staff know what they want to accomplish and speak a common language to achieve their aims.

Working Together

A common language is the foundation for attaining collaborative impact. It is the pivotal step in bringing a faculty together. Building clarity using specific terminology sets the stage for shared expectations and identifying effective instructional strategies.

To begin a professional development program using this book, organize and schedule a regular book study group. Appoint an administrator, coach, or teacher to lead the group and assign the tasks.

The book study group leader should guide teachers through the three-step process of **I Do, We Do, You Do** with each chapter. Plan for twenty-three weeks of meetings, equaling one chapter per week plus the introductory meeting.

Ideally, the administrator, coach, or teacher group leader during the week, visits classrooms to assess and assist when needed as teachers implement what has been discussed with the group.

I Do: Provide the Background

THE Classroom Instruction Book is about how to teach the curriculum effectively. It is not about a program or some philosophy. It presents well-researched techniques and strategies used to improve the chances that students will learn.

- At the introductory meeting, read through the Contents and Introduction. Discuss any questions and observations.

- Explain the I Do, We Do, You Do process.

- Organize the book study group to read one chapter a week, in sequential order, beginning with Chapter 1.

We Do: Guided Practice

One week later, reconvene the group.

- Appoint two teachers to lead a brainstorming session of the key ideas from the chapter.

- Ask teachers to suggest a few ideas from the chapter that could be attempted at the school and in classrooms.

- Have the appointed teachers lead a discussion on how the ideas could be implemented.

- Before ending the meeting, come to a group consensus on the ideas to try in the next week.

You Do: Independent Practice

- Teachers incorporate the ideas agreed upon in their instructional plans and implement them in their teaching practice.

- If possible, teachers should be encouraged to visit other classrooms to learn now the ideas have been implemented and used by their colleagues.

- Results are shared and feedback is discussed at the next week's meeting before starting the next chapter in the book.

Professional development centered on _THE Classroom Instruction Book_ will result in collaborative practices based on a common language and shared goals.

It will empower teachers and establish schoolwide consistency.

Implementation Guide

A free, in-depth Professional Development Implementation Guide for **_THE Classroom Instruction Book_** is available at www.EffectiveTeaching.com or scan the QR code.

A Common Language

Ruby Zickafoose was principal of an underachieving Title 1 school in Florida. As she observed teachers in their classrooms, she discovered they were using many systems and variations for guided reading. The teachers, many of them newly hired, were doing their best to achieve results in student learning, but each student group in the school was being exposed to different formations and strategy talk.

Teachers were all working on their own with no common language to unite their efforts. This created a confusing and fragmented learning environment for both teachers and students that created ambiguity within and among grade-level teams.

Ruby knew it was her leadership role to ensure her teachers were on the same page in order to achieve

learning gains. She knew that if teachers worked together and aligned their work, students would perform better.

She was able to bring structure and uniformity to her school through professional development that established a common language and a collaborative culture of "We Are All in This Together." Teachers observed and were observed by their colleagues and became part of networks and study groups where they shared experiences, grew together, and learned to respect each other's work.

Becoming an effective educator cannot take place overnight or in a single workshop session. Teamwork, collaboration, and time will yield positive, lasting outcomes for you and your students.

Be Purposeful in Building Your Career

These are the MUST HAVE books for every professional library. Put the three characteristics of all effective teachers into practice. Learn skills that will result in being a successful, effective, and happy educator.

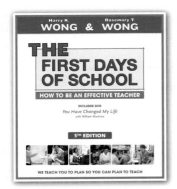

The FOUNDATION book that is based on the three characteristics of effective teachers.

CLASSROOM MANAGEMENT
LESSON MASTERY
POSITIVE EXPECTATIONS

Bestselling book for teacher training—more than 4.25 million copies sold. It works!

Learn in depth how to reduce discipline problems and organize a classroom for student learning and success.

Step-by-step with examples for all grade levels, from before the first day to the last day of school.

It's the companion book to our eLearning course—
THE Classroom Management Course.

Forthcoming book

Learn how to teach your students the skills needed to succeed in school.

With ten detailed techniques students can use in school and life.

HARRY K. WONG PUBLICATIONS, INC.
www.EffectiveTeaching.com